The Acquisition of
Syntactic Knowledge

The MIT Press Series in Artificial Intelligence
Edited by Patrick Henry Winston and Michael Brady

The Acquisition of Syntactic Knowledge

Robert C. Berwick

The MIT Press
Cambridge, Massachusetts
London, England

PUBLISHER'S NOTE

This format is intended to reduce the cost of publishing certain works in book form and to shorten the gap between editorial preparation and final publication. The time and expense of detailed editing and composition in print have been avoided by photographing the text of this book directly from the author's typeset copy.

Second printing, 1986

Copyright © 1985 by The Massachusetts Institute of Technology.

This book was typeset with Donald E. Knuth's TEX and Leslie Lamport's LATEX.

Printed and bound in the United States of America.

Library of Congress Cataloging in Publication Data

Berwick, Robert C.
    The acquisition of syntactic knowledge.

    (The MIT Press series in artificial intelligence)
    Bibliography: p.
    Includes index.
    1. Artificial intelligence. 2. Linguistics—Data processing. 3. Language acquisition. 4. Learning—Mathematical models.   I. Title.   II. Series.
Q335.B48 1985   401.9   85–11460
ISBN 0-262-02226-5

CONTENTS

Part II: A Theory of Acquisition

SERIES FOREWORD

Artificial intelligence is the study of intelligence using the ideas and methods of computation. Unfortunately, a definition of intelligence seems impossible at the moment because intelligence appears to be an amalgam of so many information-processing and information-representation abilities.

Of course psychology, philosophy, linguistics, and related disciplines offer various perspectives and methodologies for studying intelligence. For the most part, however, the theories proposed in these fields are too incomplete and too vaguely stated to be realized in computational terms. Something more is needed, even though valuable ideas, relationships, and constraints can be gleaned from traditional studies of what are, after all, impressive existence proofs that intelligence is in fact possible.

Artificial intelligence offers a new perspective and a new methodology. Its central goal is to make computers intelligent, both to make them more useful and to understand the principles that make intelligence possible. That intelligent computers will be extremely useful is obvious. The more profound point is that artificial intelligence aims to understand intelligence using the ideas and methods of computation, thus offering a radically new and different basis for theory formation. Most of the people doing artificial intelligence believe that these theories will apply to any intelligent information processor, whether biological or solid state.

There are side effects that deserve attention, too. Any program that will successfully model even a small part of intelligence will be inherently massive and complex. Consequently, artificial intelligence continually confronts the limits of computer science technology. The problems encountered have been hard enough and interesting enough to seduce artificial intelligence people into working on them with enthusiasm. It is natural, then, that there has been a steady flow of ideas from artificial intelligence to computer science, and the flow shows no sign of abating.

The purpose of this MIT Press Series in Artificial Intelligence is to provide people in many areas, both professionals and students, with timely, detailed information about what is happening on the frontiers in research centers all over the world.

Patrick Henry Winston   Michael Brady

PREFACE

How do people learn language? How can we get a machine to learn language? This book is an investigation into these central questions of human and machine cognition. Its approach is computational, drawing on studies of language acquisition from linguistics and psychology, but ultimately using the tools and techniques of computational theory and modeling as its investigative probe. The computational approach to language acquisition has two parts. First, we build an explicit computation model of language acquisition. This computer procedure can actually learn rules of English syntax given a sequence of grammatical, but otherwise unprepared, sentences. From the standpoint of work in artificial intelligence and the design of "expert systems" this work is exciting because it shows how extensive knowledge might actually be acquired automatically, without outside intervention. From a computational point of view, the work shows how constraints that may be reasonably assumed to aid one of the tasks of language use—sentence processing—also aids another—language acquisition. Evidently, natural languages are designed to be easily learned and easily processed. Part I shows how.

In the second part of this book we apply the methods of computer science to the general problem of developmental growth—how a complex ability like language can arise by the interaction of internal constraints with the external environment. We might call this "computational embryology." One of the long-standing puzzles of developmental biology focuses on how information needed to reproduce the complexity of the adult organism can possibly be encoded in the initial genetic endowment. This problem has its counterpart in language acquisition: How can we account for the range of adult human languages, given some initial knowledge that children start with and the evidence about language that they receive? Here we advance a general, computational scaffolding on which to build theories of ontogenetic development. By looking at development as if it were a kind of computer program that "builds" the organism or a grammar, we can use some of the methods to analyze programs to study developmental questions, particularly the thorny problem of the interaction between innate genetic endowment and environmental input. Our aim is to uncover the computational constraints on the acquisition of knowledge—syntactic knowledge. The results here should be of interest to developmental biologists, geneticists, or anyone that wants to understand how a complex organism can be "output" as the result of a sequence of decisions that unfold over time.

Like all computer modeling, and more acutely, like all work that tackles a subject as rich as language, corners have been cut in order that the work could proceed. Only the acquisition of syntax has been studied. Large areas obviously relevant to language growth have been assumed fixed, or have been ignored. For example, the acquisition of knowledge about words is only hinted at. (For a concrete proposal on this score, see Berwick 1983; 1984.) Likewise, knowledge about what are sometimes called *conceptual* or *thematic* roles—for example, that the subject of the sentence is often the "agent" or "doer" of an action—was assumed known for at least simple sentences. This simplification was deliberate. Plainly, the constraints from these other domains can aid and abet the acquisition of syntactic knowledge—as was assumed here. But it was felt that only by understanding in full one part of language acquisition, one part where rich constraints are known, could progress be made on the whole. The reader may judge whether this strategy has paid off. There are many pieces to the puzzle of language acquisition, and many ways to attack it.

On the other hand, even this modest attack has demanded a diversity of "mini-theories" of learning, each a substantial effort in its own right. A side benefit of this diversity is that the results should appeal to a wide range of interests, covering as they do everything from general learning theory to phonology to syntax. The mini-theories include:

- How lexical categories are learned;

- How phonological rule systems are learned;

- How phrase structure rules are learned;

- The role of semantic-syntactic interaction in language acquisition;

- How a "parameter setting" model may be formalized as a learning procedure;

- How multiple constraints (from syntax, thematic knowledge, or phrase structure) interact to aid acquisition;

- How transformational-type rules may be learned;

- The role of lexical ambiguity in language acquisition.

A word about the history of this work and the organization of this book. Chapter 1 summarizes the whole story. It can be read for a quick overview of the remainder. Part I continues with details on the computer model. Chapter 2 presents the assumptions behind the model, and chapters 3 and 4, detailed discussion of the model's performance and limits. Part II turns to the computational analysis of acquisition. Chapter 5 outlines a general theory of development, using the computer program model, and chapter 6 applies this model to some case studies drawn from phonology and syntax. Chapter 7 concludes with a study of the relationship between parsing and language acquisition.

The book is a revision of my 1982 PhD thesis. The basic outline and implementation of the computer model were completed during the spring and summer of 1979, and first presented at a workshop on language learnability held by Ken Wexler and Peter Culicover at the University of California at Irvine in June 1979. The model was refined over the next year; details here are given in the 1980 conference proceedings of the Association for Computational Linguistics and M.S. thesis of June, 1980. The bulk of this material makes up Part I of this book. Part II is a revised version of material from the June, 1982 PhD thesis. One chapter of that thesis (originally chapter 4), on a general theory of modularity, has been omitted here. Chapter 5 of the thesis, on parsing and language acquisition, has been substantially revised and expanded here as chapter 7.

Acknowledgments

This book on learning has been above all a learning experience for its author. Would that it had been as easy as language acquisition itself! Among those who helped in setting the right parameters at the start were key figures at the MIT Artificial Intelligence Laboratory: Patrick Winston, Director of the Lab; and Mitch Marcus, advisor in the earlier stages of this work. Thanks are also due to the Defense Advanced Research Projects Agency of the Department of Defense, for its generous support of the Laboratory.

Ken Wexler and Peter Culicover provided more positive examples of the right kind in the workshop held in 1979 sponsored by the University of California, Irvine. The only thing better than a good start is continuing good direction. Here I have been blessed with a wealth of advice and scholarship. I am particularly indebted to Noam Chomsky, whose unshaken belief in rationality remains, even though he knows that our capacities are limited; to Ken Wexler for his unflagging interest and good scientific sense; to Patrick Winston and Mike Brady for the special environment of the A.I. Lab; and to Amy Weinberg, for her boundless enthusiasm unmatched only by her linguistic energies. Aravind Joshi, Sam Pilato, Craig Thiersch, and Dan Brotsky also contributed to this book's final form, in mysterious and not so mysterious ways.

Robert Cregar Berwick
Cambridge, Massachusetts
January, 1985

Part I:

The Computer Model

Chapter 1

Computation and Language Acquisition

One of the important goals of modern linguistic theory is to explain how it is that children can acquire their first language. On many accounts the "evidence" that children receive to learn language is quite impoverished and reinforcement by adults haphazard. Yet the process of first language acquisition seems relatively easy and strikingly uniform. Children with enormously disparate sensory environments all seem to learn the same parts of what linguists call a grammar (Newport, Gleitman, and Gleitman 1977; Gleitman and Wanner 1982). How is this possible? In this book we shall try to answer this question *computationally*, by describing a specific computer model that acquires language.

This computational approach to language acquisition draws heavily upon linguistically-based descriptions of languages, or *grammars*. Modern linguistics' answer to the puzzle of language acquisition is to characterize so narrowly the class of possible human grammars that the language learner's burden is eased, perhaps trivialized. In Chomsky's metaphor, hypothesizable grammars should be "sufficiently scattered" from one another so that children can easily select the one correctly corresponding to the language of their caretakers (Chomsky 1965). Restrictions aid the learner because they rule out countless faulty hypotheses about which possible grammar might cover the language at hand. For example, suppose there was but a single human grammar. Such a situation would be optimal from the standpoint of language acquisition: no matter how complex the grammar, it might be built-in, and no "learning" required. More realistically, current theories of transformational grammar are usually motivated and evaluated against the demand of learnability. In these theories the possible rules of grammar (and thus the possible human grammars) are restricted as much as possible to just a few actions plus universal constraints on their application. The business of linguistics for the past several years has been to uncover these universal principles from the "data" of grammaticality judgments, and so advance, indirectly, an explanation for language learnability.

The metaphor of a child searching through a restricted hypothesis space of grammars has proved to be an enormously fruitful one for modern linguistic theory, drawing us closer toward the goal of characterizing what is distinctively human about the complex behavior that is called "language." Yet the study of generative grammar as developed over the past few decades has, for the most part, deliberately abstracted away from the study of language use or the real-time course of language acquisition. As Chomsky has often pointed out, this is a scientific idealization of the usual sort— an assumption known to be false, yet one that allows researchers to focus on questions central to the theory of grammar while ignoring presumably inessential questions about human processing mechanisms.

This way of explaining language acquisition has its limits. It deliberately tells us only what knowledge of language is, not how it is used or how it is acquired. We might think that understanding *what* can often take us most of the way—perhaps all of the way—to understanding *how*, just as knowing the data structures involved in an algorithm will often tell one all one needs to know about how the algorithm using those representations actually runs. So one is left with these questions: Just how would one incorporate a theory of generative grammar into an account of how knowledge of language is acquired? How do computational constraints interact with language acquisition, if at all?

The goal of this book is to probe these questions in an explicit *computational* setting. First we shall outline a computational model for the acquisition of English syntax. This is an implemented LISP program that learns how to parse English sentences. Based on the Marcus parser (Marcus 1980), the procedure is able to "project" a substantial number of the parsing rules for English syntax given an initial knowledge about possible grammars plus simple, well-formed sentences of English as input data.

This is both an engineering and a scientific accomplishment. The acquisition procedure demonstrates that one *can* naturally embed a generative grammar into a working model of language acquisition. Part I of the book gives the details of this model, its capabilities, and its limitations. More important than simple engineering success, perhaps, is the discovery of interrelationships between learnability and parsability. Modern linguistic theory interprets the theory of universal grammar (UG) as part of a theory of language acquisition. By restricting the class of available grammars compatible with evidence assumed available to the child, we advance toward an explanation of how it is that children can "fix" a grammar for the language of their caretakers.

This focus on the functional demand of learnability has been criticized by computationalists. Why, they ask, should one concentrate on learnability and ignore the possibly equally constricting demands of parsability or sentence production? Evidently, not only are natural languages learnable, but sentences of natural languages are easily parsable and producible—or at least those sentences that are observed in natural discourse. How then do the multiple functional demands of learnability, parsability, and producibility interact? After all, learnability constraints might be different from parsability constraints. In this case learnability and parsability constraints would simply turn out to be incomparable. Or it might be that the constraints that make languages learnable also make languages easily parsable; or, the reverse might hold. Without a specific model it is impossible to test any of these possibilities.

A second, key goal of this book—described in Part II—is to specify a learning model in enough detail so that learnability and parsability constraints may be compared. The main result here shows that the two kinds of constraints are closely related: the same constraints that guarantee efficient parsability also guarantee "easy" learnability. From this standpoint natural grammars are particularly well-designed.

More generally we can ask how grammatical knowledge "grows." A complex interaction between environment and internal structure yields the complex skill we call language. How should we understand the time course of this skill's development? Psycholinguists have long sought to understand this unfolding pattern via a battery of linguistic constraints, psychological abilities, and general cognitive processes like rote memorization. This book takes a somewhat different tack. It uses the most sophisticated model we have of a complex time-changing process, a computer program, as its model for language growth. Think of the process that learns a grammar as a computer program that "writes" a grammar as its output. The amount of information required to "fix" a grammar on the basis of external evidence is identified with the size of the shortest program needed to "write down" a grammar.[1] The term *program* here is deliberately ambiguous, denoting either a computer program for producing a grammar, given some input data, or a developmental program in an ontogenetic sense.

The program metaphor provides insight into grammar growth or "real-time" acquisition. Like any computer program, a program for fixing a grammar will have a definite *control flow*, corresponding roughly to an augmented flowchart that describes the implicational structure of the program. The flow diagram specifies a series of "decision points" that actually carry out the job of building the rule system. These decision points form the "developmental envelope" of real-time acquisition.

For example, evidently one of the choices that fixes the phrase structure system of a natural language is whether Noun Phrase (NP) Objects appear the left or to the right of their verbs. In English, a Subject–Verb–Object language, NP Objects appear to the right of the verb (*I gave Mary flowers*). In other, so-called Subject–Object–Verb languages (Japanese, German), NP Objects appear to the left of the verb. The learner fixes Verb–Object or Object–Verb order presumably by analyzing sentences it hears. Observational data indicates that this choice is indeed made early, perhaps without error. But once this order is set for the expansion of Verb Phrases, there is a grammatical constraint forcing this order to apply across *all* categories—e.g., Prepositional Phrases, Noun Phrases, and Adjective Phrases. For example, Japanese has postpositional structure for its categories; English has prepositional structure. Put another way, all that is learned is a general *operator–operand* or *function–argument* order that is applied to all phrases.

The implicational structure of the developmental program is such that *one* binary decision, Verb–Object order, cements a whole set of developmental patterns. Thus a propagating cluster of effects results from just a single decision. It is this cluster of effects that is actually "observed" on the surface. A claim of the program metaphor is that this is the general pattern: developmental stages are just clusters of such implications, in turn reflecting the underlying decision points of the grammar-writing program.[2] This redun-

---

[1] The use of program size measures in inductive inference was introduced, so far as I know, by Solomonoff (1964) and studied in a general context by Biermann (1972); see also Biermann and Feldman (1972).

[2] So far, nothing has been said that gives one kind of information, say, information about Verb–Object order, priority over another kind of information for acquisition.

dancy in information coding compresses the amount of information needed to learn a grammar. Consider the Verb–Object decision. Instead of having to learn separately the rules for Verb Phrases, Noun Phrases, Prepositional Phrases, and so forth, there is just a single binary choice to make.

Clusters of variables, then, represent information theoretic redundancies. Chapter 5 advances a formal model of this phenomenon. We shall see that this same property holds generally, in that all linguistic generalizations can be interpreted as implying specific developmental "programs" as described above. In particular, the acquisition of phonological rule systems contains substantial information-theoretic redundancies of this kind. By interpreting these redundancies as a developmental program, one can actually explain the observed distribution of possible natural phonological systems as a side-effect of a simple model of acquisition.

The program metaphor also resolves the tension between *instantaneous* and *noninstantaneous* models of acquisition. An instantaneous model assumes that acquisition can be properly idealized *as if* all the input data were presented all at once to the learner. On this view, there are no important acquisition constraints that follow from the *ordering* or sequence in which input data are presented to the acquisition device. This idealization has been the subject of much controversy. It has frequently been claimed that developmental sequencing has an important role to play in the acquisition of grammar. Intuitively, sequential learning eases grammar identification, because at each step the learner faces fewer choices, and new hypotheses can be built on the foundations of past choices.[3] This concern also surfaces in the claim of psychologists who suggest that the data input to children is richly structured, in the sense that mothers' speech to children is simple, highly inflected, repetitious, and so forth, an almost Berlitz-like training sequence. We shall see in chapter 6 that there *are* cases where an acquisition model with a rigid order in which knowledge is acquired gives a better account of why a natural rule system is the way it is rather than some other way.

In summary, this book aims to carry out the research program of generative grammar in a computational setting. We start with a characterization of *what* constitutes knowledge of language, and then go on to describe *how*

---

[3]The definition of *noninstantaneous* as used here means that a certain implicational structure is "projected" into a temporal domain, i.e., that $P \rightarrow Q \equiv P$ *precedes* Q. This is not a necessary condition. Actually all that is required of a noninstantaneous model is that it contain implicational statements; these need not map over into an externally observable developmental sequence.

that knowledge is acquired. Before plunging on with the details of the acquisition model, it is worth pointing out just what the computational viewpoint contributes to the theory as a whole.

Generative grammar's "division of labor" into *what* and *how* has sometimes been taken to mean that one cannot proceed with a computational theory of grammar acquisition without first settling upon, in detail, the "right" theory of grammar. Such an interpretation might well be too strong. It is often possible to take a non-computational theory whose details are not fully worked out (such as a theory of generative grammar), and embed that theory in a computational framework in order to gain additional insight into the representations implied by that theory. In the best case, such a move even allows one to admit additional sources of evidence, for example, assessments of processing time complexity, or other psychophysical measurements, to guide the construction of a better theory.[4]

We can compare this approach to a similar research strategy, that chosen by D. Marr and his colleagues in the study of early visual processing. As Marr notes, in any research effort that is attempting to explain a complicated information processing system explanations may be pitched at any one of several different *levels of description*:

> ... in a system that solves an information processing problem, we may distinguish four important levels of description .... At the lowest, there is basic component and circuit analysis—how do transistors (or neurons), diodes (or synapses) work? The second level is the study of particular mechanisms: adders, multipliers, and memories, these being assemblies made from basic components. The third level is that of the algorithm, the scheme for a computation; and the top level contains the theory of the computation .... [T]ake the case of Fourier analysis. Here the computational theory of the Fourier transform ... is well understood, and is expressed independently of the particular way in which it might be computed. (Marr and Nishihara 1978)

---

[4]This is not to say, of course, that this approach is necessarily *easy* or that it will always succeed. In fact, as discussed in Berwick and Weinberg (1982), there have been numerous *unsuccessful* attempts to use psychophysical evidence to bear on the choice among alternative theories of grammar, attempts vitiated, for the most part, because of a failure to consider alternative computational instantiations.

In Marr's view, one may distinguish the *abstract theory of a computation* from the *particular algorithms* that realize that computation. This is the analogue of a distinction observed in the study of grammar. A theory of grammar corresponds to Marr's abstract theory of a computation: it tells us only *what* knowledge an ideal speaker-hearer has of language, abstracted away from any particular procedure that *uses* that knowledge (e.g., procedures for understanding or uttering sentences). And just as the abstract theory of a computation—for example, the mathematical theory of the Fourier transform—makes no reference to actual computational processes (indeed, makes no reference to *time* at all), the theory of generative grammar does not involve the notion of *time*, and hence actual language use, at all. The theory of grammar is to be "expressed independently of the particular way in which it might be computed."

Given that Marr's and the generative grammarian's research strategies are so much alike, it is perhaps surprising that considerable dissatisfaction has been voiced with the grammarian's stance of abstraction, but much less with Marr's. It is hard to distill this uneasiness into a single line or two, but at bottom, it seems to amount to this: these critics of generative grammar (or even of particular theories of grammar) sometimes seem to be saying that a theory that begins and *ends* with grammar cannot be a true account of the human language faculty. Marr, it should be noted, does not stop in his account of early visual processing at the abstract theory of the computation; he goes on to probe alternative algorithmic realizations of that theory, and a range of possible machine implementations for those algorithms, ultimately aiming for a full account of the *psychophysical* behavior of human visual perception. Isn't it then possible, these critics go on to say, that by *ignoring* the exigencies of computation—associated algorithms and machine implementations for grammars—that one could arrive at a theory of grammar that literally could not be incorporated into the human nervous system, i.e., a theory of grammar that could not be "psychologically real"? Note that, in Marr's terms, this would mean that we would have arrived at a theory of the abstract computation for which there was *no* associated algorithm.

This book shows that these fears of "nonrealizability" are unfounded. The acquisition model does the double-duty of first, accounting for language processing via a system closely tailored after the structures provided by generative grammar; and second, accounting for the unfolding of those processing abilities over time. Indeed, if the connections between learnability and parsability are correct, then not only can generative grammars for natural language be "realized" in models of parsing or acquisition, they can be *efficiently* realized. Evidently one can adapt Marr's levels-of-representation framework to the study of language and explore alternative algorithmic realizations of theories of grammar as models of sentence processing, acquisition, or sentence production.[5]

1.1   The Acquisition Model is Simple

With this background behind us, we can now move on to outline the acquisition model itself. Simply put, the system builds a series of *parsers* of increasing sophistication. Figures 1.1 and 1.2 give the overall picture. The parsers map English sentences to syntactic descriptions of those sentences— parse trees. Like any learning model, this one consists of three components: (1) some initial state of knowledge (what the system knows before it is exposed to any input data); (2) some specification of allowed input data (what the system can use as evidence to build new knowledge); and (3) an acquisition procedure that starts from the initial state and uses the input evidence to map to some desired target state of knowledge.

In the language learning system the initial state of knowledge corresponds to an initial set of parsing abilities and a knowledge of what counts as a valid rule of parsing. The system's initial parsing abilities are in fact nonexistent, but it does have a rudimentary ability to classify words as nouns or verbs and a crude representation of the semantic content of sentences. Words are assumed presegmented; the system does not have to learn how to chop up the sound stream into individual tokens. On the other hand, the system knows quite a lot about the constraints on possible parsing rules. As we shall see, it is these constraints that make learning possible. The input data consists of simple, grammatical sentences of English but is otherwise unprepared.

---

[5]Some have questioned just why a single process model should be made to serve both as a model of language use and as the cornerstone of an acquisition model. For instance, Fodor, Bever and Garrett (1974) suggested that substantially different mechanisms ("rule systems") are involved in language acquisition and in language use. One problem with this suggestion is that if language acquisition and language use are completely disassociated, then it would be difficult to explain how the mechanisms engaged in language use are acquired or why knowledge of language should be acquired in a form that is not used. Without adopting this radical proposal, one can formulate other, intermediate models that distinguish between acquisition and use. Fodor, Bever, and Garrett proposed that the representations (roughly, data structures) might be the same for acquisition and language use, though the actual algorithms operating with those data structures in parsing or production could differ, perhaps widely.

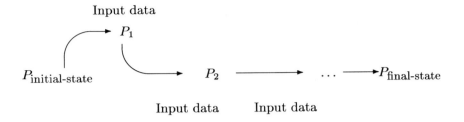

Figure 1.1: Acquisition as modeled by a sequence of parsers

We say that the system receives only *positive evidence* or positive examples. The sentences are simple because they contain at most two embeddings. No explicit correction, so-called *negative evidence*, is given, and sentences may be input in any order. These constraints were explicitly introduced to mirror corresponding constraints in human language acquisition.[6]

The acquisition procedure is incremental and failure-driven by its attempts to parse input sentences. Figure 1.2 sketches the idea. At any stage in the learning process, the system has some knowledge about how to parse sentences, P_i. Suppose it is given a new input sentence to parse. If it can already analyze the sentence without error, then nothing happens. If, on the other hand, it fails at some point in the left-to-right analysis of the sentence because none of its existing rules apply or because known rules fail, then it stops and appeals to its acquisition component. The acquisition module tries to build a single new parsing rule that will bridge the current gap in the parser's knowledge. If it can succeed, then this new rule is added to the parser's data base, perhaps after generalization with existing rules. If it does not succeed, then the analysis of the sentence is abandoned for the moment. This process is then repeated for the next input sentence.

The target state of knowledge is a "mature" parser that can handle a wide variety of constructions of English, the Marcus parser (Marcus 1980). As a working definition of "mature" we shall adopt the parsing abilities of Marcus's system, though this is by no means a complete set of rules to syntactically analyze all of English. The acquisition procedure constructs a sequence of new parsers, incrementally adding to or modifying the knowledge base of

---

[6]For additional discussion on the validity of these constraints, see chapter 2.

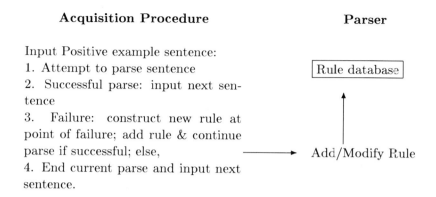

Acquisition Procedure

Input Positive example sentence:
1. Attempt to parse sentence
2. Successful parse: input next sentence
3. Failure: construct new rule at point of failure; add rule & continue parse if successful; else,
4. End current parse and input next sentence.

Parser

Rule database

Add/Modify Rule

Figure 1.2: Outline of the acquisition procedure

parsing rules in response to a set of input data. The intent is that this sequence will in fact home in to a correct target parser, where by "correct" we mean a parser that will build appropriate syntactic analyses. The following list gives an idea of the range of sentences analyzable after the acquisition procedure has been exposed to sufficient examples of the same kind. None of the sentences were analyzable prior to this, of course. The sentences are arranged in roughly ascending order of acquisition.

John scheduled a meeting for Tuesday. (Simple declarative sentence)

A meeting was scheduled for Tuesday. (Passive sentence)

Was a meeting scheduled for Tuesday? (Yes-no question)

John said that Bill scheduled a meeting for Tuesday.
(Embedded sentence)

Who scheduled a meeting? (*Wh* question)

I want to schedule a meeting for Tuesday.
(Embedded missing subject sentence)

As one can see, the acquisition system acquires primarily knowledge of syntax, though certain categorial information about individual words is also learned. How well does it work? One reference standard is the original Marcus parser. By that measure, by the time the system has processed several hundred sentences, it has acquired approximately 70% of the parsing rules originally hand-written for that parser.

With the bare-bones outline of the procedure in mind, let us turn to an actual example of acquisition. Since the system is grounded on the Marcus parser, we shall first give the briefest of descriptions of that processor and follow with a simple example of acquisition. Further details about the model and its operation are given in chapters 2, 3, and 4.

The Marcus parser: the target for learning

The Marcus parser is basically a variant of a left-to-right, bottom-up deterministic parser. In fact, it is both a restriction and an extension of the most general of deterministic bottom-up parsers, the LR(k) parsers (Knuth 1965).[7] The parser analyzes words left-to-right. It is deterministic in the weak sense that at any point in a sentence analysis, at most one parsing rule can apply. It is deterministic in the stronger sense that it is a deterministic *transducer*. It never "takes back" any of its parsing decisions. This constraint aids acquisition, as we shall see.[8] The parsing machine is bottom-up because it waits to see what is in the input sentences it analyzes before deciding what parsing rule to use. This is in contrast to a *top-down* parser that would first "guess" what rule to apply and then check that guess against the input.

The parser is divided into two parts, one a set of *grammar rules* that specify parsing actions and the other a grammar rule *interpreter* and set of *parser data structures* that work with the rules to actually build sentence

---

[7]It is not as general as the full-blown LR(k) parsers because of restrictions in the way in which grammatical information can be encoded in the state descriptions of the machine. It extends the LR(k) parsing method by using lookahead information encompassing full phrases as well as just single words. Chapters 2 and 7 have details.

[8]A machine that pursued possible syntactic analyses in parallel—as in standard versions of Earley's algorithm for context-free parsing—would thus fail to be deterministic in this sense. The Marcus parser is deterministic in the strong sense that any syntactic analysis it builds cannot be retracted. That is, the information written out as a sentence analysis is monotonically preserved. A deterministic simulation of a nondeterministic machine fails to be deterministic in this stronger sense because it must from time to time "backtrack" when one of its alternative decisions fails.

Before *reduce*:
Pushdown
stack:

After *reduce*:
Pushdown
stack:

Figure 1.3: Before and after a *reduce* action

analyses. This much is common to all parser designs, and we shall describe
each part in turn. We must also describe just what the output of the parser
is. Acquisition is modeled by assuming the learning system already knows
about the parser's working data structures and what grammar rules should
look like. The system learns the grammar rules themselves.

The Marcus parser uses two basic data structures, a *pushdown stack*
and a *lookahead buffer*. First, like general bottom-up parsers for context-
free languages, the Marcus parser has a pushdown stack in which to save
partially built phrases. The use of the pushdown stack can best be understood
by a simplified example. Suppose the grammar contained the re-write rule,
$S \rightarrow NP\ VP$—that is, the rule that a Sentence consists of a Noun Phrase
followed by a Verb Phrase. In a bottom-up analysis we wait to assemble a
larger phrasal unit, like a Sentence, until all its subparts are in place. Here,
this would mean waiting until both the Noun Phrase and Verb Phrase have
been assembled. These intermediate subparts are saved on the pushdown
stack. The VP would be on top of the stack, and the NP the second element
down. In the basic step of bottom-up parsing, these two subunits would be
combined, or *reduced*, to form the Sentence phrase. The parser replaces the
VP and NP units on the stack with a new unit, the S(entence). We can also
build the syntactic analysis tree at the same time by gluing the NP and VP
to the S node. Figure 1.3 depicts the action.

Of course, the Noun Phrase and the Verb Phrase itself will contain
internal syntactic details that are not shown here. In addition, the Marcus
parser does not slavishly adhere to the "wait until done" bottom-up analysis
strategy. It would actually attach the NP and VP separately. These differences
are discussed in chapters 2 and 7.

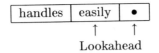

Figure 1.4: How the Marcus lookahead buffer stores information

Second, like the class of LR(k) parsers, the machine also uses *lookahead* information implemented by a buffer; this is its second data structure. That is, it can peer ahead into the input sentence—a stream of words—in order to make current parsing decisions. This information is useful because it can narrow down the choice of what to do next. For instance, in the sentence below, the parser would like to determine whether *handles* is the main Noun of the Subject NP or the main Verb, but this cannot be determined until the word after *handles* is seen:

    The cover handles...

If the next word is an adverb, say, *easily*, then *handles* is a verb; if the next word is a verb, say *are*, then it is the Subject. The examples are from Milne (1983):

    The cover handles easily.

    The cover handles are stainless steel.

The Marcus lookahead buffer is three cells long. Typically words from the input sentence fill the positions in this array by entering the buffer on the righthand end. The leftmost buffer position holds the input element currently under analysis. The other two positions contain lookahead words. In this book we shall distinguish between currently analyzed token and lookahead information by separating the leftmost buffer cell slightly from the other two. Figure 1.4 shows how the input buffer would be filled at the time *handles* is analyzed in the sentence *The cover handles easily*.

    Finally, the real heart of the parser lies in its grammar rules, those action statements that actually say what operations to carry out. The Marcus parser represents its grammar rules in an IF-THEN format. The IF part of the rule is a trigger that examines the pushdown stack and the input buffer and fires off the THEN portion as a parsing action. The IF portion of a grammar rule is a predicate that must hold of the tokens in the buffer, the top element in the pushdown stack, and perhaps of a fixed number of other elements in the stack. If that predicate holds, the THEN portion of the rule is executed. An executable action builds or labels the analysis tree, reads a new word into the input buffer, removes an element from the leftmost buffer position, or moves an element from the top of the stack to the leftmost buffer position.[9] For example, consider the following pushdown stack–input buffer configuration corresponding to the Sentence rule described earlier. Suppose that the Verb Phrase (VP) has been completely built and now resides in the leftmost buffer cell. Now following the actual Marcus parser design, we suppose that the NP is already attached to an S(entence) node. An end of sentence marker is in the second buffer cell. What should the parser do next? A reasonable action is to *attach* the VP to the S, removing it from the leftmost buffer position. A reasonable trigger for this action is precisely the configuration described. The resulting grammar rule looks like this:

> IF:
>
>> Top of stack is S with an NP attached;
>> Leftmost buffer cell contains VP;
>> Second buffer cell contains the end-of-sentence marker;
>
> THEN:
>
>> Attach VP to S.

Figure 1.5 depicts all the pieces of the parser: the two data structures (pushdown stack and input buffer); and the finite set of grammars rules that "drives" the parsing machine. Some additional details about the parser's operation will be presented in chapter 2.

The Marcus parser contains many dozens of rules in its database, denoted by the deceptively small box labeled "grammar rule control" in figure 1.5. Since grammar rules must build the sentence parse tree, it is not surprising that the majority of these rules carry out tree-building functions. There are rules that say when to start building a new piece of the analysis tree, when to stop building a part of the tree, and where to put a newly-completed portion of the analysis tree. There are also rules that label tree fragments (we may want to label a sentence as a *question*, for example), insert particular words (in an imperative sentence, we could supply the implicit *you*), and

---

[9]There are a few other actions, but the details do not matter at this point in the discussion.

Finite-state grammar
rule control

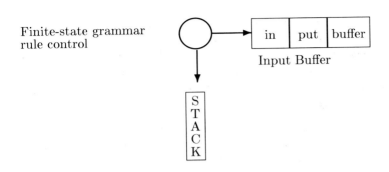

Figure 1.5: The Marcus parser in schematic form

undo the effects of local changes to simple sentences (this is what happens in a *yes-no* question, such as, *will John schedule a meeting?*). There are also special rules that initiate and stop the sentence analysis.

Finally, we sketch the output representation the parser builds. The machine constructs a *parse tree* representation of the hierarchical phrase structure of the input sentence. The tree is annotated by additional information as to whether the input sentence is declarative, imperative, and so forth. In addition, the analysis tree mimics the suggested representation of the underlying form of sentences proposed by modern transformational grammar. For our simplified discussion here, the major difference this makes is that the analysis tree is augmented with special markers indicating the location of "missing" arguments. A missing argument is just a Noun Phrase that has been moved from its ordinary position. For instance, in English the Object of a verb is usually immediately after the verb: *John likes ice cream.* But if we form the question *What does John like?* there is nothing after the verb. This "missing" argument is *what*. The analysis tree indicates this by inserting a dummy placeholder NP (dominating no words).

How rules are learned

The Marcus parser contains on the order of 100 grammar rules. Given example sentences, the acquisition system must learn these rules on its own. For any particular grammar rule, it must therefore discover which IF and THEN statements should be glued together. This is where failure-driven acquisition come into play. As mentioned, if at any point during the analysis of a sentence no known grammar rule applies, the system attempts to build a new grammar rule to do the job. We now know what a new grammar rule must look like. It will have an IF trigger and a THEN rule action. The acquisition system must decide what these should be.

For the new rule trigger, the acquisition procedure simply adopts the buffer cell and top-of-stack contents present at the point of failure.[10] Determining the new rule action is also easy. There are only four possible actions. One is to ATTACH the item in the left-most buffer cell to the node currently on top of the stack. We shall discuss the other three actions later on. What is crucial for the acquisition system is that an action's applicability can be simply tested and that two different actions cannot apply at the same time; these key learnability properties are also described in later chapters. For now though, it is enough to note that the system can just test each candidate action in turn, and pick the one that can apply. This becomes the new action. The new rule is possibly generalized against its current rule database. Rule generalization is possible when the new rule's action is the same as an existing rule, and the new rule's trigger partially matches an existing rule trigger. The exact conditions under which generalization operates are described in chapter 2. If generalization is possible, the revised generalized rule is simply the intersection of triggering features in the older, known rule and the newly acquired rule. (Again, just what the set of possible features of a rule can be is taken up in chapter 2.) After generalization with the other rules it already knows about, the system executes its new rule and continues with its analysis of the current input sentence.

Let us follow this procedure step-by-step for the NP–VP setting pictured earlier. We enter on the scene with the machine having a partial set of grammar rules. Assume the system has analyzed a given sentence, for example, *John scheduled the meeting for Tuesday*, as far as building the Subject NP *John* attached to the main S(entence) node, and the main Verb Phrase node *scheduled the meeting for Tuesday* as far as assembling the VP as a complete unit. The machine's top of stack element would then be an S (with the Subject NP attached). A VP would reside in the leftmost buffer cell. Now suppose that no known grammar rules can trigger. The acquisition procedure runs

---

[10]This is not entirely accurate. In fact, besides the top of the stack, one additional stack element can be involved.

Stack: $\boxed{\text{S}}$

Input buffer: $\boxed{\text{Will}}\ \boxed{\text{John}}\ \boxed{\text{schedule}}$

Figure 1.6: Initial machine state for *Will John* ... sentence

through its list of four possible actions. As it happens, ATTACH passes muster because the system knows that a Verb Phrase may be attached to a Sentence Phrase.[11] It assembles the trigger and action together as a new rule. In this case, no generalization is possible since there are no other known rules in common with this combination of trigger and action. The system executes the ATTACH and continues with the sentence analysis. In our running example, the obvious next step will be to recognize the end-of-sentence marker and finish off the parse.

The same procedure works for more complicated sentences. Let us look at just one more example now before continuing with a discussion of computational constraints on learnability. This second example will introduce another possible rule action, leaving just two others to be covered later.

For our second example, suppose that the grammar rule database includes all and only the rules necessary to successfully analyze a sentence such as, *John will schedule a meeting for Tuesday*. Now assume that the system receives as input the sentence, *Will John schedule a meeting for Tuesday*. Figure 1.6 shows the initial stack–input buffer configuration. Details of the features associated with each word have been suppressed.

No known grammar rules can trigger, because the only known rules handle sentences that begin with a Subject Noun Phrase. The system enters its acquisition phase. It first tries to ATTACH the leftmost buffer item, *will*, to the top of node element, S. This fails. Previous examples have fixed the order Noun Phrase–Verb Phrase for Sentences, and *will* is assumed known as a verbal element, not a Noun Phrase. It therefore cannot be attached as the Noun Phrase portion of the Sentence. The acquisition procedure next tries the action SWITCH. As its name suggests, SWITCH interchanges the contents of the leftmost buffer cell and the cell next to it, subject to certain constraints. A SWITCH succeeds if and only if some already existing grammar rule can

---

[11] Again, this is a gloss on what actually happens. The acceptability of attachment is actually derived from other quite general constraints. The system does not know specifically that the VP can attach to the S .

execute after the SWITCH. In this case, of course, a known rule can trigger: the very same rule used to analyze the beginning of *John will schedule a meeting*. The *switch* succeeds. The acquisition procedure saves the stack–buffer configuration as the trigger of the new rule, and *switch* as its action. This is a grammar rule to handle Subject-Auxiliary verb inversion.

Note that the new rule is quite specific. It calls for the token *will* to be in the leftmost buffer cell. Later examples, for example, *Did the official schedule the meeting?* will generalize this rule to permit any *auxiliary verb* to be in this position, and any Noun Phrase to be in the second buffer cell. Further, as we shall see in chapter 4, the acquisition procedure does not go overboard and permit inversion in any context. For instance, inversion does not occur in an embedded sentence context: *John thought that did Sue schedule a meeting* is not a grammatical sentence of English. The system properly acquires this distinction as well.

These two examples illustrate but do not exhaust the four kinds of syntactic knowledge that the learning system acquires. The system also learns:

1. The ordering information implicit in traditional phrase structure rules. The knowledge acquired here corresponds to the basic order and structure of (English) phrases, e.g., that a Verb Phrase consists of a verb followed by a possibly optional Noun Phrase. (Note that no commitment is made to precisely *how* this ordering information is expressed; one need not use explicit phrase structure rules.) The learning system fixes these rules by a "parameter setting" approach. All phrases are assumed to be assembled out of three pieces, based on the so-called $\overline{\mathrm{X}}$ theory of phrases: a *Head* or *Operator*; the *Arguments* to the Operator; and a *Specifier* for the Operator. The Head or Operator is the "core" of the phrase—the verb, if a Verb Phrase, the preposition, if a Prepositional Phrase, and so forth. The Specifier is something like *the* in a Noun Phrase; the Arguments are the "operands" of an Operator—the Objects of a Verb, Preposition, or Adjective Phrase. The system initially has the information that these three elements are unordered {Head, Arguments, Specifier}. It learns their order from example sentences.[12]

2. Lexical insertion grammar rules. This knowledge amounts to valid contexts for the insertion of terminal elements into a phrase structure tree.

---

[12]There are other initial constraints that aid in this task. See chapter 2.

One example is that a transitive verb like *kiss* must appear with a Noun Phrase Object.

3. Movement rules. This knowledge corresponds to particular movement operations, inversions, and the like, e.g., Noun Phrase movement; *wh* questions (*Who did Mary kiss?*); other fronted elements (*How many meetings did John schedule?*); Subject-Auxiliary verb inversion in questions. Chapter 4 gives detailed example scenarios.

4. Lexical categories. The system learns that words like *the* can be a part of a Noun Phrase, but that, e.g., *dogged* is a verb in *John dogged Mary*. To do this, it has a set of finite, binary-valued ($\pm$) *features*, initially grounded on an assumed known correspondence between objects and the feature $+N$, and actions and the feature $-V$. For example, a word known as an action in a particular sentence has the features $-N, +V$. An unknown word may be unmarked for either or both features,[13] and is coerced to a particular feature pattern according to a set of syntactic restrictions described in chapters 2 and 3. Sometimes, then, depending on what information is most secure, the learning system uses syntactic information to fix lexical categorization; in other cases, it is semantically-grounded information that fixes syntactic knowledge.

There are many syntactic constructions of English that cannot be acquired by the current system. A prime example is conjunction. It is hard to write grammar rules at all to handle conjunction. Part of the problem is that phrasal syntax seems to be a poor representation for the grammatical constraints on conjunction. Rather, conjunction seems best expressed in terms of the union of non-tree type structures.[14] Since rules for conjunction are hard to write at all, learning them automatically is even harder.

In general, since the system makes minimal use of semantic information, it cannot choose between alternatives that appear to demand some kind of "semantic" information. For example, given a sentence like, *John hit the guy*

---

[13]In effect, then, a "0" value is possible for a feature, resulting in a three-valued system.

[14]See Goodall (1984). More precisely, the familiar constraint that one can conjoin only phrases that "look alike" seems more readily described by the union of phrase markers, not trees.

with the hammer, it is impossible to tell whether the Prepositional Phrase modifies *guy* or serves as the instrumental argument of *hit*.[15]

The role of semantic information

The acquisition system learns syntax. What role do other kinds of linguistic knowledge play in this process? Besides its understanding of the proper form for grammar rules and the basic parsing machinery, several kinds of knowledge have been tacitly assumed. First, the system receives predigested words. This presupposes phonological knowledge and a feature system for word classification. Some of these features can themselves be learned, as suggested above. Chapters 4 and 5 have additional examples of this kind of learning. Second, at least in the early going, the system must appeal to a rudimentary representation of what the input sentence "means." This has sometimes been dubbed "semantic bootstrapping" (Grimshaw 1981). Since the role of bootstrapping is open to dispute, it is worthwhile to say just what this extra information comes to and how essential it is. Chapter 2 explores the use of semantic information in more detail.

What the system gets in addition to an input sentence is a crude representation of "who did what to whom." This information has also been called the *thematic role* structure of a sentence, and we shall use this term interchangeably with the term *predicate-argument structure*. Thematic roles are ubiquitous in linguistic theory, though a satisfactory theory of thematic roles remains elusive (see, e.g., Jackendoff 1972; Fillmore 1968). As an example, in the sentence, *John hit the vase with a hammer*, *John* is the AGENT of the action *hit*; *vase* is the AFFECTED OBJECT or PATIENT; *hammer* is the INSTRUMENT. Thus a thematic role representation provides an association of objects and actions. For simple sentences, this tight association is used to "fix" certain syntactic parameters that describe the most basic ordering constraints of a language. The assumption here is that at the very beginning of acquisition there is a 1-1 correspondence between thematic and syntactic representational units. This correspondence has been often noted (see Jakobson 1961; Limber 1973). In the learning system, it is used to fix the basic left-to-right order of phrases for main sentences (NP–Tense or Inflection–VP) and to tell when certain syntactic phrases are complete. Note that there is

---

[15]The point is that there are other, unambiguous sentences where the instrumental argument possibility can be acquired, e.g., *John hit Bill with a hammer*. These succumb using the minimal semantic information provided, as discussed immediately below.

nothing that says that it is semantic information that must provide this kind of information. In reality, any source of information—intonation perhaps, as suggested by Morgan and Newport (1981)—could be used to aid syntactic acquisition. All that is required is some confident alignment between syntactic units and these other representations. This is really what the "bootstrapping" hypothesis is all about.

Actually, "bootstrapping" (semantic or otherwise) *follows* from a general principle of acquisition from positive-only examples, the Subset Principle. This basic constraint on learning, described in later in section 2 of this chapter and in chapter 5, seems to account for a variety of ordering constraints proposed in the language acquisition literature. Briefly, the Subset Principle states that learning hypotheses are ordered in such a way that positive examples can disconfirm them. For many cases, the ordering will force the narrowest possible *language* to be hypothesized first, so that no alternative target language can be a subset of the hypothesized language. More precisely, no other target language compatible with the triggering data that led to the new hypothesis language can be a proper subset of that language. Importantly, the Subset Principle is necessary and sufficient for acquisition from positive examples.

A 1-1 syntactic/thematic correspondence follows from the Subset Principle. The most rigid, narrowest possible surface language is one where syntactic and thematic units are strictly aligned: for example, AGENT and Subject Noun Phrase come first; followed by the action; followed by the AFFECTED OBJECT. Suppose now that a strict superset of this language was a possible target language. For example, suppose that in addition to the basic order just described, some other order was possible—say, that the AFFECTED OBJECT could come first, as it most often does in passive sentences—and after the main verb. Then a wider language would be possible. If the learner hypothesized this language and was wrong, there would be no way to retract this guess using positive evidence alone. The Subset Principle states that this broader alternative is considered only *after* the 1-1 hypothesis is refuted. Thus the Subset Principle predicts that the *first* hypothesis will be thematic-syntactic alignment. This is in fact the case for children, as is well known (Slobin 1966; Brown 1973). Later sentences relax the alignment.

While thematic information is important, its role has been minimized here. The reasons for this are twofold. First, the theory of thematic roles is undeveloped. It is problematic to base a learning theory on a promissory note, however tempting its possible rate of return. It seems safest to rely on minimal information that can be argued to be plausibly available in undegraded form. Second, too much thematic information "gives away" the problem by indirectly encoding the syntax of sentences. Note that the thematic role representation of a simple sentence does not directly encode syntax; we might think of it as an unordered set of associations. For complex (embedded) sentences though, a thematic role structure would partially encode the hierarchy of the sentence, since an embedded sentence would itself have a thematic role structure. So for example, given the sentence, *John thinks that Bill believes that Mary wants to leave*, whereas what John wants is a complex sentence (*that Bill believes* ...), this sentence itself has an Agent (*Bill*), the thing believed, and so forth. In this case the thematic representation replicates hierarchical phrasal structure.

We avoid this problem by using thematic role information only for simple sentences. This is arguably more plausible. The syntactic structure of embedded sentences is parasitic on that of simple sentences. As more grammar rules are acquired, the need for thematic role information declines, and syntactic and thematic representations diverge. Eventually, the system can use its syntactic knowledge to infer thematic representations, rather than the other way around.

1.2   Constraints Make Learning Possible

Aside from engineering aspects, the acquisition model is important for what it says about the constraints that make learning possible. Simply put, what makes the rules easy to acquire is that the choices that must be made are few. The acquisition program is limited to constructing rules only of a certain kind, built from but a handful of possible actions. The success of this approach confirms a truism in artificial intelligence: having the right restrictions on a given representation can make learning simple.

Two kinds of constraints have been investigated. The first kind is tightly linked to other restrictions that make parsing fast. The second kind of constraint involves the ordering of hypotheses. The next sections review each of these in turn.

Learnability constraints and parsability constraints

Learnability and parsability constraints can only be compared within specific models of learning and parsing. The parsing model we shall use is essentially the Marcus parser. As for learning models, besides the computer model described earlier, there is a carefully articulated existing mathematical model for the acquisition of a generative (transformational) grammar, that of Wexler and Culicover 1980.[16] The computer model was developed independently of the Wexler and Culicover work. Nevertheless, there are striking similarities between the two approaches that stimulated a more careful investigation of the relationships between the two. Let us review these.

First of all, similar constraining principles figure in the success of both the computer and the Wexler and Culicover models. This is not coincidental. Both approaches incorporate essentially the same constraints on permissible grammatical rules. For Wexler and Culicover, the key learnability criterion that must be met is that the target grammars must exhibit what they call "bounded degree of error" (BDE). Informally, the BDE property is a claim about language "separability." BDE asserts that a sufficient condition for the learnability of a family of grammars is that they be distinguishable by simple data. The idea is that the learner must pick out a correct target from some family of potential targets using just example sentences drawn from the target as evidence. BDE claims this can always be done after seeing a finite number of sentence examples *if* the space of possible errors the learner could ever make is exhausted by the possible errors the learner could make by looking just at simple sentences. Here, a "simple" sentence is one that is limited in its depth of embedding: Wexler and Culicover allow sentences that contain embedded sentences, and these embedded sentences may themselves contain embedded sentences. For example, *John persuaded Bill that Howie believed the world is flat* is the most complex sort of sentence allowed.

Wexler and Culicover's incremental learning model works jointly with error detection as follows. They base their work on a model of transformational grammar current in the mid 1960s. Within this framework, a "grammar" consists in part of a set of *transformational rules* that map simple tree structures (deep structures) to derived surface sentences. Thus any legal

---

[16]The Wexler and Culicover work was also done with H. Hamburger (Hamburger and Wexler 1975), but, for convenience, this joint research will be referred to simply as "Degree-2 theory," because the acquisition model it posits uses only input sentences of degree of embedding 2 or less.

surface sentence s has at least one underlying, associated deep structure, b. Deep structures are generated by some context-free grammar. Wexler and Culicover's procedure learns the transformational mapping, T carrying b to s, given a sequence of (b, s) pairs.

Suppose the learner has acquired some set of transformational rules T_t up through time t. Now suppose the learner is given a new pair (b', s'). It applies its known mapping T_t to b'. If this yields the sentence s', then all is well. If not—the mapping yields a sentence $T_t(b') = s'' \neq s'$ (possibly no valid surface sentence)—then we say that a *detectable error* has been uncovered. Stimulated by the error, the learner adds or subtracts one transformational rule to its T_t. The depth of embedding of b' is the *degree of the error*. BDE can now be stated precisely:

> Let T be a family of transformational grammars. T is BDE if, for any deep structure grammar B, there exists a finite integer k such that for any possible target transformational mapping T_{adult} and hypothesized mapping T_{child}, if there is a detectable error on any underlying deep structure b generated by B, then there is a detectable error on deep structure b' generated by B, with the depth of embedding of b' at most k.

Wexler and Culicover must advance a whole host of restrictions on a family of grammars in order to ensure that it meets the BDE condition. Without going into detail on these now, it is enough to note that the effect of each constraint is to guarantee that errors will remain localized. For example, consider a rule that looks at a domain of 5 embedded sentences deep in order to work properly. Plainly, a system with this rule cannot be acquired by looking at sentences only 3 deep. We may conclude that any system that meets the BDE condition must ensure that any single rule does not look at unboundedly complex sentences for its proper operation. Wexler and Culicover call this the *Binary Principle*.

Now consider the computer model. The analog of the Binary Principle is the model's restriction on its triggering *if* conditions. Just as Wexler and Culicover restrict single rules to operate locally, the computer model's grammar rule triggers look only at the contents of the three buffer cells, the top-of-stack cell, and one additional stack element. There is no grammar rule that uses potentially unbounded triggering contexts for its operation—

IF:

> top of stack is an S;
> leftmost buffer cell holds an NP;

THEN:

> attach NP to the S.

(a) A possible grammar rule.

IF:

> top of stack is an S;
> 2nd element in stack is an S;
> 7th element in stack is an S;
> leftmost buffer cell holds an NP;

THEN:

> attach NP to the S.

(b) An impossible grammar rule.

Figure 1.7: Only some grammar rules are possible

for example, a rule that looks down ten elements into the pushdown stack. Figure 1.7 compares a possible grammar rule to an impossible rule.

In fact, each one of Wexler and Culicover's constraints is reflected in the computer model. Table 1.1 summarizes the comparison. The reader should consult chapter 7 for further explanation of the Wexler and Culicover constraints.

Our first comparison, then, shows that two learning models—the Wexler and Culicover model and the computer model—are close cousins. A related result shows that learnability and parsability constraints are closely yoked. To carry out this comparison we must propose a model of efficient parsability. We take as our paradigm the class of parsers defined by Marcus type machines. This class is formalized as the Bounded Context parsers (BC parsers), deterministic, bottom-up parsers that use bounded right and left context patterns based on actual grammar symbols.[17] All that *literal* context means is that the symbols in the pushdown stack and buffer are just the unalloyed symbols that would be part of the grammar—symbols like S, NP, words, or grammatical features. We are not permitted to use symbols that do not otherwise appear in the grammar. We say that a grammar is bounded context parsable (BCP) if there is a BC parser that can analyze all the sentences generated by the grammar and assign the same descriptions (parse trees) that the grammar does to these sentences. This "transparency" is particularly attractive because it insists on a close connection between grammatical knowledge and how that knowledge is actually put to use. Further, this class of parsers serves as a good proxy for "efficiently parsable" because in most cases such machines operate in time linearly proportional to the length of sentences.

Suppose now that we have a finite family of BC parsable grammars, defined in the right way so as to represent the learner's possible target guesses about the language it is encountering. Chapter 7 shows that this family already meets the BDE condition. In this sense, then, once we have a family of (natural) grammars that meet a reasonable criterion for being efficiently parsable, then that family will also be learnable. Two key functional properties of language are thereby ensured. Given this result, it is no surprise that the a learning model based on the Marcus machine, a bounded context parser of an extended kind, would mirror the Wexler and Culicover BDE constraints.

---

[17]These parsers are related to the Bounded Context Parsers of Floyd (1964) as extended by Szymanski and Williams (1976). Chapter 7 gives the details.

Wexler and Culicover Constraints	Acquisition Procedure Constraints
Incremental rule acquisition	Incremental rule acquisition
No negative evidence	No negative evidence
No memory for past sentences	No memory for past sentences
(only current sentence used	(only current sentence used
as data)	as data)
Small number of	Small number of
new rule hypotheses	new rule hypotheses
Simple sentences used	Simple sentences used
Deterministic generation	Deterministic parsing
Binary principle	⎫ Determinism plus locality
Freezing principle	⎬ restrictions imposed by buffer
Raising principle	⎭ and pushdown stack context
No bottom context	

Table 1.1: Wexler and Culicover constraints compared to computer model

Ordering constraints in acquisition

Besides illuminating the learnability–parsability connection, another contribution of the computational point of view is its analysis of developmental ordering effects. To see just what is at stake here, consider the "abstract" picture of language acquisition outlined in Chomsky's *Aspects of A Theory of Syntax*:

> A child who is capable of language learning must have
>
> (i) a technique for representing input signals
>
> (ii) a way of representing structural information about these signals
>
> (iii) some initial delimitation of a class of possible hypotheses about language structure
>
> (iv) a method for determining what each hypothesis implies with respect to each structure
>
> (v) a method for selecting one of the (presumably, infinitely many) hypotheses that are allowed by (iii) and are compatible with the given primary linguistic data. (1965:31)

> This [language acquisition] device must search through the set of
> possible hypotheses $G_1, G_2, \ldots$, which are available to it by virtue
> of condition (iii), and must select grammars that are compatible
> with the primary linguistic data, represented in terms of (i) and
> (ii). It is possible to test compatibility by virtue of the fact that
> the device meets condition (iv). The device would then select one
> of these potential grammars by the evaluation measure guaranteed
> by (v). (1965:32)

It is easy to see what the computer model and the *Aspects* model have in common. Both presume an ability to represent the speech signal as a highly structured set of input tokens—in the case of the acquisition procedure, as the segmented individual words input to the parser. Both propose to represent those signals as highly abstract, labeled tree structures. Finally, both approaches assume restrictions on the possible hypotheses about those structures—on the one hand, initial constraints on grammars, and on the other, universal constraints on the parser's operating principles and a knowledge of what counts as a valid rule of parsing.

It is true though that the *Aspects* model has deliberately (and even legitimately) abstracted away from the actual time course of acquisition in its attempt to arrive at a perspicuous idealization. In a word, it is an instantaneous model of acquisition: it lumps all possible candidate grammars and data together, and, using a selection function (the evaluation measure, or evaluation metric) picks out the "best" grammar (the "correct" G_i) at one fell swoop. As Chomsky notes in the footnote to the passage quoted immediately above, this is once a again a scientific idealization of the usual sort, an assumption known to be false, yet apparently innocuous:

> What I am describing is an idealization in which only the moment of acquisition of the correct grammar is considered .... it
> might very well be true that a series of successively more detailed
> and highly structured schemata (corresponding to maturational
> stages, but perhaps in part themselves determined in form by
> earlier steps of language acquisition) are applied to the data at
> successive stages of language acquisition. (1965:202)

The computer model pursues the consequences of an explicit developmental approach. There are at least two possible rewards to this approach. First of all, a problem for any "learning theory" is to account for how a learner is "driven" from one stage of knowledge to the next. This is a major hurdle for developmental models:

> There is, however, a very general problem with practically all studies of language development, whether investigated from the standpoint of rule acquisition, strategy change, or elaboration of mechanism. The problem arises both for accounts that postulate 'stages' of development (i.e. a finite number of qualitatively distinct levels of organization through which the organism passes en route from molecule to maturity), and for accounts that view development as a continuous function of simple accumulation. The difficulty is this: No one has seriously attempted to specify a mechanism that 'drives' language acquisition through its 'stages' or along its continuous function. Or more succinctly: there is no known learning theory for language. (Marshall 1979:443)

The current model is designed to remedy at least part of this problem: it is the parser's attempts to interpret sentences that provides a specific driving mechanism for acquisition. In this sense, this model constitutes a true theory of acquisition.

Second, even though a developmental approach need not necessarily provide any new insights into the structure of grammar, it could be useful in its own right as a theory of the actual time course of acquisition. In other words, if one was interested in explaining what actually *happens* in acquisition, then a theory that attends to the time course of events would seem to be crucial. Such a theory is of obvious interest to those who are interested in developmental processes in and of themselves. Thus, those who are interested in why what looks like a rule of "truncated passives" (*John was kissed*) is acquired earlier than a rule for full passives (*John was kissed by Mary*), or why auxiliary verb inversion appears to be acquired at different times depending on which *wh*-question word is involved, must look to an essentially developmental theory, perhaps of the kind described here. Note that there is no necessary contradiction between the instantaneous and noninstantaneous viewpoints, but simply a difference in research aims.

Finally, but more speculatively, by incorporating the actual time course of events into an acquisition model, we may hope to gain further insight into what distinguishes the class of natural languages from arbitrary symbol systems. As discussed above, the belief here is that there may actually be developmental dependencies that further restrict the space of hypothesizable grammars—dependencies such that earlier choices constrain the choices that must be made at a later stage. The advantages are uncertain. Staging contingencies are, of course, quite common in the development of other biological structures, but whether such dependencies play a crucial role in the acquisition of grammars is open to question. Chapter 6 explores this issue.

What does it mean for the notion of *time* or *developmental stages* to play an essential role in an acquisition process? In the "search space" metaphor of acquisition, it amounts to the claim that grammars are separable (hence acquirable) in part as the result of the *order* in which certain decisions are made. Put another way, it asserts that once, say, part of the rule system for grammar G_i has been fixed, then certain other options, say those that are part of grammars G_j or G_k can never be acquired, or are inaccessible. Chapter 6 draws on the particular case of regularities in phonological systems (from Kean 1974) to show that this developmental account may in fact actually explain why certain phonological systems do not occur naturally.

To say then that ordering plays an essential role in acquisition is to say, analogous to the embryological case, that once certain pathways have been selected (on the basis of specific triggering evidence), other options may be cut off forever (or at least severely restricted). To say that ordering plays an *essential* role is to make the stronger claim that restricting developmental pathways in this fashion is necessary for the successful identification of grammars for natural languages.[18]

As an example, consider again knowledge of the "canonical" ordering of constituents in an English Noun Phrase. As several authors have noted,[19] the basic order of Article-Noun or Adjective-Noun—such as in *a bottle* or *big dish*—appears early in a child's productions. Furthermore, once these forms are established, gross errors such as **book a*, do not arise. One could account for this rapid fixation on the right phrase structure by postulating the

---

[18]Some care is required in the discussion of ordering effects. There are certain results of formal learnability theory (Blum and Blum 1975) suggesting that order-dependent language identification can be replaced by order independent learning functions. This is done essentially by allowing the order independent learning machine to enumerate all data sequences until it finds the sequence used by the order dependent learning machine. If this kind of enumerative strategy is not allowed, then this construction does not really apply to the natural language case, however.

[19]See e.g., Williams (1981c).

existence of a structural "parameter" of all Noun Phrases that would permit, say, Articles to appear to either the right or the left side of the Noun, but not both sides. The decision as to right or left attachment could then be left to the actual evidence the child hears: upon encountering (innumerable) forms like *the doll*, one could conclude that the sequence Article–Noun is the "right" setting of the option, the sequence Noun-Article, not so allowed.[20] This "parameterized" view of acquisition reflects directly the so-called $\overline{\text{X}}$ theory of phrase structure.

Here is how the $\overline{\text{X}}$ theory works with the acquisition model. All phrase structure rules for natural grammars are assumed to be expansions of just a few templates of a rather specific form:

$$XP \to \ldots X \ldots$$

Here, the X stands for a lexical category, the word that forms the core of the phrase. In most accounts of $\overline{\text{X}}$ theory, the ellipses are filled in with complete phrases of other categories or specified grammatical formatives, such as Articles, Noun Phrases, Adjectives, or Prepositional Phrases, among others. Actual phrase structure rules are fleshed out by choosing a particular lexical category as the X (also called the *head* of the phrase) and fixing some way to fill out what may precede or follow it. We also call the head the Operator in this book, since semantically it acts like one. The other components of the template are the *arguments* to the head or Operator, sometimes called the *Complement* of the phrase, and particular elements that externally *specify* the Head (the so-called Specifiers, such as the determiner *the* in a Noun Phrase.) The key idea of $\overline{\text{X}}$ theory is that this triple {*Head, Arguments, Specifier*} is ordered in the same way for all phrase types.

For example, by setting $X = V$(erb) and allowing some other XP to the right of the verb as an argument we would get one possible Verb Phrase rule,

$$VP \to Verb\ NP$$

But this would also fix the order for Noun Phrase or Prepositional Phrase arguments. Other choices give other languages. In German the object Noun

---

[20]Plainly, this is the "ideal" case; one must leave room for the acquisition of patterns where articles appear on both sides of the Head Noun. These could well be acquired on the basis of "brute force" induction; see Chapter 5. Since, as Chapter 5 shows, "brute force" induction can make large demands on data input and computational resources, there would be a high cost to such variation away from the ideal case.

Phrase is arguably attached to the left of the verb.[21] The space of possible natural phrase structure systems is thereby delimited.

Given this template-filling approach, the problem for the learner is essentially reduced to figuring out what items are permitted to go in the slots on either side of the X. Note that the XP schema tightly constrains the set of possible hierarchical tree structures generated by the base phrase structure rules. For instance, no Noun Phrase rule of the form.

$$NounPhrase \rightarrow Article\ Adjective\ Noun\ Noun$$

would be admissible as a core part of phrase structure.

To see in outline how the $\overline{X}$ constraints can simplify the phrase structure induction task, suppose that the acquisition procedure has already acquired a phrase structure rule for English main sentences,

$$Sentence \rightarrow NounPhrase\ VerbPhrase$$

and now requires information to determine the proper expansion of a Verb phrase.

The $\overline{X}$ theory cuts through the maze of possible expansions for the right-hand side of this rule. Assuming that Noun Phrases are the only other known category type, $\overline{X}$ theory tells us that there are only a few possible configurations for a Verb Phrase rule:

$VerbPhrase \rightarrow Verb$ or

$VerbPhrase \rightarrow NounPhrase\ Verb$ or

$VerbPhrase \rightarrow Verb\ NounPhrase$ or

$VerbPhrase \rightarrow NounPhrase\ Verb\ NounPhrase$

etc.

Now suppose that the learner can classify word tokens as Nouns, Verbs, or "other" (perhaps by at first linking items to some semantic grounding as objects and actions, as suggested earlier). Then by simply matching an example sentence such as *John kissed Mary* against the array of possible phrase structure expansions, the correct Verb Phrase rule can be quickly deduced. Only

---

[21]Thiersch (1978).

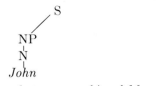

words to come: *kissed Mary.*

(a) Before VP construction.

words to come: *Mary.*

(b) After VP construction

Figure 1.8: $\overline{\text{X}}$ acquisition of a VP expansion.

one context-free tree can be fit successfully against the given input string. Omitting much detail (see chapter 3), the parse proceeds left-to-right with *John* first built as a Noun Phrase and recognized as a valid part of the expansion of the already-known rule $S \rightarrow NP\,VP$. (Note that *John* is attached as an NP by a grammar rule, as discussed earlier.) The resulting tree is depicted in figure 1.8(a).

Since *kissed* is supposedly recognizable as a non-Noun action—a Verb—the $\overline{\text{X}}$ schema is entered with $X = V$. The head of the $\overline{\text{X}}$ schema must, by definition, be a verb; only *kissed* meets this criterion. Consequently, *kissed* can be attached as the V portion of the growing tree (again by a lexical insertion rule). See figure 1.8(b). (Note that one might have required that the insertion of *kiss* be made contingent upon the presence of a Noun Phrase to the right of *kiss*. This test can be automatically accommodated in the parser via the lookahead buffer. One temporarily suspends processing of *kiss* to analyze the tokens to its right into (possibly) a complete Noun Phrase.)

At a stroke, the other options that attach Noun Phrases to the left of the head in a Verb Phrase are ruled out. The only choice left open is whether the given input example is compatible with Noun Phrase attachment to the right of the head. The next move of the parser shows that it is: *Mary* is recognizable as a name, hence a Noun and Noun Phrase; it is available for attachment to the Verb Phrase under construction, completing construction of the parse tree.

The correct expansion is fixed. A single simple example has provided positive evidence sufficient to establish a major English phrase structure rule. Although this is but a simple example, it still illustrates how phrase structure rules can be acquired by a process akin to "parameter setting": given a highly constrained initial state, the desired final state can be obtained upon exposure to very simple triggering data. The additional examples in chapter 3 show how the entire phrase structure system can be reduced to the fixing of just a few basic parameters within the $\overline{\text{X}}$ framework.

One immediate question about the "parameter fixing" approach is its resilience to error. Suppose the learner gets examples that do not follow the canonical Head–Complement order of English, for example, imperatives or *wh*-questions. These are certainly common enough examples (though it is widely suspected by adults, perhaps correctly, that children immediately map all imperative examples to the null string). Or it might be that the learner gets examples where the categories of lexical items is unknown. How are the $\overline{\text{X}}$ parameters fixed in these cases? The answer is that parameters are fixed and grammar rules acquired only in "clear cases." If we regard a parameter system as a set of simultaneous equations, then there can be at most one "unknown" for acquisition to proceed. This conservative acquisition strategy also follows the Subset Principle. Consider what happens in an imperative sentence, e.g., *Give Bill the ball.* If the category of *give* is unknown, then there is no problem because the parameter fixing procedure is underdetermined. (If some parameters are already fixed, then in fact this may be used to infer the category of *give*, as we shall see in chapter 4.) If *give* is known as a verb, then we must somehow guarantee that the order Verb–Subject–Object is not inferred. But this is not a problem, since initially we fix a thematic–syntactic correspondence between AGENT (in this case, the person addressed) and Subject. The system knows that *Bill* is not the AGENT. Fixing *Bill* as the Object is permitted, and in fact establishes the correct Head-Complement order. Evidently the system is tightly constrained to avoid errors and possible backtracking. Examples in chapters 3–5 give additional examples of this property.[22]

Of course, once the basic order of phrases is fixed, then variations are permitted, following the incremental acquisition procedure. It is this gradual relaxation of constraint that produces the surface evolution of the system's

---

[22] A more subtle example of this kind is the presentation of auxiliary inverted sentences, e.g., *Will John give* ... before ordinary declarative sentences. Here we must block a decision of AUX NP VP as the "basic" sentence order for English. We want the system to fix the order NP AUX VP as the correct basic order. We shall see that the incorrect basic order is again prevented by an underdetermination of constraint: the INFL category is not initially known, but is parasitic on the basic sentence order NP VP. Therefore, this basic order is fixed before the inverted sentences can be correctly analyzed and so cause difficulties for acquisition.

abilities. By establishing an order in which parameters may be fixed, the $\overline{\text{X}}$ theory also delimits the possible "developmental envelopes" for acquisition, providing a theoretical framework for interpreting actual ontogenetic data.

Just how does developmental sequencing matter in the acquisition of grammars? Formal analysis and experience with the acquisition procedure itself has led to the formulation of a set of specific *ordering criteria*, part of the temporal structure of the "program" that fixes a grammar on the basis of positive-only evidence:

- Rules that fix basic phrase order are acquired before rules that fix local movement rules. In turn, rules that fix local movement are acquired before rules that fix general movement of constituents.

- Rules cannot contain arbitrary Boolean predicates on their triggering conditions. (Suggested in Marcus 1980.)

- Rules are assumed obligatory until positive example sentences show that they are optional.[23]

- Arguments to verbs are assumed obligatory until proven otherwise.

- Arguments are assumed to appear immediately adjacent to Verbs (more generally, their operators) until proven otherwise by positive examples.

In fact, each of these constraints turns out to reflect a necessary and sufficient condition for acquisition from positive-only evidence (given a certain mathematical model for that acquisition), the *Subset Principle*. This principle is one of conservative acquisition: the learner should hypothesize languages in such a way that positive evidence can refute an incorrect guess.

More precisely, the Subset Principle ensures that a family of languages will be identifiable in the limit (in the sense of Gold 1967) from positive-only examples. Informally, by "identifiable in the limit" we mean that (1) assuming the learner is getting example sentences one at a time, there is some point after which which the learning system never changes its hypothesized grammar; and (2) the hypothesized grammar is a correct grammar for the target language. The Subset Principle says that such learning is guaranteed just in case for all target languages L_i of a family of recursive languages L, there exists an (effective) procedure that can enumerate positive examples

---

[23] Also proposed by Roeper (1981).

$S_1, S_2, \ldots$ such that (i) $S_i \subseteq L_i$; and (ii) For all $j > 1$, if $S_i \subseteq L_j$, then $L_j \not\subseteq L_i$. It is because the alternative targets L_j *cannot* be subsets of the guessed L_i that this is dubbed the "Subset Principle." This constraint has been implicit in the linguistic literature for several years (see, e.g., Baker 1979) and was also formulated, apparently independently, by Angluin (1978) in a more formal recursive-theoretic setting. The condition as formulated above is taken from Angluin 1978. Chapters 5 and 6 discuss the implications of this principle in detail. We shall see that the Subset Principle accounts for the ordering principles implicit in the acquisition model as well as several observed linguistic constraints. We gave one example of its application earlier, in an account of "semantic bootstrapping."

The difficulty of acquisition given positive-only evidence also interacts with program model of acquisition. In particular, it is shown in chapter 5 that rule systems that are *disjunctively complete* (in a sense to be made precise) are difficult, sometimes impossible, to acquire from positive-only evidence. This result serves as a strong constraint on possible notational systems for grammars. For example, it means that one cannot admit notational devices that can be interpreted as disjunctive into the statement of rules, such as the use of braces in phonological or phrase structure systems. As a case in point, the constraint against disjunction implies that rules of the following form are to be avoided:

VP → V {NP *or* S} e.g., VP → V NP; VP → V S

The elimination of such disjunctions in rules has recently received independent support in the work of Stowell 1981. What the formal analysis shows is that these linguistic proposals can be independently justified on grounds of acquisition. As case studies of the interaction between the information-theoretic developmental model and acquisition constraints, three separate rule systems are analyzed: Kean's (1974) theory of markedness in phonological rule systems; the $\overline{\text{X}}$ system for English; and the system of English Auxiliary verbs (chapters 5 and 6).

1.3   Evaluating the Model

Any psychologically oriented learning model must pass a stiff set of evaluation criteria. First, it must *work* and actually learn a correct target grammar.

Second is the issue of psychological plausibility. The system must acquire its knowledge using information and computational resources plausibly available to children. We take the following constraints as one account of what is psychologically plausible (postponing further discussion until chapter 2):

- No negative evidence (correction)

- No (or very small) memory for previous sentences

- Convergence using simple sentences, after a fixed, finite number of data examples

- Active construction of new grammars rather than enumerative guessing

- Minimal use of extra-syntactic information

- Integration of language processing and acquisition

- Robustness under different orders of data presentation

Some of these constraints may appear too severe. Surely children remember some of the sentences they hear, although this may not seem so to adults. The intent, though, is to impose constraints as severe as possible to determine the "boundary conditions" on learning. If some previous sentences can be remembered, then the effect of this relaxation might be determined by loosening the "no memory" condition.

A third criterion of evaluation centers on the predictions the models makes regarding the course of child language acquisition. Such predictions are fraught with familiar dangers. One is the problem of concurrent cognitive development. This often leaves so much free variable slack that predictions can be freely changed to suit the available data. Still, there are some general areas where the Subset Principle makes testable predictions, and some specific instances where the computer model itself is suggestively accurate.

Let us now backtrack and review each of these criteria in turn.

How well does it learn?

How well does the procedure fare in actually acquiring parsing rules? Starting with *no* grammar rules, the currently implemented procedure acquires many of the grammar rules in an originally handwritten "core grammar" of

English. The currently acquired rules are sufficient to parse simple declaratives, much of the English auxiliary system including auxiliary verb inversion, simple passives, many *wh* questions (e.g., *Who did John kiss?*), imperatives, and negative adverbial preposing. Carrying acquisition one step further, by starting with a relatively restricted set of context-free base rule schemas—the $\overline{X}$ system—the procedure fixes the proper order for many of the phrase structure rules for English, including some recursive rules. Acquired base rules include those for Noun Phrases, Verb Phrases, Prepositional Phrases, embedded sentences, and a substantial part of the English auxiliary verb system. On the order of 70–100 rules total are learned from a corpus of several hundred sentences.

This short list of acquired rules is not, of course, even close to a "complete" knowledge of English syntax. Many rules lie beyond the current procedure's reach. Some of these gaps in acquisition are the result of corresponding gaps in computational machinery, while others probably signal a deeper deficit in the grammar-as-parser approach. Some examples, like conjunction, were described earlier. In addition, rightward movements, such as rightward extraposition—*A book yesterday appeared about nuclear war*—cannot be represented in the current framework. Therefore, these rules cannot be currently acquired.[24] The same holds for so-called "gapping" constructions (e.g., *I gave Fred a dollar and Sue a dime*); "right-node raising" (*Did Joe admire, and Sue buy, the book you were talking about*); and other types of coordinate conjunctions (*The meat is ready to heat, serve, and eat*).

More generally, the present model cannot capture *all* "knowledge of language" in the sense intended by generative grammarians. For example, since the weakest form of the acquisition procedure does not employ backup, it cannot re-analyze certain sentences as people appear to do, and so deduce that they are grammatically well-formed.[25] No knowledge about "logical form" is acquired—for example, the ambiguous quantifier readings of *Everyone loves someone*. Since the parser does not recover any representation of quantifier scope, currently this knowledge cannot even be internally represented.

---

[24]A more recent version of the parser does have rules for rightward extraposition. See Berwick (1983).

[25]For instance, such an acquisition procedure could never determine that the "garden-path" sentence, *The horse raced past the barn fell* is grammatical. Additional machinery must be added in order to accommodate such behavior.

Psychological fidelity

The computer model meets most of the psychological plausibility criteria by fiat:

• No negative evidence (explicit correction). The model uses only positive examples.[26]

• No memory for previous sentences. This restriction is also met by fiat. The model uses only its current "grammar" (rule database) plus current input sentence to arrive at its augmented grammar. (The procedure is thus "intensional" in the sense discussed by Wexler and Culicover (1980).)

• Convergence using simple sentences, after a fixed, finite number of data examples. The acquisition system uses only sentences of depth of embedding two or less. There are only a finite number of such sentences. We could thus use the following method adopted by Wexler and Culicover to ensure convergence: when an error is detected, add or delete a rule at random. If all example sentences are presented (so that all sentences have a positive chance of appearing), then convergence is guaranteed: there are only a finite number of ways to go wrong. Note that this system, like modern transformational theory, posits only a finite number of possible grammars.

• Active construction of new rules. On the other hand, the "guess and try again" approach seems unintelligent. The acquisition procedure's new rules are actually based on repairs of what is going wrong when an error is detected.

• Minimal use of extrasyntactic information. Nearly every grammatical theory posits something like thematic role information. The acquisition proce-

---

[26]One might in fact distinguish at least two types of "negative evidence." (1) *Explicit* negative information is the (perhaps methodical) pairing of positive (syntactically well-formed) and negative (syntactically ill-formed) sentences with the appropriate labels *well-formed* and *ill-formed*. It could also include correction of ill-formed utterances (alternatively, parses) via (a) explicit negative reinforcement (e.g., *That's wrong*) or (b) tacit negative reinforcement (e.g., responding with the correct pattern, or not responding). (2) *Indirect negative evidence*, the inference that if a linguistic construction P can appear in simple sentences and is not observed to appear, then P does not occur in any sentence, no matter how complex. Chapter 5 shows that every case of indirect negative evidence can be reduced to one where only positive evidence is used.

For additional remarks see chapter 2; Wexler and Culicover (1980). For evidence that children do not receive reinforcement for syntactic well-formedness, see Brown and Hanlon (1970); or Newport, Gleitman, and Gleitman (1977). However, children might (and seem to) receive negative evidence for what is a semantically well-formed sentence. This sort of input might prove to be of value in acquisition; for further discussion, see Brown and Hanlon (1970).

dure uses this information, but only for simple sentences, and only to fix a few syntactic parameters early in acquisition. We might compare the amount of "semantic" information required here to the complete underlying base structures posited in the Wexler and Culicover model.

• Integration of language processing and acquisition. The acquisition system unites a processing model (a parser) with language acquisition. The interaction between language processing and acquisition is made explicit: at each stage, the system uses its current parser to direct learning.

• Robustness under different orders of data presentation. Acquisition in children seems invariant (within certain developmental envelopes) with respect to the order of examples received, as seems appropriate given the uncertain nature of the input. In several cases the system is resilient to the order of examples because of its basically conservative acquisition strategy. By not learning a new rule or setting a parameter in underdetermined situations, we have seen that certain problematic decisions about Head–Complement order can be avoided. This is a rather surprising property, and is certainly not characteristic of most "search" procedures. It says that acquisition decisions can, for the most part, be made locally and incrementally. Yet the system can still arrive at the "correct" target grammar. It follows that there should be no cul-de-sacs or local maxima in the search space of grammars. It remains to establish this property as a characteristic of the space of possible natural grammars.

Model predictions

Subject to the general caveats of all simulation models, there are some general points to make about the system's learning behavior.

First of all, the procedure is deliberately designed to be able to glean more information from simple example sentences (of limited embedding) than more complex examples. This is accomplished in two ways. The acquisition procedure cannot be recursively invoked: if, during the process of acquiring a new grammar or base rule the procedure discovers that it must acquire yet another new rule, the attempt to acquire the first new rule (as well as the second) is abandoned. This ban on recursion has the beneficial effect of keeping the procedure's new rules "close" to those it already knows, imposing a certain incremental and conservative character on its developmental history. Second, the grammar rule patterns themselves are restricted under the conventions of Marcus's parser to examine only local context in order to decide what to do next. Together these restrictions mean that if an input datum is too complex for the acquisition program to handle at its current stage of syntactic knowledge, it simply parses what it can, and ignores the rest. The outcome is that the first rules to be acquired handle simple, few-word sentences and expand the basic phrase structure for English; later rules deal with more sophisticated phrase structure, alterations of canonical word order, and embedded sentences. Although this is clearly part of the desired result—current parsing abilities suggest new rules of parsing, as discussed in Limber 1973—it is a picture without much detail. An important area for future research will be to investigate more thoroughly the patterns of over- and under-generalization implicit in the model, comparing them to observed patterns of human language ontogenesis and error production.

Third, the Subset Principle forces a number of predictions that appear plausible, at least on a superficial analysis. One is the initial assumption of a fixed AGENT-ACTION assignment of thematic roles. This has been widely observed, as mentioned. Another prediction of the Subset Principle is that arguments to verbs will be assumed obligatory until proven otherwise by explicit positive examples showing their absence. This too has been suggested as an operative principle in child language acquisition; see Roeper (1981).

With these general constraints in mind, table 1.2 gives some of the particular predictions of the model. A question mark in column 2 indicates that the empirical result is unknown. One example of this kind of prediction centers on passive. As we shall see in chapter 4, the incremental character of the acquisition system tends to favor the acquisition of "short" passives, without *by* phrases (as in, *John was kissed*), over "long" passives (*John was kissed by Mary*). This order has been suggested as a part of child acquisition, though matters are far from clear.[27]

As another example, the parametric acquisition of phrasal constructs implies that once Operator–Argument structure is fixed for one sort of phrase, then it is fixed for all phrases. In particular, consider Prepositional Phrases using *for*: *This ice cream is for you.* As we shall see in chapter 3, once an example like this can be analyzed, then *for*-Sentence constructs can be also, since this will just be another Operator–Argument structure. At this

---

[27]See Maratsos (1978). There are other accounts of this phenomenon. It is not even clear that "short" passives *are* acquired earlier. Rather, it seems that the problem is due to problems in learning the morphology of words in passive constructions: the *ed* ending is confusing. See Berwick and Weinberg (1984).

Phenomenon	Source	Prediction
Early thematic–syntactic alignment	Various authors	Chapters 3, 4
Parsing-driven phrase learning	Gleitman & Wanner (1984)	Chapter 3
Subjectless infinitives acquired before overt case	Roeper(1981)	Chapter 4
Truncated passives with clear thematic roles acquired before reversible passives	Maratsos (1978)	Chapter 4
Basic $\overline{\text{X}}$ rules acquired before movement rules	Lightfoot (1982)	Chapter 3
For acquired as Operator in PP constructions before use as Complementizer	Roeper (1981)	Chapter 4
Object relatives acquired before Subject relatives clauses	? ?	Chapter 4
Demonstrative *there* acquired before existential	?	
Why and *how* acquired first as *wh*	Labov and Labov (1976)	Chapter 4
Object "controls" subject by default (minimal distance principle)	Chomsky (1969)	Chapters 3, 4
It taken as full NP	Baker (1979)	Chapter 3
AUX–modal errors with *do*	Mayer, Erreich, Valian (1978)	Chapter 3

Table 1.2: Some predictions of the computer model.

stage the system could analyze as grammatical (or produce, if the model were turned around to generate sentences) sentences such as, *This is for you hold it*; *It's too big for you eat*; and others like this. These sentences and others of this kind are attested by Roeper (1981). They are ungrammatical, of course: presumably, the relevant positive examples have not yet been analyzed to block the appearance for *for* and insert *to* instead (in examples like *It's too big for you to eat*; *I want you to hold it*). Chapter 4 shows how the Subset Principle interacts with this early stage to prompt a shift to the right rule system.

1.4 Summary of Key Ideas

• A working computer program has been developed that can acquire substantial syntactic knowledge of English under restrictions faithful to what is known about human acquisition (simple, positive-only example sentences). This knowledge is acquired in the form of an explicit process model of language use (a parser) during the on-going, left-to-right analysis of individual sentences. The syntactic knowledge acquired is of three sorts: order of constituents for context-free base rules, lexical classes, and so-called grammar rules that handle forms such as passives and *wh*-movement.

• The model shows how a transformational theory can be embedded in a theory of language use and language acquisition.

• The acquisition process (rule acquisition) is driven by the parser's attempt to interpret example sentences. It thus provides an explicit "learning theory" for the acquisition of knowledge of syntax. It avoids an unrealistic, "guessing" model for acquisition. At all times, the system maintains a procedure that can actually analyze sentences.

• The procedure required for acquisition is by itself simple. It is constraints on representations rather than any sophisticated, general learning "heuristics" that play the key role in the success of the acquisition model.

• The interaction between the functional demands of learnability and parsability have been studied using the specific models of acquisition and parsing proposed here. The same locality principles that ensure efficient parsing—the no-backtracking and bounded lookahead conditions imposed by Marcus—also aid acquisition. Bounded look-ahead helps ensure that the "search space" for new rule hypotheses is finite (in fact, small); the no-backtracking condition helps pinpoint the exact place in the analysis of a sentence to build a new rule of parsing.

• A simple version of the $\overline{X}$ theory has been advanced as a theory of the acquisition of base phrase structure rules. The $\overline{X}$ theory has also proved useful as a model for lexical acquisition and as a source of testable hypotheses about the actual developmental course of human acquisition. The theory is a modular one, in which core cases are determined by fixing a small set of parameters This combination of acquisition procedures eliminates the heavy data demands of complete reliance on inductive procedures. A system of context-free re-write rules is eliminated as an explicit representation of the knowledge that is acquired when the system "fixes" a grammar.

• The locality principles proposed for the acquisition model mirror the structural constraints advanced in several current linguistic theories of grammar, as well as the Bounded Degree of Error (BDE) condition of Wexler and Culicover (1980). It is demonstrated that under certain assumptions the bounded context parsability condition implies BDE. It seems that natural languages are well-designed for both parsing and learning.

• The constraints of developmental sequencing have been analyzed in the framework of incremental models of acquisition based on positive-only evidence. A general constraint on learning from positive examples, the Subset Principle, is proposed as an explanation for various ordering constraints previously advanced. This principle seems powerful enough to explain a variety of linguistic ordering constraints suggested by a range of different research. The Subset Principle works with the principle of acquisition from clear cases to guide the joint use of syntactic and semantic information if acquiring rules and fixing parameters.

• The explanatory power of "noninstantaneous" acquisition models has been investigated. In certain specific linguistic settings it appears that earlier developmental decisions can constrain later acquisition choices, thus providing an additional source of constraint on the identification of rule systems. In other words, by assuming a noninstantaneous model, we can actually better explain just why natural languages are the way they are. This "parametric" view of acquisition may account for apparent developmental stages observed in child language acquisition.

An outline of things to come

Chapter 2 discusses each of the components of the acquisition model: the initial state of knowledge that is assumed; the input data used to acquire new rules; and the acquisition procedure itself.

Chapter 3 explores the acquisition of phrase structure rules.

Chapter 4 turns to the acquisition of transformational-type rules.

Chapter 5 presents a formal theory of evaluation measures, using the notion of program size complexity. It applies this theory to the acquisition of base phrase structure rules and phonological rule systems.

Chapter 6 continues with several scenarios illustrating the program size model and the use of noninstantaneous acquisition models. Our case study is that of phonological systems. Chapter 6 then goes on to explore the implications of the Subset Principle.

Chapter 7 examines the relationship between efficient parsability and Wexler-Culicover learnability.

Chapter 2

The Acquisition Model

This chapter describes the acquisition model in detail. The model has three components:

1. An *initial state* of knowledge;

2. A *target state* of knowledge;

3. An *acquisition procedure* that drives the system from initial to final state. The procedure subdivides into:

   (a) The *input data* the learning system uses;

   (b) The *acquisition algorithm* itself.

This chapter's sections outline these components, one by one. Section 1 opens with a discussion of the initial state of the learning system. Revisions to the original Marcus parser are sketched here. Section 2 continues with a discussion of the assumed target machine—the "mature" parser's grammar rules. Section 3 follows with an outline of the acquisition system, reviewing assumptions about the input data available to the acquisition procedure, and section 4 describes the acquisition algorithm itself. The next chapter turns to examples of the acquisition procedure in action.

2.1   The Initial State of Knowledge

The final state of the parser's knowledge about syntax is its ability to analyze sentences. This knowledge is packaged into the parser's grammar rules plus the machinery to execute those rules. The initial state amounts to removing the grammar rules, leaving behind just the rule execution machinery (pushdown stack plus buffer), as well as a knowledge of the proper format for base phrase structure rules, lexical insertion grammar rules, and transformational-like grammar rules. See figure 2.1.

No specific instantiations of rules are known. The rest of this section will be devoted to describing the initial interpreter and its knowledge of grammar rules and words. (A final part of what is "given" to the system—the input sentences plus thematic information for simple sentences—is described in a later section.) Aside from the parser's knowledge of grammar rule form and the information contained in the acquisition algorithm itself, the following knowledge is assumed as the initial state of the acquisition procedure:

- The major data and control structures of the parser. These include a pushdown stack and input buffer as well as procedures that maintain the data structures and perform routine matching tasks.

- A dictionary. Initially, the dictionary classifies words as objects (automatically nouns) actions (automatically verbs), or *unknown*. The following feature system is used: $\pm$N, $\pm$V. If neither value is given, it is assumed to have no value, or 0. This "semantic" grounding can be relaxed and additional categorizations made.

- Verbs and arguments. The system knows that verbs assign thematic roles to objects, and this stock of thematic roles is fixed (presumably grounded in a conceptual subsystem that refers to notions such as AGENT or AFFECTED OBJECT). The system does not know what the detailed entries for any particular verb, but does know that thematic role assignments must be made, if they are required (see below).

- A finite stock of syntactic feature primitives. These are various familiar grammaticalized elements that may serve as predicate tests for the parser's grammar rule triggers. For example, the word *Sally* might come attached with the features *Name, Singular, Animate, Feminine*, and so forth. We leave open the question of just how these features, rather than others, are learned, and just how one would learn to attach them to words.[1]

---

[1] The list of primitives is of course open to empirical review; see Keil (1979) for a discussion of the development of children's ontological categories. Chapter 5 has a formal model of how such categorization systems might develop.

Fixed	Acquired
Rule execution loop	Context-free base order
Data structures	Movement rules
Rudimentary word classification	Lexical rules
Feature primitives	
$\overline{\text{X}}$ constraints	
Simple thematic structure	

Figure 2.1: The parser interpreter is fixed and grammar rules acquired

- An unordered $\overline{\text{X}}$ template, {Head, Complement, Specifier}.

- A "saturation" constraint on sentences. Full sentences consist of *complete* predicate-argument structures, as determined by thematic constraints (see below).

- A thematic structure for sentences with at most one embedding. This structure assigns thematic roles to NP or S arguments. For example, the sentence *John kissed Mary* would assign *kiss* as the PREDICATE, with the NP *John* filling an AGENT role and the NP *Mary* as the AFFECTED OBJECT.

In the remainder of this section we shall discuss each of these components, one by one. We first discuss the operation of the parser as originally designed by Marcus, and then several revisions that aid acquisition. The revisions include the addition of the $\overline{\text{X}}$ theory to the parsing model, a must for the "parameter setting" model of phrase structure acquisition that follows. The $\overline{\text{X}}$ theory also figures in the acquisition of lexical categories, the final topic of discussion.

The initial state: the parser interpreter

To understand the parser that is used for acquisition, we must first understand the design of the original machine. As chapter 1 mentioned, the parser acts as an *interpreter* for simple pattern-action g   es. The patterns are predicates that hold of tokens in the parser's input buffer or stack. The actions are the basic operations that build the parse tree itself.[2]

The Marcus parser was designed primarily to handle syntactic phenomena, producing as output a modified form of *annotated surface structures* as described by mid 70s transformational grammars (Chomsky 1975; Fiengo 1974; 1977). Formally, the parser is a function that maps *strings of words* to *syntactic parse trees*. *Semantic* processing is not strictly within the parser's realm.[3]

A parse proceeds by making a single left-to-right pass through a given input sentence, with the interpreter executing any grammar rules that happen to match on the environment of the parse (features of the input tokens and portions of the already-built parse tree), ending with an annotated tree as output. The restriction to a single sweep through the sentence was specifically designed by Marcus to reflect the exigencies of human sentence processing. One modification to strict left-to-right processing was permitted. The parser is free to postpone the processing of an item and process material to its right for a *finite* (and fixed) distance. In effect, one can backtrack a finite amount to return to the processing of the postponed item.

The parser: data and control structures

Because the parser's data structures and the primitive operations are given ready-made to the acquisition system, it is important to understand their role in parsing a sentence. The parser is built around two major data structures motivated by Marcus's theoretical goal of *deterministic parsing*. The output of the parse of *Sally will kiss John* might look like that in figure 2.2(a) below. Figure 2.2(b) shows a "snapshot" of this same tree while under construction by the parser. The emerging tree structure is stored as a *pushdown stack* of constituent nodes. The stack is designed to hold the phrases of the sentence in proper hierarchical order for their assembly into a complete parse tree. Phrases held there are either not yet completely built or else their attachment to some higher (still active) phrase has not yet been determined. We invert the pushdown stack to show its correspondence to the parse tree. In the figure the S(entence) node (labeled S20) is on the top of the stack and is

---

[2]For a formalization of the machine as a two-stack parser, see chapter 7.

[3]Note that the parser does *not* recover multiple structural analyses of ambiguous sentences.

active because in the snapshot as given the entire sentence has not yet been analyzed. More daughter phrases, in particular a Verb Phrase, are still to be attached to the Sentence node.

Figure 2.2(b) also shows two nodes, a Noun Phrase (NP) node and an Auxiliary Verb (AUX or INFLection) node, already attached to the main Sentence node. The attachment of these two phrases to the Sentence node signifies that by the time this snapshot was taken the parser had already determined the grammatical role of these two phrases in the sentence. Note that the Noun Phrase and Inflection nodes are not part of the active node stack, but are simply part of the graphic representation of the emerging annotated surface structure tree.

The bottom node in the stack diagram (the top node on the stack in a conventional stack representation) is the Verb Phrase node, VP22. Just like the Sentence Phrase, it too is active because it has not yet been completely built. Although the verb *kiss* has already been attached to the Verb Phrase node, the Noun Phrase object *John* has not. Typically only the top node of the stack is subject to grammar rule actions. In figure 2.2(b), VP22 is the focus of the parser's efforts. In Marcus's terminology, it is the *current active node* (denoted C), and grammar rules that execute will attempt to build structure under this node. Once the Verb Phrase node is completely built (the object Noun Phrase attached), the parser will attach it to its place in the S node above, removing it from the stack of active nodes, and assigning the S node current active node status.

The second major data structure of the parser is the three-cell lookahead buffer. The buffer holds either incoming words from the sentence string or phrases whose grammatical function has not yet been completely determined. Each cell in the buffer can hold a single word or several, if these words all form a single phrase.

The parser delays deciding about what syntactic structure should be built—what nodes or tokens to attach to what other nodes in the pushdown stack—until it has had the opportunity to use (if necessary) the local context information in the buffer. Marcus's *determinism hypothesis* claims that the easily parsed sentences of natural languages can be analyzed using lookahead in this way so that parsing decisions can always be made correctly, without backup.[4]

---

[4]Formally, what does determinism mean? Conventionally, a language is deterministic if it can be recognized by a deterministic machine, and a machine is deterministic if its

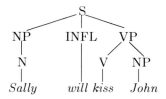

(a) Surface structure tree

Pushdown stack (inverted)

s20
NP:*Sally*
INFL:*will*
VP22
VERB: *kiss*

(b) Emerging node stack representation of tree.

Figure 2.2: Surface structure tree and snapshot of stack representation

The necessity for lookahead facility in a parser that operates left-to-right can be seen from a cursory examination of pairs of sentences like those below, from Marcus (1980:15):

Have the boys who missed the exam take the makeup today.

Have the boys who missed the exam taken the makeup today?

To quote Marcus,

> It is impossible to distinguish between this pair of sentences before examining the morphology of the verb following the [noun phrase] *the boys*. These sentences can be distinguished, however, if the parser has a large enough "window" on the clause to see this verb; if the verb ends in *en* (in the simple case presented here), then the clause is a yes/no question, otherwise it is an imperative. Thus, if a parser is to be deterministic, it must have some constrained facility for lookahead. (1980:17)

Grammar rules do all the work of building the parse tree. The typical action of a grammar rule is to remove an item from the first cell of the buffer and attach it to the top node on the stack (the current active node). There are also rules to label phrases, insert items into the buffer, and perform other housekeeping chores. Figure 2.3 displays the pattern and action for the Subject-Auxiliary verb inversion rule informally presented in chapter 1. The version in the top half of the figure is written in English, while that in the bottom half gives the form quite close to that actually processed by the Marcus parser. It is not important to understand all the notational details of the abbreviated pattern language of part (b).[5]

In simple English, the rule in figure 2.3 says that *if* the first item in the buffer has the feature AUXILIARY, the second is a Noun Phrase, the third

---

transition mapping is deterministic, i.e., a function that maps a state, input pair to a unique next state. For example, a deterministic context-free language is one accepted by a deterministic pushdown automaton. Reconstructing Marcus's claim, we want to say that a certain subset of a natural language (English) that can be processed "without conscious difficulty" is deterministic with respect to the pushdown automaton described by the parser interpreter. Marcus's machine is actually a transducer: it writes an output representation, namely, a parse tree. So Marcus is in fact claiming that a subset of English can be transduced deterministically.

[5] The original parser did not have a SWITCH operation. Instead, there was a grammar rule that attached the second element in the buffer to the top node of the stack.

Item examined   **Feature to match against**
current active node: Major sentence
1st buffer cell: Auxiliary verb
2nd buffer cell: Noun Phrase
3rd buffer cell: none

    Rule action: SWITCH first and second buffer items

(a) English description of grammar rule.

Pattern: Current active node   Buffer
                                     1st   2nd   3rd
        [**c; * is S Major]   [=Aux]   [=NP]   [ ]   →

Action: SWITCH

(b) Abbreviated form

Figure 2.3: A grammar rule and its abbreviated form.

item is anything, and the top of the stack node is a main S(entence), *then* interchange the first and second items in the buffer.

Finally, in the original Marcus parser, functionally related grammar rules are grouped into *packets*. The packet system provides a way of controlling whether entire sets of grammar rules should be made available for matching against the buffer items. For example, all the grammar rules that analyze Subject Noun Phrases can be clumped together, and unless this Noun Phrase packet is *activated*, the parser will not even attempt to match the grammar rules in this packet against the buffer. When the parse of a constituent is complete, that packet is *deactivated*. The system is discussed in more detail in appendix 1 to this chapter. There it is shown how the activation and deactivation process can be formally associated with base phrase structure rules, reducing the acquisition of this information to the acquisition of base rules.[6] Going a step further, the base phrase structure rules themselves can be eliminated in favor of a representational structure based on regularities in phrase structure—the $\overline{X}$ theory. No information about packets need be learned, only easily acquired information about the *order* of basic constituents. We describe the $\overline{X}$ system and its role in acquisition in the next subsection.

The parser's operation can be completely characterized by a sequence of "snapshots" that depict the contents of its pushdown stack, buffer, and the currently active packet. Following the terminology of automata theory, such a snapshot will be referred to as an *instantaneous description* (or ID). Thus a (successful) parse will consist of an ordered sequence of valid ID's, commencing with an empty stack, buffer, and active packet and ending (if the sentence is grammatical) with a complete S as the only entry in the node stack and a buffer containing an end of sentence marker.[7]

Note that the information encoded in successive ID's is of course finite. Like all automata, the control table that dictates what new state the machine

---

[6]This approach was first implemented by Shipman (1979).

[7]A more formal presentation is given in chapter 7. Briefly, one can define the machine as a restricted 2-stack parser, a 5-tuple (Q, L, R, T, P) of states, left-stack symbols, right-stack symbols, terminal symbols, and productions, respectively. The right-stack is the analogue of the parser's input buffer; the left-stack is the Marcus parser's pushdown stack. The productions are limited to (1) moving elements from the top of the right stack (=the left most element of the input buffer) to the top of the left-stack (=the current active node), or vice-versa; (2) using the lookahead and changing state; or (3) reading new tokens. The system is less general than an unrestricted 2-stack deterministic pushdown automaton because (1) it is designed to halt on all inputs and (2) it possesses certain local error-detecting capabilities.

should enter given some existing state and input is finite. The grammar rules are the "control table" in this case. Thus the grammar rules make reference to only a finitely representable amount of information.

To summarize, there are two major data structures crucial to the operation of the Marcus parser. The pushdown stack provides the usual computational power required for handling the recursive syntactic structures typical of natural languages. The lookahead buffer serves as a window to hold constituents or individual words under current analysis, reducing the parser's guesses about what the next parsing decision should be. If Marcus's determinism hypothesis is correct, a small lookahead can actually reduce the amount of guessing to zero, so that a single left-to-right sweep through a sentence with finite backtracking will suffice for correct parsing of English, that is, that the language handled is deterministic. The grammar interpreter deals with two different kinds of rules that direct the parse. Grammar rules are unitary pattern-action productions that perform the real work of the parse, actually building tree structure, labeling nodes, and the like. Base rules, corresponding to packets in the original parser design, dictate when certain bundles of grammar rules are permitted to apply. Both these types of rules are acquired.

Revising the Parser

The "target machine" to be acquired is a modification of the original Marcus parser. The modifications were prompted for two basic reasons, first, to bring the Marcus design into line with standard models of parsing and second, to simplify the machine to make it easier to learn. The basic alterations are: conversion of the parser to more standard bottom-up form; elimination of the packet system; removal of what Marcus called "attention shifting"; and creation of and labeling of phrasal nodes via the $\overline{X}$ theory. The discussion is lengthy, and is contained in appendix 1 to this chapter. Here we shall instead focus on just one sample grammar rule of the old parser, and what it looks like in the new parser. We continue with a discussion of $\overline{X}$ theory, since it is central to the learning model. Next is a comparison of the way that the original parser and the new parsing design would analyze a simple example sentence. This example lays out all the new machinery that is used, if not its justification, and is all the reader needs to know to understand the acquisition model.

To get some feel for how grammar rules in the new and old parsers differ, let us take a look at just a portion of the original rule that analyzed main verbs. In English form, it looked something like the description in figure 2.4. Rule actions are in small capital letters.

This is only about half of the actual verb rule. Note that it contains multiple actions and conditionals. It explicitly activates packets, runs rules, creates new phrase structure nodes, and tests for complex properties of the elements in the buffer. It has an explicit priority, in case of a conflict with another rule that might match against the buffer element specified as a trigger.

The new rule eliminates all of these details, because they are difficult to learn. Here is what the new version of the main-verb rule looks like. There is just one action, to attach the verb to the active node that is the top element on the stack. There are no priorities, or explicit packet activation or deactivation. (This new rule is not quite in correct form because we have not yet introduced the feature bundle replacement of the conventional node names like VP.) *All* the actions such as activating and deactivating packets or selecting the argument structure of the verb are carried out via automatic activities of the grammar interpreter, not the grammar rule system. For example, the lexicon is always consulted when a predicate like a verb is encountered, and the requirements for its arguments are made part of the features of the VP, thus ensuring that the right grammar rules will execute later on. It should be obvious that this modified parser is easier to learn. We simply note here that this simplification strategy parallels that of modern linguistic theory: specific conditions on rule application have been "factored out" into general constraints that need not be learned.

Table 2.1 displays a summary of the major modifications to the parsing design compared against the original machine design. We can divide the surgery into two groups: changes to grammar rules and changes to the interpreter. Again, these details are most readily appreciated by following the example immediately following the next subsection. To see how important these revisions are, consider the elimination of the entire set of packet rules, functioning as a large set of context-free phrase structure rules. They are replaced with just a single $\overline{X}$ template. At the same time, packet activation/deactivation is no longer carried out by grammar rules.

Rule **Main-verb**   in packet *parse-vp*
                       priority: 10

IF: The first element in the buffer is a verb
THEN:

                       DEACTIVATE packet *parse-vp*;
                         if the active node is a major sentence
                           then ACTIVATE packet *ss-final*;
                         else if the active node is a secondary clause
                           then ACTIVATE packet *emb-s-final*.
                       CREATE a VP node.
                       ATTACH the VP node to the S.
                       ATTACH the first element in the buffer to
                         the active node as a verb.
                       ACTIVATE the clause level packet *cpool*.
                         if the verb is labeled *passive*
                           then ACTIVATE the packet *passive*
                           and RUN the grammar rule *passive* next.
                         if the verb takes an infinitive sentence object
                           then if the verb takes an infinitive without *to*
                           then ACTIVATE the packet *to-less-inf-obj*.
                       etc.

Rule **Main-verb**
IF:

                       current active node is S
                       current cyclic node is nil
                       1st buffer cell is V
THEN:

                       ATTACH

                Figure 2.4: Old-style and new-style rules compared

Original	New
Grammar rules	
1. Multiple actions per rule	One action per rule
2. Labeling of nodes by grammar rule	Labeling of nodes by feature percolation
3. Activation/deactivation of packets by rule	Activation/deactivation of packets by interpreter
4. Arguments to grammar rules	No arguments (defaults assumed) to grammar rules, plus new SWITCH action
5. Packet control of rules	No packets
6. "Run rule next" grammar rule action	Replaced by interpreter control
7. Create node and complete (drop) node grammar rule actions.	Replaced by $\overline{\text{X}}$ control
Parser interpreter	
8. No automatic annotation of active node	Active node annotated with grammar rule execution
9. Case frame check of verb arguments	Check of verb arguments by percolation (Projection Principle)
10. Many category features allowed (e.g, NPSTART)	Finite stock of features based on $\overline{\text{X}}$ theory
11. "Attention shifting" to parse NPs	No attention shifting except phrasal projection from first buffer cell
12. $\overline{\text{N}}$ always created	$\overline{\text{N}}$ created on demand
13. Buffer cells filled on demand	Three buffer cells always filled
14. S node always created first	S node created on demand
15. Cyclic node and active node sometimes the same	Cyclic node always distinguished
16. Numbered rule priorities	Rules ordered by specific before general triggering order

Table 2.1: Summary of changes to parser design

X̄ theory: the basics

All of the changes to the parser make learning easier. This is especially true of the X̄ theory. Instead of having to learn a set of context-free rewrite rules of a base grammar (as implicitly encoded in the Marcus packet system or explicitly coded in a form described in appendix 1), the X̄ theory tells us that the base phrase structure system of a particular language is fixed by a few simple template-filling decisions. Basically, we replace the long list of packet names in the original parser with a single template packet consisting of three elements: *Parse-specifier*, *Parse-head*, and *Parse-complement*. These packet names control sets of grammar rules, as before. In addition, these three packets are parameterized by a set of feature values that distinguish, for example, properties of nouns from those of verbs. All that is learned are the properties of nouns and verbs—these must be learned anyway—and the relative order of the three elements of the template. The net effect is that the grammar rules themselves no longer activate and deactivate packets, and the packet structure itself is learned. Let us see how the X̄ theory can do all this.

The basic idea of X̄ theory is that the space of possible base context-free rules is greatly limited, much more restricted than if one could write down context-free rules at will. The context-free rules for noun, preposition, adjective, and verb phrases look very much alike (these rules are approximations):[8]

$$
\begin{aligned}
\text{Noun Phrase} &\rightarrow \quad \ldots \text{NOUN} \ldots (\text{PP})^* \ (\text{S}) \\
\text{Verb Phrase} &\rightarrow \quad \text{VERB NP} \ (\text{PP})^* \ (\text{S}) \\
\text{Prepositional Phrase} &\rightarrow \quad \text{PREPOSITION NP} \ (\text{PP})^* \ (\text{S}) \\
\text{Adjective Phrase} &\rightarrow \quad \text{ADJECTIVE} \ (\text{PP})^* \ (\text{S}).
\end{aligned}
$$

Evidently all these phrases are built upon a single central scaffolding that includes a basic *Head* lexical item that fixes the type of the phrase.[9] A Noun Phrase is headed by a noun; a Verb Phrase by a verb; a Prepositional Phrase

---

[8] In particular, we write S here instead of S̄.

[9] Other constraints account for the apparent surface differences between these phrases. One difference between Noun and Verb Phrases is that NPs do not allow "bare" NP complements whereas VPs do: *destroy the city* is fine, but not, **destruction the city*. One familiar explanation for this is that verbs and prepositions, but not nouns or adjectives, assign an abstract "Case." Thus, in order to realize *destruction the city* one must insert a dummy preposition so that *the city* receives Case and can surface: *destruction OF the city*.

by a preposition; and so on. There are no Verb Phrases headed by, say, prepositions. In effect, there are no separate rules for these different phrases, but just a single rule, $XP \rightarrow Head\ Complement$, where $Head=$ noun, verb, adjective, or preposition, and $Complement=$ a string of optional arguments, here NP PP S. The key $\overline{X}$ constraint is that a phrase of type X gets all the features of the word that forms its core. We may imagine the phrase receives the feature $+N$ (for *Noun*) by "percolation." Note that we may think of this features percolation as operating even in the case of a stem and its affix, as when a verb is inflected via its affix. In this case, a root plus affix combine to form a node X that has the feature of an inflection, plus its verbal qualities. As we shall see, percolation can be implemented directly in the computer model.

In the usual exposition of $\overline{X}$ theory, trees have a kind of ternary branching structure. The central core of the tree consists of the X skeleton, as we have discussed. In addition, the phrase can contain *Complements* (COMP), serving as "arguments" of the phrase, or *Specifiers*, (SPEC) further modifying the phrase. For example, Noun Phrases can contain sentential complements (the guy *that I know*). They can also contain determiners or adjectives preceding head nouns, as in *the big book*; these are Specifiers. Note that Specifiers and Complements are not themselves constituent nodes, but rather template variables that may be occupied by actual constituents such as NP, AP, and so on.

A key insight of the $\overline{X}$ theory is that the possible tree shapes accommodating Specifiers and Complements are fixed from category to category: the possible complements of verb, preposition, adjective, and Noun Phrases are roughly the same, and occur in the same order. In English, Complements of all these phrases can be NP (PP)* (S). In other languages, this Complement structure can appear to the *left* of the head verb of a Verb Phrase, or the preposition in a Prepositional Phrase, and so forth.[10]

For any particular language one must learn whether Complements appear to the left or right of the head X. The relative position of Specifiers must also be learned. Of course, one must also be able to tell when a constituent is a COMP or SPEC. We assume that COMP elements are arguments of the head of the phrase in which they are located, while SPEC elements do not play this

---

[10]Some languages, as Lightfoot (1982) observes, deviate from this strict template: COMP may appear both before and after the HEAD. As Lightfoot goes on to say, this represents a "marked" case—i.e., one that requires more positive evidence to learn. German is one example, since it is verb final and prepositional.

(a) Permitted phrase structure tree   (b) Prohibited phrase structure tree

Figure 2.5: $\overline{\text{X}}$ theory rules out many tree configurations

argument role. The learner is given the unordered set {HEAD, SPECIFIER, COMPLEMENT} and has only to order these relative to one another to fix much of the basic tree structure in its language.

In the full $\overline{\text{X}}$ theory, lexical categories are defined by bundles of distinctive features. Which features to use is still a matter of debate—we shall propose our own modifications below—but for our purposes here we follow Chomsky (1970) and identify the following basic features. First, we have $\pm$N and $\pm$V—the binary valued features *Noun* and *Verb*. Actual nouns are marked +N −V, and verbs, −N +V.

For purposes of acquisition we identify the semantic categories of *Object* and *Action* with +N and +V features, respectively. Learning categories then becomes a matter of fixing feature complexes starting from this initial assignment. (As we shall see, the learning procedure in effect introduces a third zero value alongside the $\pm$ possibilities.) The next chapter gives several examples of how features values are learned.

Several other components of the $\overline{\text{X}}$ theory play a leading role in the acquisition model. We outline these here and return to how the acquisition procedure uses them later on in this chapter.

First, the theory greatly restricts possible phrase structure rules: their shapes, their nonterminal vocabulary, and their number. There can be at most *one* core lexical item that fixes the identity of a phrase—its Head. That is, we cannot have a rule $NP \rightarrow Determiner\ Noun\ Verb$, or, more generally, $XP \rightarrow X_1 X_2$ where X_1 and X_2 are both the Heads of the phrase (either different categories, like N or V, or even the same category), or where the features of XP do not match those of its Head. Figure 2.5 illustrates.

Besides this restriction, the $\overline{\text{X}}$ theory actually determines the inventory of possible base phrase structure trees by fixing the labels of tree nodes (NP, VP) and the branching structure of the trees themselves. Possible tree node labels correspond to projections of possible lexical categories such as N or V. Following a conventional phrasal system, we admit the following lexical node categories: N; A (adjectives and adverbs); DET (determiners and quantifiers like *the*, *every*); V; P (prepositions); COMP (a complementizer, such as *for* or *that*; and INFL (inflectional elements).

To accommodate these additional categories we need more that two binary-valued features. In our model, we assume two additional features: A, for *argument* and P, for *predicate*. The prototypical argument is NP and the prototypical predicate is VP. An argument is a thematic-role bearing phrase, and a predicate is a function-like phrase that assigns thematic roles. These two features are properties of syntactic constituents, rather than lexical items: it is a phrase that serves as an argument or acts as a function-like constituent. In part, this distinguishes the A and P features from the pure lexical properties of N and V. Our correspondence between traditional category names and feature complexes is as follows. (We discuss the status of S afterwards, which will prompt some revision for the INFL, COMP, and ADJ complexes.)

N	Adj	Det	V	P	Infl	Comp	Particle
+N	+N	+N	−N	−N	−N	−N	−N
−V	−V	−V	+V	−V	+V	−V	−V
+A	+A	−A	−A	−A	+A	+A	−A
−P	+P	−P	+P	+P	+P	+P	−P

There remains the question of how to fit the Sentence node (S) into the $\overline{X}$ system. Some have considered S to lie outside the $\overline{X}$ system (see Jackendoff 1977); others place it squarely within the conventional bar level notation. There is no accepted standard. Since learning is eased by uniformity, we adopt the approach that makes S just like any other constituent. Intuitively, a sentence must be "complete" in the sense that it is a complete predicate-argument structure. We honor this intuition by assuming that the Inflection marker INFL is the Head of S. INFL governs a Subject NP, acting as a kind of predicate; hence its +P status. But S can also play the role of an argument. Saturation demands that both an NP and a VP appear with INFL; otherwise, the S is ill-formed. This view suggests that we regard the feature values for *A* and *P* for INFL as undetermined, or 0, fixed by "percolation" from NP and VP. The saturation constraint then amounts to saying that no feature value be left undetermined.

Similarly, we say that COMP functions as the Head of $\bar{\text{S}}$, with a complement S (now $\text{INFL}^{\max}$). Like INFL, the status of this node is fixed partly by percolation from the lexical features of the syntactic elements that it dominates. We note this by changing the + markings to an indeterminate value. The implications of these choices for learning are taken up below and in the next chapter.

Having addressed the question of node labels, we turn next to a remaining point of tree topology. One thorny problem in $\bar{\text{X}}$ notation also poses a barrier for learning. In most versions of $\bar{\text{X}}$ theory, one supposes that there are several numbered *levels* of phrase structure, X^0, X^1, X^2, ... up to some prespecified maximum, usually three or four. The additional levels are required because of evidence that, e.g., in a Noun Phrase there must be some constituent that acts the way a Verb Complement acts in a Verb Phrase. But if this is so, then this element must attach to some point below the top level of the NP itself. Thus we must posit an additional layer of tree structure to receive this complement constituent. This is sometimes called a "bar level," since the new node is called an $\bar{\text{X}}$.

While the need for additional layers of tree structure is plain enough, problems arise for acquisition. How do we know how many levels to use? One could always fix the number of levels in advance—at, say, three—but then unused levels are superfluous. Further, there is no explanation why the number of levels should be three, rather than four or five; and in fact all of these possibilities have been raised in the literature.

To solve this problem we must understand what a bar level is. If we use the framework of automata theory, then we know that a distinguished nonterminal category represents simply a distinguishable state for a machine. If all we really need is a way to tell that we are at the top of a tree—$\text{X}^{\max}$—or at the bottom—X^0—then we do not need any other features to distinguish between other levels. A "bar level" in between these two extremes is neither maximal nor lexical (corresponding to the usual single bar level).

Any additional levels may be interpolated "on demand." That is, if there is evidence that a distinct phrase must be inserted between a tree top and tree bottom, then a node is created for it. For example, consider a name, such as *Sally*. This is lexical and maximal; hence, no additional bar levels need to be inserted and the name is dominated by just an $\text{X}^{\max}$ node. As an example, we shall see that simple sentences without an explicit inflectional element, such as *John kissed Sally*, will not force the system to posit a separate inflection node.

This will only come via evidence such as *John has kissed Sally*. Evidently, this is what children do (Tavakolian 1981). This also predicts that there might not be a distinct, lexicalized node INFL in some languages.

What is the categorial status of the Specifier or Complement elements themselves? Whatever the element, we note that in order to be attached to a tree a constituent must be *complete*. In general, this means that the constituent must be a maximal projection. For example, only maximal constituents like NPs and PPs appear as arguments to a verb. The exceptions are elements that cannot form phrases, including determiners like *the* or particles like *up*. These single tokens are complete; also note that they cannot be iterated (**the the book*; **pick up up*). Finally, Specifiers or Complements may be optional.

With the description of the $\overline{\text{X}}$ system behind us, we can now describe how the parser incorporates the $\overline{\text{X}}$ features.

In the original parser, phrases were built in three main steps corresponding to the beginning, middle, and end of phrase assembly. First, a phrase would be CREATED by the action of some grammar rule. For example, if a determiner occupied the first buffer cell, then a grammar rule could execute to create an NP node and push it onto the active node stack. Next, all other grammar rules for parsing NPs would come into play, controlled by the packet sequence to follow the context-free constituent structure order for NPs. During this middle stage, other pieces of the NP would be assembled by attaching them to the NP nodes; in addition, an $\overline{\text{N}}$ node would be created and elements perhaps attached to it. Here the ATTACH grammar rule action played the most prominent role. For example, given a phrase *the young student with red hair* the determiner *the* would get attached to the NP, then *young* would get attached as an adjective, and so forth. Finally, when the parser detected that the end of the NP had been reached, the phrase would be completed by DROPping the phrase back into the first buffer position.

These three stages—phrase creation, construction, and completion—have their $\overline{\text{X}}$ counterparts. Phrase creation is initiated whenever a HEAD or SPEC of a particular type is encountered. Once a phrase is created, grammar rules are guided by the SPEC–HEAD–COMP order (in English). This is done by keeping a special pointer to one part of the SPEC-HEAD-COMP triple. This triple labels the current active node, recording progress in analyzing the phrase. Whenever a subcomponent of the triple has been completely analyzed, the pointer is advanced through the triple. When a new phrase is created, the pointer is first set to SPEC, unless it was a head element in the first buffer cell that prompted the phrase's creation. Next, when the head is encountered, the pointer is advanced from the SPEC to the HEAD. The label on the current active node changes accordingly. Once the head is attached to the current active phrase, the pointer moves to COMP. Finally, a phrase is completed whenever a complement is completed; this prompts the interpreter to drop the phrase into the first cell in the buffer.

We must also link the new phrase analysis to the remaining grammar rules. When either grammar rules or phrase creation can apply, we let the grammar rules have a chance to execute first. For example, if an NP is in the first buffer position, and a preposition in the second buffer position, then rules that attach the NP as, say, the object of a verb will be allowed to trigger before the creation of a new projection. Then, once these rules have had their say (perhaps none of them match), a new maximal projection may be initiated via the first, second, or third buffer cells, in that order. The effect of this protocol is to try to build as few new nodes as possible—something like the Frazier (1979) rule of Minimal Attachment. Finally, if a node is completely built, then it is dropped into the first buffer slot, without running any grammar rules.

The easiest way to describe the new parsing machinery is to present a running example, comparing the operation to that of the original parser design. Our example is a simple sentence, *the student will buy a book*. Only enough of the sentence analysis will be presented to give the reader a feel for the difference in operation between the old and revised parsers. Section 2.2 presents the actual grammar rules for the new parser. Appendix 1 to this chapter has additional discussion of the packet system of the original parser and its relationship to phrase structure rule systems such as $\overline{\mathrm{X}}$ conventions.

Step 1. We shall assume that the first input buffer cell is filled with the token *the*.

Old machine: An S (sentence) node is always placed on the active node stack before any analysis occurs. The packets Ss-start, containing rules that analyze the beginning of simple sentences, and Cpool, containing general clause level grammar rules, are activated.

New machine: No nodes are created at this point. S nodes are created when evidence for them is encountered.

Step 2. *Old machine*: *The* is marked *det* and *npstart*—an element that starts a Noun Phrase. The parser creates a Noun Phrase and pushes it onto the active node stack. The packet to parse subject NPs, **Parse-subject-NP**, is activated; it also activates packet **Parse-det** and a packet to parse quantifier and measure phrases, **Parse-qp-1**.

New machine: *The* is marked $+N$ $-V$ $-A$ $-P$. This prompts creation of an X^{max}, with lexical features $+N$ $-V$ percolated. The packet name **Parse-specifier-$[+N$ $-V]$** is associated with this active node.

Step 3. *Old machine*: A grammar rule in the packet **Parse-det** triggers to attach *the* as a determiner. The packet **Parse-det** is deactivated and the packet **Parse-adj** is activated (so that the machine is primed to parse any adjectives). Here is the pattern and action of that rule.

> packet **Parse-det**
> [Det][*][*] →
> ATTACH 1st to C as Det
> activate **Parse-adj**

New machine: A grammar rule triggers to attach *the*. The active node (denoted C) is annotated with the name of the rule that has just executed. This annotation will play a valuable role in recording transformational operations (though none occur here).

> C is $+N$ $-V$; **Parse-specifier**
> $[+N$ $-V-A$ $-P][+N$ $-V+A][$ * $]$ →
> ATTACH

This step reveals most of the differences in grammar rule format between the two parser designs: the action here needs no "arguments" since it is always the first buffer element that is acted on. Pattern matching looks at the $\overline{X}$ name associated with the active node C, duplicating the work of the packet name in the old format. The features in the second buffer cell include $+A$ (since this position will hold either an adjective or a noun); Note that the **Parse-specifier** packet remains active.

Step 4. *Old machine*: With *student* now occupying the first buffer cell, and the packet **Parse-adj** active, the only grammar rule that can trigger simply deactivates the **Parse-adj** packet and activates the packet to analyze nouns, **Parse-noun**.

New machine: No action this step.

Step 5. *Old machine*: The grammar rule to attach nouns triggers. It creates an $\overline{\text{N}}$ node and attaches the Head *student* to it as a noun. It then deactivates the **Parse-noun** packet and activates packets to parse clauses and the end of NPs.

New machine: The grammar rule to attach nouns triggers. The noun is marked $+\text{N} -\text{V} +\text{A}$, and so meets the feature requirements for a Head of this projection:

> C is $+\text{N} -\text{V}$; **Parse-specifier**
> $[+\text{N} -\text{V}+\text{A} -\text{P}][-\text{N} +\text{V}] \rightarrow$
> ATTACH

Because the attached item can be a Head of this maximal projection, it is attached as such and the grammar interpreter marks the active node with the new "packet name" **Parse-comp**. The parser is now ready to parse the complements of a noun.[11]

Step 6. *Old machine*: With *will* in the first buffer cell, no rules in **Parse-NP-complement** trigger and the default rule for this packet fires, completing the NP and placing it back into the buffer.

New machine: Essentially the same action takes place here, but it is the grammar interpreter that does the job: no rules can trigger, so the completed X^{max} is dropped into the first buffer position.

How is it known in general when a phrase is completed? First of all, the end of a constituent is unambiguously marked by the end of a sentence. For example, the PP, *with red hair* is unambiguously terminated in the sentence, *I kissed the girl with red hair.* Note that the end of sentence marker also terminates the NP (and the VP) in this case. Second, a phrase is unambiguously

---

[11]This example also shows how potential ambiguity is handled by the feature percolation machinery. Suppose that the example was a genitive construction, say, *the student's book*. Then the noun *student* would be followed by the genitive marker *s*, which has the inflectional features 0A 0P. Thus the above rule does not trigger. Instead, another grammar rule will execute that creates a maximal projection with an Inflectional head (but with $+\text{N}$ features). This new phrase will absorb the *s* as its Head, and *student* will be attached to it instead.

terminated if it is a single name, such as *Bill*. So for example, in a sentence such as, *I kissed Sally behind the barn*, the PP *behind the barn* cannot be a part of the NP *Sally*. But what happens in truly ambiguous cases, e.g., sentences where PPs can be attached either to NPs or to a matrix VP, as in the classic, *I saw the man on the hill with the telescope*? Is this a problem for acquisition?

While these sorts of examples might pose a problem for deterministic parsing, they do not pose a problem for *acquisition*. While there are ambiguous cases where the trailing edge of, e.g., an NP, cannot be pinpointed for certain, there are other examples where the boundaries of the NP are clearcut. Ambiguities can arise out of the interaction of these two separately acquired pieces of knowledge. For example, one piece of knowledge is that NPs can have PP complements; this knowledge is triggered by unambiguous positive examples such as, *The boy with red hair is sick*. Here, it is known for certain that the PP *with red hair* ends the NP, assuming that it is already known that VPs cannot appear as NP complements (as must be already known in order to handle simple declaratives successfully). Similarly, an acquisition procedure can acquire the knowledge that VPs can have PP complements, via examples such as, *I saw Bill with the telescope*. No difficulties are encountered *learning* these constructions, but together they form a potent combination. The grammatical system that is induced is ambiguous:

$$NP \rightarrow \quad N \ (PP)$$
$$PP \rightarrow \quad P \ NP$$
$$VP \rightarrow \quad V \ NP \ (PP)$$

Since this grammar is ambiguous, it cannot be parsed by a deterministic pushdown automaton. This is not a paradoxical result. There is no reason to expect that the entire system of linguistic knowledge that is acquired must be easily "processable." To take a more familiar case, consider the existence of center-embedded sentences. As Chomsky and Miller (1963) observe, such sentences cannot be easily processed, if at all, by people; yet they are perfectly well a part of the system of knowledge that is acquired.

Step 7. *Old machine*: S is now the active node, on top of the stack. The packets associated with it become active once again. This means that the grammar rule for declarative sentences, **Major-decl-s**, can trigger. It does so, labeling the sentence node a major declarative sentence. The packet **Parse-subj** is activated, to pave the way for analysis of a subject NP.

New machine: The $-$N $+$V 0P item *will* triggers creation of an X^{max} marked with the features $-$N $+$V; it is made the current active node. **Parse-spec** is active. Note that this X^{max} plays the role of the S node.

Step 8. *Old machine*: The NP is attached to the top node in the stack, now the S. This rule also activates the packet **Parse-aux**, to get ready to analyze an auxiliary verb if one is present, and deactivates **Parse-subj**.

New machine: The grammar rule that attaches X^{max} elements labeled $+$N $-$V executes, attaching an NP to the X^{max} on the top of the stack. This node is also annotated with the name of this rule; this annotation replaces the labeling of the sentence as a major declarative sentence. Since the X^{max} has "zero" features for A and P, the $+$ feature on the NP is percolated to set this value.

Step 9. *Old machine*: The packet **Parse-aux** contains a grammar rule that creates an auxiliary node, transfers person and number features from the first item now in the buffer to that node, and then activates a packet of rules that will actually analyze the auxiliary elements. A rule in this packet attaches the modal *will* to the AUX node. A final rule in this packet (which triggers on any element but is ordered last so that all other rules have a chance to fire) drops the completed AUX into the buffer. At that point, the rule *aux-attach* executes, attaching the AUX to the S, deactivating the aux-building packets and activating a packet to parse verb phrases, **Parse-vp**.

New machine: *Will* is attached as the Head of the X^{max} (since its features agree with those of the maximal projection). Automatically, the interpreter increments the $\overline{X}$ template to point at **Parse-comp**. Note that no separate AUX node is created.

Step 10. *Old machine*: The grammar rule *main-verb* executes (it triggers on a verb in the first buffer cell). This rule creates a VP, attaches the verb to the VP, and then activates a packet appropriate for the argument structure of the verb (whether it is intransitive, ditransitive, takes a sentential complement of a certain kind, and so forth). In this case, *buy* takes one obligatory NP argument, so a packet for simple sentences is activated, and the packet to parse verbs deactivated.

New machine: The verb sparks creation of an X^{max} labeled $-N$ $+V$. The Specifier portion of the $\overline{X}$ schema is activated, but the first element in the buffer is of course the verb itself; its $+P$ $-A$ features prevent its attachment as a part of the Specifier. The grammar rule to attach a Head executes, advancing the $\overline{X}$ pointer to the Complement segment. Finally, the $+P$ annotation prompts consultation of the lexical entry for the verb; this retrieves the entry $+N$ $-V$, which is placed on the active node for later reference.

Step 11. *Old machine*: The token *a* is now in the first buffer cell. As before, this will force an interrupt-driven parse of an NP. The details will not be covered here. The NP will be created; *a* attached as a determiner, the Head Noun attached, and then the complete NP put back into the buffer. Next, a grammar rule will execute to attach the NP as the object NP to the VP. Finally, the now completed VP will be returned to the first buffer cell, where a final grammar rule will attach it to the S, completing the parse. (The original parser also attached a final end-of-sentence marker to the S.)

New machine: An X^{max} of type $+N$ $-V$ will be created as before. Once again, Specifier and Head Noun will be attached to the X^{max}. At this point, no further grammar rules trigger, and the X^{max} is therefore known to be complete according to the interpreter; it is returned to the first buffer cell. A grammar rule now executes that matches on the following features: (i) an active node that points to **Parse-complement**; (ii) an argument demanded by the active node that matches the type of the first buffer cell; and (iii) an $+A$ element in the first buffer cell. After this rule triggers, the X^{max} (the VP) active node is complete. It is automatically dropped into the first buffer cell. The **Parse-complement** part of the new active node (INFL) is now exposed. A grammar rule triggering on a $-N$ $+V$-type X^{max} now executes, attaching the VP to the active node, setting its OP feature, and completing the parse. This is an accepting machine configuration, and the parse succeeds.

Here is a summary of the new parsing machinery:

- Node creation and completion. Phrases are created in a "data driven" way from evidence in the input. A new maximal projection is created when either:

    - The item in the first buffer cell is a Head of type X; or

- The item is a nonargument or nonpredicate of known type X (e.g., a DET); or

- The complement of a predicate calls for an obligatory maximal projection of type X.

- Nodes are completed under the following conditions:

  - No grammar rules can execute and

  - A known thematic role assignment indicates that the argument is complete.

- Active node annotation. The node that is currently on top of the stack is always labeled with the names of whatever grammar rules executed to build up that node.

- $\overline{X}$ annotation. The top of stack node is also labeled with an updated SPEC, HEAD, or COMP specification. This replaces a packet name.

- Feature percolation. Features of Heads are "percolated" to their maximal projections. Features of Specifiers are checked for compatibility with maximal projections (this includes number and gender features, if these exist). Ambiguous lexical entries are forced to be compatible with what is required by the maximal projection.

- The Projection Principle. The argument structure of verbs is projected to label their maximal projections, and is "checked off" as obligatory arguments are encountered.

- Rule priorities. There are no explicit priorities. Instead we use the general production rule (or "elsewhere") principle that more specific rules fire before more general rules.

- Simple grammar rule actions. There is just one action per grammar rule.

The feature projection machinery has several advantages over an explicit phrase structure approach, even if one is just talking about parsing. Lexical (part of speech) ambiguity can be handled more easily. The remainder of this subsection explores this point in more detail. This material is only tangentially related to the acquisition model—though it does enter in at some points—and so may be omitted.

Consider part-of-speech ambiguity. Here one can often simply project whatever features of the lexical item are known, and then filter out impossible combinations later as more information is received, perhaps using information about what is expected given the current state of the parse. For example, in a sentence such as,

Did John dog Bill?

dog is either a noun or a verb. But in context the choice is plain. At the time that *dog* is analyzed, the parser will have parsed *did* as an inflectional element, and *John* as an NP, also taking note of the inversion via a rule that need not concern us here. Now, *dog* is a lexical Head item, either $+N$ $-V$ or $-N$ $+V$. But we know that it cannot be projected to an $+N$ $-V$ maximal projection, because the complement of the inflectional projection demands a $-N$ $+V$ element. This is the feature complex forced on the lexical item. Some words are born nouns, some words achieve nounhood; and some words have nounhood thrust upon them.

Let us consider a few other examples. The node creation protocol occasionally leads to ambiguities on account of the homophonic status of *that* and *for*, but these ambiguities can be resolved, by and large, through local context. Consider, for example, sentences such as,

That children hate spinach is well known.

That child hates spinach.

The lookahead buffer reveals the difference between the singular and plural forms of child. The feature complex that includes $+N$ $-V$ SINGULAR will be incompatible with the Head in the first case, but compatible with it in the second, thus resolving this example.

To take another case, consider *to*, which can be ambiguous between a prepositional or verbal Head (a locative preposition, as in, *to* NP, or an infinitive, as in, *to go home*). Here again the lookahead buffer is used as a diagnostic. If the element after *to* is unambiguously an NP, then *to* must be a preposition; if the element is verbal, it is an infinitive.

These two examples suggest that the automatic creation of phrases must be monitored by a process of feature agreement or compatibility. Roughly, a Specifier must agree with the features of its Head, where the set of features may be taken as Person, Number, and Gender in English. (This array of features must be acquired, obviously.) To guarantee this, as a Specifier or Head is attached to its XP, the parser checks to see if any agreement features specified conflict with existing agreement features. In the example above, *that* may be assumed to have NUMBER SINGULAR, and so cannot be attached to an XP of type +N −V with features PLURAL, as dictated by the Head *student*.

The postponed decision about *that* is exactly the same kind that occurs in the analysis of the sentence, *Have the students* .... An item of vague category status is placed on the active node stack, and its identity is resolved by the analysis of the next input constituent.

Other parser changes: grammar rules

Our last job in this section is to discuss the changes made to grammar rules beyond the packet system itself. These include the removal of the rule priority system and limiting the grammar rule actions.

Removing rule priorities. In the original parser, rules could be ordered by a priority system whereby grammar rules with higher priority were allowed to execute before those with lower priority. The revised model eliminates an explicit priority scheme. In its place is a general principle that specific rules execute before general rules. By "specific" we mean a ranking of predicate specificity in terms of the number of pattern matches called for in the first buffer; if that does not resolve matters, then the second buffer is examined using the same criterion, and so on. For example, figure 2.6 shows that an Auxiliary inversion rule is more specific than a rule that simply attaches the Inflectional item.

The principle that specific rules should get a chance to execute before general ones is grounded in widespread experience with production systems like this one; see McDermott and Forgy (1978). Its rationale is simple: if general rules are allowed to be tested before specific rules, then a possibly-matching specific rule might always be prevented from executing. This could happen, for example, if there were a very general rule that matched almost any input pattern. But if specific rules are tried first, then a very general rule will still get a chance to run, if all its specific relatives fail. From a slightly different point of view, such a system imposes an "elsewhere" condition, as discussed

Subject-Auxiliary rule

IF: [Auxiliary verb][NP][*]
THEN: ATTACH second item as an NP subject

Auxiliary attachment rule

IF: [Auxiliary verb][*][*]
THEN: ATTACH first item as Auxiliary.

Figure 2.6: Ordering rules by specificity

by Kiparsky (1973). It has also been advanced in Lasnik and Kupin's (1977) formalization of transformational grammar.

This principle has interesting consequences for acquisition. For one thing, it ensures that the system will attempt to first use specific rules, generally recently-acquired, before its older, more generalized grammar rules. These implications are discussed in more detail in chapters 3 and 4.

Restricting grammar rule format. The format of grammar rules is revised in three more ways. First, grammar rules are forbidden to have more than a single action. This is in contrast to the original parser's rules, which could consist of a sequence of actions.

Second, rule patterns are defined to uniformly mention items (if any) in all three buffer cells. In the original parser a grammar rule could have a pattern that referred to just the first or second buffer cell.

Finally, the repertoire of rule actions in the revised parser is limited. As the discussion of automatic node creation suggests, there is no need to label nodes via grammar rule actions. Rather, feature sets of a Head item are required to percolate to the top XP of the phrase that they head; likewise, agreement between Specifiers and Heads is enforced automatically. Therefore, a LABEL action is not required. It is still obviously necessary to move items from the input buffer to the partial tree under construction (if a tree representation is selected), or to indicate that such items have been analyzed; thus an ATTACH action is still required. Node CREATION has been covered by

Grammatical Operation	Corresponding Rule Action
local syntactic inversions	SWITCH
long distance movement	INSERT TRACE
lexical insertion	INSERT ⟨lexical item⟩

Table 2.2: Grammar rule actions other than ATTACH

the automatic projection of XPs given lexical items in the buffer; therefore, an explicit CREATE action is not required. Nor are ACTIVATE and DEACTIVATE, since these deal with the packet system, and packet activation and deactivation has been made automatic. We are left with the following possibilities: (1) local syntactic modifications, e.g., inversions; (2) "long distance" syntactic movements, e.g., *wh* movement, as in, *What did John think that Mary ate?*; and (3) specific lexical insertions, as in (*You*) *kiss Sue!* Each of these is handled by a separate grammar rule action. Table 2.2 summarizes.

As its name implies, SWITCH interchanges the first two items in the buffer. There are certain conditions on its operation; ordinarily both items must be complete constituents. INSERT TRACE puts an (unbound) NP trace into the first cell in the buffer. INSERT ⟨lexical item⟩ puts one of a small finite number of designated lexical items into the first cell in the buffer. It should be pointed out that the location of all actions is fixed. Attachment is always to the top item of the stack (the current active node), interchanges involve the first two buffer items, and insertions are always into the first buffer cell. Therefore, none of these actions demand arguments, except the insertion action; even this one consults only a small list of elements: *you, there, it, of*.

This completes discussion of changes made to the Marcus parser design.

The initial state: the lexicon

The lexicon plays an important role in the acquisition model. We have already seen that since there are no explicit phrase structure rules, information about the argument (complement) structure of phrases and the properties of their Heads is "projected" from features attached to lexical items. For example, each verb contains information about its argument structure—whether it is transitive or not, and, if transitive, whether it takes one or more arguments. In addition, the verb's dictionary entry will state whether the subject of the verb controls the subject of an embedded infinitive complement (such as *promise*) or whether the subject of the infinitive is controlled by the object of the verb (such as *persuade*).

Initially, none of this information is attached to a lexical entry. The acquisition system has an inventory of features it knows may be applied to a lexical entry. Part of learning consists in acquiring (i) the feature identity of a lexical item (including ambiguous feature complexes); (ii) the argument structure of a verb, including the number of arguments it must or may take, and (iii) the other lexical items that behave like this one, its "equivalence class."

The inventory of syntactic features includes those described in the previous section plus a finite set of grammatically relevant *agreement features* including TENSE, NUMBER, and GENDER. In addition, we allow a small set of features for describing selectional restrictions, including ANIMATE and HUMAN.[12] For the most part, agreement features are binary valued. We draw a distinction between an item that is marked either plus or minus for some feature and an item that is simply not marked for a feature. For example, the auxiliary verb *will* is marked +*tense*, whereas *be* is marked −*tense*, but *apple* is not marked either plus or minus for *tense*. Figure 2.7 has a (mature) sample lexical entry for *persuade*.[13]

We will sometimes use the label *persuade* as a gloss for the entire equivalence class of words lumped with *persuade*. Where a mature grammar rule mentions *persuade* explicitly, any member of the class will do.

---

[12]We will not further justify the selection of these features at this point, though these recur in natural grammatical systems.

[13]Information that *persuade*'s sentential complement can have a missing subject is still encoded in grammar rule triggering patterns, as we shall see.

ARGUMENTS:	NP, +ANIMATE, $\overline{S}$
THEMATIC ROLES:	Subject is AGENT;
	Object is AFFECTED OBJECT;
	Propositional complement is THEME
CLASS:	*convince, tell ...*

Figure 2.7: A lexical entry

Particular grammar rules will say whether a verb's sentential complement must contain a complementizer of a particular sort (e.g., that *know* selects for propositions, indirect questions, or exclamatory complements, as described by Grimshaw (1981)). Finally, information about a verb's NUMBER and GENDER is carried on the inflectional endings attached to verbs. This information is then "percolated" to the Head of the verb, becoming accessible to the VP as a whole.

Mistakes are possible in learning about words, but they are also correctable. This is one category of errors that frequently shows up in actual acquisition. For example, it is possible to get the system to assume that *promise* acts like *tell* in assigning the missing subject of an embedded clause to the object of the matrix clause. That is, in the absence of contrary evidence, in a sentence such as *John told Bill to leave Bill* will be chosen as the subject of *to leave*. This is C. Chomsky's (1969) well known Minimal Distance Principle (MDP). Children apparently apply this principle quite generally, evidently taking *promise* to be like *tell* and interpreting *John promised Bill to leave* incorrectly for a time.

As we shall see, this effect has a quite natural interpretation in the computer model, and it is to be expected.[14] Similarly, after analyzing sentences such as *John got a cookie after dinner* the system will quite naturally lump *got* together with other main verbs, leading to its appearance in forms such as *John don't got one*. Many errors of this kind arise from the misanalysis of

---

[14]It is only by examining independent thematic structure or the meaning of *promise* that the system deduces that the true subject of the complement clause is the matrix subject.

morphological information; see Berwick and Weinberg (1984) for an example drawn from the acquisition of passive constructions.[15]

As will be discussed later in this chapter and chapter 5, the acquisition procedure makes certain assumptions about the number of arguments a verb will take, or whether these arguments are obligatory or not. A verb is assumed to take no arguments until positive evidence appears that indicates that it can take an argument; this holds for NP, PP and $\bar{S}$ arguments. Once an argument appears, it is assumed obligatory unless explicit positive evidence shows that it is optional. Finally, the $\bar{X}$ expansion itself does not specify that any particular *number* of arguments must be present; this information is part of a lexical entry. That is why the $\bar{X}$ expansion itself uses simply an "indefinite repetition" notation: if one argument PP is allowed, for example, an indefinite number are.

In the "mature" parser, the order of arguments in English could be encoded directly, by expanding the Complement as a rule in the form $(\text{NP})^*-(\text{PP})^*-(\bar{S})$. Our approach will be to list any such information unique to a particular verb in the lexical entry of that verb.[16]

To conclude this section, we give the initial lexicon that the system has for analyzing the sentence, *Sue kissed John on the lips*. Section 2.2 gives the target lexicon and grammar rules for this same sentence. The next chapter shows how these rules may be acquired.

Note in particular that the inflectional morphology of *ed* is not known, or any details of the adjective *red*.

---

[15] Berwick and Weinberg show how confusion over past participle forms leads to difficulties in learning passives. More generally, it seems that difficulties in acquisition arise from ambiguous morphological-syntactic linkages such as this one. For example, Baker (1979) discusses child overgeneralizations regarding pronouns for dative and particle movement (*I turned off it*) as a by-product of the child's misunderstanding of the clitic status of these elements. That is, children do not know a (morphophonetic) feature for *it* that blocks such a rule; this feature is ultimately learned from positive evidence. There are similar difficulties with other homophonous elements: uses of *for* as a preposition spill over to its distribution as a complementizer. Again, we shall see in chapter 3 that this has a natural explanation in the computer model.

[16] Note the use here of the Kleene star "indefinite repetition" notation. There are alternatives to encoding Complement order directly. Since it is evidently derivative, one approach might be to use whatever principles determine this order and simply refer to those principles. For example, one could impose a requirement of adjacency on NP arguments. This approach has not been adopted here; see Stowell (1981).

Sue:	Object (+N, −V), singular, female, name
John:	Object (+N, −V), singular, masc, name
kissed:	Action (−N +V)
the:	Nonaction, nonverb, nonargument
lips:	Object (+N, −V), singular
on:	Nonaction, nonverb

Initial thematic information

The acquisition system also has a rudimentary representation of the "meaning" of at least simple sentences, in the form of a case frame or thematic representation. This is a "picture" of the sentence's predicate-argument semantics, identifying the major action of the sentence and the objects that play major roles: AGENT, AFFECTED OBJECT, INSTRUMENT. The inventory of thematic roles follows the major expositors of this theory, starting from Fillmore (1968). Since a full discussion of this representation more property belongs to the input data the system gets (section 2.3) we postpone further discussion until then. We note here only that access to a thematic representation for simple sentences is assumed in most models of acquisition (Wexler and Culicover 1980). We also give the thematic representation supplied for the sentence *Sue kissed John on the lips.*

Verb:	kiss
Kisser:	Sue
Kissee:	John
Loc. Modifier:	on the lips

2.2   The Target Grammar

The "mature" target grammar has two parts: base phrase structure grammar rules (for the most part fixed by the $\overline{\text{X}}$ theory) and transformational-type grammar rules. We list separately here the grammar rules and lexical information required to analyze the simple sentence, *Sue kissed the boy on the lips.* This sentence (and others like it) takes center stage in chapter 3, as one

$\overline{\text{S}}$	$\rightarrow$	Comp S
S	$\rightarrow$	NP INFL VP
NP	$\rightarrow$	(Det) (Adj)* N (PP)* ($\overline{\text{S}}$)
PP	$\rightarrow$	P (NP) (PP)* ($\overline{\text{S}}$)
AdjP	$\rightarrow$	Adj (PP)*($\overline{\text{S}}$)
VP	$\rightarrow$	V (NP) (NP) (PP)*($\overline{\text{S}}$)
Comp	$\rightarrow$	*that*, *for*
Infl	$\rightarrow$	(Modal)(Have en)(Be en)

Table 2.3: Conventional phrase structure rules

of the examples initially tackled by the learning procedure. Appendix 2 for this chapter lists the full complement of target grammar rules. All of these are learned by the acquisition procedure.

Target base rules

The target base phrase structure system contains rules for NPs, VPs, auxiliaries (inflection), main sentences, PPs, and embedded sentences. Adjective phrases could be easily added to this list. In general, for each type of phrase, creation of the phrase (pushing a new node onto the active node stack) and completion of the phrase (dropping it into the buffer) is carried out by the interpreter's $\overline{\text{X}}$ protocol. Beyond this, there must be a separate grammar rule for each portion of the righthand side of a phrase. We give first a conventional list of the base phrase structure rules (table 2.3). Tables 2.4–2.7 follow with the base grammar rules required for analyzing a simple sentence, using a feature-based notation. Appendix 2 to the chapter has the rest of the base grammar rules. There are no DROP NODE type rules in the new format. Therefore the only possible grammar rule action for base phrase structure rules is ATTACH. The star (*) is a "wild card" predicate that matches any feature or feature combination. C denotes the the top of stack node, or current active node, while CYC is the current cyclic (NP or S) node above that node.

The rules for analyzing verb phrases discriminate among verbs that take different kinds of complements, e.g., those that take certain kinds of *wh* complements vs. those that take *that* complements; verbs that take only tensed

Rule attach-det

CYC is *

C is X^{max} +N −V +A −P—SP$\overset{\downarrow}{E}$C—HEAD—COMP

[+N −V −P −A][+N −V +A][*] →

ATTACH

Rule attach-noun

CYC is *

C is X^{max} +N −V +A −P—SPEC—H$\overset{\downarrow}{E}$AD—COMP

[+N −V −P +A][*][*] →

ATTACH

Rule attach-pp

CYC is *

C is X^{max} +N −V +A −P—SPEC—HEAD—C$\overset{\downarrow}{O}$MP

[X^{max} −N −V][*][*] →

ATTACH

Table 2.4: Rules for parsing NPs

sentential complements (*know*, *believe*) vs. those that can take either tensed or infinitival sentential complements (*expect*); those that take missing or lexical Subjects in sentential complements (*want*) vs. those that take only a missing subject embedded sentential complement (*try*, *believe*). In addition, the lexical entries for verbs may distinguish between verbs that take, e.g., one NP argument from those that take either S or NP arguments or those that take both an NP and an S argument, and so forth. All this information was coded in the Marcus parser packet structure, which is not used here.

Target transformational rules

Transformational rules fall into two groups: simple local transformations like Subject-auxiliary inversion and major movement rules like *wh* movement. None of these are needed to analyze a simple declarative sentence, but we give some examples here in table 2.8. See the appendix for a complete list.

2.3 The Input Data

Having reviewed the "end product" of acquisition, we turn to the input data that the acquisition procedure gets. We assume that the acquisition procedure uses only *grammatical* example sentences, dubbed *positive* evidence. We prohibit the use of *ungrammatical* sentences followed by an indication that the example was ungrammatical, or explicit correction of the learner's syntactic mistakes, what is usually called *negative data*. We further limit the procedure to *simple* sentences that contain no more than two embedded sentences.

The assumption that only positive data is exploited for the acquisition of syntactic knowledge may well be too strong. On the other hand, most psycholinguistic experiments indicate that it is not (Brown and Hanlon 1970; Brown 1973:387; Newport, Gleitman, and Gleitman 1977; for a summary see Wexler and Culicover 1980). If acquisition can proceed using only positive data, then it would seem completely unnecessary to move to an enrichment of the input data that is as yet unsupported by psycholinguistic evidence. Beyond this point, limiting the procedure to positive evidence does not hinder learning—it helps, since we can focus on the important matter of constraints needed so that learning can proceed.

Rule attach-subject

CYC is nil

C is X^{max} $-N$ $+V$ $+A$ $+P$—SP$\overset{\downarrow}{E}$C—HEAD—COMP
$[X^{max}$ $+N$ $-V$ $+A$ $-P][-N$ $+V$ $+tense][$ $*$ $]$ $\rightarrow$
ATTACH

Rule attach-infl

CYC is *

C is X^{max} $-N$ $+V$ $+A$ $+P$—SPEC—H$\overset{\downarrow}{E}$AD—COMP
$[-N$ $+V$ $+A$ $+P][-N][$ $*$ $]$ $\rightarrow$
ATTACH

Rule attach-vp

CYC is *

C is X^{max} $-N$ $+V$ $+A$ $+P$—SPEC—HEAD—C$\overset{\downarrow}{O}$MP
$[X^{max}$ $-N$ $+V$ $+P$ $-A][$ $*$ $][$ $*$ $]$ $\rightarrow$
ATTACH

Table 2.5: Rules for parsing sentences

Rule attach-prep

CYC is *

C is X^{max} —N —V—SPEC—HE$\overset{\downarrow}{A}$D—COMP
[−N −V][+N −V][*] →
ATTACH

Rule attach-pp-object

CYC is *

C is X^{max} —N —V—SPEC—HEAD—CO$\overset{\downarrow}{M}$P
[X^{max} +N −V][*][*] →
ATTACH

Table 2.6: Rules for parsing PPs

We assume then that the procedure receives as input data a sequence of grammatical surface strings derived from a mature grammar in presegmented form—as words with whatever associated features are assumed to be recognizable. Initially, the set of recognizable features includes just ±N, ±V. For example, the string consisting of the three tokens ordered as *Sally—kissed—John* would get input roughly as, [+N −V][−N +V][−N +V][+N −V] (note the extra −N +V for the *ed* marker).

Admitting a structured input of this form clearly presupposes that some grasp of individual words (their segmentation and feature labeling) precedes the development of parsing abilities. This is an idealization demanding some justification.

Segmentation and words

The assumption that segmentation precedes more sophisticated parsing abilities can be supported on several grounds. First of all, it allows work to proceed, concentrating on just a single aspect of language acquisition. But it also appears to be logically justified. An ability to *parse* presumes some ability at assigning different words to different parts of a tree (or labeled

---

Rule attach-verb-kiss

CYC is *

C is X^{max} −N +V +P −A—SPEC—$\overset{\downarrow}{HEAD}$—COMP

[−N +V *kiss*][*][*] →

ATTACH

Rule attach-object

CYC is *

C is X^{max} −N +V +P −A—SPEC—HEAD—$\overset{\downarrow}{COMP}$

[X^{max} +N −V +A −P][*][*] →

ATTACH

Rule attach-pp

CYC is *

C is X^{max} −N +V +P −A—SPEC—HEAD—$\overset{\downarrow}{COMP}$

[X^{max} −N −V][*][*] →

ATTACH

Table 2.7: Rules for parsing VPs

Rule subject-aux-inversion
CYC is nil

C is X^{max} $-N$ $+V$ $+A$ $+P$—SPÉC—HEAD—COMP
$[-N +V +A +P+\text{tense}][X^{max}+N -V +A -P][-N +V] \rightarrow$
SWITCH

Rule passive
CYC is * Rule passive-be

C is $X^{max}-N +V +P -A$—SPEC—HEAD—CÓMP
$[\quad * \quad][\quad * \quad][\quad * \quad] \rightarrow$
INSERT TRACE

Table 2.8: Some transformational rules

bracketing). It is hard to see how the notion of a syntactic rule for parsing can even be made coherent without some way to pick out individual words from the continuous speech stream. If so, then since this research is about the acquisition of syntactic rules it is a reasonable methodological simplification to take some ability at segmentation as given, since it is logically prior to the syntactic rules to be acquired.

It at least makes sense then that a rough grasp of the categorization features of *some* individual words should precede the development of parsing abilities manipulating them. In fact, this appears to be the case for children: production of single words precedes connected speech (although the complicating effects of developing processing abilities suggest the usual likelihood of confounding effects) (Brown 1973:390). Likewise it is plausible that the initial categorization of lexical items as nouns or verbs can be accounted for by the obvious (and often suggested) proposal that nouns can be identified with objects and verbs with actions.[17]

---

[17]It should be emphasized that the recent Government-Binding theory of Chomsky (1981) is actually designed to maintain this close connection between syntactic and semantic representations. As we shall discuss later on in this section, in early child language the correlation between a supposed canonical predicate-argument form and surface order of words is nearly exact: as has been often observed, children produce utterances as if they

The same kind of story can be told about segmentation. Once again, we appeal to a principle of inference from clear cases. We assume that only unambiguous examples of word segmentation are exploited for the acquisition of new syntactic knowledge. As has been frequently observed, speech to very young children is punctuated by features that would serve to ease the extraordinary burden of separating out individual words in the sound stream: use of single words, special intonation and stress, slow delivery (Brown 1973; Newport, Gleitman and Gleitman 1977). Such characteristics would tend to ensure that the developing child gets the sort of input that we have assumed for the acquisition procedure: a segmented input stream. Once certain clear cases of words have been recognized, then their psychophysical cues might be relaxed. We shall see that as designed the acquisition procedure actually exhibits this "filtering" effect. Since its acquisition is incremental, sentences that are "too complex" or that require the simultaneous inference of segmentation boundaries and grammar rules are simply left uninterpreted until the proper time comes for their acquisition.[18]

In any case, the assumption of prior development of segmentation and word classification leaves the door open to a more sophisticated theory that

---

followed a fixed Agent–Action–Object order (Brown 1973; Limber 1973). Adherence to a strict order strategy sets the stage for the detection of deviations from this rigid word order (e.g., inversions in yes-no questions), because everything can be held fixed save for a single deviation. Government-binding theory is helpful in this regard because it assumes that semantic structure, in particular the predicate argument structure of verbs, is projected through to the level of annotated surface structure.semantic "bootstrapping" In effect, the Government-Binding theory claims that simple N-V-N strategies never have to be abandoned, because syntactic form never deviates from semantic form, contrary to surface impressions. This confluence of representational levels has a prima facie appeal from the standpoint of acquisition, of course.

[18]See Brown (1973:390) for discussion. Of course, for this account to be made precise one must supply a more fully-developed theory of adult processing of speech. This is a research topic in its own right. It could be that recent developments in the metrical theory of phonology (the theory of syllabification and weak-strong stress contours) (Liberman and Prince 1977) could play some role in advancing our understanding of early development of speech segmentation. It is well known, for example, that infants mimic the stress contours of full sentences before producing them complete with words. (A fact that might be due however entirely to unfolding processing capabilities.) The metrical restrictions might presumably aid learning because they provide a narrower characterization of the valid syllabification patterns of human languages, and possibly the boundaries of words and phrases themselves. Acquisition of the syllabification patterns for a particular language could even parallel the template-instantiation used by the acquisition procedure to flesh out context-free base rules. The same sort of "parameter setting" outlook may also provide an account for the unfolding of phonological feature categories; see chapter 6.

specifies a detailed interaction between phonological and syntactic development. As discussed in the previous footnote, constraints on possible phonological representations could supplement those provided by syntactic representations, providing an additional "forcing function" that aids the learner.

Features and adult correction

One assumption about the form of the input data remains: the labeling of words with features drawn from a finite, semantically-grounded stock of primitives such as *singular* and *animate*—features potentially available to the parser as its basis for constructing triggering patterns for grammar rules. The procedure knows what universal set of features is possibly relevant for its grammar rules simply because it has been told what the members of that set are. How can this be justified?

A simple-minded proposal is to adopt a corollary of the Subset Principle outlined in chapter one: if possible target languages can be proper subsets of one another, then guess the narrowest possible language consistent with positive evidence seen so far, such that no other possible target language is a subset of the current guess. How does this translate into the domain of features? Since additional features can only limit when a grammar rule can be executed, application of the Subset Principle demands that one err on the side of providing too many features for the grammar rule pattern. For suppose otherwise, that is, suppose too few features are supplied for the triggering pattern of a grammar rule. Then that rule will be too general; it will execute in too many environments and hence lead to a larger possible class of surface strings that are acceptable. If a more restricted rule is the correct one, it will generate too large a language. But then, given positive-only evidence, it cannot know that it has acquired too large a language.

An over-supply of features is not a severe computational burden, and can quickly be remedied by rule generalization. The details of generalization are covered later in this chapter, but the basic idea is simple. Whenever a new grammar rule is constructed that specifies the same ACTION as an already-known rule(s), and at exactly the same point in the left-to-right parse, merge the rules by intersecting the features that the two rules have encoded in their patterns. This has the beneficial effect of quickly pruning away irrelevant features. For instance, suppose that the Subject-auxiliary inversion grammar rule encodes as part of its triggering pattern a possibly superfluous set of *Sally*'s features, e.g., that NAME, GENDER and so forth. Given the generalization scheme, the presentation of an additional example sentence like *Will John kiss John* will eliminate via set intersection the gender feature, leaving only the tag NAME on the triggering pattern for the grammar rule. Provided that the stock of features is finite (perhaps this can be guaranteed by limitations on inherent conceptual abilities) and that the supplied examples are consistent (the adult contributes, error-free, the regularities), then this method settles many of the encoding problems that will come up in the context of this book.

Note that because this technique has been designed to select bundles of features across a sequence of sentences, it cannot solve the additional problem of finding the correct triggering features to select within a single sentence. Consider for example Subject-Verb agreement in English: the Subject Noun Phrase must agree in Person, Number, and Gender with the main verb. How is the procedure to know that this agreement must be observed and that it is these features that do the work of encoding agreement?

Once again, one could resort to a stop-gap conservative strategy. If the number of features that can ever be attached to a single token is finite, then one way to proceed is to simply err on the side of overlabeling, attaching all possible features to both the Subject and Verb of an example sentence. Then regularities can be observed by comparisons across sentences: if an agreement feature is not observed—say, a sentence occurs with a masculine-marked Subject and an feminine-marked verb—then that feature is struck from the surviving list of agreement features.

Such a method is almost certainly too simple-minded to be completely correct. If it is not carefully controlled it can lead to serious problems of over-generalization because certain sentences may not exhibit agreement paradigms that are observed elsewhere. For example, in English, case agreement is often dropped in *wh* questions (e.g., *Who did Sally kiss* instead of *Whom did Sally kiss*). But it is not dropped following prepositions, e.g., *I know of her*—**I know of she*. Therefore, the acquisition procedure should not drop case agreement for pronouns just because it is dropped for *wh* elements. To avoid this problem, the acquisition procedure has been deliberately designed to be conservative in its generalization. Roughly, two sentences prompt a generalization only if they are one feature different (with respect to the parser state). So for example, *Who did Sally kiss* and *Whom did Sally kiss* would tell the acquisition procedure that the Case feature could be dropped for *wh* elements; however, since no positive examples exhibiting a lack of case agreement would be encountered for *she/her*, case agreement would *not* be dropped in this situation.

Fortunately, because the set of potential features is finite (and perhaps not even very large), one could supplement (even replace) the guess-too-large-and-prune strategy with sheer brute-force enumeration; one could simply try all the possible combinations. Unfortunately, if the acquisition of semantically-grounded features for syntactic rules actually proceeds in a trial-and-error fashion, then the acquisition procedure in itself will not be of much theoretical (and computational) interest. It would however predict that there should be a sharp distinction in the kinds of errors observed in child acquisition, paralleling the syntactic rule-parameter setting/ trial-and-error distinction. On the one hand, the parameter setting framework implies a largely monotonic, error-free course of acquisition: the basic (and correct) settings for rules for sentence phrase structure are acquired early, and, once fixed, are never withdrawn. On the other hand, trial-and-error learning would leave the child open to outright blunders that should be easily detected. The target should be a system that makes errors in just those places where children make errors. As has been noted, children do not make gross errors in their hypothesis of base phrase structure rules, except where these are the result of faulty lexical categorizations (e.g., assuming that *it* is just like an ordinary Noun Phrase; see Baker 1979); they do make errors with morphological patterns that are, in essence, memorized. But it also appears that the areas where children make errors are precisely those where there is abundant positive evidence, and even adult attempts at negative reinforcement.[19]

The tight restrictions on the form of syntactic rule acquisition proposed here also makes several highly specific predictions as to the errors that can possibly be made during the course of acquisition. Since acquisition proceeds

---

[19] A purely enumerative strategy should probably be supplemented by a theoretical structure of its own, for brute-force trial-and-error does not seem to account for certain inflectional errors made by children. See chapter 6 for a formal model of these cases. For instance, Brown (1973:140) observes that (English language) children overgeneralize all verb inflections to inappropriate verb stems, save for one: the progressive *ing* is employed correctly on only "process" verbs (e.g., *hitting*), and never attached (incorrectly) to stative verbs such as *want*. The implication is that children develop quite early a distinction between the two classes of verbs. But this separation into verb classes cannot be directly expressed in the current model for the acquisition of syntactic features. A richer theory might exploit Lieber's recent work (1980) on the structure of the lexicon.

S. Pinker (1982) has also independently proposed a modified brute-force approach that attempts to deal with some of these problems.

by altering the atomic components of a single parsing rule at a time, an error must be representable as some combination of elementary mistakes in a complete rule. Whether or not this prediction is supported by observational data in children is a matter still open to dispute: see Mayer, Erreich, and Valian (1978).

There is some evidence in the child language acquisition literature that would argue for this more groping, trial-and-error acquisition for a proper subset of feature predicates, though only in strictly limited contexts. First, in some special situations adults can be observed to at least attempt the correction of a narrow class of syntactic errors—intriguingly, just the sort of errors that might require acquisition by brute-force methods. For example, it is a commonplace that adults will respond to a child's errors in Subject–Verb agreement or the over-generalized use of certain morphological markings with negative reinforcement of some sort. (e.g., *Don't say, "Mommy are hungry," say, "Mommy is hungry"*; *Don't say "Mommy goed home," say....*) However, it is not at all apparent just what the impact of these mini-training sequences is. For the classic example of a mother's repetition having no apparent effect see McNeill (1966:69); also quoted in Wexler and Culicover (1980:509) or Braine (1971).[20]

Errors in the input data and resiliency

There is yet another way in which the assumption of positive-only evidence is an idealization: The assumption of positive-only input abstracts away from the realities of normal discourse, scattered as it is with ungrammaticalities, false starts, and the like.[21]

---

[20] What is crucial to note is that the sort of syntactic error that is the target of these brave attempts is typically exactly those cases involving (language particular) flags for features such as Person, Tense, Gender, and the like. For example, in English we are told that the morpheme *s* is appended to verbs to mark the use of the third person singular case: *John likeS Sally* is fine, but not *John like Sally*. Likewise, the association of a particular phonological shape with a particular morpheme is arbitrary (and language particular); there is no apparent way for the child to know that it is *s* that must be appended (rather than some other morpheme).

[21] A significant percentage of utterances the child receives may be ill-formed—see Wexler and Culicover (1980:77). However, as is so often the case in the child developmental literature, the evidence is most unclear. As cited in Brown (1973:387), Labov (1970:42) suggests that after removing obvious ellipses and false starts, only a few percent of utterances are ungrammatical. Brown's view (1973) is that adult speech to children is mostly well-formed. This does not quite answer the question, however, since it could well

How can the acquisition procedure deal with these realities? Suppose we define noise as a finite number of intrusions from the sample of another language other than the target language (this might even be a nonnatural languages, since the errors could be the result of performance defects in adult speech). At one extreme, this "noise" could definitely lead an acquisition procedure astray, since one could, for example, intend the system to learn English rules and then present as its first thousand examples the "noise" of Chinese sentences. We want the system to fix on Chinese in this case, even if this is wrong. Conversely, if it gets just a few errors, it should be able to either ignore or recover from these.

We rule out the "Chinese error" situation by assuming that our system gets a representative sample of sentences generated by the target grammar in question. More precisely, the sentences are correctly parsed by the target parsing machine we have assumed for the language in question. We understand "representative" to mean the following two conditions: (i) in order to successfully parse all the sample sentences, all grammar rules of the target machine must be exercised at least once, and all left- and righthand parsing contexts must appear often enough to distinguish all possible lexical classes relevant for the grammar rule; (ii) these contexts appear with uniform probability, and with greater frequency than errors.

The acquisition system is actually designed to both ignore and recover from single (as opposed to systematic) errors. Two properties ensure this: first, the system proposes new grammar rules only in unambiguous situations. Often, an error will result in an ungrammatical sentence that would demand two or three new grammar rules to parse correctly. The system just ignores these cases. Second, the system adopts a uniqueness principle: if there are two or more alternative settings of a single parameter, only one is permitted to survive.[22] An error that leads to the setting of an incorrect $\overline{X}$ parameter either appears after the $\overline{X}$ order has been set—in which case it is set aside as deviant—or it appears before the true $\overline{X}$ order has been encountered.

---

be that even though just a few utterances are ill-formed, these are the crucial examples that "trigger" major acquisition decisions. For example, one would not want to literally fix base phrase structure order on the basis of a single example, the first one heard, since that might be ungrammatical. Again, the obvious way out of this problem is to add some kind of "strength" requirement—fix a rule only if it is encountered ten, or a hundred, times. We take up this question in the main text.

[22] This constraint is closely allied to Wexler's *Uniqueness principle* (1981), which forces a single surface form for every deep structure in the unmarked case. See chapter 6 for more discussion on this principle.

This last case is the thorniest one, since it allows sentences from other languages to appear, perhaps throwing off acquisition. Here we rely on the uniqueness principle and distributional uniformity. Consider a sentence that violates the correct $\overline{\text{X}}$ HEAD–COMPLEMENT order, for instance, a topicalized sentence such as, *Beans, I like.* If the surface order of this sentence is used to fix the $\overline{\text{X}}$ parameters, then they might be set, incorrectly, to the order COMPLEMENT–HEAD. But there will be many other simple examples occurring in the order HEAD–COMPLEMENT—including the order *I like beans.* Given uniqueness, then the order COMPLEMENT–HEAD must be excluded, since it cannot cover the order found over all PPs, APs, or NPs.

Closely tied to the issue of error correction is the question of data ordering. It has often been noted that language learners arrive at the same target grammar regardless of varying environmental conditions. Indeed, their developmental trajectories seem broadly similar, with individual differences falling within a narrow range. There are two "solutions" that would force this uniformity in the face of varying data input.

First, any pair of acquisition decisions d_1, d_2 might be commutative— that is to say, order independent. Second, the acquisition device itself might act as a filter to order an otherwise randomly presented data sequence. We investigate both of these constraints. Section 3.4 shows that pairs of transformational-type grammar rules can be acquired in either order. In addition, we shall show that the basic $\overline{\text{X}}$ parameters may be fixed in a certain order so that data that is "too complex" will be filtered out and not play a role in acquisition. We call this second type of ordering *intrinsic.* Examples in chapters 3 and 4 cover specific examples of this effect.

Formal learnability and negative evidence

Besides its lack of empirical support, negative evidence is dangerous on yet a final ground. From mathematical results in inductive inference it is known that positive and negative examples paired with the appropriate labels "grammatical" and "ungrammatical" enable one to learn *almost any* language (see Gold 1967).[23] While this result might seem fortunate, implying that nega-

---

[23]More precisely, any recursively enumerable set of recursive languages is "identifiable in the limit" from positive and negative examples. However, the result is abstract, and so sets a very weak (though important) upper bound on what can be expected from computational methods; there are many psychologically unsettling aspects to Gold's result that make it unsatisfactory as a "realistic" model of acquisition. For one thing, it

tive evidence would be a boon, it also implies the existence of an *informant* who is carefully guiding the learner through some reinforcement schedule. As mentioned above, the possibility of explicit reinforcement seems hardly likely in the case of human acquisition of syntactic knowledge. Children simply do not seem to receive correction of this sort.[24] Interestingly as well, the assumption of informant presentation in a sense places the burden of language acquisition implicitly on the adult, not the child, since in order to determine the next piece of data to present, the adult must somehow know the internal state of the child's grammar.[25]

In short then, the reliance upon positive-only evidence is a key part of the methodological strategy of this research. Its aim is to see what constraints must be postulated on a representation in order that acquisition be possible *even with* impoverished input data. Note that this viewpoint is in sharp contrast to most artificial intelligence models of learning. For example, Winston's concept learning program (1975) made essential use of negative examples as a powerful source of evidence for hypothesis formation. Perhaps the most important discovery of the current research is that in certain domains the limitation to positive-only evidence need not be debilitating. In fact, at least for the acquisition of syntactic knowledge studied in this report, quite the reverse is true. One can make considerable progress by discovering what sorts of constraints must take up the slack that negative evidence (supposedly) provided.

---

relies on an enumeration of the class of languages (or grammars for those languages), as if the full details of each possibility were known in advance, rather than the construction of the proper grammar via the fixing of various parameters. As a result, the Gold procedure takes enormous amounts of time, approaching the correct identification only in the limit. Secondly, the approach permits the wholesale rejection or acceptance of grammars based upon single input examples, a fact not really compatible with what is known about human acquisition.

[24]Brown (1973:387-388): "... judgment and correction are not a royal road to the child's grammatical knowledge." See also Wexler and Culicover (1980).

[25]As pointed out by Newport, Gleitman, and Gleitman (1977); see also Wexler and Culicover (1980:69, 75).

But note that children apparently do receive negative reinforcement for *semantic* well-formedness—the adult says "Huh?" in response to a meaningless string. As Anderson (1977) shows, this *semantic* supplement can add (in principle) sufficient information to establish learnability from just *syntactically* correct sentences.

Semantic, pragmatic, and contextual information

In addition to a surface string already divided into words, there are other sorts
of input data that have traditionally been assumed helpful to a hypothetical
child acquiring syntactic knowledge, and therefore of possible importance for
an acquisition program. Foremost among these is what is usually dubbed
"semantic knowledge" or sometimes, "contextual" or "world knowledge"—all
the information that might contribute to one's understanding of an utterance
besides the properties of the utterance's surface string. The way such information could in principle be of assistance to the learner is clear: if syntactic
knowledge involves the mapping of surface strings to mental representations
(including perhaps what some might loosely call "meaning"), then at some
level the acquisition of syntactic knowledge means the acquisition of the correct function to carry out this mapping. Contextual information could help
because in certain cases it might independently specify (part of) the underlying representation, pinning down one end of the mapping. Extra-syntactic
information is most easily used precisely when supposed "semantic" forms
are close to syntactic forms, and all the more so when syntactic forms are
isomorphic to literal surface strings of words. This close correspondence between surface and "semantic" form typically holds only in the earliest stages
of acquisition, when (as often observed) there is but a single surface form for
every underlying semantic structure. But this is simply the observation that
the Projection Principle holds in early child language. In fact, one common
strategy of children at this early stage is to simply "read off" the thematic
roles of AGENT, ACTION, and OBJECT in a fixed sequence directly from the
surface order of words (Fodor, Bever, and Garrett 1974). There is simply
no need for any other "strategy" because the structural relationships among
constituents is reflected in the linear ordering of words themselves.

But what happens when surface form and meaning part ways? The ob-
servations above suggest that any *large* deviations between surface form and
known syntactic/semantic relationships is likely to render an utterance simply
uninterpretable.[26] Suppose, however, that semantic and syntactic form never
"part ways," because syntactic form is augmented with abstract structure
so that it always reflects underlying predicate-argument structure. Roughly
speaking, suppose that sentences "wear their meanings on their sleeves." This
constraint—amounting to the Projection Principle—would seem to be *prima*

---

[26]See Limber (1973:179) for an earlier exposition of this position.

facie the right assumption to make, and it is the one that will be adopted here.

The Projection Principle still leaves us with the problem of how the assignment of arguments to structural positions is made initially. For instance, what tells the child that *ball* in *John kicked the ball* is the GOAL or PATIENT rather than the AGENT of the sentence? The first question to answer is whether this information is required for syntactic acquisition at all. That is, why should it matter whether an argument is assigned the thematic role of GOAL or PATIENT? For many cases it seems not to matter. So for example, consider the case of an Agentless passive, e.g., *John was kissed*. The acquisition procedure does not need to know anything about the proper assignment of thematic roles in this case, if it also knows that *kiss* demands an NP argument as a complement, and that these arguments go after the Head verb. For then, some kind of empty category placeholder must be placed into the input. The only antecedent for this empty element is *John*. If in addition there is a constraint saying that an argument can bear just one thematic role, then there is a conflict: according to the usual rules for reading thematic roles off of structure, *John* cannot be both the Object of *kiss* and the Subject (Agent). As we will see, the answer is plain if other Agent-less sentences have been encountered, e.g., *It was raining, John was sick*. These *be* forms are associated with Subject NPs that do not get interpreted as bearing thematic roles. Thus there is a precedent for interpreting this new *be* form in this way as well.

What if thematic role assignments are required? Here it appears that there is just one approach that has been suggested in the literature, though in various forms (for example, by Anderson (1977); Wexler and Culicover (1980)). This is to assume that, to some degree or another, the acquisition procedure can recover the correct assignment of thematic roles to verbal arguments independently of the usual linguistic rules used to recover thematic role assignments. So for instance, in a sentence such as, *John kicked the ball*, it is assumed that the acquisition procedure knows that *John* is the AGENT of the sentence, and has had some effect in some way or another on the GOAL or RECIPIENT, the *ball*. In Anderson's work, this assumption is explicitly made in the form of providing the acquisition procedure with a "semantic network representation" of the input sentence.[27] Wexler and Culicover do not assume that thematic structure is explicitly furnished, but they do assume that the

---

[27] In fact, Anderson assumes that this semantic network is a minor structural deformation of a labeled bracketing of the surface string.

learner is provided with a base phrase marker (a deep structure representation) of each surface string. Assuming that thematic roles are "read off" a deep structure tree, this is actually a stronger condition than simply positing that correct thematic role assignments can be recovered. It is a stronger condition because it assumes that structural relationships among thematic roles are also independently recoverable. Wexler and Culicover's theory is set within an *Aspects*-style transformational theory, where deep structures are used for semantic interpretation. A base phrase structure represents canonical predicate-argument structure, and so satisfies (trivially) the Projection Principle. Fixed positions in the deep structure tree are associated with certain grammatical relations, e.g., the NP under S is the Subject, the first NP under the VP is the Direct Object, and so forth.[28]

How exactly could thematic role assignments be determined without recourse to linguistic knowledge? It has often been supposed that there is an initial association mediated by some kind of "interaction" with the real world—either visual observation, or participation in the actual act involved. However, since such proposals are not very precise and entirely speculative, we shall just leave this question as an unresolved problem, and simply assume that the association between certain linguistic representations (roughly, Noun Phrases) and thematic roles (such as AGENT, PATIENT, GOAL, INSTRUMENT) can be made. Note that several researchers (Keil 1979) have observed that concepts such as Agency, Instrumentality, and the like, are acquired quite early by children, as seems reasonable. Thus it would be at least natural for children to be able to assign these characteristics to objects in the world, however that is done.

It should be stressed again that this approach does not necessarily imply that the predicate-argument structure must *always* be independently recoverable from extra-syntactic context alone in order for acquisition to proceed. In many cases the proper assignment of thematic roles to the constituent Noun Phrases in a particular sentence is not a prerequisite for the formulation of parsing rules, as in the case of passives discussed above. This is true since the absence of a needed rule of parsing can often be signalled by the detection

---

[28] However, it should be noted that Wexler and Culicover realize that the assumption that a complete base structure is furnished with every example string is a strong condition that might perhaps be dispensed with. In fact, they propose that base structures could be inferred directly from thematic assignments plus conditions on properly formed base phrase structures rules, roughly, $\overline{X}$ theory. This proposal is quite close to the approach adopted here.

of a missing item in the input string of words itself—a "gap"—and this can sometimes be done no matter what the thematic role assignment of the missing material. Examples like these indicate that syntactic predicate-argument structure in conjunction with the Projection Principle could be used to infer new thematic roles, rather than, as is usually assumed, the other way around.[29]

Once simple passive forms like these have been acquired, then acquisition of the full passive analysis (*Sally was kissed by Bill*) may not be so mysterious. If the gap after *kissed* can still be assumed detectable, then its binding to *Sally* can be effected by exactly the same rule as in the truncated, Agentless passive. However, some additional interpretive rule is required to determine that the agentive *by* phrase serves as the first argument to *kiss*.

In summary, thematic role assignments are assumed to be available, but are used only as a last resort, to check whether constituents alleged to be completed are in fact completed or whether bindings have been correctly made. The acquisition procedure knows the following.

1. The correct assignment of constituents to thematic roles in simple sentences with at most one embedding.

2. By default, that any arguments to a verb are obligatory until proven otherwise. This rule follows the Subset Principle for acquisition from positive-only evidence (see chapters 5 and 6 for discussion).[30] Plainly, assuming that arguments to verbs are obligatory generates a smaller set of surface strings than assuming that the constituents may be obligatory or optional. If a procedure first guessed that an argument was optional, and if the argument was obligatory, it would never receive disconfirming evidence; there would be no way for a procedure to recover from a faulty hypothesis of optionality. On the other hand, by guessing a more restricted language (namely, one where all arguments are obligatory), it could protect itself: if the procedure finds itself to be wrong (it receives a piece of input data where the item is not present) it can still retreat to the broader position of optionality.

---

[29]See Berwick and Weinberg (1984) for a more complete discussion of the acquisition of passives, and chapter 4.

[30]Roeper (1981) has also suggested a default obligatory requirement for arguments to predicates, based on the same learnability motivation.

3. Also by default, that repetition of a constituent in phrase structure is disallowed unless a positive surface string indicates it. But if any repetition is observed, the procedure permits arbitrary repetition (in apparent violation of the Subset Principle). The choice is whether an item of a given type allows an indefinite number of immediately adjacent elements of the same category in surface form. The system is designed so that we cannot state in a phrase structure rule that, say, a Prepositional Phrase can be repeated exactly three times. According to this approach, phrase structure rules cannot "count." This observation seems to be descriptively correct, for most (perhaps all) linguistic phenomena. One justification for the inductive leap from PP to PP* is simply that natural grammars do not have access to "counting predicates." There are no rules of grammar that refer to "three" or "seven" elements. See Berwick and Weinberg (1984) for a discussion of this property of natural grammars.[31]

2.4 The Acquisition Procedure

Having sketched the knowledge to be acquired, the target machine, the initial state of knowledge, and the input data to be used for the construction of new rules, it remains to outline the acquisition procedure itself. Earlier in chapter 1, figure 1.1 depicted the course of acquisition as the development of a sequence of parsers. The initial parser P_0 has no grammar rules. A sequence of grammatical example sentences is then given to the acquisition procedure, which proceeds according to the following steps. Figure 2.8 gives the toplevel flowchart.

The acquisition procedure itself splits into five main steps. First, the sentence may be successfully analyzed with existing rules. In this case, no acquisition takes place. The net effect is that the acquisition procedure does not change its rule system without evidence that it must do so. This strategy is unlike the general Gold (1967) model of language identification. In that formal framework, a learning machine could alter its guess even if its current rule system was consistent with the evidence it had seen so far. On the

---

[31]Berwick and Weinberg show how this "noncounting" property can help explain the existence of a constraint like Subjacency. Beyond this, noncounting languages seem easier to learn. For example, counter-free parenthesis grammars seem to be more easily inducible from sample evidence (Crespi-Reghizzi, Guida, Mandriolo (1978); Crespi-Reghizzi (1971)).

other hand, this strategy of change-if-failure matches that of most acquisition models, such as Wexler and Culicover's (1980).

The remaining steps of the acquisition procedure come into play when the parser's existing set of rules fails at some stage in the analysis of an example sentence. Step 2 records the instantaneous description of the parser's state for later use. In step 3 the procedure tries to see whether the new sentence demands a new $\overline{\text{X}}$ parameter setting, or a new nonterminal node or modification of an existing lexical entry. A new parser grammar rule is written to encode these changes. If it succeeds, it moves on to step 5 to generalize the rule; otherwise it marches to step 4. In step 4 the procedure attempts to build a new transformational-like rule to handle the situation. Once again, if it succeeds, it proceeds to generalization in step 5; otherwise, it drops the analysis of the current sentence. After generalization, the procedure simply goes back to step 1 and starts the whole procedure over again.

We now backup and cover the same ground in more detail. We begin with a description of Steps 1 and 2.

OUTLINE OF ACQUISITION PROCEDURE

STEP 1: Attempt to parse the sentence left-to-right in a single pass, using currently known grammar rules. If there are no failures while processing the sentence (the parser is never blocked because there are no grammar rules that can trigger) and afterwards (the output is a complete parse tree with a valid thematic role assignment), read in and attempt to parse the next sentence. If the parse fails at any point during the analysis (no currently known grammar rules trigger), go to Step 2.

STEP 2: Acquisition phase. Note instantaneous description (ID) of the parser at the point of failure (whether SPEC, HEAD, or COMP is currently active; the node on top of the stack and the cyclic (S or NP) node immediately above the current active node, annotated with the names of previously executed grammar rules that built up these nodes; and the contents of the input buffer).

The next step of the acquisition procedure is to try to build a new base phrase structure rule, using the ATTACH action. These rules are tried before any transformational-type actions, in accordance with the Subset Principle as discussed later in this chapter and in chapter 5. The idea is to hypothesize

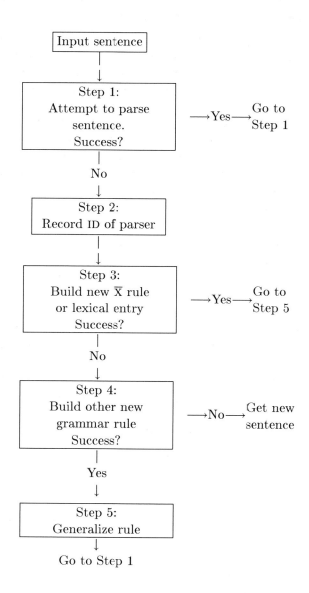

Figure 2.8: Toplevel flowchart for the acquisition procedure

as narrow a language as possible in the case where the target languages may be proper subsets of one another, so as to avoid overgeneralization. Note that in this situation a learner using positive-only evidence cannot recover if the larger language is guessed.

First the ATTACH is checked for compatibility with $\overline{X}$ constraints—if a Head, then this element must be the Head that prompted the creation of this projection. Also, the attached item must agree with the current maximal projection's features; if a Complement, then it must be a maximal projection and a possible argument to the maximal projection, and so forth. Then the $\overline{X}$ pointer is advanced. Some care must be taken to check for an optional Specifier or Argument. If all else fails, yet the given thematic structure indicates a complete constituent, then the current active node is just dropped into the first input buffer cell. Otherwise, the procedure moves on to step 4.

STEP 3: Attempt to build a single new base phrase structure rule corresponding to the $\overline{X}$ constituent currently active, by trying ATTACH. The procedure tries to attach the item in the first buffer cell to the $\overline{X}$ constituent currently active. (If $\overline{X}$ order is not yet fixed, then the conditions set out below are used to set it.) If successful, it stores the new rule as an instantiated $\overline{X}$ template (via the parser action ATTACH). Success is defined as follows:

STEP3A: If the current $\overline{X}$ component on the X^{max} active node is SPEC, then the syntactic features of the attached element must be compatible with those of the X^{max}. If they are, attach as SPEC and go to Step 5, rule generalization. If $\overline{X}$ order is not yet set, place SPEC first relative to HEAD or COMP if HEAD or COMP have not been processed; place SPEC after HEAD if HEAD was processed, and so on. If $\overline{X}$ order is set, attachment fails, and this SPEC was marked as obligatory, mark it as optional, advanced the packet pointer, and go to Step 1. (The system will now attempt to parse this item as HEAD, if this is the next element.)

STEP 3B: If the current $\overline{X}$ component is HEAD, then the attached element must be the lexical item that prompted the creation of this projection, and match the X^{max} features exactly. Set HEAD order as appropriate, if $\overline{X}$ order is not yet set. Advance the packet pointer to the next part of the $\overline{X}$ component, if $\overline{X}$ order is known, and go to Step 5. If the attach fails, go to Step 3c.

STEP 3C: if the $\overline{\text{X}}$ component is COMP, then the features of the attached element cannot be the same as those of the X^{max} and must be compatible with the given thematic structure constraints, if any. Set $\overline{\text{X}}$ order if as yet unknown and go to Step 5. If all arguments to this HEAD are attached, and the current token cannot meet the attachment criterion, then drop the current active node into the buffer and go to Step 1; otherwise go to Step 4. If this attachment completes the arguments to a HEAD, as indicated by the thematic representation, then make any previously obligatory arguments not presently attached optional for this HEAD.

Step 4 considers new transformational-like rule actions. It is invoked only when $\overline{\text{X}}$-rule building fails. The three remaining rule actions, SWITCH, INSERT LEXICAL ITEM and INSERT TRACE, are tried in turn. These actions are ordered to obey the Subset Principle, being arranged from most conservative to least conservative rule action. The success criterion is different here from $\overline{\text{X}}$ type rule actions: they pass muster if an already known grammar rule can execute after the tentative rule action is tried. If all actions fail, syntactic analysis of the current sentence is abandoned; successful rules get passed to Step 5, rule generalization.

STEP 4: Try to build a new grammar rule using SWITCH, INSERT LEXICAL ITEM, or INSERT TRACE. Test each action for successful triggering. The criterion for success is basically that a known grammar rule can execute after the tentative rule has fired: after 4(a) SWITCH, 4(b) INSERT LEXICAL ITEM, or 4(c) INSERT TRACE. Note that SWITCH demands that the second buffer cell be projected to a full X^{max}, and so prompts the creation of a new maximal projection that is parsed and returned to the second buffer cell if possible. If this "attention shift" parse fails, then the SWITCH itself fails; the acquisition procedure is not called recursively. If a rule succeeds, go to Step 5. If not, and if the current active node is complete as indicated by thematic structure, drop it into the buffer and return to Step 1. Finally, if no rules can be built, project an X^{max} from the second buffer cell and go to Step 1; if this fails, try the third buffer cell. Otherwise, no new rule can be built. Abandon the syntactic analysis of the current sentence and return to process another sentence. (Note that nonsyntactic interpretation is still possible.)

Step 5 executes and then generalizes any new rules. The key idea is an extension of the method of *k tail* induction, as described by Biermann and Feldman (1972) for finite automata. Biermann and Feldman note that a two states of a finite automaton are equivalent if and only if they have the same suffixes. That is, given that the automaton is in state s_1 or s_2, then $s_1 \equiv s_2$ if and only if for all suffixes ("tails") of length k, z, then $\delta(s_1, z) = \delta(s_2, z)$.

Roughly, two rules are merged by extending this condition to parsing states. Two rules are merged if they have the same action and are at the same points in the parse of similar sentences, and have the same lookahead. By "same point" we mean same left context of the parse—the same cyclic node and top of stack (current active node). By insisting that the two rules have the same lookahead, we demand that their length-2 suffixes (the two lookahead cells) be the same. This is a length-2 "tail" as defined by Biermann and Feldman. (For additional discussion of this restriction, see chapter 6.)

To begin the generalization procedure, the system first checks to see if there are already any known rules with the same action and with the same current active node and packet pointer. If not, nothing need be done and the parse continues. Otherwise, there are two main subcases, depending upon whether the first buffer cells of the two corresponding rules are the same or not.

If the corresponding first buffer cells of the two rules are the same, then there are two further subcases. If both left- and righthand contexts are different, then the rules are kept separate, since this corresponds to distinct rule contexts. If either left or right context is the same, then the rules are merged by intersecting features of the two rule patterns and saving the resulting generalized rule. This corresponds to forming a new lexical equivalence class. If *both* left and right contexts are exactly the same, the two rules are identical; this case should not be encountered because the previously stored rule should have triggered, but if it is, the system simply does not save the new, identical rule.

Otherwise, the first buffer cells of the candidate merger rules contain different items. The procedure then checks both left- and righthand contexts. If both are the same then the lexical classes of the first buffer cells are equivalent. The tokens in the first buffer cells of the two rules are placed in the same equivalence class. If either context is different, and the tokens were previously placed in the same equivalence class, then the two words are now separated.

STEP 5A: If successful, update the rule database. First check if the new grammar rule performs the same action as an already-known grammar rule with the same current active node and packet pointer. If not, go to Step 5d. Otherwise, retrieve all such grammar rules.

STEP 5B: If the first buffer cells of the new rule and retrieved rule(s) are the same, then check their left- and righthand contexts. If their righthand contexts are the same, then merge their lefthand contexts by feature intersection, store the single new generalized rule, and go to Step 5d to continue the parse. If their lefthand contexts are the same, merge their righthand contexts, store the new rule, and go to Step 5d. If both contexts are the same, this is the same rule as a previously stored one; do not store the new rule and go to Step 1. Otherwise, store the new rule as is and go to Step 5d.

STEP 5C: If the first buffer cells are different, and if both left and right contexts are identical, then place the two first buffer cell tokens in the same equivalence class. If either context is different, and if the two first buffer cell tokens were previously placed in the same lexical equivalence class, then separate them. Otherwise, do nothing and store the new rule as is.

STEP 5D: Prompt the user for a name for the new rule. Go to Step 1 to continue the parse.

Several properties of this procedure are worthy of note.

- *Process model realization.* At each step in the acquisition sequence, the model always has its knowledge of syntax available in the form of a working parser. The procedure provides a functionally realized representation of syntactic knowledge of ever-increasing sophistication.

- *Constructive and incremental acquisition.* (*"One error-one rule"*) The system adds only a single new rule at a time to its knowledge base, rather than hypothesizing and rejecting whole sets of rules (or grammars) at a time. Thus the procedure does not proceed by *enumerating* the sets of possible parsing rules (or grammars), and testing each for adequacy in turn, the method that was used by many previous acquisition programs for syntactic rules (see Feldman (1972); Horning (1969, 1971); Biermann and Feldman (1972); Fu and Booth (1975); review in Pinker

(1979)). Rather, the program is *constructive*, building the right parser by filling in the details of an initially-provided set of base rule templates and assembling one at a time a set of pattern-action grammar rules. As will be shown, this incrementality condition (working in conjunction with a restriction on recursive calls to the acquisition procedure) has the effect of imposing an intrinsic order to the sequence in which rules are acquired. The net effect is that "simpler" sentences where there are fewer changes from what is already known will be handled before more "complex" sentences that require several novel rules to analyze. (Note that this definition of what is "simple" or "complex" need not have any straightforward correspondence to surface string complexity, since it could be that a single new rule has dramatic surface effects.)[32]

- *No recursive entry into the acquisition procedure.* The procedure cannot call upon itself to construct a new rule while already in the midst of constructing a rule. This stipulation ensures that only one new rule can be constructed for each detection of a missing rule ("one error-one rule"). If recursion is necessary, the current acquisition attempt is abandoned. In part, this stipulation is justified by the principle of finite error detectability: if an error is detectable, it should be detectable in a "local" radius about a failure point. That the finite error condition is a proper characterization of the class of (humanly) learnable grammars is the centerpiece of the formal learnability work of Wexler *et al.* (Hamburger and Wexler (1975); Wexler and Culicover (1980); for further discussion, see chapter 7).

---

[32]Incremental acquisition may well prove to be far too strong a theory in the case of child acquisition: if there can be dramatic "radical reorganizations" of grammars—for example, the abandonment of one whole set of phrase structure rules for another then the model proposed here will not suffice. To take another example, consider the case of German. If simple German declarative sentences are all in S-V-O order (perhaps the result of a "verb second" rule), then an acquisition procedure hearing only S-V-O sentences must be driven to the conclusion that German is a Head-Complement language. But then it will later hear sentences in embedded clauses where the order is S-O-V, and so must abandon its previous conclusion. This is only an apparent contradiction, however. Thiersch [personal communication] has observed that in fact most simple German sentences used in conversation are in fact Verb final.

On the other hand, incremental decisions, such as the decision that Heads follow Complements, can have significant impact on the appearance of surface strings. It follows therefore that an incremental acquisition model does not necessarily rule out the possibility of apparent radical reconstruction.

- *Conservative acquisition.* Each new parser P_i is determined by the *current* input example sentence plus the previous parser, P_{i-1}. This implies that the acquisition procedure does not store previous example sentences it has encountered (though it does so indirectly via the knowledge in its rule base). Conclusions about the structure of a new rule are made by drawing upon knowledge of past rules, the current example sentence, and specific constraints about the form of all rules. It is this reliance on past knowledge that provides an incremental, conservative basis to the system's development. See chapter 5 for a formal discussion of incremental acquisition.[33]

- *Base rules acquired before other grammar rules.* The details of basic phrase structure rules are set before more particular grammar rules are acquired. For instance, the system would assume that the basic word order of a sentence is generated via phrase structure rules before assuming that the ordering was generated via the movement specified by some grammar rule. This ordering follows from the hypothesis of *attachments* before any other kind of rule, a constraint that in turn follows from a property of acquisition from positive-only evidence, discussed below and in chapter 5.

- *Lexical acquisition as equivalence class formation.* Items that behave alike with respect to parsing, e.g., the class of modals (*should, will, can...*) are placed in the same category.

This completes an outline of the acquisition procedure. The next chapter moves on to take up actual examples of the procedure in action. Four points about the acquisition model deserve further discussion. These details are not essential to an understanding of the model, and one may skip ahead directly to chapter 3 to see the procedure in action. The details cover: (1) rule generalization; (2) the order in which rule actions are attempted; (3) annotation of the active node with the names of rules that build that node; and (4) the order in which rules are executed.

---

[33] Thus the acquisition procedure is intensional, in the sense of Chomsky (1975:119–122): the current parser plus the new input datum (grammar in Chomsky's discussion) fixes the next parser, rather than the next language. For a discussion, see Wexler and Culicover (1980:93–94).

(1) *Rule Generalization and the Acquisition Procedure.*

New lexical categories can be formed via the collapse of terminal items into equivalence classes. To see this, note that the ATTACH rule is simply the reverse of the expansion $A \rightarrow \alpha/\Phi\_\_\_\psi$, that is, α is reduced to A in the context Φ on the left and ψ on the right. Equivalence class formation is based on the notion of "state" and "suffix" from automata theory, a matter that is taken up in detail in chapter 5. Call the *state* of the parse simply the left-context plus the item being analyzed; parsing actions map between states. The *suffixes* of a state are simply the possible buffer configurations (righthand contexts) that appear with the state.

Now consider two parser states q_i and q_j, and the succeeding states of the parser prompted by the attachment of the input tokens a or b respectively; call these new states q_{i+1} and q_{j+1}. If the two initial states and the two succeeding states are equivalent ($q_i = q_j$ and $q_{i+1} = q_{j+1}$) then, since the parser is deterministic, a must be in the same equivalence class as b *with respect to the operation of the parser*; such inputs are indistinguishable based on just lefthand context. For example, consider the sentences, *John could kiss Mary*; *John will kiss Mary*. *Could* and *will* are followed by the same lookahead strings (hence must lead the parser through the same sequence of states, leading to acceptance, at least given this example); the parse up to the point where *could* and *will* are encountered is also identical in both cases, so the parse state at the point where each is attached to the parse tree must be the same. Thus the conditions for equivalence are fulfilled, and *could* and *will* should be placed in the same (lexical) equivalence class. Conventionally, this set is called the class of *Modals*. In this case, because we are talking about single linear tokens, this example reduces to conventional approaches for the induction of finite state automata (Biermann and Feldman 1972). Sometimes, however, buffer cells or lefthand contexts may include complete phrases or subtrees, generalizing finite state induction to the context-free case. Chapter 5 gives details.[34]

---

[34]Two tokens are declared to be in the same equivalence class (hence are denoted by identical nonterminal labels in the acquired grammars) just in case their trailing k-cell suffixes are identical. If the buffer can hold complete constituents, or subtrees, as in the Marcus parser, then this method actually induces a restricted class of tree automata. This formalization allows one to calculate bounds on the running time and correctness of the acquisition procedure.

Later examples may force the *splitting* of a merged class. For example, consider the examples, *I did go* and *I will go*. This example forces *did* and *will* into the same class. However, a later example, such as, *I will have gone*, along with the *absence* of the example, *I did have gone* shows that this merged class must be split. Now, it is in general impossible to tell from positive evidence that an example of a certain type has not appeared. A supplementary principle is required that lets the procedure conclude that *if* a certain example has not appeared by a certain point in time *then* it never will appear. If it makes sense at all, this principle of "indirect negative evidence" makes sense for simple sentences that would have an *a priori* high probability of appearing, as in this case.[35] This example underscores two major and often-noted problems with purely "inductive" generalization procedures: (1) the requirement for a complete data sample, that is, all and only the positive examples; and (2) the low probability of occurrence of certain positive examples, e.g., complex auxiliary sequences. Chapters 5 and 6 discuss these matters in more detail.

For the other grammar rule actions, SWITCH and INSERT TRACE, no token is attached, but the basic equivalence class approach is still used. The method is as follows. If the trailing suffix in the buffer is identical for two grammar rules, and the $\overline{X}$ context is the same, then the rules are merged to yield a new, generalized rule by forming the intersection of the features in the remaining lefthand context. If the first buffer cell contents are different for the two rules, and the left- and right- contexts are the same, then place the items in the first buffer cell in the same lexical class.

It is not obvious why these rule generalization procedures should work. Indeed, the claim that class merger can be determined just by inspecting the buffer and the local lefthand context of the parse is a strong one; it plays the same role here as the notion of Finite Error Detectability does in the Wexler and Culicover work. The claim is that a 3-constituent buffer plus two-cell lefthand context actually suffices to detect all cases of nonequivalent states.[36] This constraint is intimately connected to Wexler and Culicover's

---

[35]This principle was introduced by Rizzi (1980). For additional discussion, see chapter 5, where the relationship between indirect negative evidence and hypothesis ordering is discussed.

[36]It is also not clear whether the three-cell limit is psycholinguistically significant or not. Given the assumption that an S consists of NP INFL VP, then the input buffer can hold an entire S. In addition, grammar rule patterns can access two nodes of the active node stack, the current active node and one cyclic (S or NP) node above the current active node. At most then a grammar rule can access an S as the cyclic node, an S as the

demand that all possible transformational errors be locally detectable on *some* phrase marker. Again, for details, see chapter 7.

(2) *Rule action ordering by the acquisition procedure.*

Above it was stated that the acquisition procedure attempts to find a single new action by trying the following sequence of actions:

ATTACH

SWITCH

INSERT LEXICAL ITEM (e.g., *you*)

INSERT TRACE

Why is this ordering of actions attempted and not some other? This order has been designed to follow the Subset Principle, introduced in chapter 1 and described in detail in chapter 5. This ordering of hypotheses guarantees that there is no legitimate rule system that could produce a target language narrower than the hypothesized set. In this particular case, the tightest assumption possible is that no movement is permitted; i.e., that all surface strings are base generated unless evidence is provided to the contrary.

From another point of view it seems unnecessary to invoke any ordering at all, because the possible actions seem to be in nearly complementary distribution. Consider first what it must mean to be forced to order the DROP INSERT and ATTACH actions. There are just two possible orders: try ATTACH and then TRACE, or vice-versa. Suppose the second ordering is incorrect. This implies that there must be some case where this order leads to the incorrect acquisition of a rule that would be correctly acquired by the reverse ATTACH-TRACE ordering. But this in turn means that there must be some case where a correct attachment rule is blocked by the insertion of a trace. If an attachment rule is correct, this means that the current element in the first cell in the buffer passes all tests for compatibility with the current active node. If a TRACE rule is correct, this means that INSERT TRACE followed by an ATTACH succeeds as well. Otherwise, the attempted TRACE would fail, and the ATTACH attempted, just as if the order were reversed.

---

current active node, and the constituents NP INFL VP in the input buffer—roughly a two-sentence range, the current S being parsed plus the S dominating the current S.

Is there a case that meets this condition? We seek a situation where both an ordinary lexical element and a trace can be attached to the same $\overline{X}$ node in the active node stack at the same point in the parse. Interestingly, such cases do not seem possible. The reason is basically that traces appear where lexical NPs cannot appear, and vice-versa. In particular, traces appear in so-called noncase-marked positions, after verbs with adjectival status such as *was hit*, while lexical NPs must appear in case-marked positions, e.g., after ordinary verbs as in *hit John*. Accepting this complementary distribution as a fact, the implication is that the ATTACH and INSERT TRACE actions cannot conflict. Just where a lexical NP cannot be inserted, a trace can be inserted, and vice-versa.[37] We may conclude, then, that the relative ordering of the ATTACH action with respect to TRACE does not matter—assuming that it is known that *kissed* does not assign Case to the NP it subcategorizes for. How could an acquisition procedure know this? There are simple positive examples where the choice between ATTACH and INSERT TRACE never arises, because there is no alternative lexical NP to attach. For example, consider truncated passives, such as, *John was kissed.* Here, only the action INSERT TRACE can possibly succeed. But this example indicates exactly what the procedure needs to know: that the quasi-adjectival form *was kissed* "absorbs" Case, since no overt NP appears. Assuming that such "clear" examples are acquired first—as seems to be the case (see Berwick and Weinberg (1984))—then no problems arise.

What about the relative ordering of ATTACH and SWITCH? The same kind of logical analysis of output possibilities can be applied. If the relative ordering of ATTACH and SWITCH matters, then there must be a case where an incorrect parsing rule is acquired if the actions are ordered (i) try switch then (ii) try attach, rather than the other way around. What kind of case would this be? Suppose that the surface order of constituents is B–A. Assume that a SWITCH in this case is successful; otherwise, we would simply try ATTACH, and the order of actions would not matter. If SWITCH succeeds, then this means that the inverted order A–B is a possible phrase structure order, since a SWITCH succeeds just in case it is followed by an ATTACH. Thus B–A and A–B must be allowable surface constituent orders. If ATTACH is tried first, then there are two possibilities. First, the ATTACH could fail. In this case we

---

[37]This does not cover the situation where the empty element functions as an empty pronominal. But here there cannot be a conflict in actions either, since this NP gap is always in the Subject position and the next element in the sentence is the infinitive *to*. An ATTACH is never possible at this point.

are back in the first situation, and so there is no difference in ordering ATTACH before SWITCH. So suppose the ATTACH succeeds. This means that B–A is an allowable base phrase structure order. But then both A–B and B–A are allowable surface structure orders, as before (A–B must be allowable since a SWITCH is assumed to be valid.) We conclude that the relative ordering of SWITCH and ATTACH does not matter, in terms of parsing rules.

Finally, we consider the ordering of SWITCH and INSERT TRACE. If a SWITCH is made, then this must mean that the first item in the buffer cannot currently be attached to the X^{max} active node. But a trace is just like an NP, except that it is phonologically null. Therefore, if the item in the first buffer cell is an NP, then inserting a trace will not help matters in terms of attachment. What if the item is not an NP? Then inserting a trace might work, as in, *Did John go home*. Here, *did* cannot be attached as the Subject NP of the sentence, but an empty category NP could be. This would block the SWITCH to follow. Note that in this case, however, this does not happen, since the resulting sentence, [empty NP] *did John go home*, will not match any known grammar rules for attachment of the first NP. Thus trace insertion does not work, and the relative ordering of the attempted actions does not matter. It is not apparent whether this analysis can be extended to other cases where SWITCH applies, but if it does, then we have demonstrated that the relative ordering of attempted rule actions does not matter for the construction of a new rule. Basically, the reason is that the actions are mutually exclusive.

(3) *Annotation of the active node.*

As described above, after a grammar rule executes we label the currently active node (the node on top of the active node stack) with the name of the rule just executed. (In the case of a newly acquired rule, the name is a uniquely generated name.) This is done for two reasons: (1) to mark the current left-hand context of a parse, so that certain rules will execute properly and (2) to provide an annotation for a (hypothetical) semantic translation routine to distinguish between sentence variants, e.g., declarative and auxiliary-verb inverted forms.[38] The name of the rule is simply attached as one of the features of the currently active node.

As an example of the first use of annotation, consider a rule for a passive construction, such as, *John was kissed*. When the parser reaches the point where it is analyzing the complement of the verb *kissed*, a passive rule triggers.

---

[38]The annotation approach was suggested by M. Marcus.

Note that at this point the currently active node is the VP. The maximal $\overline{\text{X}}$ phrase, the INFL node, has been labeled with features percolated from its HEAD lexical item (*was*).

The basic action of the passive grammar rule is to drop a trace into the input buffer; the trace acts as a dummy NP, a placeholder for the missing NP Object of *kiss*. The pattern for such an action is roughly, an active node of VP, labeled +*ed* and some record that a passive *be* has been encountered. (See chapter 4 for the acquisition scenario for passive.) How is this done? By assumption, the VP node is labeled with the names of rules that attach items to it. In this case, for example, the VP will be labeled with the name of the rule that attached the verb *kissed* to it. Similarly, the INFL node (actually, the maximal projection of Inflection) will be labeled with the names of the rules that attached the NP Subject and some form of the verb *be*.[39]

As a result, the passive rule will require that the left-context of the parser contain an INFL node marked +*be* and an X^{max} node marked +*ed*. (The X^{max} is also marked with an argument structure percolated from the verb's lexical entry—namely, that it marks an NP as the affected object.) Why is annotation important? Later examples, such as *Sally was kissed by Bill*, force a rule generalization so that passive triggers on a buffer pattern of the following form:

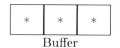

Buffer

This rule will trigger on any kind of element in the buffer. Given just this buffer pattern, the passive rule would trigger erroneously in a sentence such as, *Sally has kissed John*. What prevents it from doing so is the left-context of the parse, stored as part of the rule trigger. In the case at hand, the cyclic node above the $-\text{N} +\text{V} \ \text{X}^{\text{max}}$, INFL, will not have the proper *be* annotation, thus blocking rule application.

---

[39]This annotation is automatic. By convention, and in accord with ideas developed by Williams (1981b), the features of the Head of a phrase are percolated through to the projections of that phrase. For instance, the features of INFL, by assumption the Head of the Sentence phrase, are automatically passed through to the S node; the features of a verb are passed through to label the VP node. This percolation mechanism has also been adopted in recent theories of word formation; see Lieber (1980) or Farmer (1980).

As an example of the second function of annotation, consider the yes-no question, *Will Bill kiss Sally?*. According to the actions of the grammar rules acquired by the system (see later in this chapter), a SWITCH is used to convert this sentence into the form, *Bill will kiss Sally*. Then the parse proceeds as in a simple declarative sentence. But if this is so, then there would be no way to distinguish between the structure built by this sentence and its declarative counterpart. Therefore, any later or concurrently active semantic interpretation routines would be unable to distinguish between declarative and question forms. Since these sentences obviously differ in meaning, there must be some way that the parser marks them as different. A straightforward marking method is the annotation device. The yes-no question will mark the S node with the name of the switch rule, while the declarative sentence will not. (Note that the currently active node at the point where the switch is performed is in fact S.)

(4) *Specific and general rules.*

The passive rule illustrates another principle that was discussed earlier, namely, that specific rules have a chance to execute before general rules. Suppose that the passive rule has triggered, and has dropped an NP trace into the buffer. Presumably, the next rule that should execute is one that will attach the NP trace to the VP node, as the argument of the verb. The trigger for this rule is just that for the ordinary NP attach-object grammar rule.

We now have two rules that match after the NP trace is inserted: the Object attachment rule or the passive rule itself. To block this possibility we invoke a general principle that specific rules execute before general rules. In the case at hand the Object attach rule is "more specific," since it calls for the element filling the first buffer position to be at least an NP, whereas the generalized passive rule demands nothing at all about the first, or any buffer position. Therefore, the Object attachment rule will execute, attaching the NP to the current active node, the VP. As usual, the system will then check to see whether the current active node has been completely built; in this case it has, since the subcategorization frame of the verb is satisfied and the input buffer holds the end-of-sentence marker in its first slot. As a result, the completed node is dropped into the input buffer, deactivating the rule packet that holds the passive rule; the passive rule will never get a chance to repeat its execution in this phrasal domain. (This also demands that active rules be acquired before passive rules, evidently the empirically correct result.)

There are other situations where the specific-general ordering principle applies. One is when a so-called "diagnostic" rule executes. A diagnostic rule is one that decides among one of several (usually two) alternative parsing actions. For example, the rule that decides whether *have* is a main verb or an auxiliary verb in, *Have the students* . . . by looking at the morphology of the verb following the NP is a diagnostic rule. Without the specific-before-general rule principle it is difficult to see how one of Marcus's diagnostic rules could ever trigger without some explicit information about rule ordering. In short, the rule ordering principle is justified both from the standpoint of acquisition and from an engineering point of view.

Appendix 1

The New Parser Design

The main text noted several major changes to the original Marcus design that were prompted to make the system easier to learn. This appendix justifies these changes. First, we show how the packet system may be eliminated. Second, we consider how to integrate the prediction of new phrasal nodes into a standard bottom-up parsing regime. Third, we remove Marcus's "attention shifting" mechanism.

Parsing, parse trees, and the packet system

To begin we show how the parser's construction of a parse tree is related to the packet system. The Marcus parser builds a derivation tree for an input sentence as it goes, and its rules refer to a description of that tree for their proper operation. This means that the parser uses its own output in order to decide what to do next. In other words, its transition function looks like $\delta(\text{ID})$ where ID includes an encoding of the parse tree built so far. But how much of this tree must be encoded? If one looks carefully at the grammar rules, one discovers that rules may refer to the category and feature labels of nonterminal nodes in the stack, e.g., S or NP, and occasionally to the existence of a node of a given type attached to nodes in the stack, e.g., an NP attached to an S. Exact tree relationships other than these are specifically not required.

This limited use of a tree encoding suggests that one could resort to the usual way of storing information about the parse used by standard bottom-up or general context-free parsers rather than an explicit representation of tree structure. Namely, one could simply store a representation of how far one has gotten in the parse in the form of a more complex nonterminal symbol called a *dotted rule*. What is a dotted rule? Informally, a dotted rule is simply an ordinary context-free rewrite rule with a marker *dot* placed at some point in the righthand side of the expansion indicating how far we have gotten in the recognition of a rule of that type. For example, suppose we assume that sentences are always of the form, $S \rightarrow NP \ VP$, and that we have analyzed a string such as *John kissed the girl* as far as the NP *John*. We can indicate this by the dotted rule $S \rightarrow NP \bullet VP$. Note the dot placed to the right of the NP constituent, denoting that the NP has been recognized. When the VP constituent is recognized, the dot will be moved past the end of the righthand side of the expansion rule, indicating that the lefthand side constituent, an S, has been completely recognized. In the Marcus parser this completion of a constituent was signalled by dropping the now completely-built constituent back into the first cell of the buffer, where it could then be operated on by additional grammar rules. In the usual case, the very next grammar rule would attach the completed unit to its proper mother node—namely, the lefthand side nonterminal (here, the S).

The suggested change, then, is to place dotted rules on the active node stack rather than simple nonterminal names like S or NP. Plainly, this dotted-rule information subsumes that of simple nonterminal names, since a simple nonterminal name is a degenerate dotted rule without the dot. But it also suffices to replace whatever tree representation might be built, since the dotted rules encode precisely a representation of the constituents that could have been already recognized at a certain point.

Interestingly enough, the parser already manipulates an encoding of dotted rules, under the guise of the packet names. As observed by Marcus, packet names stand in a one-to-one correspondence with base phrase structure rules. For instance, consider the sequence of packets activated when the original Marcus parser analyzes a simple declarative sentence. At the main sentence level these include in turn: (1) SENTENCE-START, (2) PARSE-SUBJECT, (3) PARSE-AUX, and (4) PARSE-VP. But since dotted rules are just a static representation of all the possible places the parser could be in this expansion, they encode this sequencing information directly. For example, corresponding to the packet sequence above we have an associated rewrite rule $S \rightarrow NP \ AUX \ \ VP$, with dotted rules (1) $S \rightarrow \bullet NP \ AUX \ VP$, (2) $S \rightarrow NP \bullet \ AUX \ VP$, (3) $S \rightarrow NP \ AUX \ \bullet VP$, and (4) $S \rightarrow NP \ AUX \ VP \bullet$. One can see that packets and dotted rules are indeed in a 1-1 correspondence in this case.

More generally, let $A \rightarrow w_1 \ldots w_n$ be a (context-free) rewrite rule. Construct the corresponding set of dotted rules. Then for every dotted rule in this set of the form $A \rightarrow w_1 \ldots w_j \bullet \ldots w_n$ there exists a packet name P_{w_j}, for $0 \leq j \leq n - 1$. (We do not need a packet name corresponding to the dot at the extreme righthand end of the rule, because at that point the entire phrase A is complete and control returns to whatever packet was active before the A rule was entered.) Conversely, suppose we are given a sequence of packet activations and deactivations, $P_1, \ldots, P_n$, where a node of type X is created before entry to P_1, and where a node of type X is completed (dropped into the buffer and then attached to some higher node) while packet P_n is activated. If there is no such sequence, then the original decision to create a node of type X was incorrect, which is impossible by the assumption of determinism. Therefore, there must be such a sequence. Further, this sequence must be finite, also by the assumption of correct parsing, since otherwise there is some valid input on which the parser will loop forever. Since this sequence may include the possibility of other phrases being created and completed, these must be "spliced out."[40]

The Marcus parser manipulated packet names (hence dotted rules) by placing them onto its pushdown stack along with nonterminal names like NP or VP. Since a packet name corresponds to a dotted rule, this has the effect of pushing dotted rules onto the stack. Consider the expansion $NP \rightarrow$ *Article Adj N* as an example. The dotted rule expansion of this rule is:

- Article Adj N
- Article ● Adj N
- Article Adj ● N
- Article Adj N ●

We do not need to encode the last dotted rule, as mentioned. The others all have their corresponding packets in the Marcus parser. Figure 2.9 shows the correspondence.

Note that in the Marcus parser sometimes more than one packet could be active at a given point in a parse. For example, in the original parser, the

---

[40]That is, suppose the sequence $P_1, \ldots, P_n$ contains a subsequence that creates and completes a node of type Y; this subsequence is removed. Continuing in this fashion, we obtain a sequence with no create-complete subsequences, with X created at the start of the sequence and completed at its end; call this sequence $P'_1, \ldots, P'_m$. We can then form the rewrite rule $X \rightarrow P'_1 \ldots P'_m$ with its corresponding dotted rules.

Dotted rule		*Packet name*
• Article Adj N	$\leftrightarrow$	Parse-Determiner
Article • Adj N	$\leftrightarrow$	Parse-Adjective
Article Adj • N	$\leftrightarrow$	Parse-Noun
Article Adj N •	$\leftrightarrow$	*no packet; return*

Figure 2.9: Dotted rules and packets compared

packet CPOOL, or clause level packet, was always active. But this simply follows from the assumption that a toplevel S is being parsed, no matter where one is in a derivation. Besides this information, in the revised parser no more than one packet is active at any given point.

In summary, putting aside the question of complex feature information, one can see then that the information placed on the parser's pushdown included (1) a nonterminal name NT, corresponding to the expansion of NT; and (2) the righthand part of a dotted rule, in the form of a packet name. But this means that we can form the true dotted rule $NT \rightarrow$ *righthand portion*, and dispense with (1) and (2).

Top-down and bottom-up parsing

Next we compare the order of attachment of items to the parse tree in the original parser to a more standard bottom-up parser. The Marcus parser seems to deviate in two ways from standard bottom-up operation. First of all, in a standard bottom-up parse, the output for a rule of the form $A \rightarrow XYZ$ is not produced until all three subconstituents, X, Y, and Z, are analyzed. This is done by pushing all three constituents onto a stack and then bundling them together as a phrase of type Z. For example, in a strict bottom-up parse, we would push NP and VP onto the stack and *then* combine or *reduce* them to an S (if the rule $S \rightarrow NP\ VP$ were available). Things are slightly different in the Marcus parser, thanks to deterministic operation. We do not have to wait until Z is analyzed to do something with X or Y, since in the usual case the Marcus parser has already predicted just what the mother node of these subconstituents will be. This integration of prediction into a standard bottom-up parse will be discussed below, but for now, we need only observe that with this change, items whose mothers are already known need not be explicitly pushed onto a stack as separate entities. Instead, one can simply attach them to a parse tree under construction, if a tree representation is used (the Marcus design). For example, we can *predict* an S, and then attach the NP and VP to the S in turn. Alternatively, if a dotted rule approach is adopted, one can simply replace e.g., the dotted rule $S \rightarrow \bullet NP \ VP$ with the dotted rule $S \rightarrow NP \bullet VP$, signifying that NP has been attached to the S.

The second difference between the Marcus parser and a strict bottom-up parser was alluded to above. This is the interspersed prediction of phrasal nodes. While node attachment does nothing to disturb the basic bottom-up recognition of phrases, node prediction would at first seem to be more problematic. As it turns out, however, the order in which phrases are completed does not change, so that bottom-up recognition order is not altered.

This is perhaps best explained by an example. Consider how the Marcus parser predicted the existence of certain phrases. Suppose the following items are in the parser's input buffer:

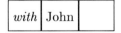

The relevant Marcus grammar rule would create a Prepositional phrase node triggered by the "leading edge" of the phrase, the preposition *of*:

IF:

    [Preposition] [   ][   ]

THEN:

    create a new PP node.

The new Prepositional Phrase node will be pushed onto the stack, becoming the new top node of the stack. A new nonterminal node is predicted given the current machine state (top of stack element plus lookahead).

Many phrases in English that can be predicted by looking at just their "leading edges."[41] For example, Prepositional Phrases, Verb Phrases, and

---

[41]This observation is advanced, for example, in Kimball (1973) as a way to parse sentences: "function words start phrases."

Adjective Phrases generally begin with prepositions, verbs, and adjectives, respectively. Noun Phrases need not begin with Nouns, but when they do not, they often begin with articles (such as *the*) that serve equally as well to predict the existence of a Noun Phrase. (The same holds when an adverb appears before a verb.)[42] The deeper reason for this Operator–Operand pattern is the $\overline{\mathrm{X}}$ theory, which predicts that English phrases should uniformly pattern in this fashion.

A strict bottom-up parser does not predict the existence of nodes in this way. It waits until a constituent has been built before recognizing what kind of constituent it is. Hammer (1974) observed that the introduction of prediction does not change the basic bottom-up order of phrase recognition. Rather, all that changes is that the new, predicted nodes are inserted onto the pushdown stack. (See chapter 7.) One can see that this is so by examining a simple example. Suppose we have the following simple grammar.

$$
\begin{aligned}
&\mathrm{S} \rightarrow \mathrm{NP\ VP} \\
&\mathrm{NP} \rightarrow \mathrm{Determiner\ Noun} \\
&\mathrm{Noun} \rightarrow \textit{boy, girl} \\
&\mathrm{Determiner} \rightarrow \textit{the, a} \\
&\mathrm{VP} \rightarrow \mathrm{V\ NP} \\
&\mathrm{V} \rightarrow \textit{kissed}
\end{aligned}
$$

A rightmost derivation of *a girl kissed the boy* is given below.

> S
> NP VP
> NP V Determiner Noun
> NP V Determiner *boy*
> NP V *the boy*
> NP *kissed the boy*
> Determiner Noun *kissed the boy*
> Determiner *girl kissed the boy*
> *A girl kissed the boy*

---

[42]Complementizers such as *for, that* and so forth can ambiguously introduce Noun Phrases or Sentences, but we shall see that the parser can usually remain agnostic as to the identity of the phrase in this case.

A strict bottom-up parse of this sentence would proceed in the reverse order, building leftmost complete subtrees. The phrase completion order would be, Subject NP, Object NP, VP, S. Now consider a similar system where nodes are predictively inserted into the stack as soon as they can be recognized. A trace of the analysis of the same sentence would be as in the bottom half of figure 2.10.

The confirmation (completion) of phrases is exactly the same as before: Subject NP, Object NP, VP, S. The introduction of this kind of phrase prediction does nothing to alter the basic bottom-up order of phrase completion. The Marcus parser, then, is a bottom-up parser, with the introduction of predictively created nodes that do not alter this basic recognition order.

The Marcus parser and "attention shifting"

Marcus's parser incorporated one additional extension to the usual bottom-up parsing machinery. This was what Marcus dubbed "attention shifting." The point of an attention shift is to deliberately postpone the processing of an item in the first cell of input buffer so that a complete constituent can be parsed starting in the second buffer cell position. The canonical case is a sentence such as *Have the students take the exam today!* vs. *Have the students taken the exam today?*. The determination of *have* as an auxiliary or main verb must be deliberately postponed until the NP starting in the second position is analyzed as a complete constituent; then, the morphology of the following verb dictates the proper answer. Marcus implemented this postponement operation by temporarily suspending the analysis of the item in the first buffer cell and effectively starting a new parse as commencing with the element in the second buffer cell.

All that has been done here is to reduce the second leftmost complete constituent (the NP) before the first leftmost constituent (the main or auxiliary verb). One could encode this postponement directly so that constituents are always analyzed starting in the first buffer cell position. The method is as follows. Simply stack a postponed item on the active node stack *with its features determined as completely as possible*. For example, we do not know whether *have* is an auxiliary or main verb in the *the students* sentence, but it is at least a verb. Again using the $\overline{X}$ theory, we can create a phrase with at least the feature of a verb. Now the leading edge of the NP *the students* is in the first cell of the buffer; predict a constituent of the appropriate type (in

Step 1:   Push Determiner, *a*, onto stack
    2:    Push Noun, *girl*, onto stack
    3:    Reduce the top two items on the stack to a complete NP
          NP is now the top item on the stack
    4:    Push Verb, *kissed*
    5:    Push Determiner, *the*
    6:    Push Noun, *boy*
    7:    Reduce top two items on stack as a complete NP
          etc.

Step 1:   Predict an S (always carried out for root S)
    2:    Predict NP (based on Determiner, *a*)
  3–4:   As before (confirming N)
    5:    Predict VP (based on Verb, *kissed*)
    6:    Stack Verb
    7:    Predict NP (based on Determiner)
    8:    Stack Determiner
    9:    Stack Noun
   10:    Confirm NP, completing the NP
          etc.

Figure 2.10: Phrase completion in bottom-up and Marcus parsers

this case an NP) as before. When complete, put the NP back into the buffer. Now, as before, use the morphology of the verb now in the second buffer cell to decide how to add to the features of the the topmost item in the stack, the postponed phrase *have*. Note that at no point do we violate the "monotonic" property of determinism. We never undo past decisions.

For a formalization of this method, see chapter 7. The basic result described there (established by Szymanski and Williams 1975) is that if a finite number of such "attention-shifting" postponements are permitted, then the resulting language can be analyzed by a deterministic pushdown automaton, and hence is a deterministic context-free language.

Appendix 2

Target Grammar Rules

Rules for parsing $\overline{\overline{S}}$s

Rule attach-comp

CYC is *

C is X^{max} $-N$ $-V$ $+A$ $+P$—SPEC—HEAD$\overset{\downarrow}{}$—COMP

$[-N$ $-V$ $+A$ $+P$][*][*] $\rightarrow$

ATTACH

Rule attach-sent

CYC is *

C is X^{max} $-N$ $-V$ $+A$ $+P$—SPEC—HEAD$\overset{\downarrow}{}$—COMP

$[-N$ $+V$ $+A$ $+P$][*][*] $\rightarrow$

ATTACH

Rule attach-wh-comp

CYC is *

C is X^{max} $-N$ $-V$ $+A$ $+P$—SPEC—HEAD$\overset{\downarrow}{}$—COMP

$[wh][-N$ $+V$ $+A$ $+P][+N$ $-V]$ $\rightarrow$

ATTACH

Rules for parsing sentences

Rule attach-subject

CYC is nil

C is X^{max} $-N$ $+V$ $+A$ $+P$—$\overset{\downarrow}{SPEC}$—HEAD—COMP

$[X^{max}$ $+N$ $-V$ $+A$ $-P][-N$ $+V$ $+tense][$ $*$ $] \rightarrow$

ATTACH

Rule attach-embedded-subject

CYC is X^{max} $-N$ $-V$ $+A$ $+P$

C is X^{max} $-N$ $+V$ $+A$ $+P$—$\overset{\downarrow}{SPEC}$—HEAD—COMP

$[X^{max}$ $+N$ $-V$ $+A$ $-P][-N$ $+V$ $\pm tense][$ $*$ $] \rightarrow$

ATTACH

Rule attach-infl

CYC is $*$

C is X^{max} $-N$ $+V$ $+A$ $+P$—SPEC—$\overset{\downarrow}{HEAD}$—COMP

$[-N$ $+V$ $+A$ $+P][-N][$ $*$ $]$

ATTACH

Rule attach-vp

CYC is $*$

C is X^{max} $-N$ $+V$ $+A$ $+P$—SPEC—HEAD—$\overset{\downarrow}{COMP}$

$[X^{max}$ $-N$ $+V$ $+P$ $-A][$ $*$ $][$ $*$ $] \rightarrow$

ATTACH

Rules for parsing NPs

Rule attach-det

CYC is *

C is X^{max} +N $-$V +A $-$P$\overset{\downarrow}{—}$SPEC—HEAD—COMP

[+N $-$V $-$P $-$A][+N $-$V +A][*   ] $\rightarrow$

ATTACH

Rule attach-adj

CYC is *

C is X^{max} +N $-$V +A $-$P$\overset{\downarrow}{—}$SPEC—HEAD—COMP

[+N $-$V +P +A][+N $-$V +A][*   ] $\rightarrow$

ATTACH

Rule attach-noun

CYC is *

C is X^{max} +N $-$V +A $-$P—SPEC—$\overset{\downarrow}{HEAD}$—COMP

[+N $-$V $-$P +A][*][*] $\rightarrow$

ATTACH

Rule attach-relative-clause

CYC is *

C is X^{max} +N $-$V +A $-$P—SPEC—HEAD—$\overset{\downarrow}{COMP}$

[$-$N $-$V +A +P][*   ][*   ] $\rightarrow$

ATTACH

Rule attach-pp

CYC is *

C is X^{max} $-$N +V +P $-$A—SPEC—HEAD—$\overset{\downarrow}{COMP}$

[X^{max} $-$N $-$V][*   ][*   ] $\rightarrow$

ATTACH

The rules for analyzing verb phrases discriminate among verbs that take different kinds of complements: verbs that *wh* complements; verbs that take *that* complements; verbs that take sentential tensed only sentential complements (*know, believe*); those that can take either tensed or infinitival sentential complements (*expect*); those that take only infinitival complements (*want*); and verbs that take only a missing subject embedded sentential complement (*try, believe*). In addition, the lexical entries for verbs distinguish between verbs that take, e.g., one NP argument from those that take either S or NP arguments or those that take both an NP and an S argument, and so forth. All this information was coded in the Marcus parser packet structure, which cannot be used here.

Rules for parsing VPs

Rule attach-verb-want

CYC is *

C is X^{max} $-N$ $+V$ $+P$ $-A$—SPEC—HEAD—COMP

$[-N +V$ *want*$][$ * $][$ * $] \rightarrow$ ATTACH

Rule attach-verb-try

CYC is *

C is X^{max} $-N$ $+V$ $+P$ $-A$—SPEC—HEAD—COMP

$[-N +V$ *try*$][$ * $][$ * $] \rightarrow$
ATTACH

Rule attach-verb-believe

CYC is *

C is X^{max} $-N$ $+V$ $+P$ $-A$—SPEC—HEAD—COMP

$[-N +V$ *believe*$][+N][$ * $] \rightarrow$
ATTACH

Rules for VPs, contd.

Rule attach-verb-know

CYC is *

C is X^{max} $-N$ $+V$ $+P$ $-A$—SPEC—HEAD—COMP
$[-N +V \ know][+N][\ * \ ] \rightarrow$
ATTACH

Rule attach-verb-expect

CYC is *

C is X^{max} $-N$ $+V$ $+P$ $-A$—SPEC—HEAD—COMP
$[-N +V \ expect][\ * \ ][\ * \ ] \rightarrow$
ATTACH

Rule attach-verb-kiss

CYC is *

C is X^{max} $-N$ $+V$ $+P$ $-A$—SPEC—HEAD—COMP
$[-N +V kiss][\ +N -V \ ][\ * \ ] \rightarrow$
ATTACH

Rule attach-verb-eat

CYC is *

C is X^{max} $-N$ $+V$ $+P$ $-A$—SPEC—HEAD—COMP
$[-N +V \ eat][\ * \ ][\ * \ ] \rightarrow$
ATTACH

Rules for VPs, contd.

Rule attach-verb-persuade

CYC is *

C is X^{max} $-N$ $+V$ $+P$ $-A$—SPEC—HEĀD—COMP
$[-N +V$ *persuade*$][$ * $][$ * $] \rightarrow$
ATTACH

Rule attach-object

CYC is *

C is X^{max} $-N$ $+V$ $+P$ $-A$—SPEC—HEAD—CŌMP
$[X^{max} +N -V +A -P$ $][$ * $][$ * $] \rightarrow$
ATTACH

Rule attach-pp

CYC is *

C is X^{max} $-N$ $+V$ $+P$ $-A$—SPEC—HEAD—CŌMP
$[X^{max} -N -V$ $][$ * $][$ * $] \rightarrow$
ATTACH

Rules for parsing INFL (Aux)
Rule to-infinitive CYC is X^{max} −N +V +A +P C is X^{max} −N +V +A +P—SPEC—HEAD$\downarrow$—COMP $[to$ −N +V +A +P$][$−N +V +P −A −tense$][$ * $]$ → ATTACH ### Rule perfective CYC is * C is X^{max} −N +V—SPEC—HEAD$\downarrow$—COMP $[have$ −N +V $][$−N +V +en$][$ * $]$ → ATTACH ### Rule progressive CYC * C is X^{max} −N +V—SPEC—HEAD$\downarrow$—COMP $[be$ −N +V$][$ −N +V $ing][$ * $]$ → ATTACH ### Rule modal CYC is * C is X^{max} −N +V +A +P—SPEC—HEAD$\downarrow$—COMP $[could$ −N +V +A +P$][$−N +V−tense$][$ * $]$ → ATTACH

Rules for parsing INFL, contd.

Rule do
CYC is X^{max} $-N$ $+V$ $+A$ $+P$

C is X^{max} $-N$ $+V$ $+A$ $+P$—SPEC—HEAD$^{\downarrow}$—COMP
$[do -N +V +A +P][-N +V +P -A -\text{tense}][\quad * \quad] \rightarrow$
ATTACH

Rule passive-be
CYC is $*$

C is X^{max} $-N$ $+V$ $+A$ $+P$—SPEC—HEAD$^{\downarrow}$—COMP
$[be][-N +V +P -A +\text{Sed}][\quad * \quad] \rightarrow$
ATTACH

Rule infl-attach
CYC is $*$

C is X^{max} $-N$ $+V$ $+A$ $+P$—SPEC—HEAD—COMP$^{\downarrow}$
$[X^{max} -N +V +A +P][\quad * \quad][\quad * \quad] \rightarrow$
ATTACH

Rules for parsing PPs

Rule attach-prep
CYC is $*$

C is X^{max} $-N$ $-V$—SPEC—HEAD$^{\downarrow}$—COMP
$[-N -V][+N -V][\quad * \quad] \rightarrow$
ATTACH

Rule attach-pp-object
CYC is $*$

C is X^{max} $-N$ $-V$—SPEC—HEAD—COMP$^{\downarrow}$
$[X^{max} +N -V][\quad * \quad][\quad * \quad] \rightarrow$
ATTACH

Transformational rules fall into two groups: simple local transformations like Subject-auxiliary inversion and major movement rules like *wh* movement.

Rule subject-aux-inversion

CYC is nil

C is X^{max} $-N$ $+V$ $+A$ $+P$—SPEC—HEAD—COMP
$[-N +V +A +P+\text{tense}][X^{max}+N -V +A -P][-N +V] \rightarrow$
SWITCH

Rule Imperative

CYC is nil

C is X^{max} $-N$ $+V$ $+A$ $+P$—SPEC—HEAD—COMP
$[-N +V +P -A -\text{tense}][\quad * \quad][\quad * \quad] \rightarrow$
INSERT YOU

Rule passive

CYC is * Rule passive-be

C is X^{max} $-N$ $+V$ $+P$ $-A$—SPEC—HEAD—COMP
$[\quad * \quad][\quad * \quad][\quad * \quad] \rightarrow$
INSERT TRACE

Rule *wh*-insert

CYC is *

C is X^{max} $-N$ $+V$ $+P$ $-A$—SPEC—HEAD—COMP
Rule attach-wh-comp
$[-N +V][\quad * \quad][\quad * \quad] \rightarrow$
INSERT TRACE

Rule insert-want-NP

CYC is X^{max}——$-N$ $+V$ $+A$ $+P$ Rule attach-want

C is X^{max} $-N$ $+V$ $+A$ $+P$—SPĒC—HEAD—COMP

$[to$ $-N$ $+V$ $+A$ $+P][-N$ $+V$ $+P$ $-A$ $-$tense$][$ * $]$ $\rightarrow$

INSERT TRACE

Rule insert-try-NP

CYC is X^{max} $-N$ $+V$ $+A$ $+P$

C is X^{max} $-N$ $+V$ $+A$ $+P$—SPĒC—HEAD—COMP Rule attach-try

$[to$ $-N$ $+V$ $+A$ $+P][-N$ $+V$ $+P$ $-A$ $-$tense$][$ * $]$ $\rightarrow$

INSERT TRACE

Rule insert-know-NP

CYC is X^{max} $-N$ $+V$ $+A$ $+P$

C is X^{max} $-N$ $+V$ $+A$ $+P$—SPĒC—HEAD—COMP Rule attach-know

$[to$ $-N$ $+V$ $+A$ $+P][-N$ $+V$ $+P$ $-A$ $-$tense $be][$ * $]$ $\rightarrow$

INSERT TRACE

Chapter 3

Learning Phrase Structure

This chapter shows how the grammars rules for parsing the basic phrase structure of English are learned by the computer model. The next chapter covers the acquisition of transformational-like grammar rules.

Phrase structure rules account for the bulk of grammar rules in Marcus's original grammar. Roughly one half of the hundred or so grammar rules in Marcus's published grammar (1980) are base phrase structure rules.[1]

We begin with the acquisition of a very simple sentence that fixes the Head-Complement order of English. This initial example will be somewhat laborious to work through, because so little syntactic information is known; the procedure draws correspondingly more heavily on the given thematic representation. Following this example, section 2 shows how the system learns grammar rules to handle prepositional phrases, inflectional elements, and embedded sentences. Section 3 continues with a detailed look at the acquisition of the inflectional (auxiliary verb) system of English. Finally, section 4 rounds off the chapter by looking at what happens if the first example sentences are received in a different order or with multiple part-of-speech categorization. What will be demonstrated is that when there are too many uncertainties then acquisition cannot proceed—but that this is a desirable result that prevents mistakes from being made. If word classes are uncertain *and* new grammar rules must be acquired, then the incremental character of the acquisition procedure has the effect of stopping the system from making an unsure inference. If however basic NP-VP order is established (by clear examples where word class identity is on safe ground), then new lexical classes can be formed.

---

[1]Excluding special-purpose rules written by Marcus to handle peculiarities of time expressions and dates, case-frame interpretation rules, and so forth.

3.1   Learning to Parse a Simple Sentence

Our first example sentence clears a simple but important hurdle, since no grammar rules are known: *John kissed Sally*. The initial state of the system and what will be learned follows.

Base rules assumed known: none.

Thematic representation: PREDICATE: kiss;
                             AGENT: John;
                             AFFECTED OBJECT: Sally

Lexical categorization: *John, Sally* are objects;
                             kiss is an action

Base rules: Specifiers to the left of the Head
                             Complements to the right of the Head
                             Rule to attach NOUNS to NP
                             Rule to attach NP as subject of S
                             Rule to attach VERB to VP
                             Rule to attach object NP to VP
                             Rule to attach VP to S

We shall now go through the acquisition procedure's analysis, step by step, showing how each of these new rule is acquired. To begin the parse, the first three cells of the input buffer are filled with the tokens *John, kissed*, and *Sally*. *John* is assumed known as an Object and not an Action, hence is marked $+N -V$. Therefore, a maximal projection of type $+N -V$ is created and placed on the active node stack, and *John* is marked as the HEAD of this phrase. In addition, the $\overline{X}$ template {Head, Spec, Comp} is associated with the maximal projection; note that as yet this template is unordered.

Next, the system attempts to match one of its currently known grammar rules against this parser state. It has no rules, so this attempt fails. We move on to Step 2 of the acquisition procedure, and note the parser's instantaneous description in preparation for acquisition. The *left context* of the parse has a cyclic node that is nil (empty) and an active node that is the $X^{\max}$ marked $+N$ $-V$. The *right context* consists of the 1st buffer cell marked $+N -V$ and noted as the HEAD of the current active node; the 2nd buffer cell item is labeled −N +V, since *kiss* is a non-Object and an Action; and the third buffer cell is filled with an +N −V element.

Step 3 of the acquisition procedure tries to build a new grammar rule using the constraints of $\overline{\text{X}}$ theory. The $\overline{\text{X}}$ template is so far unordered, so there are no constraints on attachment from that quarter. The procedure first tests the action ATTACH: can it attach the +N −V to the current active node, using the compatibility constraints of the $\overline{\text{X}}$ theory? In this case, the answer is yes, since the features of the +N −V match those of the maximal projection. Since the attached element is the HEAD of the phrase, the HEAD portion of the $\overline{\text{X}}$ template is checked off (SPEC and COMP remain). The system moves to Step 5 of the acquisition procedure, and stores its new grammar rule:

Give me a name for new rule being created
in packet parse—X^{max}—+N −V.
Pattern of rule is:

CYCLIC NODE: nil
ACTIVE NODE: X^{max}—+N −V—{Head, Spec, Comp}

John +N −V	*kissed* −N +V	*Sally* +N −V

BUFFER:

ACTION: ATTACH

>attach-noun1

The ATTACH now executes, moving *John* underneath the N^{max} (and labeling the N^{max} with the rule just run). The parse proceeds. The verb *kissed* now fills the first buffer cell, *Sally* the second cell, and • the third. The −N +V item in the first cell can project to a phrase, as it is assumed known as an action, but, following our uniform procedure for $\overline{\text{X}}$ analysis, the system first checks to see if the current active node is completely built. The check is carried out by looking at the thematic representation confirming that *John* is a complete unit. The N^{max} is therefore dropped into the buffer, displacing *kissed* to the right. Note that the order of HEAD, SPEC, and COMP is not fixed by this constituent analysis.

No known grammar rules now trigger (the active node stack is empty). Running through the acquisition procedure, Step 3 fails because there is nothing to attach the NP to. Likewise, since there are no known grammar rules besides the one to build names, all other attempted actions fail. Following protocol, the procedure moves on and considers the second buffer cell. This is a $-$N $+$V item; according to the $\overline{\text{X}}$ creation routine the $-$N $+$V maximal projection is pushed onto the active node stack and *kissed* marked as its head. The parser returns to step 1.

The parser next tries to see if any known grammar rules handle the N^{max} in the first buffer cell. None match (there is only one known grammar rule, the one just acquired to attach names). The acquisition procedure is entered. Step 2 of this procedure records the parser's ID: a left-context with an empty cyclic node and an active node of $-$N $+$V (with unordered HEAD, SPEC, and COMP); a right context consisting of an X^{max} labeled $+$N $-$V; a $-$N $+$V in the second cell; and an $+$N $-$V in the third. Next, the procedure tries each grammar rule action in turn. Can ATTACH succeed? The system tries to attach the N^{max} as HEAD but cannot, since the maximal projection is marked to have a $-$N $+$V HEAD. What about attachment as SPEC or COMP? Given what has been learned so far, either one would be acceptable: there are no known agreement features and the N^{max} does not have the same features as the V^{max} current active node. Both conditions are met here, so the ATTACH wins for certain no matter what. If one wanted to settle the question, and if only COMPs are true (internal) arguments, we know from the given thematic representation that the N^{max} cannot be a COMP. On the other hand, if one considers the evidence to be uncertain, then the procedure could simply not fix the N^{max} as either SPEC or COMP at this point; only later evidence from other examples would do so. We adopt the first course here. Step 5 saves the resulting grammar rule. It attaches subject NPs in root sentences—an **attach-subject** rule. Note that the cyclic node of the rule's pattern is empty.

| CYCLIC NODE: | nil |
| ACTIVE NODE: | X^{max} $-$N $+$V SPEC$\overset{\downarrow}{—}$\{HEAD, COMP\} |

BUFFER:	$+$N $-$V	*kissed* $-$N $+$V	*Sally* $+$N $-$V

| ACTION: | ATTACH |

With the N^{max} attached, the verb and remaining lexical token *Sally* remain unanalyzed. What next? No known grammar rules can work at this point. The only other attach rule works only with a packet pointer at SPEC, and now the pointer is at HEAD. The parse stops at this point, and the acquisition procedure attempts to construct a new grammar rule. It tries ATTACH first. Can ATTACH work? Yes, because the first item currently in the buffer, *kiss*, is marked $-$N $+$V and prompted the creation of the X^{max} currently the active node. The ATTACH is carried out, with the HEAD portion of the $\overline{X}$ template checked off.

Give me a name for rule being created
in packet parse—X^{max}——$-$N $+$V.
Pattern of rule is:

CYCLIC NODE:	nil
ACTIVE NODE:	X^{max} $-$N $+$V SPEC—HEAD$\downarrow$, $\{$COMP$\}$

BUFFER:

$-$N $+$V *kiss*	*Sally* $+$N $-$V	•

ACTION: ATTACH

>attach-verb

Note that *kiss* is placed in a lexical equivalence class of its own for now. The new rule runs, leaving *Sally* as the first element in the input buffer. (As always, the active node, the X^{max} $-$N $+$V, is annotated with the name of the rule just executed.) In effect, the procedure has built a sentence that collapses the INFL and VP nodes into one—because it does not recognize a distinct INFL constituent. Later in this chapter we shall see how this combined VP/INFL node is split into its correct pieces. For now, though, this collapse means that the current cyclic node is identified with the VP/INFL projection.

Next, *Sally* stimulates the automatic creation of an X^{max}; note that the current active node is tested for completion before this happens, but that the V^{max} currently on the stack is by no means complete (as known by a check of the thematic representation, since the V^{max}'s arguments are not all present). This new X^{max} of type $+$N $-$V marks *Sally* as its Head.

As before, the procedure now checks if any known grammar rules can execute. The closest match is the previous rule attach-noun1, but its buffer pattern calls for a $+$N $-$V in the first cell, but a $-$N $+$V in the second. So the acquisition procedure must be invoked again. A second ATTACH rule is built:

Give me a name for new rule being created
in packet parse—$X^{\max}$—$+N$ $-V$.
Pattern of rule is:

CYCLIC NODE: $X^{\max}$ $-N$ $+V$ SPEC—HEAD, $\{$COMP$\}$↓

ACTIVE NODE: $+N$ $-V$ SPEC—HEAD↓, $\{$COMP$\}$

BUFFER:

Sally $+N$ $-V$	•	

ACTION: ATTACH

>attach-noun2

Moving on to Step 5 of the acquisition procedure, the system checks for a
possible rule generalization. Precisely speaking, the rules cannot be merged,
because the first buffer cells for the two are different: one holds *John* and
the other *Sally*. To speed things up a bit, we will assume that a second
sentence is received with *John* as the Object. This *will* allow merger (subject
to certain caveats)[2], so by Step 5b, the rules are merged: their buffer features
are intersected, resulting in a generalized grammar rule for nouns.

CYCLIC NODE: *

ACTIVE NODE: $+N$ $-V$ SPEC—HEAD↓, $\{$COMP$\}$

BUFFER:

$+N$ $-V$	*	*

ACTION: ATTACH

>attach-noun3

Note that this is basically the correct rule for attaching any kind of Head
noun to an NP. As the previous footnote points out, the ordering of COMP
after the HEAD takes a few additional examples. Thus the model predicts

---

[2]In fact, merger won't occur because the packet name of the first attachment rule calls
for an unordered $\overline{X}$ template, and an empty cyclic node, while the newer one has ordered
a specifier first and has a filled cyclic node. But this is a detail. A repeat of the first
example sentence would force the first noun attachment rule to have a specifier first as
well. An additional example like *Sally kissed the boy with red hair* forces the second and
third buffer cells to be wild cards. This revised noun attachment rule may be merged
with one that handles *The boy with red hair*..., arriving at the right target rule.

that such rules will be acquired early and without error, which is empirically correct (Lightfoot 1982).

Given its relatively impoverished feature markings for nouns, it also predicts certain errors that *are* made by children. As far as the parser is concerned, a pronoun like *it* has the same status as a name or other NP. Therefore, given the relevant additional grammar rules, the system would blithely parse *John turned off it* just as it would parse *John turned off the lamp*. This is what is actually observed (Baker 1979). Not until *it*'s enclitic status is recognized would there be some reason to split off a new lexical category or feature marker.

Now the parser faces the end of sentence marker • in the first buffer cell. This item cannot be projected as a new maximal phrase. No known grammar rules fire. The system attempts to ATTACH the marker to the N^{max} active node as its SPEC or COMP, but this fails the $\overline{X}$ constraints.

SWITCH obviously fails because the second buffer cell is empty, and the two INSERT actions cannot succeed because no known grammar rule fires after an insertion. The procedure passes to Step 4 of its algorithm and checks to see if the current active node is complete. It is, according to its thematic representation. The current active node is thus dropped into the buffer, displacing the end of sentence marker to the second cell. The current active node becomes the now-exposed top of stack element, V^{max}.

Once again, no known grammar rules fire. The acquisition procedure is entered. ATTACH succeeds because the N^{max} may be attached to the current active node as either SPEC or COMP. (This time, the X^{max} is a complement, as dictated by its argument status in the thematic representation, but we might leave this unsettled if need be.)

CYCLIC NODE: nil

ACTIVE NODE: $-N +V$ SPEC—HEAD—COMP↓

BUFFER:

N^{max}	•	nil

ACTION: ATTACH

>attach-object1

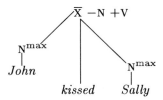

Figure 3.1: Parse tree built for early input sentence

This action is the same as the attach-subject rule's, so one might ask just why this grammar rule is not generalized. The key difference is that the packet pointer is at a different point, as encoded by the $\overline{X}$ template form. In the original Marcus parser, the packet names of the two rules would be different. According to the generalization protocol, merger is not attempted.

One last task remains in Step 5: update a lexical entry if required. In this case, we add to the entry for *kiss* that it must take an X^{max} +N −V argument (following the protocol of assuming arguments obligatory until proven otherwise). We also create an equivalence class of lexical items that holds just *kiss*.

With the N^{max} attached, only the • marker remains in the first buffer cell. Again no rules trigger, and the acquisition procedure runs through its repertoire of actions. Each one fails. Step 4 of the procedure checks for completion of the current active node. This time completion passes muster, because all thematic roles have been accounted for. We drop the phrase into the input buffer. The active node stack and cyclic nodes are now empty. This is an accepting configuration, so the machine halts, ready to read in a new sentence.

Figure 3.1 shows the output tree. It has several distinctive properties. First, it has a relatively flat NP–V–NP order. This result is compatible with findings by Tavakolian (1981) that children's first tree structures are shallow. This is a natural result given the $\overline{X}$ theory. Maximal projections are based on the category of their Heads. If *kissed* has both the features of a verb (an action) and TENSE, then its maximal projections will have both INFL and verb-like properties, a kind of composite nonterminal. If we regard nonterminal names as just the equivalence classes of the states of a machine as it analyzes sentences, then this is perfectly acceptable. It simply means that not enough information has been received to warrant distinguishing these categories. A separate "concept" of INFL has not yet been acquired. This is also a natural result since the evidence that there is a separate INFL node is quite scanty in sentences like *John kissed Sue*. All the operations that act on a VP as a separate unit—such as fronting—act only if there is a separate INFL element.

3.2   Prepositional Phrases and Verb Complements

With this first sentence behind us, in this section we shall see how the acquisition procedure can fill out its knowledge of phrase structure rules. We assume that HEAD-COMPLEMENT order has been fixed by an earlier example sentence, like the one above. We first consider a sentence with a Prepositional Phrase, and then a sentence with a sentential complement. The Prepositional Phrase examples show how rule generalization works, while the acquisition of verb complements shows how the argument structure of different verbs is learned. The following section turns to a detailed look at how the auxiliary verb phrase structure of English is acquired. We defer the important question of how input sentence order affects the acquisition procedure until the end of this chapter. There we show that even though the *external* order of sentence presentation may vary, the acquisition procedure acts as a filter to render all learning sequences identical up to certain allowable permutations.

A Prepositional Phrase example

Learning to parse Prepositional Phrases is easy once the basic HEAD-COMP order is fixed. Suppose that the system has already successfully tackled the *John kissed Sally* sentence and now receives the sentence, *The girl kissed John on the lips*.

We begin as usual with *the* in the first buffer cell, *girl* in the second, and *kissed* in the third. We assume *the* to have the features $-V$ $-A$, that is, it is at least known to be a nonaction and a nonargument. We do not know that it is $+N$. Since it is not marked as either an argument or a predicate, it does not prompt the creation of an X^{max}. Since the active node stack is empty, all attempted acquisition actions will fail. ATTACH has nothing to work with; SWITCH and INSERT fail because no known grammar rules match if they are tried. (All known rules demand that the active node be nonempty.) Moving to the second buffer cell, *girl* is assumed known as $+$N $-$V, and does force an X^{max} creation; *girl* is also marked as the HEAD of this phrase. The $+$N $-$V features are percolated to the X^{max}.

This is a perfect example of how embryonic syntactic analysis can force lexical category identification. *The* is forced to be part of the NP because of its context and known $\overline{X}$ constraints. The learner is actually assisted by what it already knows about NPs. If its category information is impoverished, then it may be assisted by syntactic configurations. Conversely, syntactic analysis is aided by category learning.

Next, the system attempts to execute its only known grammar rule in the $X^{max}+$N $-$V packet, attach-noun3. This is the pattern of that rule:

CYCLIC NODE:	nil
ACTIVE NODE:	$+$N $-$V SPEC—HĔAD, {COMP}

BUFFER:	$+$N $-$V	*	*
ACTION:	ATTACH		

This rule does not match, for two reasons: (i) the pattern demands $+$N $-$V in the buffer, and *the* is not marked as such; (ii) the pattern's packet pointer is set to HEAD, and the current parser's is SPEC. The acquisition procedure is entered. First, the procedure checks if ATTACH can work. It can: the features of *the* are compatible with $+$N $-$V. Since the order HEAD-COMPLEMENT is now known, attachment as SPEC is the only possibility. This forces downward percolation, setting *the*'s features to $+$N $-$V. The new rule is stored.

Rule attach-det

CYCLIC NODE:	nil
ACTIVE NODE:	X^{max}
	$+$N $-$V-SPĔC—HEAD—COMP

BUFFER:	*the* $+$N $-$V	*girl* $+$N $-$V	*kissed* $-$N $+$V
ACTION:	ATTACH		

With *girl* now in the first buffer cell, the existing rule attach-noun3 can trigger (note that it was marked as the HEAD of this phrase earlier and the remaining pattern matches that of the buffer). *Girl* is attached as the HEAD of the X^{max}, and the packet pointer is advanced to COMP.

At this point, no further grammar rules trigger, so we check for constituent completion against the thematic structure. Since *the girl* is a complete argument, we drop it into the input buffer. Just as with the first sentence, the verb will now trigger creation of an X^{max}, a combination INFL/VP node. The existing rule attach-subject fires, fixing *the girl* as the subject of this phrase. The verb gets attached as before. Next, *John* triggers creation of an $+N -V$ X^{max} and is attached as the head of this phrase by rule attach-noun3, leaving *on* in the first buffer cell. *On* is marked as neither noun nor verb (object or action): $-N -V$. It creates a maximal projection with these features, which is pushed on the active node stack as the current active node; the packet pointer is set immediately to the head portion, and *on* is noted as the HEAD of this phrase.

The system now checks to see if any known grammar rules execute. The answer is no (none match the features of the current active node). The acquisition procedure is entered. ATTACH works because *on* is feature-compatible with the phrasal head (and is marked as the head). (SPECs are hence assumed not required for this kind of phrase.) Since the $\overline{X}$ order HEAD-COMPLEMENT is known, the packet pointer is advanced to COMP.

As before, *the* cannot be attached to COMP (it is not a maximal projection). No tentative action will work. Moving to the second buffer cell, the head noun *lips* prompts creation of a new X^{max}. It becomes the current active node, with the packet pointer at SPEC. *The* will be attached as the SPEC of this phrase. Note that this attachment rule will be slightly different from the previous rule for *the*, since the cyclic node is filled with a VP/INFL, while the third buffer cell is occupied by a final punctuation mark (in contrast to the first attach-determiner rule). Several other examples are needed to generalize this rule properly. Basically we need examples such as *the tall block* ... in order to get the third buffer cell to be filled with a wild card pattern. Such examples will also force the cyclic node for the attach-noun rule to become a wild card.

Returning to the current example, the head noun *lips* will be attached by the attach-noun3 grammar rule, leaving the final punctuation mark as the first element in the buffer. The packet pointer is now set to COMP. No further grammar rules execute. Checking the thematic representation, we see that the N^{max} is complete. Following the acquisition procedure, the current active node is therefore dropped into the input buffer.

Once again, we see if any grammar rules can execute. The rule to attach objects comes close, but calls for an active node that is $-N +V$. Here the active node is $-N -V$. Slavishly, the acquisition procedure is entered. This time ATTACH succeeds because the N^{max} can be attached as the COMP of a $-N -V$ phrase (via Step 3d). The new rule is saved as **attach-pp-object**.

Rule **attach-pp-object**

CYCLIC NODE:	X^{max}— $-N +V$
ACTIVE NODE:	X^{max} $-N -V$—SPEC—HEAD—CÓMP

BUFFER:	$X^{max} +N -V$	*	*

ACTION: ATTACH

With the final punctuation mark back in the first buffer cell, no further grammar rules fire. The acquisition procedure fails, as before. Following its default protocol, the X^{max} is dropped into the input buffer, exposing the N^{max} as the active node, with its packet pointer at COMP. No grammar rules match. Following the acquisition procedure, we check to see if this phrase is complete. The thematic structure tells us that it is: *John* is the AFFECTED OBJECT.[3] The N^{max} is dropped into the input buffer, pushing the P^{max} to the right. Now a grammar rule will be acquired that attaches the N^{max} to the INFL/VP. The known rule **attach-object1** will not work because it calls for a final punctuation mark in the second buffer cell, but this time around this is a P^{max}. Call the new rule **attach-object2**. Following the rule merger protocol, since this rule's action is the same as that of the old **attach-object1**, and since the element in the first buffer cell and left-context is the same in both cases, we combine these two rules to get a single, generalized object attach rule:

CYCLIC NODE:	nil
ACTIVE NODE:	$-N +V$ SPEC—HEAD—CÓMP

BUFFER:	$X^{max} +N -V$	*	*

ACTION: ATTACH

---

[3]Alternatively, the system could know that all names are semantically complete.

Now VP/INFL is the active node with its packet pointer at COMP. No grammar rules match; the acquisition procedure's ATTACH action can succeed, since the PP can be attached as a COMP. This becomes the rule attach-pp. As before we need an example in Subject position, such as, *The girl with red hair kissed John* in order to generalize the cyclic node left context to a wild card, as required.

The remainder of the parse will proceed as before. The V^{max} is completed, and a final punctuation mark is in the first buffer cell, so the parse is accepted.[4]

With the analysis of this first PP out of the way, other phrases of this kind may now be parsed. Another prepositional phrase example serves to generalize the lexical class of *on*. For instance, given the (emotionally rather distinct) sentence *The girl kissed John near the lips*, *near* will be placed in the same class as *on*.

To complete this section, we shall see how to acquire a rule to handle simple adjectives. This process demands two modifications to the basic system, one in the way that maximal projections are created, and another in how left context is represented. Suppose that the procedure gets the sentence *The big girl kissed John*. We have a rule to attach *the*, but no maximal projection to attach it to. In the Marcus parser, this problem was solved by permitting single-token specifiers such as determiners to create maximal projections. So far, we have allowed only Heads this status. To alter the $\overline{X}$ node creation protocol, we augment every non-maximal attached SPEC (like *the*) with information about the maximal projection it may be attached to. (This information is encoded as the type of the current active node in its rule pattern.) If no such node with empty SPEC, HEAD, and COMP exists, then the SPEC creates one. There is no danger of successfully parsing just *the* without a head, for if one is not found, then the analysis fails.

Applying this modification to our current dilemma, *the* sparks creation of an X^{max} of type $+N -V$ of which it is the SPEC. The packet pointer is

---

[4]We might contrast this example with a sentence that has a PP modifying an object NP, e.g., *John kissed the girl with blue eyes*. In this sentence, *the girl with blue eyes* plays an affected object role, so the NP fragment *the girl* is not dropped, completed, into the input buffer. Instead, the P^{max} is attached to it as part of the phrase's COMP. Note that this strategy will always attach a constituent to a phrase if it can. An ambiguous sentence such as *I saw the blocks in the street* is always parsed with *in the street* attached to *blocks*, not the VP. This strategy, essentially Frazier's Minimal Attachment Principle (1979), seems adequate for acquisition.

at SPEC. Since an adjective, not a noun, is in the second buffer cell, a new determiner attachment rule must be built. This rule will have the same left context and same current input as the first determiner attachment rule, so we merge the lookahead contexts, arriving at the nearly target attach-det rule that calls for a $+N$ $-V$ item in the second buffer cell and a wild card in the third.

Now the packet pointer still stands at SPEC. With *big* in the first buffer cell, we must check to see if it can be attached as HEAD. It is not marked as such (in contrast to the usual $\overline{X}$ situation), but it is feature compatible with an $+N$ $-V$ maximal projection. So it does not pass all the tests for HEAD. We must enter the acquisition procedure and build a new rule for a SPEC attachment. Note that via the rule merger procedure, the order *the*–adjective–noun will be permitted, but not adjective–*the*. Why? The *the* attachment rule always triggers on an X^{max} .with a pointer to SPEC but *no* other node labelings prompted by previously run attachment rules. In contrast, while adjectives may appear with no such labelings, they may also trigger with the label attach-det present. Therefore, the attach-adj rule will not be merged with the attach-det rule. Alternatively, one may simply note that the attach-det attachment rule calls for adjective or nouns in its second buffer cell. We can build a set of adjectives and nouns as an equivalence class directly; by positive examples, this class would not include *the*. Of course, it would be better to have some feature labels, say, $+A$, that both adjectives and nouns have in common but not determiners. Here this is so: both adjectives and nouns can be arguments to predicates, but determiners cannot be. This strategy might be used as confirmation of the second buffer cell's pattern. The target rule in chapter 2 uses this second approach. Whenever an element serves as an argument to a predicate, it gets marked $+A$.

Save for a rule to parse inflectional elements, this rounds out the entire list of 12 rules for simple sentences presented in chapter 2.

Learning verb complements

So far, we have not had to expand the $\overline{X}$ system to include embedded sentences or Inflectional elements. That is topic we'll take up now, while section 3.3 turns to the acquisition of auxiliary verb sequences. Let's consider sentential verb complements. Here are some examples.

For Bill to go would be foolish.
I promised John to go.
The man that left early is sick.

The usual analysis of the first two kinds of sentences extends S to a higher level bar category, $\overline{\text{S}}$ adding a Complementizer (COMP) in the form of *for* or *that* (see Bresnan 1972). Note that this structure of $\overline{\text{X}}$ follows the HEAD-COMP order fixed by other examples in English, if we consider *for* or *that* to be operators. This is a natural assumption. *For* assigns case to its NP argument in Prepositional Phrases; *that* is a deictic operator. Moreover, this choice makes the Complementizer the Head of $\overline{\text{S}}$. (INFL^{max} is S.) One advantage to this is that it makes *for* the governor of *John* in sentences such as *For John to leave would be terrible.* Then all cases of government fall under a canonical operator-operand pattern, the core notion of government: Preposition–NP; Verb–NP or $\overline{\text{X}}$; and Complementizer–S.

Additionally, some theories claim that *wh* elements fill the Complementizer position, intuitively acting like operators:

Why–did Sally kiss John?
    Opr–Operand

How–will you get home?
    Opr–Operand

Who–will Sally kiss?
    Opr–Operand

How is this extension of the $\overline{\text{X}}$ system acquired? Consider an example such as, *Sally bought a candy for Bill to eat.* Assume that *bought* has already been successfully analyzed in other constructions, so that it is known that it takes an argument. Assume further that *for* has been analyzed in PP constructions as described in the preceding section.

The parse proceeds smoothly until the point where *a candy* has been analyzed as the beginning of an NP. *Candy* is attached as the HEAD of this phrase; the packet pointer is set to COMP. Next, *for* is projected as an X^{max}, just as if it were the beginning of a PP. *For* is attached as the HEAD of this phrase, and the packet pointer set to COMP. The +N −V *Bill* prompts creation of an N^{max}. The details of this analysis will be (mercifully) skipped here; suffice it to say that this analysis proceeds without incident and returns the N^{max} to the first buffer cell. We now have an N^{max} in the first buffer cell; *to* in the second; and *eat* in the third.

The attach-pp-object rule triggers, but violates the given thematic representation. No other rules can trigger, and the other possible rule actions fail as well. Following standard procedure, *to* is projected as an X^{max}. Note that this may be done even though *to* is ambiguously a preposition or an inflectional marker; in both cases, it is $-N$. The packet pointer is set to SPEC, as usual.

What next? A grammar rule to attach the N^{max} *Bill* as the SPEC of the new X^{max} can trigger; this is the rule attach-embedded-subject:

CYCLIC NODE	X^{max} $-N$ $-V$ $+A$ $+P$
ACTIVE NODE:	X^{max}
	$\quad\quad\quad\quad\quad\quad\quad\quad\quad\downarrow$ $-N$ $+V$ $+A$ $+P$—SPEC—HEAD—COMP
BUFFER:	$[X^{max}\ +N\ -V\ +A\ -P][-N\ +V\ \pm tense][\quad * \quad]$
ACTION:	ATTACH

The $\pm$ marking here indicates simply that the second buffer cell *is* marked for tense, rather than being unmarked. (That is, the element does not have zero tense, but must be marked either one way or the other for tense.) if tense is unknown, this rule simply does not trigger. (This would correspond to a system that analyzes *I want John goed* as OK.)

Next, *to* is attached as the HEAD of the new phrase; the packet pointer is advanced to COMP. This is done by a newly-minted inflection rule, attach-to-infinitive.

CYCLIC:	X^{max} $-N$ $+V$ $+A$ $+P$
ACTIVE NODE:	X^{max}
	$\quad\quad\quad\quad\quad\quad\quad\quad\quad\downarrow$ $-N$ $+V$ $+A$ $+P$—SPEC—HEAD—COMP
BUFFER:	$[to\ -N\ +V\ +A\ +P][-N\ +V\ +P\ -A\ -tense][\quad * \quad]$
ACTION:	ATTACH

We now have *eat* in the first buffer cell. As usual, this $-N$ $+V$ item triggers creation of an X^{max} of this type; it is made the active node. *Eat* is then attached as the head of this phrase. With the end of sentence marker in the first buffer cell, no grammar rules trigger; but the given thematic structure says that *eat* has no arguments other than the Subject *Bill*, so all is well; the completed V^{max} is dropped back into the buffer. We now have a V^{max} in the first buffer cell, while the active node is the INFL with the packet pointer at COMP. No grammar rules trigger because no rules have been acquired to attach a V^{max} to an $INFL^{max}$. The acquisition procedure's ATTACH action succeeds, though: the attached V^{max} isn't of the same category as the INFL. Importantly, we have split off an inflectional phrase from a VP.

CYCLIC NODE:	X^{max} $-N$ $+V$ $+A$ $+P$
ACTIVE NODE:	X^{max}
	$-N$ $+V$ $+A$ $+P$—SPEC—HEAD—CO$\downarrow$MP
BUFFER:	[X^{max} $-N$ $+V$ $+P$ $-A$][*][*]
ACTION:	ATTACH

The end of sentence marker now sits in the first buffer cell and $INFL^{max}$ is the current active node. No rules match; no acquisition actions succeed. Note that the cyclic node is occupied by the matrix phrase associated with *kissed*, so that the parser is not in an accepting configuration. The default drop is taken and the $INFL^{max}$ put into the first buffer cell. This finally uncovers the *for* maximal projection, with its packet pointer at COMP. We can now attach the $INFL^{max}$ as this complement, via the new rule **attach-sent**. This completes the matrix phrase; the rest of the parse works as in a simple sentence.

CYCLIC NODE:	*
ACTIVE NODE:	X^{max}
	$-N$ $-V$ $+A$ $+P$—SPEC—HEAD—CO$\downarrow$MP
BUFFER:	[$-N$ $+V$ $+A$ $+P$][*][*]
ACTION:	ATTACH

In all, four new rules are acquired: (1) The expansion of $\overline{S}$ as *for*-S; (2) the attachment of *to* as INFL; (3) the attachment of VP as the complement of $INFL^{max}$; and (4) the attachment of the $INFL^{max}$ as the complement of *for*. In addition, the system has learned to separate INFL as a distinct phrasal node from VP—because of the explicit *to*. As we'll see just below, there's some evidence that this sequence follows what goes on in children.

Evidence for embedded complement acquisition

Interestingly, there are indications that something like this is going on in child language acquisition. The key insight is that the use of *for* as a Preposition triggers its use as a Complementizer. This developmental sequence is mimicked by the computer model. Note that the computer model cannot analyze a *for*-S construction without first going through the PP stage, because this is what fixes the maximal projection (operator) required for the analysis to proceed.

Roeper (personal communication) has collected examples of sentences produced by a child 2.5–2.10 years old showing that *for* is indeed used in *for*-NP constructions quite early:

> *This one is bigger for you.*
> *There's one for Mom for to brush he's too.*

Evidently, children of this age recognize *for* in the input stream of sentences and can use it productively. It is not surprising, then, that *for*-S constructions are also found:

> *This is for I can put some light on.*
> *I want for you hold it.*
> *It's too big for you eat.*
> *It's for fix things.*

Note that the *to*-inflection is often dropped, as is often the case with inflectional elements generally at this age. The computer model would, of course, also mimic this if no separate INFL is recognized. More interestingly, as Roeper observes, these early uses of *for*-S constructions obey a clear semantics that is parasitic on that used in *for* Prepositional forms. The use of *for* as a purposive, as in, *I want this for Mom*, portends its use as a purposive in sentence complements. This is the order the model obeys.

Roeper's sample also includes many examples of *for-to* constructions. Note that these are strictly speaking ungrammatical, though they do occur in some dialects. If the acquisition procedure is flawless, we have to explain why these sentences can be produced.

Let's bring a bench for to jump in.
The milk is for to drink.
Toys are for to play with.

Why do these sentences appear? If *for* is known to be *required* as an Operator, assigning some kind of purposive thematic role, then it must be present, at some level of representation. Since there is no known rule to block its appearance in forms like *Toys are for to play with*, it will appear. Note that this surface form is not permitted in most English dialects, but that the underlying representation of *Toys are to play with* is the child's version. Thus the child's sentence is simply a "purer" representation of underlying thematic structure—as expected. Moreover, sentences such as *The milk is for to drink* will be parsed perfectly well by a (hypothetical) self-analyzer that subjects sentences that are to be generated to error checks; a trace will simply be dropped to fill the role of the NP that is missing.

Finally, there is evidence that the full *for*-S construction is acquired by this age:

It's for Daddy to look at.
Some berries for the birds to eat.

How could the adult *for-to* filter be acquired? If the child is in a dialect community that uses *for-to*, then of course it will hear such constructions and be able to parse and generate them; all is well. But what of the case where the community does not use *for-to*? As we have seen, the child still *generates* such cases, early on. This would seem to be an explicit violation of the Subset Principle: the child has guessed a language that is "too large," and there is no positive evidence that it could receive that will tell it that this is incorrect.

There is a way out of this dilemma, however. Suppose that we invoke a corollary of the Subset Principle, Wexler's uniqueness Principle (see Roeper 1981). The Uniqueness Principle is a constraint on the evaluation procedure for grammars such that the learner always maintains at most one surface form for every corresponding deep structure. Its effect is to narrow the class of possible output surface forms. In the case at hand, it would permit the existence of forms such as, *The milk is for to drink* along with, *Grandma has a present for me to blow on*, as long as there were no other alternative surface forms corresponding to the deep structures for these sentences. However, as soon as a positive example surface string such as, *The milk is to drink* can be analyzed, the Uniqueness Principle would block the generation of *for-to* from then on, because there would be an alternative surface form corresponding to this one underlying structure. The *for-to* surface form need not be used.

A model of generation of this kind, along with appropriate modifications to handle self-correction and the acquisition of filters as suggested by the Uniqueness Principle, has not been considered here. An extension of this kind would be an interesting direction for future work.

Other complement structures

Turning now to other complement structures, consider first *that* complements, e.g., *Sally knows that Bill kissed Jane*. The parse of such sentences proceeds normally until we reach a point where the input buffer holds *that*, *Bill* and *kissed*. Now we have a choice. *That* can be projected as an X^{max} of some sort, or it could be the Specifier of an X^{max} (as in, *that boy*). Suppose the latter course is taken. Then the system will project *Bill* as the HEAD of the phrase, and *that* as its SPEC. This possibility is ruled out by a check of the thematic representation, which mentions only *Bill* as a complete unit. Thus this option fails, and this example discarded. Suppose then that *that* is projected as an X^{max}. It is attached as the HEAD of its own phrase (as usual), and the packet pointer set to the COMP portion. A new grammar rule will be acquired to attach *that*.

Now the system is in good shape to finish. *Bill* will be projected as an X^{max}, as usual; we suppress the details of building this phrase (all works as before). The completed NP will be placed back in the input buffer. Now the verb in the second buffer cell will trigger creation of an X^{max} of type $-N$ $+V$. At this point the current cyclic node of the parse is still the maximal projection associated with *know*. We shall ignore details about INFL here; see the next section for additional discussion. It is easy to see that the rest of the parse will proceed as with a root sentence: the subject NP will get attached; the object Noun Phrase will get built and attached to the V^{max}. At this point, with the end of sentence marker in the first buffer cell, and no matching rules, we see that the parser is not yet in an accepting configuration because the cyclic and active nodes are not empty. So the procedure drops the completed

X^{max} into the input buffer, uncovering the *that* phrase projection along with its pointer to COMP. No known grammar rules execute, but ATTACH works. Now the *that* phrase is complete according to the thematic representation, so we drop it into the input buffer, revealing *know* and the the packet pointer set to COMP. The parse is almost done; it remains only to attach the *that* phrase as the complement of *know*. No known rules fire, but again ATTACH works and the new rule is saved.

Why is the tensed form *Sally knows that Bill kissed Sally* permitted, but not the corresponding tenseless form, *Sally knows that Bill to kiss Sally*? One explanation for this difference is that the NP *Bill* must be "Case marked" in order to appear in a surface form, and Case marking is performed by a Tense element or a Preposition. *That* is neither. In contrast, since *for* assigns Case, *Bill* can appear in a tenseless clause after *for*, as in, *I want very much for Bill to win*. This property is *encoded* by the acquisition procedure's grammar rules: note that the *for* complement rules include patterns with an NP in the first buffer cell and *to* in the second, while the *that* complement rules will not. The rules are therefore not merged. Tenseless verbs in *that* clauses will not be directly parsable, the right result. The parser left context distinguishes *that* from *for* clauses, since the X^{max} in question will be annotated with the name of the rule that attaches either *that* or *for*. This will prove important for later analysis of missing Subject sentences, discussed in chapter 4.

More complicated complement structures can now be analyzed. Consider a verb that takes an NP and an S complement, e.g., *persuade*, as in *I persuaded Bill that John should kiss Sally*. Suppose that examples where *persuade* takes just an NP have already been encountered, e.g., *I persuaded Bill*. Then *persuade* will already be marked to take an NP complement. What happens when the system attempts to parse *I persuaded Bill that he should kiss Sally*?

As in other examples, the parse proceeds normally to the point where the Complement of the V is being analyzed. *Bill* is then parsed as a complete NP, using a thematic check. Now observe that the known grammar rules to attach object NPs do not execute, since they trigger on patterns NP—• or NP—PREPOSITION—+N, not NP—THAT—+N. The acquisition procedure is entered, and an ATTACH works. At this point the buffer contains *that* in the first buffer cell, *John* in the second, and *should* in the third. This configuration is exactly like that of a simple *that* complement sentence, and the analysis will proceed along those lines. The only difference will be that the lexical entry for *persuade* will be modified to indicate that it must take both NP and S (actually a V-type X^{max}) complements.

A deeper look at some related examples highlights the acquisition of control structures. Consider first of all a *want* type complement, *I want Bill to go* (a related sentence with an empty subject NP, *I want to go*, is discussed in the next chapter, since it requires insertion of an empty element). Such examples will be acquired without incident if *want* is already known to take an argument complement, as in *I want a candy*. For then *Bill to go* is parsed as a full sentence (as above), and attached as the complement of *want*. Now consider a sentence such as *I persuaded Bill to go*. If *persuade* is now known to take two arguments, the first obligatory, then *Bill* will get attached as the complement of *persuade*.

The procedure's next move is properly a subject for the next chapter, but we include a discussion of it here. *To* will project as an INFL^{max} phrase; at this point no further grammar rules match (the packet pointer is set to SPEC). SWITCH fails, since after a SWITCH no known rules fire. INSERT TRACE succeeds, because after an empty NP is placed into the first buffer position the known attach-subject rule triggers. The remainder of the embedded sentence parses as before.

A key remaining question centers on the binding of the empty NP: is its antecedent *Bill* or *I*? In effect, this question must be settled by appeal to another cognitive subsystem, the one that maintains the thematic representation. Not surprisingly, there may be difficulties in deducing the correct antecedent. Various processing strategies are apparently involved here. For example, in C. Chomsky's classic (1969) analysis, children evidently first took the *nearest* NP as the subject of *go*—the Minimal Distance Principle. This "nearest neighbor" story is quite plausible in the parsing model, since the most accessible node in the active node stack will be the nearest NP, in this case, the object, if there is one. The Subject NP is more inaccessible.

3.3 Learning the Inflectional System

The auxiliary verb system in English has often been considered a good testbed for an acquisition theory. In this section we apply the acquisition procedure to English sentences with different auxiliary verb patterns. We shall see that the auxiliary verb system can be easily acquired by exposure to just simple positive examples. (See chapter 6 for a formal analysis of the same problem.)

Importantly, the uniform use of $\overline{\text{X}}$ theory in the acquisition model will lead directly to an analysis of auxiliary verbs as a right-branching chain of verb complements, in the manner suggested by Baker (1981).

Before beginning in earnest, we shall look at the properties of the rule system that must be acquired. The Marcus parser grammar rules for auxiliaries are displayed in table 3.1, followed by the corresponding new format grammar rules.

The English auxiliary verb system is, by all accounts, a simple finite-state language; there is no recursion. Given that one can exhibit a finite-state automaton for this system, how many states does it take? If we include a start state, a non-accepting state, an accepting state, and a state for the main verb and a trailing Object, chapter 6 shows that 10 states are minimally required.

In the corresponding Marcus grammar rules, **Startaux** corresponds to the start state of the automaton; **Complete-aux** to the accepting state. (This is not quite accurate: since we should really add the activation of the verb packet as another state, and a trailing NP object as yet a third extra state.) These two rules are replaced by the automatic node creation and completion protocols and so need not be acquired at all. The remaining attachment rules all correspond to one of the insertion contexts. There are eight of these, not counting main verb and NP insertion frames. Note that the Marcus subgrammar includes a rule for *to* infinitives that is not part of root sentence environments, so we shall not consider that rule further here. As we shall see, the acquisition system successfully cordons off that rule from root sentence analysis. Furthermore, the rules for FUTURE and other modals are represented by a single rule in the usual analysis.

This leaves us with the following rules in the Marcus subgrammar for the Auxiliary:

1. Modals   2. Perfective   3. Progressive
4. *Do*   5. Passive *be* 6. Infinitives

This system of grammar rules directly reflects the AUX grammar proposed in *Syntactic Structures*, with an additional state for passive *be* and infinitivals.

Aux → Tense (Modal) (*have* +*ing*)(*be* +*en*)

Rule Format:
Rule *rulename* (**Priority**: *priority number*) in *packetname*
pattern → *action*

Rule Startaux in Parse-Aux
[verb] →
Create a new aux node.
Activate build-aux, cpool.

Rule To-Infinitive in Parse-Aux
[*to, auxverb] [tnsless] →
Label a new aux node inf.
Attach 1st to c as to.
Activate build-aux, cpool.

Rule Aux-Attach in Parse-Aux
[aux] →
Attach 1st to c as aux.
Activate parse-vp.
Deactivate parse-aux.

Rule Perfective in Build-Aux
[*have] [en] →
Attach 1st to c as perf. Label c perf.

Rule Progressive in Build-Aux
[*be] [ing] →
Attach 1st to c as prog.
Label c prog

Rule Passive-Aux in Build-Aux
[*be] [en] →
Attach 1st to c as passive.
Label 2nd passive.

Rule Modal in Build-Aux
[modal] [tnsless] →
Attach 1st to c as modal.
Label c modal

Rule Future in Build-Aux
[*will] [tnsless] →
Attach 1st to c as will.
Label c future.

Rule Do-Support in Build-Aux
[*do] [tnsless] →
Attach 1st to c as do.

Rule Aux-Complete Priority:15
in Build-Aux
[*] →
Drop c into the buffer.

Table 3.1: Old format grammar rules for auxiliary verbs

Rules for parsing Infl (Aux)

Rule to-infinitive

CYC is $X^{max} -N +V +A +P$

C is $X^{max} -N +V +A +P$—SPEC—HE$\overset{\downarrow}{A}$D—COMP
$[to\ -N\ +V\ +A\ +P][-N\ +V\ +P\ -A\ -tense][\quad *\quad]\ \rightarrow$
ATTACH

Rule perfective

CYC is *

C is $X^{max} -N +V$—SPEC—HE$\overset{\downarrow}{A}$D—COMP
$[have\ -N\ +V][-N\ +V+en][\quad *\quad]\ \rightarrow$
ATTACH

Rule progressive

CYC *

C is $X^{max} -N +V$—SPEC—HE$\overset{\downarrow}{A}$D—COMP
$[be\ -N\ +V][\ -N\ +Ving][\quad *\quad]\ \rightarrow$
ATTACH

Rule modal

CYC is *

C is $X^{max} -N +V +A +P$—SPEC—HE$\overset{\downarrow}{A}$D—COMP
$[could\ -N\ +V\ +A\ +P][-N\ +V-tense][\quad *\quad]\ \rightarrow$
ATTACH

Table 3.2: New format rules for parsing auxiliaries

Rules for parsing Infl (Aux)

Rule dɔ

CYC is X^{max} $-N$ $+V$ $+A$ $+P$

C is $X^{\text{max}}-N$ $+V$ $+A$ $+P$—SPEC—HEAD—COMP
$[do$ $-N$ $+V$ $+A$ $+P][-N$ $+V$ $+P$ $-A$ $-$tense$][$ $*$ $] \rightarrow$
ATTACH

Rule passive-be

CYC is $*$

C is $X^{\text{max}}-N$ $+V$ $+A$ $+P$—SPEC—HEAD—COMP
$[be][-N$ $+V$ $+P$ $-A$ $+ed][$ $*$ $] \rightarrow$
ATTACH

Rule infl-attach

CYC is $*$

C is $X^{\text{max}}-N$ $+V$ $+A$ $+P$—SPEC—HEAD—COMP
$[X^{\text{max}}$ $-N$ $+V$ $+A$ $+P][$ $*$ $][$ $*$ $] \rightarrow$
ATTACH

Table 3.3: New format grammar rules for auxiliary verbs, continued

Since all grammar rules are data-driven, and since we are parsing rather than generating sentences, the optionality of the nonterminals in the *Syntactic Structures* phrase structure rule is accounted for: the system attaches *have* or *be* just in case an element of that type is present; otherwise, that particular option is not selected.

There are some apparent problems with the Marcus analysis, however. While it is perfectly adequate to handle all the occurring grammatical AUX forms, it also accepts some ungrammatical forms. This is to be expected, since the number of states in the subgrammar is smaller than that indicated by the minimal finite-state automaton for the AUX system. For example, consider the *do*-insertion rule:

Rule Do-Support in Build-Aux
[*do] [tnsless] →
Attach 1st to c as do.

All that this rule calls for is a tenseless verb immediately following *do*. A system containing only this version of *do* insertion will therefore also accept sentences such as, *I did be taking a book*. We shall see below how the acquisition procedure corrects this problem.

Second, there is a problem in distinguishing between the progressive and passive forms of verbs. For instance, Marcus's AUX rules will mark the sentence, *I could have been taking a book* as passive, the same as *I could have been being given a book*. This defect is more apparent than real, however. Actually, the sentence is marked simply as a *potential* passive. When the main verb is finally examined for an *ed* ending this ambiguity is resolved. Thus, this extra state is actually placed in another part of Marcus's grammar. In any case, one must add additional states to distinguish between the *ing* and *ed* verb forms somewhere in the grammar, either in the AUX system itself, or later on. After adjusting for these two problems one can see that the subgrammar presented by Marcus and the insertion frame grammar are the same.

The acquisition procedure can acquire this entire system of rules. In the following scenarios, we will assume that NPs are successfully analyzed by already-known rules, and, as usual, that verbs can be identified as such. Finally, we assume that *tense* is recognizable via morphological endings. The first example forces acquisition of the modal attach rule. The Marcus rule version:

Rule Modal in Build-Aux
[modal] [tnsless] $\rightarrow$
Attach 1st to c as modal. Label c modal.

The acquisition target rule:

Rule modal

CYC is *

C is $X^{max}-N +V +A +P$—SPEC—HEAD↓—COMP
[*could* $-N +V +A +P$][$-N +V-$tense][*] $\rightarrow$
ATTACH

Here, *could* is simply a gloss for all those lexical items that wind up in the same equivalence class as *could*.

The example sentence we shall use to acquire this rule is *Sally will kiss the doll*. The parse of the Subject NP proceeds as before. A key difference appears at the time the acquisition procedure acquires a new rule to attach the modal element *will*. This token is not a noun; nor is it an action. We project an X^{max} with these features, marking *will* as its HEAD. Now no grammar rules match. The packet pointer is at SPEC. The acquisition procedure attaches the N^{max} as SPEC, again acquiring a new rule. Note that this is possible because nothing rules out this attachment. Next we see if any grammar rules match on the HEAD. Again the answer is no. This time the acquisition procedure's ATTACH action succeeds, gluing *will* as the HEAD of the phrase.

CYCLIC NODE: nil

ACTIVE NODE: $X^{max}-N +V +A +P$—SPEC—HEAD↓—COMP
               (Rule attach-subject)

BUFFER:

will $-N -V$	*kiss* $-N +V$	*the* $+N -V$

ACTION: ATTACH

Note that this rule calls for *will* to be followed by a verb that has no inflectional marking; this distinguishes modals from ordinary verbs. If this information cannot be extracted from the morphological component, then this restriction is not learned at this time. This is one way that the development of syntactic analysis hinges on concurrent morphological processing. The restriction is encoded into the pattern of the ATTACH action, via the second buffer cell component. As it stands, it will accept only *kiss* in this position.

This rule is easily generalized. Suppose we have an example such as *Sally could kiss the doll.* This example will prompt creation of another attachment rule with the same left and right hand context. By the rule merger protocol, *could* and *will* are placed in the same equivalence class, because their behavior is the same in the same parse contexts. *Did* is also placed in this class by an example such as *John did kiss the doll.*[5] This is an incorrect waystation on the road to the correct final target rule system that will be repaired by other examples that split off *do* from the modals, as we shall see. In fact, it is well known that uninverted *do* forms are rarely heard. If this is so, then *do* must be acquired first by exposure in auxiliary inverted forms such as *Did Sally kiss John*. As we shall see, what this means is that *do* will be erroneously placed in the same class as *could* and *will*. The prediction is that if it were stopped here the procedure would *produce* (equivalently, be able to parse) examples such as *Sally did be kissing John.* Evidently, children do make errors with *do* more than any other auxiliary verb. The computer model mirrors this result.

Finally, an example such as, *Sally will go* reduces the third required buffer cell to a wild card pattern, since the end-of-sentence indicator has no features at all. This is precisely the target form.

Comparing this to the original Marcus rule form, in the acquired rule, the pointer to HEAD takes the place of the packet *build-aux*. The class of first cell tokens is just the set *could*, *will*, *should*, and so forth. The labeling carried out by the old rule is automatically performed by percolation of features and the labeling of the active node with the rule name.

Some points about this rule are worth noting. First of all, it correctly bars the repetition of modal items, e.g., **Sally could could eat a candy.* This is because the rule's action demands an item with features −N +V (without tense) in the second buffer cell, and this condition is violated by the modals.

---

[5] Of course, the verb in this case will itself be generalized by other examples, so that we could have *John did eat the candy.*

Second, the rule as it stands will work only in root environments, as indicated by the *empty* current cyclic node. An additional example exhibiting an embedded sentence is required for that. We need this kind of example in order to learn a rule to attach *to* as an infinitival element; such a case was covered earlier. The modal attachment rule will then be generalized to allow either a root or nonroot environment (given that identical righthand contexts are observed in both cases).

We can now turn to the next rule on our list, perfective *have*. The Marcus and acquisition target rules for this are as follows.

Rule Perfective in Build-Aux

[*have] [en] →
Attach 1st to c as perf.
Label c perf.

Rule perfective

CYCLIC NODE:	*
ACTIVE NODE:	X^{max}
	$-N +V$—SPEC—HEAD—COMP
BUFFER:	[*have* $-N +V$][$-N +V +en$][*]
ACTION:	ATTACH

(Note: we ignore differences in the various inflected forms of *have*, i.e., the differences between *has*, *have*. We also ignore the *ed/en* alternation.)

We assume two possibilities for *have*'s lexical entry: *have* is known as $-N$, but nothing more; or *have* is known as a full verb. We shall consider each.

Let us now see what happens in a sentence like *Sally has kissed John*. The parse of the Subject *Sally* proceeds as before; the N^{max} is built and dropped into the buffer. Now *have* is projected as some maximal phrase with at least $-N$ features, and possibly $-N +V$ features. The packet pointer set at SPEC. If *have* is already known as a verb, then the usual attach-subject rule triggers, attaching *Sally*, and analysis continues with the packet pointer at HEAD.

Suppose this is not true. Then no known grammar rule fires—not even the Subject attachment rule for modals, which calls for a modal phrase as the current active node. The acquisition procedure tries to see if *Sally* can be attached as a SPEC, and this at last succeeds. Note that analysis is easier if *have* has already been analyzed as a main verb in other sentences.

What next? If *have* is labeled $-$N $+$V, then the known object attachment rule cannot trigger, since it demands an $+$N $-$V element in the second buffer cell. The acquisition procedure is entered.

ATTACH works because *have* is marked as the HEAD of the $\textrm{x}^{\textrm{max}}$ that is the current active node. What is the pattern of this new rule? We assume that *kissed* in the second buffer cell is marked with *ed*. This follows a proposal of Lieber's (1980) that lexical items are in fact tree-structured, with their "heads" marked by features percolated from below, in this case, the *ed* feature. We do not say how *ed* is identified as a feature to be percolated. The procedure as implemented simply assumes that *every* property of elements in the second buffer cell is important; thus it must see another example with another verb before it actually generalizes the rule to the target pattern.

As usual, the acquisition procedure will also need to see an example in an embedded context, and an example that will generalize the third buffer cell to a wild card pattern. This is the right result. Note that this rule will *not* allow sequences such as *John could kissed*; the first buffer cell must be *have*. It also demands the *ed* feature as part of the triggering pattern.

The third rule to be acquired handles progressives.

Rule Progressive in Build-Aux
[*be] [ing] $\rightarrow$
Attach 1st to c as prog.
Label c prog.

Rule progressive
CYC is *
C is $\textrm{x}^{\textrm{max}}$

$$-\textrm{N } +\textrm{V}\textrm{---SPEC---HEAD---COMP}$$
$$[be -\textrm{N } +\textrm{V}][-\textrm{N } +\textrm{V}ing][\quad * \quad] \rightarrow$$
ATTACH

Our example sentence is *Sally should be kissing John*. As usual, the Subject NP will be parsed, dropped into the buffer, and attached properly after *will* is projected as an X^{max}. Next, *should* is attached as the HEAD of the X^{max}—but only after the acquisition procedure builds a new rule to do so. This is because the current rule to attach *should* calls for a $-N$ $+V$ in the second buffer cell and a $+N$ $-V$ element or end of sentence marker in the third, and now there is a $-N$ $+V$ item in the third cell. The new rule forces the third cell pattern to a wild card. The COMP portion of the the X^{max} is now entered. *Be* triggers creation of an X^{max}, as usual; the packet pointer is simply advanced to HEAD.

The system is now in position to acquire the progressive rule. No known grammar rule fires, since the perfective rule calls for *have* in the first buffer cell, and this does not hold. The known verb attachment rule for *be* demands something other than a verb in the second buffer cell. The tireless acquisition procedure is called on once again. An ATTACH succeeds, since *be* is the HEAD that prompted creation of the X^{max}. The rule pattern demands a verb marked *ing* in the second buffer cell, as desired.

Do support examples were briefly discussed above. If rare examples like *John did kiss Sally* are encountered, these will be lumped with modals, at least temporarily, until examples such as *John could be kissing Sally* are seen. Then, the different left contexts of the two rules (*be kissing* vs. *kiss Sally*) will force *do* and modals to be separated, via Step 5c of the acquisition procedure.

Finally, we turn to passive *be*, as in *Sally was kissed*. As usual we first give the original rule version, followed by the newer target rule.

> Rule **Passive-Aux** in Build-Aux
> [*be] [en] $\rightarrow$
> Attach 1st to c as passive.
> Label 2nd passive.

> Rule **passive-be**
> CYC is *
> C is $X^{max}-N$ $+V$—SPEC—H$\overset{\downarrow}{E}$AD—COMP
> $[be-N$ $+V][-N$ $+V$ $+ed$][*   ] $\rightarrow$
> ATTACH

Interestingly, the original grammar does not block a sequence such as *John was been kissed*. Nor does the new rule, as stated. One way to block it would be to adopt a strict equivalence class approach. If the second buffer cell includes all verbs that ever appear in that position, then *be+en* will not appear after *was*. Remember that there is no need to label the second buffer cell (the main verb) as passive, because this information will be available as a rule annotation on the lefthand context when needed.

Let us consider first a sentence such as *Sally was kissed*. In fact, as far as auxiliaries go, this sentence will be analyzed just like *Sally has left*; the end result will be to place *have* and *was* in the same lexical equivalence class (for the moment). Let us see why.

The Subject NP is parsed as usual, and returned to the first buffer cell. With *was* in the second buffer cell, an X^{max} is created. *Sally* is attached as a SPEC of this phrase, by the known subject attachment rule. No known rule matches the buffer pattern at the time *was* is to be attached; the modal rule calls for a verb without an *ed* or *ing* ending. The *have* attachment rules and the progressive rule likewise cannot match. (The perfective rule calls for *have* and the progressive rule for *ing* in the second buffer cell.) The acquisition procedure is entered. ATTACH works; *was* is marked as the HEAD of the phrase. The rule's pattern calls for *was* in the first buffer cell, a $-N +V$ item with an $+ed$ in the second, and an end of sentence marker in the third. An example such as *Sally was given a book* would show that the third buffer cell could be occupied by an $+N -V$ item. Since the righthand contexts of the *have* and *was* attach rules are identical, this suggests that *was* should be put in the same class as *have*. This is of course a (temporarily) incorrect move.

One more example will split apart *have* and *be*: *Sally has been kissed*. Then we see that *have* may be followed by *be+ed*, but *be* cannot. The acquisition procedure then separates the two lexical items. This also fixes the relative order of *have* and *be*.

We have now acquired all the rules in Marcus's rule system for auxiliaries, including improvements that block some illegal sequences the original grammar allowed. We have not yet covered the automatic creation and completion of the maximal projection for this node. It is worthwhile to go back over our tracks and see how the acquired system works.

The first point is that the acquired rule system is close to a "multiple verb" analysis, originally advanced by Ross (1967) and revived by Baker (1981). A sequence of auxiliaries is projected, naturally enough, as a series of X^{max}'s, with the complement of each phrase being the next in line; the last one is the complement position filled by the VP. Figure 3.2 illustrates.

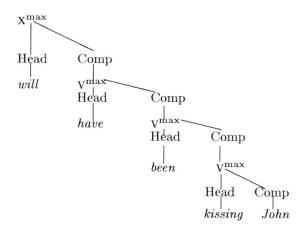

Figure 3.2: A branching verb analysis of auxiliaries

We have already seen how the rule patterns forbid multiple sequences of modals and the order of *have* and nonpassive *be*. The relative order of modals and *have* or *be* is likewise fixed because *have* and *be* demand trailing verbs.

It is easy to see how long sequences of auxiliary verbs fit into the multiple projection analysis. What is quite intriguing is that these are automatically analyzed even if they have never been seen before. This is the right kind of result, because such long sequences of auxiliary verbs are presumably quite rare. For instance, suppose an example like *Sally will have been kissing John* is encountered. The projection of the first x^{max} node and entry into its COMP portion are as before. Next, however, there is something new: *have* is projected as an x^{max} of its own. (The former active node, the x^{max} associated with *will*, is pushed down one in the active node stack.) As usual, *have* is attached as the HEAD of the new projection, and the COMP portion is entered. History repeats itself; *been* triggers the creation of a new x^{max}, *been* is attached as its HEAD, and a COMP schema is entered. This time, it is *kissing* that triggers the formation of a maximal projection. *Kissing* is attached as a v^{max} HEAD, and *John* as complement.

Other cases of multiple auxiliaries are encoded in the same fashion; the details will not be covered here. For a formal analysis of the number of examples needed to induce this system, see chapter 6. There we observe that we need only one example sentence for each modal verb, one example to set the order of *have* vs. *be*, and one for the order of modals and *have*, *be*. Thus, the auxiliary system is really not hard to acquire from positive examples. Aside from *do*, the acquisition procedure proceeds nearly flawlessly—exactly the result observed in children.

3.4   The Order of Examples

So far we have shown that learning can take place if sentences are received in some specific order. But this is patently not true of "real" language acquisition. After all, we cannot assume that sentences are presented to the child in a fixed order, consisting of first simple N-V-N sentences, then sentences with embeddings, then transformations. Indeed, as discussed by Newport, Gleitman, and Gleitman (1977), in some ways mothers' speech to children contains *more* examples of Subject-Auxiliary inversions and (simple) *wh* movement. (Questions and imperatives are a big part of mothers' lives.) How can these facts be reconciled with the rigid presentation sequence presented here?

Ordering and the acquisition procedure

A brief answer to this puzzle is that the incremental character of the acquisition procedure has the effect of *filtering* the input sentences received in random order such that the example sequences actually used for acquisition all follow the same sequence (up to a permutation among certain sentences as defined below). Roughly, sentences that fix HEAD-COMPLEMENT order appear before those requiring transformational operations defined over HEADS and COMPLEMENTS; likewise, sentences whose analysis require grammar rules that depend on particular lexical features must appear after examples that determine those features. For example, Subject-Auxiliary inversion acquisition is not learned until a distinct INFL category is acquired, as seems reasonable. Similarly, a rule to analyze passive sentences will not be fixed until after basic sentence order can be handled. This is because the passive rule cannot be acquired if the system must learn two new rules simultaneously—the new passive rule *and* the rule that attaches Object NPs after verbs. Note that these developmental dependencies are those actually observed.

It is important to see that this ordering is demanded by the success criteria of the acquisition procedure itself. New rule actions succeed just in case some already known grammar rule triggers after the actions is tried out, or, in the case of ATTACH, when certain $\overline{\text{X}}$ constraints are met. This constraint does *not* say that all base phrase structure rules must be fixed before any transformational-type operations are learned. Only base rules that are required as input to the relevant transformations must be acquired. For example, grammar rules to analyze embedded sentences might be acquired after a grammar rule to analyze passive sentences. Similarly, details of the inflectional system might remain unlearned well *after* the analysis of some *wh* questions. The *well ordering* requirement on input sequences may now be stated as follows.

Let r_i, r_j be grammar rules, with the action of r_i SWITCH, INSERT TRACE, or INSERT LEXICAL ITEM. We say that r_i is *acquisition dependent* on r_j if r_j executes immediately after r_i. If the action of r_i is ATTACH, then r_i is acquisition dependent on r_j if r_j labels the parser state with a feature required for the successful attachment defined by r_i, or advances the packet pointer so that the ATTACH can proceed.

We say that a sentence s_1 is acquisition dependent on another sentence s_2 if any of the grammar rules used to correctly parse s_1 are acquisition dependent on the grammar rules used to parse s_2.

Let $\mathcal{R}_1$, $\mathcal{R}_2$ be sets of grammar rules required to successfully analyze sentences s_1, s_2. s_1 is acquisition dependent on s_2 if $\exists r_i \in \mathcal{R}_1$ and $r_j \in \mathcal{R}_2$ such that r_i is acquisition dependent on r_j. If no such pair of rules exists, we say that s_1, s_2 are *acquisition independent*.

Well-ordering of input examples ensures that acquisition dependency follows temporal sequencing. Call a sequence of example sentences *well-ordered* if no pair of sentences s_i, s_j in the sequence exists such that s_i is acquisition dependent on s_j but nonetheless s_i precedes s_j in the sequence.

Finally, we introduce a term for a sequence of examples actually used after "filtering": call a sequence of positive examples a *learning sequence* if all examples in it can be successfully analyzed. Note that by the definition of the acquisition procedure, the example sequences the acquisition procedure successfully analyzes form learning sequences. Also note that a given sentence in a learning sequence might not prompt the creation of any new grammar rules because all the rules required to analyze them are already known. These sentences could just as well be omitted from the learning sequence, without effect. The result is a "filtered" learning sequence without these repetitions.

We can now state two important properties of the acquisition procedure: first, that the success criterion for rule acquisition guarantees that correct learning sequences are well-ordered; and second, that acquisition is invariant over permutations of a well-ordered learning sequences that preserve the well-ordering property:

(1) The acquisition procedure incorporates a filtering function f such that the resulting learning sequences are well-ordered.

(2) Any well-ordered permutation of a learning sequence that results in a correct rule set yields a grammar rule set defining the same (input sentence, output tree) parsing function.[6] A well-ordered permutation is just a permutation of a learning sequence that maintains the well-ordering property.

Let us first demonstrate the filtering property of the acquisition procedure. We must show that whatever the order of input sentences, the resulting learning sequence that is used in grammar rule formation is well-ordered. Assume that this is false. Then there is a learning sequence with two sentences, s_i and s_j, where s_i precedes s_j, and with a rule r_i used to parse s_i acquisition dependent on a rule r_j in s_j. But then, s_i cannot be parsed successfully: if r_i is a SWITCH, INSERT TRACE, or INSERT LEXICAL ITEM, then it requires rule action r_j, which is not available. If r_i is an ATTACH, then it requires that r_j label the parser state or advance the packet pointer (indirectly via its rule action). Thus the parse fails in either case, and sentence s_i is not used for learning, contrary to assumption. Our hypothesis that well-ordering does not hold must be false. See the next subsection for a particular example of this ordering effect.

Note that in one sense this is an unsatisfactory result, because a learning sequence can lead to an incorrect target. This is because even though s_i is parsed incorrectly when it appears before s_j, there might be no way for the acquisition procedure to know this. In fact, as we shall see in the demonstration of property 2 below, there is no difficulty if the rules involved include pattern generalizations, pattern splitting, or lexical class formation, because these rules may be acquired in any order. The real difficulty arises from $\overline{\text{X}}$ parameter setting. As an example, suppose that a topicalized sentence such as, *Candy, Sally likes* is given before ordinary sentence order is fixed, in particular before HEAD-COMP order. Suppose this sentence is analyzed as N^{max}–N^{max}–V^{max}, setting the order COMP-SPEC-HEAD (using the thematic

---

[6]Recall that this is a parsing *function* because only one description is output for any single input sentence.

representation as a guide). That is, basic sentence order is set incorrectly to Object-Subject-verb.

Here at least there is a remedy. Given this faulty setting, ordinary declarative sentences now cannot be parsed correctly without violating the just-learned $\overline{X}$ constraint, and all acquisition moves fail; similarly for Prepositional Phrases and Noun Phrase complements. All the acquisition procedure needs to do is to balance the competing evidence of HEAD-COMP order vs. COMP-HEAD. Something like the following format is suitable: the topicalized sentence sets COMP-HEAD order. Then, when the acquisition procedure fails on Prepositional Phrases and normal sentences, we add a procedure that (i) checks if the $\overline{X}$ parameters have been permanently set (in this case they have not been); and then (ii) considers setting the $\overline{X}$ parameter in order to deal with the current example. It then stores both HEAD, COMP orders. When other sentences are analyzed, it checks both possibilities. After a certain number of possibilities have been accumulated in favor of one choice—NPs, VPs, APs also exhibit HEAD-COMP order—then a decision is made permanently.

This definitely adds to the complexity of the acquisition procedure, giving it a more hypothesis-testing character. Fortunately, this is required only for setting two $\overline{X}$ parameters—the order of SPEC and COMP with respect to the HEAD.[7]

In the remainder of this discussion, then, we shall assume that some augmentation such as this deals with the problem of $\overline{X}$ parameter setting. We have suggested that this works in the case of topicalized sentences; it remains to demonstrate that the same method can repair incorrect parameter settings prompted by other noncanonical sentence orders, such as *wh* questions or auxiliary verb inversions. If this can be done, then we can show that the $\overline{X}$ parameters for English can be correctly set regardless of presentation order.

Now let us consider the second property, well-ordered permuations of input sentences. Suppose we are given a learning sequence, S, that yields a correct target parser, that is, one that correctly analyzes the target language. The acquisition procedure applied to this sequence yields some target rule set, g_s. Suppose that we permute the elements of the sequence while maintaining

---

[7]It is the use of an $\overline{X}$ theory that makes this possible. If we adopted a more "surface" oriented account, and said that, e.g., Subject, Verb, Object order was set independently, then problems could arise: we could take *Candy, Sally likes* or *Who does John like* as evidence for other surface sentence orders; this would be hard to refute on the basis of frequency, considering the prevalence of *wh* questions or inversions in caretakers' speech to children (Gleitman and Gleitman 1979). Using a single $\overline{X}$ template avoids this difficulty.

its well-orderedness. We are to show that the same parsing function (not necessarily with identical rules) is induced.

To demonstrate this, pick any pair of sentences whose ordering is changed by the permutation, s_i and s_j, with s_i preceding s_j. By assumption, s_i is not acquisition dependent on s_j. Since the permutation preserves the well-ordered property by assumption, s_i cannot be dependent on any sentences between s_j and s_i in the new ordering. Call the sequence from s_i to s_j a *block* of sentences. We now have two sequences:

$$S_1 = s_1, s_2, \ldots, s_{i-1}, s_i, s_{i+1}, \ldots, s_{i+j-1}, s_j$$
$$S_2 = s_1, s_2, \ldots, s_{i-1}, s_j, s_{i+1}, \ldots, s_{i+j-1}, s_i$$

Because of determinism the acquisition procedure's rule system after processing sentence s_{i-1} must be the same in both cases.

Now consider the possible differences in S_2 vs. S_1. In S_2, some rules used in sentence s_j may be acquired before some of the rules used for $s_{i+1}, \ldots, s_{i+j-1}, s_i$. We show that the rule system induced by the new sequence order s_j, s_{i+1} is the same as that induced by the original order $s_{i+1}, \ldots, s_j$; the same reasoning applies to all possible pairs where s_j now precedes a sentence it formerly followed, and, symmetrically, to sentence s_i that follows sentences it formerly preceded.

We proceed by the possible cases of rule acquisition prompted by sentences s_j and s_{i+1}.

Case 1: No new rules acquired by s_j. Then s_j has no effect on rules in s_{i+1}. We may delete s_j from the acquisition sequence without consequence.

Case 2: One or more rules acquired for s_j prompts a lexical equivalence class change compared against one or more rules acquired for s_{i+1}. We consider the case of just one rule, the case of multiple rules being similar. But lexical class formation is commutative, since the operation of takes as input two rules and checks to see if their lefthand and righthand contexts are identical. If so, then the tokens in the first input buffer cell are placed in the same equivalence class. This procedure clearly does not depend on the order in which rules are acquired, since this order is not used by the class formation procedure.

Case 3: One or more rules acquired for s_j is generalized with one or more rules acquired for s_{i+1}. Here too, rule generalization may be seen to be commutative: generalization yields the same output no matter what order two rules are given to it.

Case 4: One or more rules acquired for s_j causes a rule split with one or more rules acquired for s_{i+1}. Again, the procedure that checks for a rule split does not depend on the order of its arguments.

We have now shown that s_j and s_{i+1} may be interchanged without effect on the output rule system. Continuing this line of reasoning, it is easy to show that s_j and $s_{i+2}, s_{i+3}, \ldots, s_i$ may be so interchanged. We have now shown that S_2 results in the same induced parsing function as the sequence $s_1, \ldots, s_{i-1}, s_{i+1}, \ldots, s_{i+j-1}, s_i, s_j$. Our next step is to show that s_i may be interchanged with $s_{i+j-1}, s_{i+j-2}, \ldots, s_{i+1}$ without change in the induced parsing function. The argument is symmetric to the case of s_j and is not given here. But then we have now arrived at the sequence S_1 without changing the induced parsing function, which is what was to be proved.

This result has important implications for learning. It shows explicitly how a learning system can arrive at the same (or functionally the same) target state of knowledge in spite of varying external input. Because the system has a rich internal structure, it actually filters the data it receives. In the next few subsections we shall see how this property works in two particular situations: lexical ambiguity, and phrase structure rule acquisition.

Ambiguity, nonterminals, and order effects

The first sentence used for acquisition underscores the "bootstrapping" character of the acquisition procedure: much was assumed about word features and thematic representation so that syntactic decisions would be easier. In this the procedure follows Limber's (1973) approach that acquisition start with a nearly 1-1 correspondence between some known level of representation (here, grounded on conceptual primitives) and the representation to be learned (the syntactic representation). There are three hurdles to this approach: one is the possibility of ambiguously categorized or unknown words; another, the demand for new nonterminal categories; and the third stumbling block is the likelihood of a different order of of input sentences. Since these are all realistic possibilities, let us consider them in turn.

Lexical ambiguity

Many tokens of English are homophonically both nouns and verbs, e.g., *kiss Sally, a kiss*. How is the acquisition procedure to recognize the difference? Again, one can resort to a principle of inference from clear cases. While it is true that many lexical items are ambiguous as to their syntactic category, many are not. For example, names cannot be verbs; *John* and *Fred* never denote actions. And this is not a rare phenomenon. Other presumably frequently occurring nouns, such as *daddy, cat, boy, girl*, always seem to appear as nouns. Similarly, there are tokens that always appear as verbs, at least in input that will be plausibly be available to a child: *eat, give*, and the like. All that is needed for the system to proceed is that there be these clear cases that establish the proper argument structure for verbs in English, e.g., a sentence such as, *Mary ate candy*. This is a particular example of the filtering property of the acquisition procedure. Ambiguous cases lead nowhere, and so the system simply learns from unambiguous examples (where the notions of ambiguity and nonambiguity are of course relativized to the procedure's current rule base). Let us examine some particular cases.

What happens in a sentence with a potentially ambiguous lexical categorization, as in, *Bill kissed Mary*? (We put aside for the moment the tense feature on *kiss*.) *Kiss* could be projected as either an N^{max} or a V^{max}.

Once basic constituent order has been established by a clear example, then repetitions of previously "too complex" examples may now lead to success. (Note that the system does *not* store the example sentences it receives, and so does not have memory for past data.) To consider a simple example here, suppose that basic constituent order is established. Now suppose that the system receives the example *Bill kissed Mary* again after using *John ate candy* to acquire a verb attachment rule. This time around the assignment of the features $-N +V$ to *kiss* meets the constituent structure constraints already acquired, so the acquisition procedure can incrementally construct a new grammar rule to deal with *kiss*. Analyzing *kiss* as a Noun still requires more than one new rule, and so is avoided. Similarly, consider how the system might learn that *kiss* can be a Noun in the string, *I gave Bill a kiss*. Plainly, the system can first learn that *a* unambiguously announces the start of a Noun Phrase, via such examples as, *I ate a candy*. This, plus the knowledge that *give* demands $+N -V$ arguments, is all that is needed. Then, *kiss* could be either a Noun or a Verb, but only the $+N -V$ features are compatible with required context.

Lexical entries are formed by the dual processes of category merger and category splitting, as discussed earlier. A lexical equivalence class contains all items that "behave alike" under the invariance relation established by the parser's analysis. That is, all tokens that enter in the same way into the construction of parse trees are considered behaviorally identical with respect to the operation of the parser, and hence are placed in the same equivalence class. Note that this condition goes beyond the usual notion of simple linear string invariance used to form the equivalence classes of a finite-state automaton, in that the operation of the parser is not just one of simply concatenating strings together.[8] Rather, the parser is constructing equivalence classes according to common lefthand and righthand patterns found in the parser as it analyzes strings, and these patterns can correspond to trees rather than just strings.

To see in detail how lexical entries are built up, consider a simple case, such as the sentence, *Bill ate the candy*, and assume that *candy* is known as $+N -V$ (because it denotes a physical object). In contrast, assume that *the* is not so known—so cannot be an argument or a predicate. Earlier we observed that then we force *the* to be feature compatible with the N^{max} phrase.

What would the lexical entry for *the* look like? One way to write it down would be just as indicated above, that is, as a local context-frame indicating where *the* may be inserted. These insertion frames can be described as "local transformations," as suggested by Chomsky (1965) and formalized by Joshi and Levy(1977). On this view, lexical categorizations are dynamically defined, since they depend on the current state of the procedure's knowledge. We saw an example of this in the acquisition procedure: at first it did not know to split up VP and INFL nodes. Indeed, given different presentation orders of examples, one would expect to find stages where categories where incorrectly collapsed together, as in the example above. This would lead to predictable cases of over-generalization in certain early stages, in just those cases where not enough information has been received to distinguish among classes that are distinguishable in the adult state. This is what happens in the auxiliary verb examples. Importantly, given positive examples illustrat-

---

[8]For simple cases, such as the Inflectional system of English, the parser behaves as if it were just concatenating strings. In this case, the invariance relation reduces to that of right-concatenation. Then one can analyze the operation of the acquisition procedure as an example of finite-state induction. Only in more complex cases do we need substitution of trees. See the previous section and chapter 5.

ing all the relevant machine transitions, the right final stage would still be reached—as we demonstrated above for *do*.

Nonterminal acquisition

In our first example sentence we noted that V^{max} and $INFL^{max}$ were conflated. This is possible just when no evidence has been received that calls for the VP and INFL nodes to be "split," i.e., in just that stage of development where lexicalized proxies for INFL such as *will* or the *ed* inflection are unknown. In $\overline{X}$ terms, this means that the projection of whatever underlying lexical token it is that forms the basis of the phrase has not yet been completely distinguished from other lexical projections. As mentioned earlier, this notion of equivalence corresponds precisely to the notion of "equivalent state" from automata theory. The existence of "abstract" nodes of this sort is not surprising; for example, Aoun (1979) has suggested that discontinuous Verb and NP arguments form an "abstract" VP node in languages such as Arabic. The acquisition procedure claims simply that *all* phrases are on a par here; they are all abstract in Aoun's sense.

How do new nonterminal categories develop? In our examples we showed how INFL split from VP. This happened when evidence accumulated that these were different nodes. It is possible to imagine a more general scenario for the development of nonterminals based on Keil's (1979) analysis of the development of ontological categories in children. (See also chapter 5.) The basic notion is that new categories develop out of old ones via a process of *foliation*, the splitting of old categories into new ones. Apparently, as Keil observes, children first develop a concept by determining what it is *not*, with respect to existing categories. For instance, it might be that a concept of inanimacy could be triggered by noting that there are objects that are not animate. This negative categorization is then "reified", becoming a category in its own right, with ± assignments.

Something very much like this process could go on in the formation of the major phrasal categories. Suppose the system starts with the category *Noun*, corresponding to an object in the physical world (all such objects are nouns, but not all nouns are physical objects). There are two possible ontological categories, +N and −N. Now suppose that a verb like *eat* is identified as *not* an object—hence not a Noun. We enlist this −N element as a new category

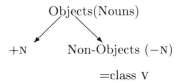

Figure 3.3: New nonterminal classes are formed by foliation

in its own right, splitting it off from the Noun class; call this class V. See figure 3.3.

Now we have two possible class names for ± assignment, the original N class and the new V class. We have four possible new feature classes: the original N and new V class, and the two other possible assignments of feature values, −N −V and +N +N. Figure 3.4 shows the collapsed categories at this point. NOUNS, DETERMINERS, and ADJECTIVES are in the +N −V class, and VERBS, INFL, and ADVERBS in the −N +V group.

We can form a new category by discovering elements that do not fit into any of these two groups. PREPOSITIONS, COMPS, and PARTICLES are neither. Prepositions are good candidates for initiating this split. We reify this class as −N −V. Note that the double + labeling is hard to pin down, since it demands an element that is both object and action.

Just two additional distinctions complete the array of required nonterminal types. We have already assumed that the procedure has access to whether an element gets a thematic role assigned to it or not. Call this feature +A. Applying this new characteristic to the +N −V class, we can split off two new groups: ADJ and DET do not get thematic roles, while NOUNS do. Turning to the −N +V class, INFL can receive a thematic role, while ADV and V cannot. Finally, COMP can get a thematic role, while PREP and PARTICLE cannot.

So far we have seen that each nonterminal category split is grounded via accessible diagnostic criteria—object/nonobject; thematic role/no thematic role. The remaining diacritic is essentially ±predicate (or, in Jackendoff's terminology, ±*Obj*). It is not so clear just how this last distinction may be grounded by positive examples. We leave this question open. Aside from

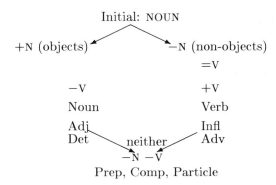

Figure 3.4: Further splitting of nonterminals leads to a prepositional class

this problem, we now have an essentially complete developmental picture of the acquisition of nonterminal categories. It makes quite specific predictions about the *order* of acquisition: the NOUN/VERB distinction is acquired first; then ARGUMENT/NONARGUMENT.

The effect of input order: an example

To conclude the chapter we give an example of invariance of acquisition with respect to the presentation order of example sentences. This example shows how the acquisition procedure "stays on course" even though it may be given sentences that vary from a canonical $\overline{\text{X}}$ order.

Why can't the acquisition system use a sentence such as *Candy, Sally likes* to fix an incorrect COMP-HEAD order? This is possible. Note, though, that by the definition of well-ordering, the correct analysis of *Sally likes candy* depends on setting the packet pointer to COMP at the time *candy* is analyzed. But then, presenting *Candy, Sally likes*, along with the order COMP-HEAD is thereby barred. Still, this solution seems problematic. Since such a sentence order may in fact occur, one must ensure that the onus of sequencing is not left to the external environment.

There is another solution in this case. Suppose we add a weighting system for $\overline{\text{X}}$ acquisition that sets a parameter value only after a certain number of instances have been seen. To this we add a version of Uniqueness: namely, that only one setting of a parameter value is admitted. When conflicting values arise, the acquisition procedure appeals to the most frequently successful parameter setting. In effect, the system will carry along a dual grammar until one version or another wins out. Applying this to our example, we see that if a COMP-HEAD order is adopted, this leads to significant difficulties with "normal" sentences. For instance, *Sally likes candy* cannot be analyzed; nor are prepositional phrases easy to handle. In contrast, the "correct" setting suffers no such problems, as we have seen earlier in this chapter.

It remains to investigate the properties of this method in detail, but at least for the basic parameter settings of the $\overline{\text{X}}$ system this seems like the right solution.

For our last example, suppose the system receives a *wh* question before it has mastered basic sentence order: *Who do you like?* There are several possibilities. First, if *do*'s properties are unknown, then the parse will fail, because the system will not be able to attach *you like* anywhere. So suppose *do* is known as an inflectional element. If *do* is projected as a maximal phrase, then *who* ought to be attached as its SPEC; there is nothing to bar this. But then, *you* can only get attached as COMP, and there is real trouble. The entire analysis will be abandoned. The next chapter tackles the full problem of *wh* sentences.

Interestingly enough, a subject *wh* question such a *who likes John* receives a different treatment. Since this example is string vacuously like an ordinary sentence, it will be treated like one if the *wh* word is taken as an NP. This follows George's (1980) analysis, arrived at on independent grounds. It also follows from the Subset Principle (chapter 5): since the surface language does not demand a movement, none is required.

Chapter 4

Learning Transformations

With the acquisition of basic phrase structure rules behind us, in this chapter we turn to the acquisition of rules that require local movement—via the SWITCH or INSERT LEXICAL ITEM action—or long distance movement—via INSERT TRACE. Because of the filtering property of the acquisition procedure, if a sentence that requires a movement rule appears before its unmoved counterpart, the movement sentence will not be successfully analyzed. Our exposition follows this order of acquisition. We begin with some local movement rules, including Subject-Auxiliary verb inversion, and then proceed to passive and *wh* movement.

4.1 Subject-Auxiliary Verb Inversion

The target rule for Subject-Aux inversion is:

Rule subject-aux-inversion

CYCLIC NODE:	nil
ACTIVE NODE:	X^{max} $-N$ $+V$ $+A$ $+P$-SPEC—HEAD—COMP
BUFFER:	$[+V$ $-N$ *aux* $+$tense$][X^{max}$ $+N$ $-V][-N$ $+V] \rightarrow$
ACTION:	SWITCH

The effect of this rule is to switch the auxiliary verb into its normal declarative position. Then the usual subject attachment rule can apply. It handles examples such as, *Was a meeting scheduled?* or *Will a meeting be scheduled?* Note that inversion is not ordinarily permitted in nonroot environments: *I thought did John schedule a meeting*. Hence the *empty* value for the cyclic node position in the rule trigger.[1]

The acquisition of this rule was outlined in chapter 1. We can now understand it in more detail. Suppose the following example is provided to the acquisition procedure after the INFL rule system has been acquired: *Will Sally kiss John?*. *Will* is assumed marked as $-N$ $-V$ and *tense*. It triggers the creation of an X^{max} marked as such, which becomes the current active node. The packet pointer is set to SPEC. From previous examples such as *The girl will eat candy* the system has set the SPEC as obligatory.

What next? Note that the known grammar rule to attach *will* as HEAD will not work here, because the packet pointer is at SPEC. The acquisition procedure is entered. ATTACH fails because *will* is a HEAD, not a SPEC. Now SWITCH must be attempted. The second buffer cell is a HEAD item, so we must project it as a phrase before the switch is carried out. Let us assume that this occurs without incident, returning an N^{max} to the second buffer cell. Now, SWITCH moves the N^{max} to the first buffer cell and puts *will* in the second. SWITCH must still check to see if any known grammar rules trigger. Yes: the old **attach-subject** rule matches. Recording its success, the system saves this new rule, and annotates the active node with the name of the SWITCH rule just built. This will prove useful as a way to distinguish this sentence from an uninverted one, important for semantic interpretation.

CYCLIC NODE:	nil		
ACTIVE NODE:	X^{max} $-N$ $+V$—SPEC—HEAD—COMP		
BUFFER:	*will* $+$tense	N^{max}	$-N$ $+V$
ACTION:	SWITCH		

---

[1] Baker (1979) observes some exceptions to this general rule, where inversion does not take place in a yes-no question:

How come he's still here?

These examples can probably be accounted for if one assumes that *how come* = an S something like, "why is it that." Then "he is still here" is in an embedded environment, and inversion is prohibited, as observed.

Note that this rule cannot trigger in nonroot environments, since it calls for the cyclic node to be empty. The procedure has built a conservative rule that it will not relax until it sees positive evidence to the contrary.

So far, the inversion rule demands that *will* must be present as the first item in the buffer before a SWITCH can take place. Further examples will generalize this rule. *Could Sally kiss John* sparks a grammar rule with the following pattern:

CYCLIC NODE:	empty

ACTIVE NODE: X^{max} $-N$ $+V$ $+A$ $+P$—SPEC—HEAD—COMP

BUFFER:	*could* +tense	N^{max}	$-N$ $+V$

ACTION:	SWITCH

The generalization protocol now applies. The lefthand and righthand context of the new rule is exactly the same as that for the previous SWITCH, save for the first buffer cell items; so the two tokens are placed in the same equivalence class. *Could* and *will* are defined to be equivalent according to their common behavior under Subject-Aux inversion—a reasonable result. This yields the correct target grammar rule.

What though, about a sentence such as, *Has John kissed Sally? Have* can be either an auxiliary verb or a main verb. At least in this case, the system is lucky, because this sentence can only have an auxiliary verb reading. More difficult are sentences like *Have the students take the exam.* It seems as though the system will take this to be an aux-inversion example as well—not a bad outcome, given the rarity of the main verb version. One way out of this bind is to consult the given thematic representation. In the imperative case, *You* is the (implicit) subject, but this will be incorrectly calculated if *have* is taken as an auxiliary verb. The system would know it had gone astray; the question is what to do about it. One fix would be to split off *have* from the other cases of inversion, as prompted by this special case. It remains to fully investigate the acquisition of "diagnostic" rules of this kind.

Alternatively, one could adopt another analysis of inversion to get around the diagnostic rule itself. Instead of saying that the leading auxiliary verb must be switched into the proper position, one could just leave it in place as an operator whose complement is the entire remainder of the sentence.

> *Did*—[*Sally kiss John*]
> Operator—Operand

This view has some appeal, particularly when one considers embedded sentences where *that* and *for* act like operators governing an entire S. This approach has not been implemented, but it is easy to see how it would work. The leading INFL element would be projected as before. Then, instead of entering the SPEC we would attach the INFL as the HEAD of the maximal projection just created. The remaining elements in the buffer would then be parsed as an S (with appropriate modifications to deal with the lack of tense in some cases). The ambiguity in the categorization of *have* could result in the often-noted *have* main verb-Subject NP inversion found in some dialects. It remains to investigate this approach in detail.

A similar grammar rule can be learned to analyze negative adverbial sentences, such as *Never have I seen such a mess!* We shall discuss this example briefly; the Marcus parser did not have a grammar rule to handle such cases. *Never* is presumably known as a $-N$ $-V$ item, but also as an operator; note that it does not require a SPEC, as shown by examples such as *I have never seen such a mess*. If this analysis is correct, then *never* will be projected to an X^{max}. Unlike the previous examples, though, it does not require a SPEC. Thus when the procedure checks to see if it can attach a SPEC and finds nothing available, it simply advances the packet pointer to HEAD. Now *never* is attached as the HEAD. The remainder of the sentence is analyzed like a Subject-Aux inverted sentence.

4.2   Passive Constructions

The effect of the passive rule is to drop a "dummy" NP node into the first cell of the buffer. Later rules will then attach this NP to its position in the Verb Phrase complement. The purpose of this rule is to analyze a passive sentence as a case of a trace-marked Noun Phrase, with the trace bound to the now displaced NP. For example, in the sentence, *Sally was kissed* the Noun Phrase *Sally* is really the Object argument of the verb *kissed*. The trace serves to express this relationship, indicating the NP's "true position" in argument structure. The target rule for basic passive constructions is as follows.

Rule passive

CYCLIC NODE:	* Rule passive-be
ACTIVE NODE:	X^{max} —N +V +P —A—SPEC—HEAD—COMP
BUFFER:	[*][*][*]
ACTION:	INSERT TRACE

It is crucial that lefthand context be marked with the feature $+ed$ as well as a *be* attachment rule—the pattern for English passives.[2]

The passive rule acquisition illustrates some key points about the acquisition procedure itself. As we shall show, the system's demand that it build only one new rule at a time has the effect of making some passives easier to acquire than others. Passives without explicit agentive *by* phrases are acquired first, if the system has no rules to parse *by* phrases. Similarly, passive verbs that are "nonreversible" are easier—the PATIENT cannot be made the AGENT without turning into semantic nonsense, as in *the eggplant was kissed*. This is because the thematic representation can be used to establish the proper linking of trace to antecedent NP.

Let us turn directly to an example. Given that the rules to handle simple declaratives are known, suppose that a truncated passive is presented to the acquisition procedure: *Sally was kissed*. We also assume, as usual, the availability of a correct thematic representation for this sentence.

The analysis of the first three tokens proceeds normally. The NP *Sally* is attached as the SPEC of the X^{max} created by *was*; *was* is attached as its

---

[2]Note that this pattern will also trigger on NP–*be*–Adj–+*ed* constructions: *The boy was unlearned*. But there is one rule feature that blocks this. The lexical entry for the verb in question must demand a complement NP object. This is precisely what is known, since *unlearned* never appears with a surface direct object: *John unlearned the boy*. Thus, the subcategorization frame for *unlearn* will not include a direct Object, and a drop trace rule will never be built to handle such cases. Rather, *unlearned* will be attached as an adjective, just as in the comparable case, *John was sick*. Alternatively, this distinction could be encoded by means of distinct packet names: a verb that demands a direct object could activate the packet parse-object, but a predicate adjective that cannot take a direct object could activate a different packet. The passive rule is cached in the packet parse-object, and so would never be triggered by the predicate adjective construction. There are other auxiliary verbs in English that allow passive (Baker **1979**), for example, *got*: *John got arrested*. The acquisition procedure also acquires this alternative construction.

HEAD. As usual, the attachment rule labels the X^{max} here. *Kissed* forms a V^{max} and is attached as HEAD. The packet pointer is advanced to COMP. (We have therefore assumed that an ordinary sentence with *kiss* has already been successfully analyzed.)

Now no known rules match. The only grammar rule known to the system with the packet pointer at COMP for a verb such as *kiss* is the rule that attaches objects, and this rule calls for an NP in the first buffer cell. But the end of sentence marker • is in the first buffer cell. Further, this is not an accepting configuration, because the thematic representation has not be satisfied; so the acquisition procedure is invoked.

ATTACH is attempted, but fails, since the end of sentence marker cannot be attached to any node. Note how clear-cut this case is; this is what makes the example easy to process. Likewise, SWITCH has nothing to SWITCH, and so cannot apply. DROP TRACE is next. An empty N^{max} element is inserted into the first position in the buffer. Can any known grammar rule now execute? Yes: the grammar rule for attaching NP Objects is satisfied, since it calls for a V^{max} active node, and a packet pointer to COMP. The new rule is saved; we label the active node V^{max} with the label *passive*. Note that the rule pattern for passive will *include* the triggering predicate be-attach annotation on the X^{max} cyclic node, since that feature was present at the time the new rule was built.

Nothing has been said about how proper thematic assignment is made in this case. *Sally* is actually the argument to the predicate *kissed*, just as *John* is the argument to *sick* in, *John is sick*. How can this be determined? Following current linguistic theory (Reinhart 1976) we assume that every empty NP must be bound to a *c-commanding* antecedent NP. A node X c-commands another node Y if the first branching phrase that dominates X also dominates Y. In addition, the antecedent can be at most one S away from the empty NP; this is the Subjacency constraint. We can now ask what NPs are in fact available to serve as antecedents of an empty NP. In general, because of the structure of the parser, at most one cyclic node can be interposed between the empty NP and its antecedent; more distant nodes are simply not visible. Thus the parser directly simulates the effect of the Subjacency constraint on movement.[3] Further, if we assume that only nodes

---

[3]This is a different approach than that taken in Marcus (1980). Marcus attempted to derive Subjacency from other constraints of the parser. He pointed out, however, that one could directly encode Subjacency in the way just described. For a different derivation

attached to the cyclic node or current active node are accessible, then the c-command constraint is also directly enforced. This occurs because once a node is completely built and attached to some other element on the active node stack, its "inside" becomes opaque. But this material is just the set of non-c-commanding nodes. See Berwick and Weinberg (1984) for further discussion.

In the case at hand, the only possible NP antecedent is *Sally*. Again there is no possibility for confusion. If the trace is bound to this NP, then *Sally* will become the argument to the predicate *kissed*, assuming that the rules that interpret arguments to predicates are held constant.[4] The thematic representation confirms this association. We now have a situation where *Sally* is linked to the argument position of the predicate *kissed*, and that move is confirmed by (assumed given) independent evidence. There is also evidence that *Sally* is not the AGENT of the sentence.

We have the following facts: *Sally* is linked and interpreted correctly as the AFFECTED OBJECT of *kissed*; *Sally* is not the AGENT of the sentence, even though it appears in the proper position to be interpreted as such. This is a case where the system of rules that assign thematic interpretations should be changed. The acquisition of this knowledge has not been the subject of this research, but something can be said here. Just as the failure of grammar rules stimulate the formation of new rules in the operation of the parser, it seems plausible to say that the failure of rules of thematic assignment could be used to prompt the formation of new thematic mappings, or even new thematic categories. This is the case here. *Sally* appears in Logical Subject position, yet is the argument to *kissed*, and is not an AGENT. Suppose we say that when an NP is in a structural Subject position but is an argument to the main predicate of the sentence, then it is the theme of the sentence. Thus *John* is the theme of *John is sick*. Interestingly enough then, in this case

---

of Subjacency from more general parsing principles that follows the acquisition model version, see Berwick and Weinberg (1984).

[4]In this sense, the Projection Principle of Chomsky (1981)—the preservation of lexical restrictions at the surface syntactic level—ensures *semantic transparency*: a slightly abstract syntactic form preserves semantic interpretation. One might, in contrast, take *syntactic* transparency as one's goal, and give up the criterion of semantic transparency. For example, instead of arguing that the surface form *I want to leave* is not what it appears to be on the surface, and is underlyingly *I want I to leave*, one could insist that the surface syntactic form is exactly what it appears to be and instead complicate semantic interpretation. This seems to be a basic thrust of lexical-functional grammar (Bresnan 1982).

one would derive the "concept" of a new thematic role from the structural relations in the passive sentence, plus existing knowledge about very simple thematic roles—in contrast to the approach that would derive a notion of passive constructions from thematic relations alone. Though this is just the sketch of a proposal for the acquisition of thematic role mappings, it appears plausible, at least in this case.[5]

What about full passive sentences? They demand prior ability to analyze Prepositional Phrases. At a minimum this means the ability to recognize *by* as a Preposition. It is not surprising then to discover that children often misanalyze such sentences, particularly in reversible passive sentences where the Subject or Object NP can be legitimately exchanged. (*John was kissed by Sally.*)

The acquisition procedure mimics this developmental staging effect. Suppose that *by*'s features are unknown and there are no grammar rules to handle Prepositional Phrases. Then, even after an NP trace is inserted the resulting pattern does not trigger an attachment rule. The system must wait until it can parse PPs. There will be a tendency for truncated passives to be analyzable before full passives.[6]

Now suppose that PPs can be successfully analyzed and that the system receives a full passive example, *John was kissed by Sally*. At the point where the NP trace should be dropped, the first buffer cell holds *by*, the second *John*, and the third, the end of sentence marker.

If we now assume that *by* sparks creation of an X^{max}, then the PP will be completely built and returned to the first buffer cell, then attached to the V^{max}. The end of sentence marker remains. No rules execute; but the parse is not in an accepting state because the requirements of the verb are not yet satisfied. From here on in, things run as in the last case. The only difference is that now there might be two possible antecedents for the trace: *John* and *Sally*. Here too the parser's design helps us. Again assuming that only attachments directly on the active node stack are visible, then the P^{max} is visible, but not its N^{max} daughter. The N^{max} *Sally* does not c-command

---

[5]Note that if other evidence conspired to make the thematic representation clear, then this too would ease acquisition.

[6]Note that it does not necessarily follow that truncated passives will become analyzable inevitably before full passives, just that it is more likely that this will happen. If a sequence of PP Complement examples is given, then the system could acquire these rules before seeing any passives at all.

the trace. It is not a candidate antecedent, because it is not visible. Thus, as before, we can only link the trace to *John*.[7]

There is one problem with this analysis: it does not force the NP object to be adjacent to the verb. In fact, this requirement is not expressible anywhere so far in the acquisition system. Evidently one must add this constraint to the system, or the system must learn it. This may be done directly, simply by checking whether the V^{max} active node has had any other rules operate on it besides the one that attached the verb. If we do this, then we will block PP attachment before trace insertion. The acquisition procedure will be entered, and trace insertion take place as in the truncated passive case. Looking at the rule generalization protocol for non-ATTACH actions, we see that we have the same lefthand contexts in both truncated and nontruncated cases, so we merge features. The first grammar rule of the to-be-merged pair has an end of sentence marker in its first buffer cell; the second rule holds a P^{max}; the intersection is a wild card predicate. An empty buffer cell and end of sentence marker likewise intersect to a wild card predicate; the third buffer cell stays *empty* since we have not yet seen examples where this was filled. Additional positive examples would generalize this position. This is just about the desired target.

One final remark. An important question to ask is why, having dropped an NP trace, the system does not immediately fire a passive rule once again. For the input buffer now matches once again the pattern of the passive rule just acquired. The annotation of the active node does not help here, so the passive rule will just execute again. Left unchecked, the machine would loop endlessly. The solution to this problem lies in the ordering of grammar rules. Remember that there is a default priority ordering of grammar rules: if two rules in the same packet match the features of the current machine state, then the most specific rule gets priority. In the case at hand, there is another rule that can execute, namely, the rule **attach-object**. But this rule demands a more specific pattern match of the input buffer: [NP][*][*]. This rule therefore has priority over the passive rule, attaching the NP trace. Now the buffer has the end marker ● in its first cell, and the V^{max} has been completely built (all its arguments are present), so it is dropped into the input buffer. In this case, looping is blocked.

---

[7]Note again that if *by* somehow remains unanalyzed then invisibility does not apply. Then the NP after *by* could be taken, incorrectly, as the Object of the verb. This seems to happen with children.

4.3   Missing Subject Sentences

This section covers the acquisition of complement sentences with "missing"
Subjects, e.g., *I want to go, I expected to go*. Here are the basic types: (i) verbs
with infinitival complements with or without overt subjects, such as *want* (*I
want Bill to win*; *I want to win*); (ii) verbs with infinitival complements not
allowing overt subjects, such as *try* (*I tried to win*); *I tried Bill to win*; (iii)
verbs with tensed complements, allowing only overt subjects, such as *believe*
(*I believe that Bill should win*); (iv) verbs allowing both infinitival and tensed
complements, such as *know* (*I know Bill to be a fool*; *I know that Bill is a
fool*); (v) verbs taking both NP and sentential complements, the complement
being inflected or not, and with a possibly missing subject if uninflected, such
as *persuade* (*I persuaded Bill to win*; *I persuaded Bill that he should win*).
The Marcus parser had separate rules for each of these verb types. The
acquisition procedure learns them all.

To see how these constructions may be acquired, suppose that *want* has
been analyzed as *want—X*, where X is an argument.[8]   Now suppose the
system gets the sentence, *I want to go*.

Again the parse proceeds without incident until the COMP portion of the
V^{max} is entered. The buffer holds the lexical items *to*, *go*, and •. Following
the node creation protocol, we first project *to* as an X^{max} and set its packet
pointer to SPEC. The ambiguity of *to* is resolved in this case by the following
$-N +V$ element *go*. *To* heads an $INFL^{max}$.

Because the HEAD *to* is first in the buffer but the packet pointer is at
SPEC, no grammar rules execute and the acquisition procedure is entered.
ATTACH fails; SWITCH fails if *go* (as a maximal projection) is placed first.
We arrive finally at INSERT TRACE. It succeeds (assuming that full embedded
sentences have been previously analyzed; here is evidently a difference with
child acquisition). The rule pattern is important to note here:

---

[8]It has been observed that sentences such as *I want to go* seem to be produced by children
before corresponding sentences with full lexical NPs, e.g., *I want Bill to go*. This would
seem to run counter to the assumption that *I want Bill to go* is analyzable before *I want
to go*. However, the situation is quite complex here, because of the uncertain status of
complements in *want–X* constructions. It could be that *to go* is an X^{max} of uncertain
categorial status, with a kind of quasi-NP status—it is *something* that is wanted, but not
a physical object, rather, a state of affairs. Note that propositions have this quasi-NP
status as well. If this is so, then *to go* would simply be analyzed as an X^{max} with an
ill-defined categorial identity, but one at least fulfilling the subcategorization demand
that *want* have some kind of argument complement.

	Rule insert-want-NP
CYCLIC NODE:	X^{max}—Rule attach-want
ACTIVE NODE:	X^{max}
	$-N +V$—SPEC—HEAD—COMP
BUFFER:	$[to -N +V][go -N +V -tense][$ • $]$
ACTION:	INSERT TRACE

To is in the first buffer cell, and a verb without tense in the second. This means that tensed forms, e.g., *I wanted should go*, are blocked. Binding is again trivial, since there is no alternative besides *I*.[9]

The insertion rule is limited to verbs in the same class as *want* by the annotation on the left context. If some other verb, in another class say, *kiss*, had been processed, then there would be no such annotation and the insertion rule would not execute, as desired. In a sense this is just good fortune, though. If the current cyclic node were really the S, not the S̄, then this information would be invisible at the time it is needed. Evidently we must modify the annotation procedure generally so that the cyclic node is labeled with the main predicate of the sentence. This is not so outlandish an idea, if we consider the saturation constraint on complete sentences to involve fixing both the predicates and arguments for that sentence. Then the annotation that one predicate had been encountered rather than another would be visible in the next lower domain via the cyclic node.

Turning from computer model to people, why should children be able to produce *John wants to go* before they can produce *I want Bill to go*? As always, the evidence is difficult to assess, but in part it seems as if the thematic structure of *I want to go* is relatively clearcut, compared to forms with an explicit lexical NP, such as *I want Bill to go*. Note that children could misinterpret sentences with an explicit lexical NP: *Bill* might be parsed as the Object NP, if, for some reason, the elements in the input buffer are neglected. Speculating, it could well be that attentional deficits limit the input buffer that children have, so that the third element, *go*, is not even seen. Since an Object NP is a legitimate alternative choice, confusion can arise.

---

[9] We have ignored here any distinction between empty NP elements—that is, between trace and PRO. Note that because lexical NPs are allowed as the subject of *to go* that the element in question must actually be a PRO, not trace; the antecedent NP is also in a position with a real thematic role, as is never the case with antecedents of NP traces.

In contrast, a sentence without a lexical NP cannot be so misinterpreted; the complement *to go* cannot be an Object NP. Thus the sentence with a missing embedded Subject is actually "simpler" according to the criterion of syntactic-semantic correspondence. It is this transparency that could explain the earlier appearance of missing Subject complement sentences.

Once examples such as *I want to go* have been successfully parsed, other verb types will now be analyzable. The details show how verb classes may be split. Consider the example, *I tried to go*. So far, *want* and *try* have been placed in the same equivalence classes. Both take NP arguments: *I want the candy/ I tried the candy*. Therefore, the analysis of *I tried to leave* will follow that of *I want to leave*: a dummy NP will be inserted as the Subject of the embedded clause following *try*.

There is a difference between *want* and *try* of course, since the former verb, but not the latter, allows a lexical NP in its embedded S: *I want Bill to win* vs. **I tried Bill to win*. Given the analysis so far, if the system collapsed these two verbs together permanently it would erroneously admit a sentence such as *I tried Bill to win*, just as if it were analyzing *want*.

This distinction *can* be captured if we are willing to use the principle that unless positive evidence appears indicating otherwise, the system assumes that a particular construction cannot be used. Let us see just how this would work. First, we must somehow limit the evidence to be used, or otherwise the system might have to wait forever for complex positive examples. In the current model this limit is expressed by the local pattern radius of the nodestack and buffer: once all three-cell buffer patterns and nodestack combinations have been seen—and these are finite in number—then acquisition ends; nothing more can be learned. This is exactly analogous to Wexler and Culicover's (1980) model of language learning from a finite (Degree 2) data sample; see chapter 7.

There is still no way for the system to know even that a particular finite parser ID has not been seen, but one can at least say that *if* a particular construction within this finite complexity bound has not been encountered *then* it may be assumed not to occur. This is what we will say here. The system could indeed analyze a verb *try** that takes an overt lexical NP as the Subject of its embedded complement, but it never sees such a verb. Likewise, it never sees *try* with a tensed embedded complement, and so never posits one.

Rule insert-try-NP

CYCLIC NODE:	X^{max} $-N$ $+V$—Rule attach-try
ACTIVE NODE:	X^{max}

$$\downarrow$$
$$-N\ +V\text{—SPEC—HEAD—COMP}$$

BUFFER:	$[to\ -N\ +V\ +A\ +P][-N\ +V\ +P\ -A\ -tense][\quad *\quad]$
ACTION:	INSERT TRACE

The lexical items *want* and *try*, then, are known to be different, since the example *I want Bill to win* is seen, but not **I tried Bill to win*. The two words have different possible suffixes: the first allows an $+N$ $-V$ item, then $-N$ $+V$ $+A$ $+P$, then $-N$ $+V$ $+P$ $-A$; the second does not admit this possibility. This indicates that the equivalence class that held both *want* and *try* should be split, as per step 5c of the acquisition procedure. If we annotate the S ($INFL^{max}$) node as suggested with the name of a verb class, then the system's rule to insert an empty category for *I want to win* will not trigger for *try*, as desired.

Let us move on to verbs such as *know*. These do not allow empty Subjects in their complement clauses. Again, this difference is picked up by a positive example: the system sees *I know John should go* but not *I know to go*. The grammar rules building the complement here will all mention a tensed lexical item, blocking the missing Subject case. No trace insertion rule will fire here; see chapter 3. Similarly, *I know John to be a fool* will attach *John* as a Subject NP, moving the packet pointer to HEAD and blocking trace insertion.

Finally, we arrive at "control" verbs such as *promise* and *persuade*. These add two new twists. Not only do these verbs take two arguments, the second a sentential complement with a possibly missing Subject, but there is a question as to what controls the missing Subject position, the matrix Subject or Object.

Consider a sentence such as *I persuaded John to leave*. The N^{max} *John* will be created as before, then returned the first buffer cell. This time, the attempted ATTACH by a newly-minted grammar rule of the N^{max} to the V^{max} *persuade* will succeed, because the thematic representation indicates that one of the arguments to the verb is in fact *John*. With *John* attached, the parser is left with *to* in the first buffer cell, and *leave* in the second.

Now things are exactly like the case of *I want to leave*. *To* will project an x^{max} with an obligatory SPEC. The *want*-type grammar rule will execute, inserting an empty NP into the first buffer cell. The key difference is how to figure out the binding of this NP. There are two possibilities accessible on the active node stack: the Subject *I* and the Object *John*. Which should be selected? There is no way to tell unless one has access to some representation of thematic structure that indicates this detail. If this level of detail is not available, then one would expect a resort to some kind of heuristic strategy. One good candidate is to pick the most recently accessible NP on the stack; we could of course add the constraint that this NP be compatible with any selectional constraints as the Subject of the embedded sentence. This is C. Chomsky's Minimal Distance Principle (1969). As modified here, this heuristic predicts that the Object NP will be taken as the controller of the embedded sentence, until other evidence is provided. Note that it does not say that the *stringwise* nearest NP to the empty position will be selected. Rather, the nearest NP *on the active node stack* will be chosen. For example, in the sentence, *I persuaded the boy that John met to leave, the boy* will be the "nearest" NP to the controlled position, because *John* will not be directly attached to an active node stack element, and hence will not be accessible.

As Chomsky (1969) discusses, verbs such as *promise* or *ask* violate this distance principle. The system must learn that the nearest NP does not control the missing subject in these cases. This seems difficult without access to an independently derived representation of the thematic structure of such sentences.[10] Great difficulty is expected with these verbs, again a natural result.

Finally, consider verbs that take *that* complements. Simple *that* complements were discussed earlier: *I believe that John kissed Sally* will be parsed just like *I know that John kissed Sally*. Thus *believe* and *know* will be placed in the same lexical class.[11] If *that* is not present, then a rule without it will also be acquired. The only difference is that no *that* is projected as a full

---

[10] *Promise* poses an additional challenge. It allows an indirect object: *I promised George a candy to eat*. Now *George* again controls the missing complement Subject, and this may even be ambiguous given another verb in the embedded sentence: *I promised George a reason to leave* can mean either *I to leave* or *George to leave*. The system can of course encode these different patterns, since the left context recording of what attachment rules have been run will serve to distinguish these cases. But this is plainly just a descriptive solution.

[11] As we will discuss below, this means that the default (unmarked) assumption is to exclude cases such as, *John believes Sally to be a fool*, that is, that $\bar{s}$ deletion is not permitted

phrase. Instead, only an S is created, by the INFL and NP present in the input. [12]

Now suppose the system gets an example such as, *John is believed to be home*, a combination of passive plus an embedded infinitival sentence. The passive rule will trigger on this example, dropping a trace into the buffer after *believed*. Now we have exactly the case of *John believes Bill to be home* or *John knows Bill to be home*. Assuming that sentence can be analyzed, then so will this sentence. Unfortunately, if this is so, then a sentence such as *John believes to be wrong* should also be analyzable. After all, we need only drop a trace and bind it to *John* in this situation. Such examples cause difficulties because the current model does not distinguish between two types of empty categories, *trace* and PRO. In current theory, these two types differ in their occurrence. Trace must be *governed*, while PRO may be ungoverned. What this boils down to is that traces are inserted after passives. PROs, on the other hand, can appear in so-called ungoverned positions, basically the Subject positions of infinitivals (except where these infinitival positions are actually governed, as with *believe*, because then there is only an S there, not an S̄). For our problem example, no trace can be inserted after *believes*, because this position would ultimately have to receive Case (as a lexical NP would) and this is impossible for a trace. So the empty position must be a PRO, but this too is impossible, since the position is governed. Note that the current system does not abide by the *trace*–PRO distinction and so cannot implement this solution. This remains a solution for the future.

We have now acquired a verb typology close to that of the original Marcus parser. A substantial portion of the complement structure of English Verb Phrases has been acquired. "Small clause" constructions have not been tackled (e.g., *I like John drunk*). Acquired constructions include *that* Complements, deleted *that* Complements, the difference between *try*, *believe*, and *want*, and some simple control verbs (*promise* and *persuade*). A summary of the Marcus verb typology follows.

---

until evidence is received to indicate otherwise. This ordering of hypotheses follows the Subset Principle; see chapter 6.

[12] This gives the *effect* of so-called S̄ deletion. That is, these verbs may appear without a full clause, though they need not. Note that we have *It is likely that John is wrong/It is probable that John is wrong; John is likely to be wrong/ *John is probable to be wrong*, so *probable* does not take a plain S complement. This may show up: *It is likely John is wrong* vs. *It is probable John is wrong*.

1. If the verb is passive then activate **passive** and run passive rule;

2. If the verb can take an infinitive-object, then:

   (a) If the verb can take an infinitive without *to*,
       then activate **to-less-infinitive**;

   (b) If the verb can take an infinitive without *to be*,
       then activate **to-be-less-infinitive**;

   (c) If the verb takes 2 objects, one an infinitive (e.g., *persuade*)
       then activate **2-object-infinitive-object**;
       else activate **infinitive-complement**;

   (d) If the verb takes an infinitive object without a subject (e.g., *want*),
       then activate **subject-less-infinitive-complement**;
       else if the verb takes a delta subject (e.g., *seem*)
       then activate **no-subject**;

3. If the verb takes a *that*-complement,
   then activate **that-comp**.

Grammar rules to handle each of these categories have been acquired, aside from categories 2(a) and 2(b). Passives were dealt with in the previous section. *To* infinitives with and without Subjects, encompassing three different classes of verbs—the *try* type, the *want* type, and the *believe* type— have been acquired. The second half of clause 2(c) and clause 2(d) of the typology above are meant to handle these cases. Verbs that take NP–S complements, e.g., *persuade*, have also been acquired; these fall under the first part of clause 2(c). *That* complements have been acquired, and are handled by clause 3 of the taxonomy.

An incremental acquisition procedure that "gives up" if a construction is too complex can be used to suggest (if not explain) certain developmental orderings in the acquisition of these sentence types. For instance, the analysis of embedded S's with empty Subjects could well be easier than that of S's with full lexical NP's because of a reduced possibility of confusion with the NP Object case, as we saw in the *I want to go–I want Bill to go* examples. This same line of argument also shows that Object embedded S's and relative clauses will have a tendency to appear before Subject embedded S's (*To leave home is upsetting*) or Subject relative clauses (*The guy John likes is leaving home*), as is apparently the case. In the context of the acquisition procedure, the reason for this is that Object embedded S's and relatives have a clear-cut S boundary, namely the end of sentence marker, that Subject S's do not have. The additional difficulty of establishing the boundary between the end of the Subject S and the root S means that these sentence types will be fixed only after the easier Object cases are successfully analyzed.

Gaps remain. One is how to deal with a PRO that is arbitrary in reference. In the current system all empty elements have been required to have antecedents. The system cannot handle cases where there a phonologically empty NP is "arbitrary" in reference, as in, *To go home would be foolish.* Therefore, these *to*-infinitives in Subject position cannot be acquired.

Finally, so-called "small clauses" have not been considered, constructions such as, *I think Bill a fool* or *John seems unhappy.* In Marcus's parser, these constructions were analyzed by inserting a *to be* into the input buffer, as appropriate.

4.4 Simple *Wh* Questions

We now turn to *wh*-questions. There are some simple examples to deal with first. The "easiest" cases of *wh*-constructions are those that already fall under the core Operator-Operand structure acquired in the analysis of $\bar{\text{S}}$s. Consider for example:

> *Why—did John kiss Sally?*
> Opr—Operand
> WH—S

> *How—did John kiss Sally?*
> Opr—Operand
> WH—S

If sentences such as *I know why John kissed Sally* are encountered after the successful analysis of sentences such as, *I know that John kissed Sally*, then *know* will already be established as taking a Propositional Complement. *Why* will be analyzed just like *that* for this particular verb; it will be projected as an X^{max}. The packet pointer will be set to HEAD. Next, *why* will be attached as the head, and the packet pointer advanced to COMP. Note that somehow it must be known that the *wh* unit is not yet completed—presumably, its operator status tells us that. Let us suppose that this is what is given, as part of the thematic representation. If this important hurdle can be crossed, then the remainder of the sentence will be parsed like any other embedded sentence. As per our modification of the last section, the lefthand context at the time *why* is projected as an X^{max} includes a record of the verb, so that the parser can distinguish between verbs that take *why* as complements (*I wonder why John left*; **I wonder that John left*) vs. those that do not (**I believe why John left*).

Similarly, consider *Why did John leave*. Here too, no binding is required. This makes the analysis of these sentences quite easy. As we shall see in more detail just below, matters are different in sentences demanding a bound *wh* trace: *What did John eat?*. Here there is an additional demand in locating the antecedent of the dummy NP inserted after the verb *eat*. This will be at least as hard as the passive construction.

Given this analysis, one would expect that the very first *wh* constructions to be acquired would behave as if they were purely extensions to the $\overline{X}$ system, introduced via a rule something like, $\overline{S} \rightarrow wh$ S.[13]

In fact, Labov and Labov (1976), in an exhaustive analysis of their daughter's use of *wh* questions, observe something like this. The earliest *wh* forms act as if they were introduced via this phrase structure rule. The model prediction is confirmed.

We now return to simple *wh* questions where the *wh* element corresponds to an item displaced from its canonical argument position: *Who will John kiss*, or *Who kissed John*.

Let us suppose, as argued above, that the straightforward *wh* forms have already been acquired, so that *wh* is known to head an X^{max}. What happens with *Who did Sally kiss?* Assuming that sentences such as *Why did Sally kiss John* can already be parsed, then we may presume that *who* is recognized as a *wh* element, just like *why*. Note that again the trigger here is basically phonological, grounded on the similarity between *why* and *who*; in this respect, it is similar to the dual use of *for* as Preposition and Complementizer. In any case, the *wh* element will be attached and the trailing S analyzed, just as in the simpler *Why did Sally kiss John*. The $\overline{S}$ node heading

---

[13]Note that this rule is presented purely for illustrative purposes; it need not be explicitly represented.

the entire tree will be annotated $+wh$, as usual, corresponding to the name of the grammar rule that attaches the *wh* element to the $\bar{\text{S}}$.

With an auxiliary verb in the first buffer cell and an NP in the second, the stage is nearly set for a replay of the inversion rule. Indeed, given our representation of left context, it is the same. Since the cyclic node is the first NP or S above the current active node, this does not include the $\bar{\text{S}}$. Thus the cyclic node is still empty, signifying a root environment. The auxiliary inversion rule triggers, placing the Subject NP and the auxiliary verb in proper sequence.

When the parse reaches the analysis of the Complement of the verb *kiss*, then, just as in the case of passives, analysis halts because the buffer now holds just the end of sentence marker •, and there is no grammar rule that matches the current parser state.[14]

The acquisition procedure is entered. ATTACH and SWITCH both fail, for the obvious reasons. INSERT TRACE is then tried. It succeeds, since the Attach-object grammar rule can execute after the INSERT TRACE is performed. The new rule is saved.

Rule wh-insert

CYCLIC NODE:	nil
ACTIVE NODE:	X^{max}
	$-\text{N} +\text{V} +\text{P} -\text{A}\text{---SPEC---HEAD---C}\overset{\downarrow}{\text{O}}\text{MP}$
BUFFER:	$[-\text{N} +\text{V}][\;\;*\;\;][\;\;*\;\;]$
ACTION:	INSERT TRACE

This is not quite right, however, because it will erroneously trigger on *Did Sue kiss*. What we need is some record that the *wh* rule has applied. A natural suggestion is that the left context of a rule contains the entire stack domain up to the current $\bar{\text{S}}$, not just the active node and cyclic node. If this alteration is made, then the left context of the rule's trigger has a cyclic node annotated with wh-insert. This will become a signal for the INSERT TRACE rule to fire.[15]

---

[14]Recall that the passive rule demands the features $+be$ and *en*, but these are not present here.

[15]This approach to *wh* movement is quite different from Marcus's; he relied on a separate mechanism to bind *wh* traces, like a separate memory cell.

What about the binding of this empty NP? This is easy to deduce in a simple sentence. The only possibilities on the active node stack are the *wh* itself or the Subject NP. The Subject NP is nearest, but violates the thematic representation: we would then have something like *John eat John*. The only other possibility is the *wh* itself.[16] In sum, these *wh* sentences should appear after those like *Why did Sue kiss John*. This still leaves open the possibility that sentences like *Who likes John* are treated as simple Subject NP sentences, if the *wh* is taken as if it were a straight NP (see George 1980).

Relative clauses may now be tackled. Suppose we have an object relative clause such as, *I know the boy that Sue likes*. It is easy to see that by the time *who* is encountered, the packet pointer for the N^{max} will be at COMP. According to the thematic representation, the N^{max} is not complete, however, so it will not be dropped. Instead, *that Sue likes* will parsed just as an embedded sentence. At the time of binding, *Sue* and *the boy* will be accessible, *Sue* because it is attached to the current active node and *the boy* because it is the cyclic node. *Sue* cannot be the antecedent (then it would receive two thematic roles; it would also violate the given thematic representation). *The boy* is the remaining choice. Finally, the completed complement will be dropped into the buffer (completion now signalled by the end of sentence marker) and attached as the COMP of the NP.

What of a subject relative clause, such as *The boy who likes John is tall*? Here, the end of sentence marker does not unambiguously announce the completion of the NP. At the time we must attach *John* as the object of *likes*, there is a competing operation, namely the rule to start a new sentence *John likes*. While we may suppose that we can just let the grammar rule trigger before starting a new maximal projection (the Minimal Attachment strategy again), the lack of a clear phrase boundary may contribute to a processing difficulty with such sentences. The prediction is that these kinds of relative clauses will be acquired later than their object cousins.

We conclude this section with some brief remarks on the acquisition of rules to parse more complex *wh* questions, such as, *What did John believe that Mary liked*. These illustrate some large inadequacies in the current model. We assume a successive cyclic analysis of such sentences, with an intermediate trace in the complementizer position of the embedded clause bound to the

---

[16]This modification to the left context of the acquisition procedure has not been implemented.

wh and in turn binding the object position in the second embedded sentence.

The acquisition procedure cannot handle these cases because they demand a trace in the Complementizer position even when it is filled by, e.g., *that*. Unfortunately, the system is not allowed to adjoin a trace to an already-filled tree position. Several actions could take place by the time *Mary* is analyzed as a complete NP. The NP could either be attached as the object of *believe*; a *wh* trace could be inserted; or else a new sentence could be created. The problem is that the object attachment rule seems to take priority. If it is blocked by a thematic representation, then if the sentence were *Who does John believe Mary likes*, at least the trace insertion rule could run. Note that the *wh* trace cannot be attached as the object of *believe*, since the thematic representation forbids it. Now the parse will proceed as with a matrix *wh* sentence. A new trace will get inserted after *liked*, and bound to the previous *wh* (the only element visible in the active node stack, since the current active node will be VP and the next cyclic node the S of the embedded sentence). The problem is that this trick will not work if *that* is present. It remains to add a more general *wh* acquisition mechanism.

4.5   Some Miscellaneous Rules

To conclude the chapter, we shall briefly review a potpourri of other sentence types that can be acquired: *there* insertion; topicalization; imperatives; and diagnostic rules. (See chapter 6 for discussion of dative alternation.)

There insertion

Sentences with existential *there* are not difficult to learn to parse, but their exact analysis is harder to come by. For our purposes here, the key point about *there* is that it behaves like an NP. It enters into agreement with its Verb and Object and appears in NP positions: *There was a riot on Tuesday*; **There were a riot on Tuesday*.

One way this could come about is by phonological triggering, namely, the use of *there* as an NP in other contexts. This is the same process that we have seen in other examples, such as the introduction of *for* as a general operator. What could the trigger be in this case? Another use of *there* is demonstrative or presentational: There *is a lion* (compare That *is a lion*); *A lion is over there.*

Although these uses of *there* are different, from the standpoint of acquisition they are intimately related. Demonstrative *there* picks out a spatiotemporal location and so has a semantic grounding as a substantive thing. Thus it is natural to suppose that this *there* has the features +N −V. An example such as *The lion is over there* will prompt the creation of grammar rules to parse *there* as the HEAD of an NP. Given this analysis, a demonstrative *there* in Subject position would also be analyzed as an NP. How would agreement work? Nothing has been said so far about Subject-Verb agreement, but however that process works, in copulative sentences the Object forces agreement as well: *John is a nice guy* but not *John and Bill are a nice guy.* Thus one could simply use the features of the Object NP to force agreement, at least in these cases.

It is this analysis of demonstrative *there* that is assumed to pave the way for existential *there*. Since the acquisition procedure does not really know about the *semantic* interpretation of the structures it builds, it will simply plunge ahead and parse *There was a riot* just like a demonstrative. Agreement will be required on account of the copulative, enforced by whatever mechanism is used in other cases of copulatives. (Perhaps this mechanism is something like the device of indexing, but we remain neutral on the details.)[17]

In short then, the analysis of *there* sentences is another case where it seems likely that the acquisition of semantically clear examples precedes the analysis of grammaticalized, more syntactically-based constructions of the same type.

Topicalization

Topicalizations are constructions such as *Beans, I hate.* Their analysis was covered earlier in chapter 3 when we pointed out that such topicalized sentences are not properly parsed until basic sentence order is established. What happens then? We assume that the leading NP is completely analyzed by other rules and returned to the buffer. Next, the NP beginning in the second buffer cell is built and returned to the second buffer cell.

---

[17]Cases of apparent rightward movement—extraposition and the like—are not covered here: *There was believed to be a riot* or *It was likely* . . .

With nothing in the active node stack, the parse grinds to a halt. No acquisition action succeeds. Following the acquisition procedure, the system tries to see if a maximal projection can be built from the third buffer cell. Applied to our sentence, *hate* in the third buffer cell prompts the formation of a V^{max}. Now *beans* can be attached as the SPEC of this phrase; then *I* will be attached as well, since there is nothing blocking it. Note that this is not the right syntactic analysis, but it is the best that can be done.[18] Finally, the verb will be analyzed. At this point, with only the end of sentence marker in the buffer and the verb demanding an object, a trace will be inserted; this will require a new grammar rule (since the passive rule triggers on a different morphology). Note that this new rule will have a different and more particular left context pattern than the normal sentence rule: the V^{max} will be annotated both with a subject attachment rule and the topic attachment. Binding of the trace will be more difficult than in a simple passive case, since there are two accessible candidates, the Subject NP and the topicalized NP. If we assume that candidates are checked off as soon as their thematic role is fixed, then the Subject NP may be bypassed and the topicalized NP unambiguously selected.

Imperatives

The acquisition procedure can acquire a grammar rule to deal with imperatives. In an imperative, *you* is evidently inserted as the Subject NP of a tenseless Sentence:

> *Be quiet* → *You be quiet*
> *Go home* → *You go home*

Tag questions show that it is indeed *you* that is inserted: *Be quiet, won't you?* Tenseless sentences ordinarily do not allow lexical NP's to surface phonologically: *John is quiet* but **John be quiet*. This raises a problem for the acquisition procedure. Its rules must reject tenseless main sentences. That is, it must *not* in general be able to parse, ** You be good*.[19]

---

[18]The alternative is to insist that all sentences be of the form, COMP–NP–INFL–VP, and then attach *beans* to the COMP position.

[19]This may not be quite right, since this is a common dialect variation: *You be good while I'm gone, now!*

Marcus's grammar has this problem. It blithely parses tenseless root sentences, e.g., *I take a book* or *I be happy*, since it is designed to parse *Take a book* by inserting *you* and then proceeding just as if the sentence were a simple declarative. The conclusion is that there must be some way to encode a difference between a parse that inserts a *you* into the buffer and one that has *you* or another lexical NP presented to it via ordinary means. Since this constraint is apparently applied at a level of phonological representation—it determines whether an NP can be "pronounced" or not— then it is reasonable to suppose that a designated lexical item inserted *after* phonological analysis will not be subject to the same constraint. That is, since *you* is apparently inserted into the input buffer *after* phonological processing, it is not constrained to appear in a tensed (root) clause, as it would be if it were a phonological word.

Here is how the acquisition procedure handles this difference. Suppose it receives an imperative sentence, *Be good*. As usual, we assume that a thematic representation is supplied, with *you* as the theme. *Be* is projected as a V^{max}. No specifier is present, yet the argument structure of the verb demands one. The acquisition procedure fails on ATTACH, then tries SWITCH. This too fails, since there is only the adjective *good* in the second buffer cell.[20] Now we come to INSERT LEXICAL ITEM (ordered here since it allows the next broadest range of possibilities). We assume a small finite list of items to try. Let us say it includes *of*, *to be*, *you*. The first two fail, since no attachment can work after they are inserted. But the last insertion, *you* (as an N^{max}) does succeed, since the subject attachment rule can now deal with *you*.

Proceeding with the parse, the system must now attach *be* as the HEAD of the V^{max}. There is no rule to do this, since all previous cases either dealt with a tensed AUX of some kind or a tensed main verb, but *be* has no tense. The grammar rules that parse inflections include a *be* attachment rule, but it demands attachment as the complement of some other inflectional element (as in *John will be good*). The acquisition procedure is entered, and builds a new ATTACH rule for this case. Note crucially that the left pattern context of this rule will include the INSERT YOU annotation, by convention. Thus the tenseless verb will be allowed only when *you* has been inserted. The rule

---

Perhaps this is handled via an implicit modal: *You be good* is actually *You will be good*—as indicated by the tag question *Be good, won't you?*

[20]The thematic representation would also signal failure in cases where an object NP follows the verb, as in *Take a hike*.

to attach *be* as a tenseless main verb in a matrix sentence cannot execute otherwise. This blocks the analysis of *You be good* as a normal declarative sentence.

Diagnostic rules

In Marcus's grammar, diagnostic rules were those used to distinguish between minimal pairs such as:

> *Have the students take the exam*
> *Have the students taken the exam?*

For the most part, the job of these rules is to decide between alternative categorizations of lexical items—in the case above, between *have* as a main verb and *have* as an auxiliary verb.[21]

Can diagnostic rules be acquired? At least in this simple case, the notion of "diagnostic rule" can be replaced by invoking the ordering principle presented earlier that specific rules should execute before general rules. Suppose that the sentence, *Have the students taken the exam?* is encountered. As usual, *have* will trigger the creation of an X^{max} item, with features $-N$ $+V$ and (in this case) both tense or tenseless corresponding to its dual use as either a main verb or an auxiliary verb.

At this point the system will be parsing the Specifier of the X^{max}, and the buffer will hold the items *Have*, *the*, and *students*, respectively. Assume that the NP *the students* is parsed correctly. The third buffer cell holds the verb *taken*. Two rules now match this buffer: both the imperative rule and the switch rule. However, the buffer pattern for imperative is more general than that for SWITCH, since it calls only for a tenseless verb in the first buffer cell, while the inversion rule calls for an NP in the second cell and a tensed verb in the third. Therefore, by the protocol (derived from the Subset Principle) that specific rules should execute before general rules, the rule will get first crack at this example. In this case, it succeeds. We can use the features of the grammar rule to coerce *have* to its desired categorization as an auxiliary verb.

---

[21]Diagnostic rules could also be used to determine alternative constituent attachments. Note that the determination of category labeling and constituent attachment *exhausts* what must be done for correct parsing, so that the notion of a "diagnostic rule" is not a very precise one.

In contrast, if the sentence begins *Have the students take* then the switch rule will again be attempted first, but will fail. Now the system will attempt to match the imperative rule, and succeeds, inserting *you* as required. Thus, in this case a principle derived on grounds of learnability—the execution of specific before general rules—also solves a problem of rule ordering in parsing.

It remains to be seen whether *all* diagnostic rules can be acquired in this way. Note that diagnostic rules are all specific grammar rules that generally refer to features of the item filling the third buffer cell. Therefore, they certainly fall under the specific-before-general rule protocol.

4.6 Summary of Part I

Part I has covered much ground. It is worthwhile reviewing what has been accomplished before proceeding to the formal analysis of acquisition, the subject of Part II (chapters 5, 6, and 7).

The main aim of chapter 2 was to describe an acquisition procedure based on an online parsing model. The first sections of this chapter discussed the the assumptions behind the model, and the changes made to Marcus's original parsing procedure in order to make it more amenable as an acquisition model. These changes include: (1) the elimination of explicit rules for labeling nodes, using a "percolation" principle; (2) the removal of explicit packet activation and deactivation rules and their replacement by an automatic instantiation of $\overline{\text{X}}$ schemas; (3) the use of complex feature bundles to label nonterminal nodes, rather than standard category labels such as VP, NP, and the like; (4) the elimination of all but four actions.

The next two chapters discussed the acquisition of base phrase structure rules and the acquisition of grammar rules to handle displaced constituents. The knowledge so acquired is in the form of lexical equivalence classes, items that "behave alike" with respect to parsing contexts. No *explicit* system of context-free rewrite rules is acquired. Lexical category ambiguities, it should be noted, have a natural place within this framework; several examples were presented to show that early on a lexical item may be almost completely unknown in its features, and yet can be analyzed in a "topdown" fashion so as to establish its identity. The acquisition procedure also shows how semantic information can be usefully integrated into the acquisition of syntactic knowledge.

The movement-type rules acquired include rules to handle Auxiliary inversion, passives, missing Subjects in embedded clauses, and simple *wh* movements. Many constructions have *not* been acquired. Some demand simple extensions to the current acquisition procedure; these have been hand simulated, and include imperatives and one or two diagnostic rules. Other constructions cannot be acquired because they require extensions to the representational system assumed so far. Complex *wh* sentences call for additional machinery. Rightward movement constructions have been avoided because we have no way to bind traces that appear to the left of their antecedents. Conjunctions remain unknown territory. Despite these gaps, a substantial grammar can be acquired automatically.

Besides the plain facts of what knowledge can or cannot be acquired, the acquisition procedure is broadly compatible with the course of acquisition that one might expect. Base rules and major Head-Complement order is fixed first, drawing upon extra-syntactic knowledge as a cue. Once this basic constituent order is fixed, the acquisition procedure builds on what it knows to "grammaticalize" forms so that a reliance on extra-syntactic knowledge may be dropped. In all of this, the Projection Principle plays a major role, ensuring that semantic transparency holds. Finally, the incremental character of the acquisition procedure seems to lead to the right developmental predictions in many cases: the order of acquisition of base rules (before movement rules); how passives are learned; the use of embedded S's without Subjects before those with overt Subjects; the appearance of *why* questions before *wh* trace examples; the appearance of *for* purposives before *for* as a complementizer; a relatively "flat" initial sentence structure —all of these flow from the way that the acquisition procedure gives up if an example is too complex. This same incrementality is also crucial in ensuring that the acquisition procedure bases its guesses on clear cases, helping it to avoid overgeneralizations from which no recovery is possible.

Part II:

A Theory of Acquisition

Chapter 5

Acquisition Complexity

Part II shifts from a simulation, computer-based analysis of language acquisition to a more formal study of learnability. Chapter 5 outlines the formal analysis, while chapters 6 and 7 apply the theory to particular examples in syntax, phonology, and concept acquisition.

The formal analysis of chapter 5 has three main parts. First, it probes the use of *simplicity* in linguistic theory as a metric for acquisition simplicity. It then advances a specific theory of acquisition complexity, based on ideas from the theory of program size complexity. By thinking of the acquisition of a grammar as a program that has the job of deciding how to build a grammar, we arrive at a general model of development. In particular, this model can be used to assess the thorny issue of instantaneous vs. noninstantaneous acquisition. Linguistic theorists like to say that grammar acquisition can be thought of *as if* all the data (positive example sentences) were presented to the child at one time, because no generalization of interest about natural grammars is thereby lost. In fact, it is very hard to think of examples where a noninstantaneous model does provide explanations otherwise missed by an instantaneous one. The next chapter provides one example, drawn from the acquisition of phonological segmental systems. Crucially, the developmental model effects a considerable economy of description over an instantaneous model, where an entire phonological system is "projected" from a set of evidence in a single step.

By interpreting markedness theory as a theory of acquisition, we will be able to explain certain co-occurrence restrictions on phonological segments. Evidently, hypotheses about new phonological classes are ordered in a lattice of general to specific descriptions, triggered in a particular sequence. This structure is also common to several proposed general models of "concept acquisition." For example, this lattice-theoretic structure is also posited in Keil's work on concept acquisition in children, and in models of concept acquisition advanced in the artificial intelligence literature under the heading of *version spaces* as developed by Plotkin (1970) and Mitchell (1978).

In addition to providing an explicit developmental model of acquisition based on a theory of grammar, the program complexity approach also allows us to analyze certain formal problems in the acquisition of grammars based on positive-only evidence, what has been called "the logical problem of language acquisition" (Lightfoot 1981). Two related problems will be considered: (1) The power of ordering statements in acquisition, including the heuristic adopted in the acquisition procedure described in chapter 2 that ordered the hypothesis of $\overline{X}$ type rules before the hypothesis of grammar rules, and, within all grammar rules, the hypothesis of local movement before the hypothesis of Move α type rules; (2) The difficulty of acquiring disjunctive rule systems, e.g., the fact that verbs such as *want* take both NP and sentential complements. A formal analysis of the ordering principles that have appeared in the recent linguistic literature reveals that each of the proposals that have been advanced conspire to meet a single necessary and sufficient condition for acquisition from positive-only evidence, dubbed the Subset Principle. The Subset Principle justifies certain other design decisions of the acquisition procedure of chapter 2, for example, the requirement that specific rules execute before more general rules, or the demand that rules be either all obligatory or all optional. These requirements are entailed by the Subset Principle.

Chapter 5 concludes with a formal model for the inference of phrase structure grammars. We show how this model is connected to the computer model sketched in the previous chapters. Chapter 6 applies this model to the inflectional system of English.

5.1 Linguistic Theory and Acquisition Complexity

We begin by looking at the notion of *simplicity* as it is used in linguistic theory. Can its use be justified? How are simplicity and acquisition complexity related?

From the earliest days of the study of generative grammar there has been an attempt to formulate explicit criteria against which alternative grammars are to be judged:

> A grammar of a language must meet two distinct kinds of criteria
> of adequacy. On the one hand it must correctly describe the
> 'structure' of the language ... On the other hand it must meet
> requirements of adequacy imposed by its special purposes ... or, in
> the case of a linguistic grammar having no such special purposes,
> requirements of simplicity, economy, compactness, etc. (Chomsky
> 1951:1)

What is the import of the term "simplicity" as it used in this passage, or
more generally in linguistic theory? For the most part, it was recognized that
the notion of simplicity serves in the same role as it does in the other natural
sciences, namely, as a criterion meant to highlight law-like generalizations
while suppressing irrelevant detail. A simplicity criterion goes hand in hand
with a particular notational or representational system, a language for writing
down theories of grammar. If the notational system adequately captures the
"linguistically significant generalizations" of a language—an empirical issue—
then this success ought to be verified through a correspondence between the
laws capable of simple notation in that system and the observable regularities
of the language.

As an example, consider the following hypothetical set of phonological
rules as described in Chomsky and Halle (1968:333):

Set 1	Set 2
i → y/___ p	i → y/___ p
i → y/___ r	i → y/___ r
i → y/___ y	i → p/___ y
i → y/___ a	i → n/___ a

As is customary, the notation i → y/___ p is to be read as "i is re-written as
y if p is immediately to its right."

The first set of rules, but not the second, contains a regularity that
demands attention: i is mapped to y in an entire set of environments. In
contrast, the second set of rules contains no such regularity. This distinction
can be reflected in the notational system adopted in Chomsky and Halle since
one can use the notational device of braces (denoting disjunction) to write the
first set of rules more compactly than the second. The resulting rule system
is literally smaller.

$$i \rightarrow y \, / \underline{} \quad \left\{ \begin{array}{c} p \\ r \\ y \\ a \end{array} \right\}$$

Note that if one attempts to write down the second set of rules using braces then one winds up with an expression that is just as long as before.

So one part of what "simplicity" means hinges on the notational devices available in a language for theories that enables us to use length or compactness as a proxy for theoretical generalizations. This approach also dates from the earliest days of generative grammar:

> We want the notion of simplicity to be broad enough to comprehend all those aspects of simplicity of grammar which enter into consideration when linguistic elements are set up. Thus we want the reduction of the number of elements and statements, any generalizations, and, to generalize the notion of generalization itself, any similarity in the form of nonidentical statements, to increase the total simplicity of the grammar. As a first approximation to the notion of simplicity, we will here consider the shortness of grammar as a measure of simplicity, and will use such notations as will permit similar statements to be coalesced .... The criteria of simplicity governing the ordering of statements is as follows: that the shorter grammar is the simpler, and that among equally short grammars, the simplest is that in which the average length of derivation of sentences is least. (Chomsky 1951:5–6)

Choice of syntactic connectives such as braces, brackets, and the like, along with a particular set of rules for expanding an expression written using those connectives, plays a role in what is judged simple or not simple. But the measurement of simplicity does not end there. More generally, like any representational system, a notational scheme (or language) consists of two basic parts: a set of vocabulary symbols (such as NP, VP or p, a), and a set of connectives (such as {, }, /, [,]) along with a set of rules for expanding expressions in the notational language. As we have seen, the choice of connectives matters because we can express generalizations using braces that we otherwise might not be able to express (assuming all other aspects of the representational language are held constant). The choice of basic vocabulary symbols is also crucial, however, as Chomsky and Halle have demonstrated. For example, we want the following set of phonological rules to be compactly representable:

$$a \rightarrow æ / \underline{\quad} \quad \left\{ \begin{array}{c} i \\ e \\ æ \end{array} \right\}$$

The reason is that the environment in which the change occurs consists of just front vowels—intuitively, a "natural class" of vowels. In contrast, the following set of triggering environments ought to be unrelated:

$$a \rightarrow æ / \underline{\quad} \quad \left\{ \begin{array}{c} p \\ i \\ z \end{array} \right\}$$

To represent the first set of rules more compactly than the second demands not a change in syntactic connectives, but a change in what is considered to be a unit of the notational vocabulary. In this case, Chomsky and Halle have argued that the true units of analysis are not the phonemes a, p, z, but rather bundles of *distinctive features* into which each phoneme is decomposed. Given this approach the grouping a, e, æ can be shown to have the distinctive feature values [+vocalic, +front] in common, hence can be completely described by a small quantity of information, whereas the grouping p, i, z has no feature values in common, hence can only be described by individually listing the features of p, i, and z. This list is enormously longer than the two features [+vocalic +front]. Hence the first set of rules, but not the second, expresses a generalization of the environment in which the a → æ rule operates. We shall show that this intuitive distinction in length actually completely characterizes, in an information-theoretic sense, the distinction of an *explanation* vs. a *stipulation*.

To preview those results here, let us say that a description of a set of surface data expresses a *regularity* or constitutes an *explanation* if the description of the data is shorter than a simple list of the data itself. Thus the distinctive feature analysis expresses a regularity in the first set of a→ æ rules, because just two features (two bits of information) are sufficient to characterize the class of front vowels, whereas if we consider there to be 7 front vowels, then an outright list of the front vowels would take at least 7 bits of information to store in a table. One can see then that the distinctive feature characterization of the front vowels "compresses" the description of the front vowels. Succinct representations, then, are the hallmark of explanations. Compare in this regard Halle's definition of a "natural kind":

> N is a natural kind if fewer features are required to designate the class N than to designate any individual sound in N. (1961:90)

Chomsky's informal characterization is nearly the same:

> We have a generalization when a set of rules about distinct items can be replaced by a single rule (or, more generally, partially identical rules) about the whole set, or when it can be shown that a "natural class" of items undergoes a certain process or set of similar processes. (1965:42)

As shall become apparent in the formal analysis below, the intuition that a generalization exists when a set can be replaced by a rule in fact exhausts the notion of generalization as it has been presented in the linguistic literature. What lies behind a generalization or a regularity in a set of data is a pattern that permits a "compression" in the description of that set, beyond a simple list of its members.

Plainly then, a notation's vocabulary, connectives, and expansion rules all matter. Together they act as a kind of programming language for "writing down" sequences of strings, be they strings of phonemes, syntactic categories, or units of semantic representations, the language in which a theory of grammar is written.

The advantages of this formal approach are several. For one thing, it allows us to settle certain questions about the role of notational systems in expressing linguistic generalizations, as raised by Chomsky and others in the early study of generative grammar. As an example, consider the problem of whether the choice of notation matters in the ranking of alternative theories. In one sense it clearly does; witness the first pair of examples above, where the brace notation permitted a considerable economy of notation.[1] This example

---

[1] But see later in this chapter, where it is suggested that the brace notation in particular is dispensable if one is permitted to reformulate vocabulary categories appropriately.

shows that if a notational system is not sufficiently rich then there may be some regularity that is inexpressible in that system, but easily captured in another.

This observation immediately leads to the question of whether one can define more precisely the notion of "sufficiently rich." Note that this question makes no sense without a formal framework in which the expressive power of a theory can be calculated. The framework chosen here will be drawn from that of automata theory, in which the expressive power of a theory is measured by the class of languages that the grammars specifiable by the theory can generate. For example, in this framework a theory that can specify grammars for every recursively enumerable set is greater in expressive power than a theory that restricts its grammars to consist of rewrite rules that are just left-linear or right-linear (and hence can generate only regular languages). Other hierarchical distinctions, e.g., in terms of machine classes or time and space bounds, are also possible under this account of expressive power.

It is obvious that a weaker system may be unable to even *describe* certain sets—as is the case if a notation that uses context-free grammars attempts to describe a strictly context-sensitive language. Second, and less obviously, it may also be true that while a weaker notational system can describe a set, it cannot do so compactly, but only via what amounts to a list of the elements of that set. In this case the weaker notation is inherently incapable of capturing descriptive generalizations about the set.

Given this programming system approach, then the answer to Chomsky's question regarding the effects of notational changes can be expressed more precisely by replacing the term "sufficiently rich" with "possesses a universal partial recursive function," that is, a "program" that can simulate all other partial recursive functions, hence all other notational systems, assuming that notational systems are identified with the partial recursive functions. Let us call such a system a *universal notation*.[2] Let us now reconsider the possible effect of altering one's notational system. Consider the following example discussed in Chomsky (1965:43), regarding the formulation of a "compact" set of rules for the English Auxiliary system:

(15) Aux → Tense (Modal)(*Perfect*)(*Progressive*)

---

[2]Given an enumeration of the partial recursive functions, $\Phi_0, \Phi_1, \ldots$, denote a universal partial recursive function by $\Phi_{univ}(i, x) = \Phi_i(x)$.

Rule (15) is an abbreviation for eight rules that analyze the element Aux into its eight possible forms. Stated in full, these eight rules would involve twenty symbols, whereas rule (15) involves four (not counting Aux, in both cases). The parenthesis notation, in this case, has the following meaning. It asserts that the difference between four and twenty symbols is a measure of the degree of linguistically significant generalization achieved in a language that has the forms given in list (16), for the Auxiliary Phrase, as compared with a language that has, for example, the forms given in list (17) as the representatives of this category:

(16) Tense, Tense–Modal, Tense–*Perfect*, Tense–*Progressive*, Tense–Modal–*Perfect*, Tense–Modal–*Progressive*, Tense– *Perfect–Progressive*, Tense–Modal–*Perfect– Progressive*

(17) Tense–Modal–*Perfect–Progressive*, Modal–*Perfect– Progressive*–Tense, *Perfect–Progressive*–Tense–Modal, *Progressive*–Tense–Modal–*Perfect*, Tense–*Perfect*, Modal–*Progressive*

In the case of both list (16) and list (17), twenty symbols are involved. List (16) abbreviates to rule (15) by the notational convention; list (17) cannot be abbreviated by this convention.

Chomsky observes that the set described in (17) *can* be abbreviated if a different set of notational conventions is admitted, namely, some notion of cyclic permutation. For example, one could reinterpret parentheses surrounding a list of elements as denoting the set of cyclic permutations of those elements—a standard mathematical notation, in fact: (Tense Modal *Perfect Progressive*).

A universal notation can simulate an arbitrary program p written in any other notation A_i via the program $p_u = 0^i 1p$, where i is the index of the notational system A_i in some enumeration of all notational systems (partial recursive functions). In essence, the universal notation simply looks up the index of notation A_i and then "runs" p on that notation. But then, the size of p_u is just some constant (depending on the enumeration of partial recursive functions) larger than p. Thus, given the alternative permutation notation, (17) is described by a program of roughly the same size as the program for (16) in the usual notation. Symbolically, $|p_2|_{A_j} = |p_1|_{A_i}$. In short, given a universal notational system, we have that $|p_u|$ (data set 17) $\leq |p_2| + (j+1)$, and $|p_u|$ (data set 16) $\leq |p_1| + (i+1) = |p_2| + (i+1)$. With respect to the universal notational system, compact representations of (16) and (17) differ only with regard to whether the program for notational system i appears before that for system j. But this enumeration order is arbitrary—we could just as well have picked an enumeration of partial recursive functions that lists j before i. In this sense, a sufficiently powerful notational system renders the demand to fix notational machinery moot, because any complete notational system will do about as well as any other; shifting notational systems, while intuitively making some generalizations easy to state, actually does not matter if one uses a complete notation and the program size measure.

This result would seem to indicate that a size complexity measure is uninteresting for "complete" computational systems. However, this invariance is *not* necessarily preserved by shifts to "weaker" notations, e.g., those that can specify grammars only for context-sensitive languages, or even only just some restricted subset of all the recursively enumerable languages. This is the situation with the Auxiliary system described earlier: if we have one notational system that can describe a cyclic permutation and one that cannot, then the regularities that the two systems can pick out differ. Presumably this is the situation that holds with regard to linguistic theories; a desideratum of current theories of grammar is that they should be tightly constrained, specifying only a finite number of grammars, in some cases. In other words, it may be that the less-than-universal notational systems that linguists use actually do give different program size complexity results. Of course, we are then still left with Chomsky's point: since the choice of a notational system will now make a difference in the complexity measure, we must now be prepared to justify the choice of one notation over another.

A second advantage of the formal analysis is that it may be used to study the problem of acquisition and to justify several of the "operating principles" used by the acquisition procedure discussed in Part I. Informally, it has long been suggested that the notion of simplicity is intimately connected to acquisition, in the sense that what is simple is also easy to acquire. Children are assumed to search for regularities in the language of their caretakers, and are assumed to be predisposed to uncover certain regularities rather than others. But as we have seen, what is nonrandom is expressible via a short program; hence the linguist's criterion that short rule systems are desirable can be interpreted as a proposal about acquisition, rather than just aesthetic sensibility. This is for example the suggestion made by Chomsky in the conclusion of the passage cited above:

Hence, adoption of the familiar notational conventions involving the use of parentheses amounts to a claim that there is a linguistically significant generalization underlying the set of forms in list (16) but not the set of forms in list (17). It amounts to the empirical hypothesis that regularities of the type exemplified in (16) are those found in natural languages, and are of the type that children learning a language will expect; whereas cyclic regularities of the type exemplified in (17), though perfectly genuine, abstractly, are not characteristic of natural language, are not of the type for which children will intuitively search in language materials, and are much more difficult for the language-learner to construct on the basis of scattered data or to use. What is claimed, then, is that when given scattered examples from (16), the language learner will construct the rule (15) generating the full set with their semantic interpretations, whereas when given scattered example that could be subsumed under a cyclic rule, he will not incorporate this "generalization" in his grammar. (1965:43–44)

On this interpretation, simplicity means *acquisition simplicity*. To pick "short" grammars is to pick a grammar that is easy to acquire. But what then of other possible functional demands on the language faculty? It has often been suggested that besides the demand of learnability, the demands imposed by language use—the fact that sentences are spoken and understood rapidly—must have played a role in the design of grammars.[3] The demand of processability is typically translated into a complexity measure by keeping track of the units of space or time used by a procedure that recognizes sentences generated by a grammar—the familiar time and space hierarchies of automata theory. There are, then, at least two distinct notions of simplicity: (1) simplicity in the sense that it has usually been used in the linguistic literature (length of grammar, number of symbols) and (2) simplicity in the sense of the complexity of the resulting family of languages, in terms of time and space bounds demanded for recognition. These two measures correspond in an obvious way to the two most-often cited "functional demands" that one might imagine to be imposed on the design of the "language faculty"—the ability to acquire language—corresponding to the length of a grammar—and the ability to use language—corresponding to length of derivations in a grammar. In the remainder of this section we shall take a closer look at acquisition

---

[3]See, e.g., Yngve (1960); Marcus (1980); J.D. Fodor (1979).

complexity.[4] Chapter 7 turns to the problem of parsing complexity, showing how the functional demands of parsability and learnability are related.

One of the major aims of this chapter is to develop and apply a formal characterization of simplicity by pursuing the idea of a notational system as a programming language. The basic approach is to adopt the theory of *program size complexity* as the right yardstick for acquisition of developmental simplicity. This meets several needs. First, it serves as a formal theory of *markedness*, by equating markedness as as *the amount of external information required to fix a grammar*. Second, this theory provides a developmental model of language acquisition (or, rather, grammar identification or instantiation), identifying the evidence that is required for acquisition with a sequence of program inputs, and the complexity of acquisition with the information-theoretic content of those inputs. Since an acquisition "program" consists of a sequence of computational states, starting in some initial state as specified by the theory of universal grammar and ending in a final state that is to correspond to the identification of a "correct" grammar, such a model is able to describe alternative developmental pathways, a matter of some interest to the psychologist. Moreover, since these developmental sequences (corresponding to possible computational sequences) are constrained to occur in certain valid combinations (corresponding to the possible and impossible computation sequences of a machine), it follows that an external observer tracking the successive "states" of such a procedure would observe it passing through only certain well-defined sequences and not others.

In particular, states can be described by a cluster of properties according to the implicational structure of the underlying program. Typically, setting the value of just one variable in a program can give rise to a number of

---

[4]Recall from the material cited above that the earliest work in generative grammar proposed grammar length as a measure of simplicity, and then, within all grammars of equal length, used length of derivation. Though tentative, formal reanalysis of this early proposal shows that it is right on the mark, or nearly so. Length of derivation can be shown (Book 1970) to correspond to the time hierarchies used to classify grammars according to their weak generative capacity, and thus does serve as a proxy for recognition complexity. Similarly, grammar length serves as a proxy for acquisition complexity, as will be demonstrated in this chapter. Thus the proposal in effect lays out the following research strategy for the study of language: find all grammars adequate with respect to a criterion of acquisition complexity; then further narrow this set by applying a criterion of derivation (recognition or production) complexity. What is interesting is that this approach still seems to be an appropriate one even after 30 years of additional research, in that the constraint of acquisition appears more potent in constraining the class of possible human grammars than the constraint of recognition. For additional discussion, see Berwick and Weinberg (1984).

immediate changes, some perhaps quite distinct. For example, the call to one or another of two completely distinct subroutines can be triggered by the value of a single other variable. In this case, the "parametric" structure of the program is revealed by observing characteristic "snapshots" of variable values as the program executes. These logical dependencies among variable values can be described by saying that the execution of one statement implies an entire block of subsequent variable value changes. It is this *clustering* of variable value modifications that induces a second-order structure to the program, above the level of individual lines of code.

Summarizing so far, a characteristic of generalizations is that they possess succinct programs. Given the correspondence between succinctness and flow diagram functional units, the program form of such generalizations will contain structural clusters or implicational blocks of code. These implicational clusters, it is claimed, are what psychologists are describing when they speak of observed regularities of development—in the case of language development, what are often called "stages" of competence. An example would be Brown's (1973) taxonomy of "Stage I" and "Stage II" children. On this view, temporal regularities in language development are the reflection of underlying implicational program structure, program structure that is in turn a simple fact about the nature of succinct representations. If this is correct, it demonstrates that linguistic theory has a crucial role to play in the description of ontogenetic sequences in language development, for it specifies the key points of parametric variation that underlie the developmental program of language growth. The program model will also allow us to study more carefully the difference between instantaneous and non-instantaneous models of acquisition. As chapter 6 demonstrates, one can show that there is a particular *order* to the way in which certain portions of linguistic knowledge are acquired.

Program size complexity and acquisition

We shall now backtrack and outline more precisely an acquisition model based on program size complexity. The theory of program size complexity as developed by Kolmogorov (1965) and others, takes the *complexity* of a set S with respect to a programming language A to be the size of the smallest program written in language A that outputs S. The relationship of this approach to the generative framework should be evident. The set S corresponds to a set of strings of some linguistic level—a string of phones, phonemes, syntactic categories, and so forth. The programming language A (together with any associated interpretive procedure for "executing" statements written in A, i.e., for deriving strings of level L) corresponds to the notational system itself. (Recall the formal connection between rewrite rules, derivation sequences, and computation sequences of Turing machines.) Thus a given rule system denotes a program for a set of sentences of a linguistic level. Clearly, there is nothing to prevent us from applying these notions to any set whatsoever. In particular, we may apply it to the case where S is a set of rule systems, i.e., a family of grammars, and the programming language A is a notational system for describing grammars—a theory of grammars. A program for a particular grammar G_i then takes the following form: given a collection of grammars G, a program for G_i "reads" some input (perhaps null) and "writes" as output a representation for G_i. The complexity of G_i is then defined as the minimum size such program, among all programs for G_i.[5]

More formally, let A_i be a partial recursive function. A_i maps strings to strings, (X^* to X^*), which we may take to be the coded representations of the sets we are actually interested in. Let p denote a program written in language A_i, and $|p|$ the size of p. $A_i(p)$ denotes the output produced by running p. Then the Kolmogorov complexity of a string s with respect to A_i is defined as:

$$K_{A_i}(s) = \begin{cases} \text{minimum} & |p| \ s.t \ A_i(p) = s \\ \text{undefined,} & \text{otherwise} \end{cases}$$

Consider by way of example the string, *101101101101*, and let A_i be the partial recursive function that simulates a common programming language, say Fortran. There are at least two Fortran programs for writing out this string. One simply lists all the bits of the string, WRITE (6) '1; WRITE (6) '0; ... STOP; END. This program will be about as large as the length of the string itself—assuming that each instruction occupies one memory location. (There will be a small additional amount of storage occupied by format statements, a STOP and END instruction, and so forth.) Plainly, there is another, shorter program for writing out this same string: DO 10 I=1, 4; 10 WRITE (6) '101; STOP; END.

This second program occupies only four memory locations—plus a register to hold the loop variable I. In fact, as the number of 101's gets larger

---

[5]Note that as demonstrated by Blum (1967), the general problem of determining the minimal size program for a given set, given the full power of an acceptable programming language, is not recursive. Presumably, however, we are not dealing with the general situation that Blum considers.

and larger, the second program will increase in size only as $\log(n/3)$, where n =the length of the string. Assuming that this second program is as short as any other for this string, then the complexity of the string is four. We see then that the string *101101101101* has a program description shorter than itself. Intuitively, this is because the string contains a *regularity* that can be captured by program code that does not merely list the elements of the string. Still other strings of 0's and 1's cannot be so compressed, because they have no such regularities. Intuitively, these correspond to precisely those that are thought of as being patternless, or random. (Consider writing a short program for the string *101000110*.)[6] This intuition inspires the following standard definition:

A string s is *random* if $K_{A_i} > |s| - c$, c some constant.

The next issue to address is the choice of notational system. As described in the introduction to this chapter, if the partial recursive function chosen is a universal partial recursive function (a Turing machine program that can simulate all other Turing machine programs, i.e., all other partial recursive functions), then the complexity of a string with respect to such a universal notation is at worst a constant different from the complexity of that string measured with respect to any other partial recursive function or notational system A_i (not necessarily the same constant):

$$K_U(s) < K_{A_i} + c$$

It is immediate that the complexity of a string measured with respect to any two universal notations will differ from each other by at most a constant, namely, the maximum of the constants used to simulate one program via the other. Thus we may replace the particular A_i used in the definition of a random string above by an arbitrary universal notational system,

---

[6]There is a well-known approach for information storage and display that is a special case of program size compression: so-called *run length encoding*. In this technique, a long string of constant values (a run of 0's or 1's, say) is encoded via two numbers: the number of repetitions and the number that is to be repeated. Thus the string *101b1* would denote a string of 5 1's (*b* being a blank). If the number of changes from 1 to 0 or 0 to 1 is small— that is, if in general the data consists of long runs—then the compression achieved by this method is considerable. A string of n 1's and 0's, where the runs are of *order n* ($O(n)$), will take $O(\log n)$ storage. At the other extreme, if the string consists of an alternating pattern of 0's and 1's, then the runlength encoding expands the string, since every 1 is encoded as 11, and 0 as 10. Note that in this case a more global compression succeeds: the number of 10's suffices to store the entire string.

without affecting things. Put another way, a random string has no expressible regularity in *any* universal notational system. The only way in which
a random string can be written out is to encode the string in the program
itself, and then have the notational system to act like the identity mapping,
$A(p) = A(s) = I(s) = s$.

Turning now to the domain of linguistic theory, recall that the goal of
modern linguistic theory has been to characterize the final states of linguistic
knowledge such that these states are "projectible" from what human initial
states of knowledge must be, under the conditions of data input, evidence,
and such that are encountered. In the program model, the output string
produced corresponds to this final state of knowledge, a grammar; the initial state of knowledge is simply the information available at the start of the
computation—namely, initial tape contents plus the program itself; and the
projection function is implicit in the partial recursive function denoting the
machine on which the program "runs." There are also two distinct ways in
which one might imagine the program receiving the input data it requires:
(i) the data is written on the program's input tape to begin with; or (ii) the
data is presented sequentially over time. Below we consider whether these
different methods of data input actually make a difference in a characterization of possible developmental programs. In any case, by the usual poverty
of the stimulus type arguments, the amount of such external information is
assumed to be small—hence the goal to keep this information to a minimum,
compatible with the observed range of possible human grammars.

From this standpoint, a strict program size measure is not quite the
right one. For if acquisition complexity really measures the difficulty of selecting a grammar given input evidence about the language generated by that
grammar, then a grammar could be very large and yet acquisition could be
extremely easy, even trivial. This might be the case if, for example, there was
but a single human grammar. Then literally no external information would
be required to identify the grammar; it could be entirely "built in," with no
obvious size limitation. Such a system would have in effect zero acquisition
complexity . Similarly, suppose there were two possible grammars. Then,
following the usual definition of information content, the complexity of this
system of grammars is $- \log_2$ (number of alternatives) $= -1$. Roughly, one
decision suffices to choose between the two alternatives. (Of course, in a cognitive context this decision must be made on the basis of evidence available
to the child.) Let us call this complexity measure *developmental complexity*
(DC), and the specific value of DC associated with a grammar measured rel-

ative to some system of possible grammars its *markedness*.[7] According to a developmental measure, we are to penalize a system that requires a large number of decisions to select the proper grammar, given some initial distribution of possible grammars. This measure thus stands proxy for the cognitive demand of poverty of the stimulus. Put another way, the developmental measure attempts to minimize program size, but where the "program" is now the developmental process that starts from an initial set of possible grammars and selects a correct final state grammar corresponding to the linguistic competence of the adult community. Why then isn't the right grammar always completely encoded in the initial state of the system to begin with, thereby reducing decision complexity to zero? For one thing, as has frequently been observed, the developmental system must retain some flexibility, because the child cannot know in advance what language community it will be a member of. The "open parameters" of the initial state must be such that they cover the range of variation of possible human languages.

Second, and more speculatively, the existence of parametric variation that is fixed by external developmental decisions may reflect the advantage of placing some of the information-theoretic burden in developmental sequencing rather than in the initial state of the system itself. To see why, first observe that there is a close connection between initial program size and developmental complexity. For example, consider the following three hypothetical example grammatical systems that aim to specify the structure of verb, noun, adjective/adverb, and prepositional phrases, where a phrase is assumed to consist of a HEAD (verb, noun, adjective/adverb, or preposition), preceded or followed by a Noun Phrase, a Prepositional Phrase, and an optional $\overline{S}$, in any order. (We are therefore assuming that $\overline{X}$ cross-category generalizations do not hold.) There are 12 possible arrangements of constituents forming Verb Phrases; in all, there are 12^4 possible rule systems. Suppose that System A explicitly stores all possible systems (as part of Universal Grammar), selecting the right system based on some kind of triggering evidence that is entirely unrelated to the linguistic system itself. Thus for the Verb Phrase alone it will have to store 12 possible expansion orders. System B stores just the unordered set VP $\rightarrow$ V$\{$NP, PP, $\overline{S}\}$ or VP $\rightarrow$ $\{$PP, NP, $\overline{S}\}$ V, and fixes the right order via external evidence. Plainly, in the worst case this may take

---

[7]To my knowledge, this distinction between *descriptive* and *developmental* complexity first appears in Solomonoff (1964). Solomonoff also proposed a joint trade-off function between program size (descriptive) complexity and developmental complexity, as discussed below.

six data samples (e.g., V PP, V NP, V S̄, V NP PP, V PP S̄, V NP S̄). We may represent B's developmental program schematically as follows: (1) Fix V-Complement order; then (2) Fix PP–NP–S̄ order.

Note how program size compression is achieved in this case. Suppose that HEAD–COMP order is fixed for a Verb Phrase by a single example sentence. We can now set the remaining order by just three additional examples, no matter what the outcome of the Head-Complement decision. From a slightly different point of view, this compression is evidenced by the fact that there is a regularity about phrase structure that can be couched in terms of a HEAD–COMP metavariable. In any case, instead of 12 separate decision points, one for each possible VP system, we have obtained a more succinct program representation by breaking the selection down into two modular steps, the first consisting of two possible choices, the second, of six possible outcomes. Thus the storage for the modular, program representation is of size approximately $(6 + 2) = 8$, smaller than a list of the 12 possibilities. In this way a multiplicative number of developmental possibilities can be stored in an additive amount of space, simply by cascading developmental decisions over time. In short, by representing the selection of a grammar as occurring over time via a sequence of decision points, we have collapsed the description of the grammar. In effect we have exchanged the size of the system that must be stored as part of Universal Grammar for an increased number of developmental decisions. Note that the total amount of information required to fix a grammar remains constant; all that changes is *where* that information is allocated. This trade-off might, then, be used to reduce the size of Universal Grammar, assuming now that the space available for specifying Universal Grammar is limited.

The "compression" inherent in the definition of an abstract supercategory such as a COMP or HEAD does not exhaust the possibilities for program size improvements in phrase structure acquisition. The system that A and B describe did not obey X̄ regularities. Thus the structure of each type of phrase would have to be determined separately, four decisions for each of four phrase types for a worst-case total of 16 decisions (or 6 examples for each for 4 phrase types, for a total of 24 data points). But suppose the X̄ regularities do hold. Then the structure of Verb Phrase complements may be assumed to predict that of prepositional, noun, and adjective/adverb complements. This regularity is reflected in the reduced developmental program size required to fix an X̄ type grammar. Only four decisions (6 examples) are required to set the rule system for all phrase structure types. Equivalently, one may say that there are no separate phrase structure rules for VP, NP, PP, and AP; rather, there is just one nonterminal class of type X. The redundancy is reflected as developmental simplicity.

There is one other modification to a grammar that may impact both descriptive and developmental complexity, and that is the redefinition of phrasal categories themselves. For example, as Stowell (1981) observes, NP and S̄ often appear in alternation in the complement of a VP:

> *I believe John*
> *I believe that John is a fool*

Two developmental decisions must be made to arrive at this grammar, one to determine that NP may appear in the VP complement, and another to determine that S̄ may appear. We can reduce the size of the grammar and at the same time the number of developmental decisions that must be made if we collapse these two categories, NP and S̄, into one. In this case, Stowell suggests that NP and S̄ are members of the same natural class, sharing the property of being Case Recipients—NP is Case-marked by the verb, and S̄ by the inflectional element of a sentence. Suppose that this suggestion is correct. Then we have shortened the description of the Verb Complement from VP → V {NP or S } to VP → V Case Recipient.

Let us characterize this situation more formally. Fix some set of possible grammars. Now suppose that P is the shortest program for grammar G_i of this set. We may imagine P's initial tape to contain a sequence of input data, corresponding to a valid sequence of "external" data samples, sentences of the language of G_i, assuming positive only evidence. The control table of P holds the program that, in conjunction with the initial tape contents, is sufficient to fix G_i: P moves through a sequence of decision states, $D_1, \ldots, D_n$, outputting a representation of grammar G_i.[8] Then P is just a program for computing G_i, and say that the descriptive complexity of G_i is just $|P|$. A decision theoretic model can in this way be converted into a description of a set. Now suppose there is a program P' that also fixes G_i, but via a smaller number of decisions. By assumption P was already as small as possible. So if we reduce the external evidence required to fix G_i (as measured by the contents of the input tape), then the control table of P' must be larger than that of P. More simply, the information required to specify G_i remains constant, and

---

[8]Note once again that there may be no recursive procedure to find P, in general.

all we have done is to shift some of the burden from external data to initially encoded program.

The decision complexity model of acquisition is useful only as far as it illuminates actual cases of acquisition. We turn to these in the next chapter. In the remainder of this chapter, we take up three purely formal aspects of acquisition, the difficulty of learning disjunctions, the role of hypothesis ordering in learning, and a formal model for learning phrasal categories.

5.2 Disjunction and Positive-only Acquisition

It has long been recognized that *disjunctions* pose a special problem for acquisition. Researchers in artificial intelligence (Winston 1975; Iba 1979) and linguistics (Stowell 1981) agree that disjunctions are hard to learn and should be eliminated. In this section we show that their position is justified.

First, the acquisition complexity of disjunctive descriptions is reflected within the theory of program size complexity and the concept of a natural class itself. Recall that a notational system captures a regularity when it permits one to write short expressions describing long lists of "data." It has often been suggested that disjunctive machinery is inherently at odds with the criterion of simplicity because it in essence allows one to "explain" any set of data extensionally, via a list $S = s_1 \cup s_2 \cup \ldots$. The program size metric shows that disjunction, and hence the brace notation, is indeed nonexplanatory as conjectured. A "natural class," then, can be described in one of either two ways: as a description that is more compact than an explicit listing of a set, or as a categorization that is acquirable on the basis of positive-only evidence.

A second major and long recognized problem with the use of disjunctions is that the danger of overgeneralization becomes more acute. By definition, the conjuncts of a disjunctive description have no features in common (save for some very general root predicate). This fact is the bane of simple generalization procedures. For if we attempt to establish one half of the disjunctive clause by observing a positive example, and the other half by another example, then a simple-minded generalizer will often conclude that the correct description of the examples is the intersection of these individual descriptions, namely, the null set. For example, if the correct description of an object is $P \vee Q$, where P and Q are themselves conjunctive expressions, then one positive example can be P, and another Q; the intersection of the two can be empty.

There are two basic solutions to the problem of disjunction. One is to admit negative evidence, so that one can know if a description is too general. But what if negative examples are not available? The only other possibility is to eliminate disjunctive statements. How much disjunction is too much? The following example Angluin (1978) shows that if "arbitrary" disjunction is allowed then there exists an infinite collection of languages whose individual members cannot be identified from positive only evidence.

Suppose that a family of languages over an alphabet Σ, L, includes the "universal" language Σ^*. In addition, suppose that L contains languages defined by rule systems that can express arbitrary disjunctions in the following sense. Grammars for these languages can be of the form $A \rightarrow \alpha|\beta|\ldots|\varsigma$ with no restrictions on the righthand sides of these rules. Then each righthand side of a rule in a grammar can cover one sentence in the language. In other words, we assume the power to form the language of any member of this family as the union of individual sentences of that language. Let us call these languages the *disjunctive covering languages* of L.

From the standpoint of acquisition, the problem with this family of languages is that any finite sample drawn from a language in L is covered by two languages: the universal language and the language generated by the grammar consisting of the disjunction of single sentences making up the finite sample. Then plainly there is a sequence of positive examples drawn from a member of L that will cause an acquisition procedure to change its guess about the identification of L_i an infinite number of times, and thus the procedure will fail to identify L in the limit. For suppose that the example sequence consists simply of sentences drawn from the universal language. At each acquisition step i an acquisition procedure must guess that examples it has seen have been drawn from either the universal language or one of the disjunctive covering languages of the examples it has seen. Suppose the procedure guesses the universal language at point i; then there is a point at which no examples it sees later will force it to change its guess (Blum and Blum 1975). We can now construct a new example sequence that the procedure cannot identify in the limit.

There is some disjunctive covering language whose examples are just like those of the sequence seen up to point i: simply conjoin the examples seen so far, disjunctively. Now the acquisition procedure must fail to identify this language, since the example sequence consisting of the sequence that forced the procedure to lock onto the universal language Σ will likewise cause the procedure to lock onto this guess given the new sequence, incorrectly. (This example is a generalization of Gold's (1967) result that any family containing all the finite languages and one infinite language is not identifiable in the limit from positive-only evidence.) The crux of the problem is that the space of hypotheses is "dense" in the sense that there are collections of positive evidence compatible with an infinite number of possible guesses. Note that this is the reason that the example family of languages provided by Gold (1967), the family of all languages of finite cardinality and one language of infinite cardinality, fails to be identifiable from positive-only evidence: there is a finite collection of evidence sentences that is covered by an infinite number of languages in the family.

In summary, there are two general situations in which an incremental approach to acquisition will work:

(1) If positive and negative examples are available, then a partial ordering of hypotheses such that the accumulation points of the ordering are themselves valid hypotheses suffices.[9]

(2) If just positive examples are available, then a sparse covering of evidence sets suffices (Angluin 1978). That is, only a *finite* number of hypothesizable languages L_i can cover any possible evidence set. If general disjunctive statements are allowed—braces, in the phrase structure notation—then this condition cannot, in general, be met. (It might be that some other condition could suffice, however.)

5.3   The Subset Principle

We now turn to a key condition guaranteeing identifiability from positive evidence, the Subset Principle. The problem with overly-dense families of languages is that no matter what the positive evidence set, when data set D_i prompts a guess of language L_i, it is always possible to find another language L_j that is compatible with D_i and that can be interposed between D_i and L_i, $L_j \subset L_i$. This leads to overgeneralization difficulties. If L_j is the correct target language, then the procedure has erroneously guessed too large a language, and, given only positive evidence, no further examples will contradict the guess L_i.

---

[9]This is an approach used in the artificial intelligence literature under the heading of *version spaces*.

Suppose that this can never happen, that is, that no L_j is a proper subset of L_i. Then either one of three situations must obtain: (1) $L_i = L_j$; (2) $L_j \supset L_i$; or (3) L_i and L_j are incomparable, with both covering the data set. In case 1, no hypothesis change is required. In cases 2 and 3, $L_j - L_i$ is nonempty, and there is some (positive) example d in L_j not in L_i. If L_j is in fact the target language, then this example must eventually appear in the information presentation (under the assumption of a complete presentation), and an identification procedure will have evidence to change its guess. If L_i is the target language, then the same principle holds. Therefore, in either case identification in the limit from positive evidence can proceed successfully. Let us say that when a family of languages meets this condition that it obeys the Subset Principle (or that the family possesses the Subset Property).

In the special case where one target language is properly contained within another, the point of this condition is to ensure that the acquisition procedure always guesses a subset language if possible, that is, the smallest language that is also compatible with the positive evidence so far encountered.[10]

The Subset Principle was independently observed and formalized in a recursive-function theoretic framework by Angluin (1978). In an important theorem, Angluin demonstrated that the Subset Principle is necessary and sufficient for identifiability from positive evidence.

Theorem. Suppose we are given a family of recursive languages, L. L is identifiable in the limit from positive-only evidence iff there exists an effective procedure which on input i enumerates finite sets $T_1, T_2, \ldots$ such that: (i) $T_i \subseteq L_i$; (ii) $\forall j > 1$, if $T_i \subseteq L_j$, then $L_j \not\subseteq L_i$.

The idea is that the T_i are "trigger" sets for hypotheses, and the condition amounts to the claim that such finite triggers must exist for positive example identification to work.

Since the Subset Principle is a necessary condition for positive-only acquisition, it is not surprising to discover that it subsumes a variety of proposals that have been advanced in the linguistic literature as constraints on the order in which acquisition hypotheses should be made. Consider first the case

---

[10]Note that the sequence of guesses conforms to an incremental search from more specific to less specific languages if the lattice of languages is ordered by the subset relation. Again, what is crucial to the demonstration is the topological structure of the lattice of hypotheses. The particular details of what these hypotheses denote is irrelevant.

where the potential target languages are proper subsets of each other, i.e., $L_j \subset L_i$. Here the Subset Principle implies that the acquisition procedure should pick the narrowest possible language consistent with evidence seen so far. This situation also arises when we consider a parameter that can be set one of two ways, with the first value yielding a subset of sentences when compared to the second setting. We shall see in chapter 6 that this covers a variety of cases that have been discussed in the linguistic literature. Note that this analysis assumes that all sources of variation in the possible target languages can be held constant, with the one parameter of interest varying independently. Otherwise, the subset relationship between the two settings of a single parameter may fail to hold with parameters considered jointly, as recently discussed by Wexler and Manzini (1984).

The Subset Principle seems to exhaust what can be said about ordering constraints in acquisition. To support this claim Chapter 6 reviews several proposals that have been made regarding the ordering of hypotheses in acquisition. To consider just one here, suppose that whether or not a verb takes an NP argument is a "parameter." The language where that verb does not take an argument is a proper subset of the one where it does. If both of these languages are possible final targets, then the acquisition procedure should hypothesize the narrowest one first.

Now suppose we introduce a second parameter, whether movement of NPs is allowed or not. Plainly, if movement is allowed we have at least as large a set of possible surface sentences as when it is not allowed. Note that this parameter does not interact with the first: we can hypothesize the set {no NP arg, no movement}, and then, given positive examples, move to any of {NP arg, no movement}; {NP arg, movement}; {no NP arg, movement}.

We postpone further illustrations of the Subset Principle until chapter 6, but add here two comments of general interest. First, we note that it might appear as though it would be hard to check the application of this principle. For recall that in general the determination of whether $L_i \subset L_j$ is undecidable, for context-free languages and beyond. This is only an apparent difficulty, however. In practice, the calculation is much easier.[11] For example, suppose we limit the data that is used for acquisition to degree 2, that is,

---

[11]It should also be stressed that the hypothesis ordering need not be done by the acquisition device itself; rather, it might have been fixed over time by an outside oracle, e.g., natural selection.

only sentences with at most two embedded sentences.[12] This is the constraint invoked by Wexler and Culicover in their learnability model (1980). Now the subset computation is decidable. This is because without recursion the only way that a string can be arbitrarily long is if Kleene star repetition is admitted—e.g., rules of the form VP → V NP PP*. But then, it is a simple matter to write out the possible degree 2 sentences as those accepted by a finite state transition network, without recursion, so these sentences must form a regular set. Inclusion of regular sets is decidable.

Second, we can apply the Subset Principle to a general situation that has been discussed in the acquisition literature, that of *indirect negative evidence*. By indirect negative evidence we mean simply that a learning procedure can assume that if it has not seen a sentence s after some finite number of examples then it may assume that s is not a positive example at all. This method was used in chapter 4.

Now consider any situation where indirect negative evidence is used to set the values of a parameter P. Assume that P takes on just two values, 0 and 1, and that these parameter values result in grammars that generate different languages, L_0 and L_1, with $L_0 \subset L_1$. If indirect negative evidence is used to set the value of P, then this occurs in the following way.

We assume some default value for the parameter P, say $P = 1$. The sentences of the target language are enumerated according to some complexity measure (e.g., length or depth of embedding), such that a finite initial segment of the set of all sentences of the target language is enumerated. Given this finite sequence of positive evidence, a sentence is observed *not* to occur, and on the basis of this evidence the acquisition procedure concludes that the value of P should be changed to 0. Assume that this negative example is part of the language compatible with the parameter set to 1 (there must be some such example, or else the two languages do not differ). Given a finite sample, though, this means we could have guessed L_0 to begin with, and then changed that guess if examples from L_1 appear. Thus we may substitute hypothesis ordering for indirect negative evidence. Chapter 6 gives an application of this result to the acquisition of bounding nodes for subjacency, as discussed by Rizzi (1978).

---

[12] One must of course demonstrate that this restriction on input examples suffices to guarantee correct identification of the target language (in this case, a grammar for the target language).

5.4   X̄ Theory and Phrase Structure Acquisition

The previous sections of this chapter outlined a theory of program size complexity and a principle acquisition based on positive evidence. This section turns to the examination of a specific model of acquisition for the base phrase structure rules of a grammar. This model will combine the constraints of X̄ theory along with a simple extension of finite state automata induction suggested by Joshi and Levy (1978). Chapter 6 applies this model to the acquisition of the English inflectional system. We begin by reviewing the role of nonterminals in a grammar.

What information is contained in a context-free base rule system? There are two basic elements to any such set of rules: (1) the nonterminal labels themselves (e.g., NP, VP, INFL); and (2) the constituent boundaries of phrases (in surface strings). Together this information is sufficient to recover the derivation trees of all surface strings, and hence the underlying grammar used to derive those strings.

What about the node labels themselves? The notion of a phrase label is just an informal shorthand for a certain collection of strings that behave alike, where the notion of behavioral similarity can range from some kind of vague, semantic grounding (NPs as "objects") to a specific syntactic relation (identity under movement). In any case, the notion of a phrase is derivative, in the sense that it is definable with respect to other grammatical terms. More generally, there is precisely one way in which a phrase is formally defined (though this definition appears in many different guises in the literature) and that is as the *equivalence class of a set of elements under some (to be defined) invariance relation*. For instance, if the invariance relation R is defined as right concatenation, so that xRy iff for all z in Σ^*, xz and yz are both in the same equivalence class, and if there are a finite number of such classes, then it is well known that the resulting equivalence classes are just the states of some finite state machine M. Here, a "phrase" is just a sequence of tokens that drives M through the same sequence of states.

Behaviorally—that is, looking at a system of equivalence classes from the "outside"—the only way to tell if two strings are in the same class or not is to see if they behave alike or differently. Given just surface strings (with no bracketing), there is only one way to do that: strings s_1 and s_2 are different just in case there is some string w (perhaps null) such that $s_1 w \notin L$ and $s_2 w \in L$ or vice-versa. Since accepting (grammatical) and nonaccepting (ungrammatical) states must be distinct, a behavioral difference has been forged. This is the basic means by which the equivalence classes of a system can be determined. Note that any kind of relation could be used to establish the equivalence classes, as long as that relation separates strings into accepting and nonaccepting classes.

As is also well known, the states of a finite state automaton correspond in a direct way to the nonterminal symbols of a (strongly) equivalent grammar, namely a grammar with rules of the form, $A \rightarrow aB$, where a is the terminal element that prompts a transition from state A to state B.

For context-free grammars, the same results hold, but now we must look at tree fragments rather than the linear sequences corresponding to finite automata. In either case, the nonterminals of a grammar just denote the states of some machine. Machine states, in turn, are just a way of distinguishing among equivalence classes of externally provided strings.

The relationship between the nonterminals of a grammar and the equivalence classes of some machine accepting or rejecting strings generated by that grammar suggests that the problem of grammatical inference may be reduced to that of inducing the equivalence classes of some machine, given the machine's input-output behavior. This problem is a familiar one in automata theory. First of all, it is well known that one must at least supply the acquisition procedure with an upper bound on the number of states in the resulting minimal finite state machine (Moore 1956). This is true because without such a bound an acquisition procedure could not limit in advance the length of strings it must look at. For example, assuming an exhaustive presentation of all positive examples, one could not distinguish between the language a^* and a^n unless the string a^{n+1} appears or fails to appear. Unless a bound on the number of states is provided, an acquisition procedure will never know when to stop looking. Once the number of states is given, however, one can obtain a finite acquisition procedure by invoking a theorem stating that a finite state automaton is completely characterized by the strings it accepts of length less than or equal to $2n - 1$.[13]

Suppose then that we are given n, the number of states in the minimal (canonical) finite state acceptor for some regular target language, along with a sample consisting of all strings of length less than or equal to $2n - 1$. (As we shall see, in many real cases not all such strings must be examined.) The

---

[13]See, e.g., Starke (1972) for a proof of this basic result.

assumption that the number of states (or an upper bound on the number of states) be provided in advance is a significant one. It is not obvious why this information should be available to the language learner. For the $\overline{X}$ system this may not be such a bad assumption, because the basic categories might be simply the lexical possibilities and the metavariables SPEC and COMP. If these possibilities constitute the full range of nonterminal elements, then there at most $2 \times 2 + 2 = 6$ possible nonterminals. The number of nonterminals is much greater in a theory that assumes a single representational level for phrase structure. Such theories multiply out the number of nonterminal labels, an effect that might require many data samples for acquisition. In contrast, a modular theory that fixes base and transformational rules independently requires fewer data examples for acquisition, all other things being equal.

This induction procedure assumes a principle of indirect negative evidence. That is, the inference procedure must know which strings in the sample are in the target language, and which are not. If only positive evidence is given—all sentences in the language less than or equal to $2n - 1$—then an acquisition procedure can assume that the strings it has not seen are not in the target language, and thus obtain a complete negative and positive sample. It can proceed in one of two ways, either by assuming that all strings are in separate states to begin with and then merging equivalent states, or by assuming that all strings are in one of two states (namely, the accept and reject states) and splitting these states into new ones:

1. Assume that all positive strings are in different equivalence classes, then find strings that should be merged into the same class. This is essentially the method proposed by Biermann and Feldman (1972). For a complete positive sample of strings of length less than or equal to $2n - 1$, (denoted $S^+_{\leq 2n-1}$) identical behavior implies that $\forall s_1, s_2 \in S^+$, $s_1 \equiv s_2$ iff $\forall s, |s| < n - 1, s_1 s = s_2 s$. In Biermann and Feldman's terminology, the $n-1$ *tails* of s_1 and s_2 are the same, where a k *tail* of s_1 with respect to a positive sample S^+ is $\{s | s_1 s \in S^+, |s| \leq k\}$. Denote this set by $T_k(s_1)$. Thus to infer the states of the automaton, one need only collapse into the same equivalence class those strings of S^+ that have the same $n - 1$ tails. Denote by Q this set of equivalence classes (set of strings). To infer the transitions, observe that a transition carries the automaton from a given equivalence class or possibly to the single rejecting state. Thus for $q \in Q$, $\delta(q, a) = \{q' \in Q | q' = T_{n-1}(sa), s \in Q\}$, and $q' = $ reject state if $sa \notin S^+_{\leq 2n-1}$, for $s \in Q$. The resulting automa-

ton may be nondeterministic and nonminimal; to form the minimal (canonical) deterministic machine, one simply applies the usual subset construction and a standard minimization algorithm.

2. Assume that there are just two states to begin with, the accepting and the nonaccepting states; these states are split to yield the required number of states. Thus initially all positive strings go into the same equivalence class—namely, the accepting state: all negative strings are associated with the nonaccepting equivalence class.[14] Given this initial partition, a new partition is constructed by looking for a pair of strings, s_1 and s_2, such that s_1 and s_2 are in the same initial partition (i.e., they both lead to accepting states), but concatenating a single new symbol onto s_1 and s_2 puts them in classes already known to be distinct.

More precisely, the only classes initially known to be distinct are the accepting and nonaccepting states. Call these q_a and q_{na}, respectively. All strings in $S^+_{\leq 2n-1}$ are initially in q_a and all strings not in S^+ are in q_{na}. Now the acquisition procedure runs through all strings in S^+ to find a pair of strings s_i, s_j and a single new token a such that $s_i a$ and $s_j a$ wind up in different equivalence classes (initially, the accepting and rejecting states). If no such pair can be found, then the acquisition procedure stops, because the equivalence classes need not be further split. Suppose then that such a pair of strings and distinguishing token a is found. Then a new state is formed that distinguishes s_i and s_j.

The new partition of equivalence classes includes the original accepting and nonaccepting states. The acquisition procedure now attempts to split this new set of classes by repeating the above procedure. Informally, one can see that this procedure eventually terminates, since after each new partition we can consider strings one token longer than the last, and there are but a finite number of such strings that can be considered; moreover, there can be at most $n - 2$ new partitions.

Both methods require that an acquisition procedure examine an exponential number of examples, in the worst case. The class-merging procedure, for example, must examine all positive example sentences less than a certain length in order to form the k tail equivalence classes. For certain families of languages this can amount to an examination of an exponential number of

---

[14]As before, this assumes a single nonaccepting state—as is the case for a reduced (minimal state) automaton.

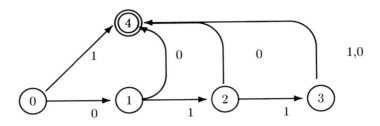

Figure 5.1: A difficult-to-learn finite automaton

strings. For instance, consider the case of a family of languages $L = \{L_n|$ all strings over $\Sigma \in L_i\} - s_n$, where s_n is of length n. The reduced finite state automaton for L_i has $n + 2$ states. An example is shown in figure 5.1, with $n = 3$, and the string 011 as the the only nonaccepted string. Note that all strings have the same k tails except for the strings 0, 01, and 011.[15]

The acquisition-by-string merger procedure must in effect find this single nonaccepting string by locating these three strings that fail to have the same k tails as all other strings. But then, given only a list of positive examples less than a certain length and the state bound $n + 1$, in the worst case the procedure would have to examine an exponential number of positive examples before finding that the k tails of λ (the empty string), 0, 10, and 011 are different from the k tails of all other strings.[16]

---

[15]This is the dual of a case suggested by Angluin (1982).

[16]Of course, the relevant information could be placed (by chance) at the head of the list of positive examples—as in this example—in which case three different states would be discovered immediately. However, one can easily design a language that places the tell-tale examples at the end of a list ordered by length: simply make the languages consist of all strings less than length $2n$, but for one string of length $2n$ that ends in a particular string i of length n.

Similarly, the refinement procedure must look at an exponential number of examples in certain cases. Consider the dual of the languages considered above, where precisely one string of length n is in each language L_n. Then unless essentially all strings of length n are examined, the acquisition procedure must sometimes misidentify a string. For suppose that in all cases the acquisition procedure uses fewer than 2^n examples. Then there must be at least two strings that are never examined, call them n_1 and n_2. But then the acquisition procedure cannot distinguish between L_{n_1} and L_{n_2}, contrary to the assumption that the procedure could tell these two different languages apart.

Since this is a "worst case" analysis, it is important to see whether these cases actually arise in natural languages. In the next chapter we shall see that in fact only a polynomial number of examples are required to learn the inflectional (auxiliary verb) system of English. Perhaps surprisingly, it is not necessary for such a system to see every possible auxiliary verb sequence in order to induce the correct target automaton: the longer (and presumably rarer) sequences such as *could have been being* are not required.

While the exact characterization of the conditions that permit such a reduction in required sentence examples is still under study, one property of the target automata seems to be implicated: they are *backwards deterministic with lookbehind 1*. A finite automaton is backwards deterministic if the inverse of its transition function is itself a function, that is, it maps to a unique state. The inverse with lookbehind 1 is defined as follows. Given a deterministic finite automaton with transition function $\delta(q, a)$ for $a \in \Sigma$, then $\delta^{-1}(q_i, a_1 a_2) = \{q | (q, a_2 a_1) = q_i\}$. This is a function if the set contains a single element. This property holds for the auxiliary verb system in English (see the transition diagrams in chapter 6). If we reverse the arrows describing the auxiliary system, we see that one arrives at a unique state after at most two word transitions. For example, if we are in a state after processing *given* then we could have arrived there via either the routes *being given*, *been given*, or *have given*, so just examining *given* is not enough. Two tokens (lookbehind 1) are enough to distinguish all such cases, however, since they all lead back to unique preceding states. Note that this property is *not* shared by the difficult-to-learn example of figure 5.1: if we reverse the transition arrows, then move backwards from state S_4, we do not always arrive at a unique state even after 4 transitions. We note here only that since the Marcus machine is more than a finite state automaton the definition of backwards determinism must be extended from the finite state case to a variant of a pushdown automaton. The same constraint appears to hold: we shall show in chapter 7 that a variant of backwards determinism, known as Bounded Context Parsability, is an important aid for acquisition.

So far our analysis has focused only on the induction of finite state automata. However, it is easy to show (as suggested by Joshi and Levy 1978) that the same partition or merger algorithms can be applied to the induction of context-free grammars if one uses tree automata instead of finite state automata. Recall that the transition function of a finite state automaton is defined as a mapping from a state and input symbols to a single new state: $Q \times \Sigma \mapsto Q$. One can picture the succession of states that a given finite state automaton enters as a nonbranching chain, $q_0, q_1, \ldots, q_f$. A tree automaton is a simple generalization allowing a mapping from a set of states (possibly none) to a new state, $Q^* \times \Sigma \mapsto Q$.

The entire theory of induction in the finite state case can now be carried over to the induction of trees. The invariance relation of string concatenation must be generalized to that of tree concatenation. In the domain of trees, the analog of k tail suffixes are k depth subtrees. The following definition establishes the connection (from Levine 1981:287):

> Suppose t and r are trees, Σ^t the set of all trees defined over an alphabet Σ, S some subset of Σ^t. (Σ includes node labels like NP as well as terminal elements.) Let the equivalence relation R^M be defined by: tR^Mu iff $\forall v \in \Sigma^t$, and for each node label x in t, the subtrees formed by replacing x in v with t are in S exactly when the subtrees formed by replacing x in v with u are in S. Then R^M is of finite index, with the classes induced by R corresponding to the states of a tree automaton accepting S. (S corresponds to a language L in the finite state case.)

In other words, to define a tree automaton, it suffices to determine, for all subtrees u and t, whether u and t are substitutable across all possible tree contexts. Joshi and Levy (1978) show that all context-free grammars are so definable. Turning now to the acquisition procedure, we can see that it provides a different definition of substitutability. At least for the case where an ATTACH acts on two items with the same left and right contexts, we have the following:

1. Initially, all sequences of states (individual tokens, plus phrase boundaries as defined by the $\overline{\mathrm{X}}$ theory and thematic information) are assumed

distinguishable.[17] In the general tree automata case, phrase boundaries are not defined by prior constraints.

2. The acquisition procedure calls two elements u and v substitutable (by placing them in the same equivalence class) whenever:

    (a) u and v are in the first buffer cell;

    (b) u and v are either single tokens or complete subtrees;

    (c) the left-contexts of the parser IDs for u and v are identical (this includes the $\overline{X}$ label and annotations for the active node and current cyclic node); and

    (d) the 2nd and 3rd buffer cells hold the same items (possibly a subtree in the case of the 2nd buffer cell).

This definition of substitutability does not demand equivalence over *all* possible subtrees, but rather only subtrees of depth 2. This is because by definition the left- and right-contexts fixed by parser descriptions cannot include more than a single root node (like an S or NP) and whatever daughters that node might have; no further details of the subtrees of the daughter nodes are allowed. Thus only trees of depth 2 are examined. Further, the right context does not include trees in the third buffer cell, though this restriction could be lifted.

What is the significance of the constraint on depth? It can be shown (see Levine 1981) that this depth restriction means that certain tree automata (hence context-free grammars) cannot be acquired by this kind of procedure. For example, context-free grammars defining a co-occurrence restriction over trees consisting of three cyclic nodes could not be learned, because evidence distinguishing these tree types could never be seen.

The general result (Joshi and Levy 1978) is that an induction procedure needs on the order of all trees of depth $2n$ in order to learn a grammar with n nonterminals. All trees of depth about $2n$ may be too many to be psychologically plausible. But how much data are actually required for "real" linguistic cases? Even here the data demands seem substantial. For example, given

---

[17]Note that such an induction procedure assumes that the full bracketing of input strings is given or can be independently reconstructed. In a more realistic setting, this bracketing might be deducible from cues such as pauses, intonation, or the like. Whether this is possible in practice, however, remains to be seen. See Morgan and Newport (1981) for preliminary psycholinguistic research on this topic.

even a simple $\overline{\text{X}}$ system, there are 4 major phrase categories plus particles, adverbs (as distinct from adjectives), complementizers, and modals. Thus all positive trees of depth less than 16 might have to be examined, a complexity that seems unrealistic.

These are the "worst case" theoretical limits on the data demands for acquisition of a phrase structure system. Turning now to the computer model, we find that its constraints are considerably tighter. The acquisition procedure can look at trees only two cyclic nodes deep. Its grammars rules can only refer to patterns that are this complex, and its notion of what is equivalent or not must be so limited. By fiat then, it need only look at simple sentences or sentences with one embedding in order to acquire its set of grammar rules. This restriction rules out many possible phrase structure grammars.

To take an artificial, but concrete example, suppose that there were a different sort of NP, call it NP*, just like an ordinary NP except appearing only in the context $[_S \; [_{VP} \; [_{NP},$ embedded under three nodes. No trees of depth two would distinguish NP*s from ordinary NPs, so there would be no way to tell them apart given simpler data. In contrast, the procedure *can* distinguish between an embedded and a nonembedded context, since this is the difference between one S and two, and a grammar rule can be written to tell these two environments apart. The current procedure forbids such rule systems. In such a system one would expect a grammar that distinguishes between root and nonroot environments—as is the case in natural grammars—but not one that distinguishes between a root environment and one that is embedded under exactly three S nodes.[18] If such grammars did exist, they would be hard to learn.

By restricting the acquisition procedure to depth-bounded trees we are claiming then that natural languages are not as general as those described by unrestricted tree automata (as far as the constituent structure of natural languages is describable by context-free grammars). While it is easy to write context-free grammars that would demand complex tree structures as evidence for their acquisition, evidently natural grammars are constrained so that they can be learned from example sentences of plausible depth. We might in fact characterize the natural grammars in part as those grammars that possess this property.

---

[18] The reason for this limit can perhaps be explained by the lack of any counting primitives in grammars; evidently, only the notion of *adjacency*, a structural predicate, is available. See Berwick and Weinberg (1984) for additional discussion of this point.

To return to the main theme of this chapter, the linguistic equation of learnability and simplicity has considerable support. Natural languages are learnable from simple examples, and this is reflected in a program-complexity description of acquisition, based on the number of decisions or amount of data required to fix a grammar. The acquisition procedure fits into this framework as a kind of tree automaton induction that is able to draw on limited data— the input buffer and stack "snapshot"—as its evidence for new grammar rules. This severely restricts what counts as learnable, simple, *and* natural. In the next chapter we apply this measure of simplicity to some actual case studies.

Chapter 6

Learning Theory: Applications

The previous chapter outlined three subtheories of acquisition: a measure of acquisition complexity based on the number of decisions to fix a grammar; a general principle of acquisition from positive-only evidence, the Subset Principle; and an induction procedure for bounded-context automata. This chapter turns to the applications of each subtheory. We first look at a model for learning segmental or sound systems. We shall see that by considering the order of acquisition decisions, we can better account for the observed distribution of natural segmental systems. This is, then, a case where a noninstantaneous model of acquisition is actually superior to an instantaneous one. The decision-based model also shows how the size of the program required to learn a rule system may be compressed by ordering decisions. Finally, we shall see that the learning of segmental systems obeys the Subset Principle.

Next we turn to a brief discussion of concept acquisition, based on the work of Sommers (1971) and Keil (1979). They advance a very general constraint on the possible shape of natural semantic networks, the *M constraint*. Briefly, Sommers has suggested that if one arranges terms such as *dog*, *cat*, *love*, and so forth into a graph structure whose terminal leaves are terms and where each node is an item that can sensibly be predicated of the all terms below it in the graph, then one never, or rarely, finds human intuitions of sensibility resulting in *M* shaped graphs. Rather, the graph structures take the form of hierarchical trees. Keil hints that this constraint is motivated for some functional reason; we shall see that in fact this constraint is compatible with the definition of a natural class and the Subset Principle.

We then consider applications of the Subset Principle to cases in linguistic theory where acquisition ordering principles have been advanced. These include: (1) dative alternation; (2) the adjacency constraint on case assignment; (3) the PRO drop parameter; (4) $\overline{\text{S}}$ deletion; (5) bounding nodes for rule application; (6) the ordering of rule action hypotheses in the acquisition procedure; (7) the identification of empty categories; (8) the acquisition of $\overline{\text{X}}$ rules; (9) the acquisition of obligatory or optional arguments to verbs; and (10) Wexler's Uniqueness Principle (Roeper 1981). In each case, we show that the Subset Principle entails the specific acquisition principle advanced. It appears that they all can be explained under the general umbrella of this single learning principle.

Finally, we take up an application of the automata theoretic model of inference developed at the end of chapter 5. We show how the English auxiliary verb system can be learned from a less-than-exhaustive sample of positive example sentences. Importantly, this result holds because the AUX system is backwards deterministic within a fixed radius of one word. Evidently, just where a "brute force" induction procedure may be required, the linguistic system is constrained to be easily learnable.

6.1   Kean's Theory of Phonological Markedness

Chapter 5 defined *markedness* in a decision theoretic way, as the amount of information that it takes to fix a particular grammar (or rule in a particular grammar). It was further claimed that the information load required to fix a grammar could be reduced by the right combination of initial constraints and developmental sequencing. But are these abstract possibilities actually realized in practice in an actual linguistic system? Is the model of program size a useful one in the study of acquisition complexity? As a concrete case study this section examines in detail Kean's (1974) theory of markedness for phonological segmental systems and phonological rules.

According to the distinctive feature theory of phonology originally developed by Prague school structuralists such as Jakobson and pursued by Chomsky and Halle in *Sound Pattern of English* (1968), all natural sound segments such as a or p can be described via a small number of binary-valued distinctive features. By and large these features have an articulatory or an acoustic grounding, with names suggestive of their place or manner of articulation, such as high, back, anterior, and the like. 24 or so features in all. Given binary values for distinctive features (+ or −), there are 2^{24} possible segments (about 16.8 million). Most of these segments are not attested in human phonological systems. Furthermore, most *collections* of segments in a particular natural language do not make use of an extensive number of these possible contrasts.

As Kean shows, in part the reason for this is that distinctive features are not fixed in isolation. Rather, certain distinctive features can be fixed *only after* certain other features are fixed. For instance, according to Kean's theory the distinctive feature **consonantal** must be fixed before the feature **back** or **continuant**. We shall see more about what this means below.

Kean developed this theory as a way to explain some of the observed restrictions on possible segmental systems and possible phonological rule systems. But there is another way to interpret such a theory, and that is as a developmental program for how a segmental system is acquired. The hierarchically-organized implicational structure involved in setting a particular distinctive feature value is in fact a developmental "program" of just the sort described abstractly in chapter 5. That is, we can identify the *markedness* of a particular rule, segment, or phonological system as the amount of information required to fix that system developmentally. This structure in turn permits a considerable compression of the information required to fix a particular segmental system, just as the program metaphor suggested. For example, as we shall see, instead of demanding a selection of the distinctive feature value settings of the segment a out of the entire space of possible settings, the developmental program can fix the features settings for a via just eight parameters.

By construing the theory in this new way, one can in fact exhibit an acquisition system in which large numbers of developmental pathways are eliminated because of the *order* in which a small number of parameters are set. Moreover, the developmental model actually *explains* the existence of Kean's constraints, constraints that, while presumably universal, are otherwise not accounted for. Put another way, taken as a model of acquisition, the Kean theory provides an explicit example of how developmental sequencing can actually be an aid for acquisition, above and beyond the constraints provided by models of acquisition that assume an "instantaneous" fixing of a system of knowledge.

To see how this approach works in detail it will first be necessary to outline Kean's theory of markedness for phonological segments. Kean states the basic aim of her theory as follows:

It is assumed here that there is a relatively small set of distinctive features with binary specifications in terms of which all the members of every segmental system can be characterized at every stage of phonological representation. The postulation of such a set of features makes a substantive claim as to the class of possible elements in phonological systems.

Of the set of possible segments characterized by the distinctive features, it is evident that some are present in nearly every language, with others only occasionally occurring. For example, the segments t and a are nearly ubiquitous in segmental systems; they are found at all stages of phonological representation in an overwhelming majority of languages, but the segments kp and u only occasionally enjoy a place in segmental systems. The simple postulation of a set of features cannot account for such facts. (1974:6)

To explain the relative frequency or rarity of certain segments, Kean posits "a hierarchy of features which is derivable from the intrinsic ordering ... of markedness conventions" (1974:81). For example, vowels are usually −anterior, consonants are +anterior. It is therefore highly unusual, or marked, for a vowel to have the feature +anterior. But a vowel also has the feature −consonantal (it is not a consonant) and consonants the feature +consonantal. Therefore, the feature anterior is correlated with that of consonantal. In the unmarked case, we have the following rule:

u(nmarked) anterior   →   +anterior/+consonantal
                          −anterior/−consonantal

Forming the complement of this rule, we obtain the convention for determining what the value of anterior should be if it is marked:

(m)arked anterior   →   −anterior/+consonantal
                        +anterior/−consonantal

To determine whether a segment is marked for anterior or not logically demands that the feature consonantal be set first. If it is −consonantal, then we would expect the segment to be −anterior (the unmarked case); if +consonantal, the segment will usually be +anterior. Pursuing this approach,

Figure 6.1: Part of a distinctive feature hierarchy based on markedness

Kean goes on to show that whether the feature **back** is unmarked (expected) or marked (unexpected) is dependent on the value of the distinctive feature **anterior**. We then obtain the hierarchy of distinctive features as in figure 6.1. Applied to all 24 distinctive features, we obtain figure 6.2.

Each distinctive feature in the network depends on those features immediately *above* it to determine whether it is marked or not. For example, to determine whether the feature **continuant** is marked or unmarked we must know the values of the the features **coronal** and **nasal**; to know whether **continuant** is marked or not, we must know the values of the features **coronal** and all features above **coronal**, **nasal**, and **sonorant**.

The Kean hierarchy as a developmental model

Although Kean did not choose to do so, we may interpret this hierarchical structure as the specification of a developmental program for acquiring a segmental system. According to distinctive feature theory, segments can be distinguished only if they have different values for at least one of the 24 distinctive features. For example, the segments a and i are distinguishable given a segmental system that sets all distinctive features for the two segments to the same value save for the feature **back**. Segment a is unmarked for **back**, while i is marked for **back** (i.e., is expected). To take another example, the segment æ is also marked for **back** (−**back**) but is distinguishable from i because it is additionally marked +**low**.

We see then that a segment must be explicitly marked in order to distinguish it from the default set of plus and minus values. Otherwise, all segments would be unmarked for all distinctive features, and hence all would possess the same array of distinctive feature values. In other words, if we regard the array of distinctive feature marks as partitioning the universe of

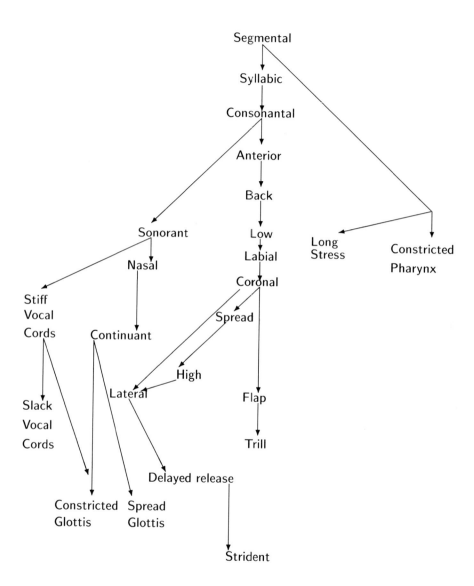

Figure 6.2: A complete markedness hierarchy of distinctive features

possible segments into equivalence classes, then if no segments were marked there would be just one class of segments, the totally unmarked segment.

This remark is not quite accurate, however, since Kean also assumes a basic syllabic/nonsyllabic distinction in addition to purely distinctive feature contrasts. As a result, there is always an initial division of all possible segments into two classes: consonants and vowels, according to the rules:[1]

> unmarked consonantal   →   +consonantal/ −syllabic
> marked consonantal   →   −consonantal/+syllabic

Given the initial partition defined by the feature ±syllabic, we can thus distinguish two classes of segments, even if no other distinctive features are used for marking segments:

(1)   { i, e, æ, u, o, œ, ī, ē, ā ū, ō } (+syllabic)

(2)   { p, t, tʸ ... } (−syllabic)

At this stage then, there are in effect just two segments, "consonants" and "vowels," as defined by local segmental context. To generate new classes, we must mark additional distinctive feature values. The key idea here is that there is a definite order in which new features are used to form new segmental classes. New classes may be formed by splitting established classes, with the split based on the order given by the distinctive feature hierarchy. Suppose we start with a division into just two classes of segments, consonants and vowels. The next partition is based on the next *unused* (previously unmarked) feature in the hierarchy. This is a natural assumption. We cannot get a new class of segments unless we explicitly mark a distinctive feature contrary to its expected value. Otherwise we would simply obtain the default feature settings for all later features in the feature hierarchy. So we must mark at least one new distinctive feature. Further, since features lower down in the hierarchy depend on the values of features above them, the natural place to look for the next distinctive feature to mark or not is the next feature below ±consonantal in the hierarchy, i.e., either the feature **anterior** or the feature **sonorant**. We cannot skip either of these features to try to mark, say, the feature **labial**, because the value of labial depends upon whether **low** and

---

[1] The initial division into ±SYLLABIC might be derived from the basic strong-weak pattern of metrical phonology. Then ±SYLLABIC might be dispensable; see, e.g., Vergnaud and Halle (1980). This matter will not be pursued here.

labial were marked or not, and these features have not yet been evaluated. So let us say that, in general, a new partition must be formed by marking exactly one of the distinctive features immediately below the last feature that was marked.

How is a split triggered? This choice must be "data driven" since different segmental systems will have different segments (from the adult point of view) that are marked for a particular distinctive feature. For example, as Kean observes, in Hawaiian only the segment n is marked for sonorant, but in Wichita, it is r that is so marked (1974:57). See figure 6.3. So a split must be triggered by the existence of some detectable difference between at least one of the members of an existing segmental class and the rest of the members of that class. Presumably, this difference could be detected on a variety of grounds—articulatory or acoustic minimal pairs; nothing more will be said here about just how this might occur. What one can say, however, is just *where* the next distinction will be made—the next available unused distinctive feature in the Kean hierarchy. Moreover, the amount of information it takes to split an existing class is also clear—it will take just one minimal pair distinction, or one bit of information.

As an example, consider again the class vowels {i, e, æ, œ, ... }. By the hierarchy diagram, the next split of the class must be captured by the value of the next feature below consonantal, namely, anterior. As it turns out, the feature combination [−cons +anterior] is an articulatory impossibility, so that in fact the feature anterior cannot be freely varied given that the value of the feature consonantal is minus. So the candidate distinctive features that may be used to split the class {i, e, a, ... } are the features just below anterior, namely, back or sonorant. The combination [−consonantal, −sonorant] is also impossible, however, so that a potential split must be pursued by considering the two features below sonorant, namely, nasal or stiff vocal cords. For now, let us make the assumption that the feature back, being the first immediately available unused feature, is elected to serve as the carrier of the new distinction. Note that in any case features lower down in the Kean hierarchy, e.g. continuant, or strident, cannot be used at this point to form new classes of segments.

Suppose then that the feature back is selected for marking, forming the basis for a new partition of segments. By marking back we obtain the following potential classes: marked back {i, e, æ, u, ... } and unmarked back {a, ... }. Note that Kean's marking convention, unmarked back → + back/−anterior,

	p	n	m	k	l	e	u	o	a	i	?	h	w
cons	u	u	u	u	u	u	m	u	u	u	m	m	m
ant	u	u	u	m	u	u	u	u	u	u	u	u	u
back	u	u	u	u	u	m	u	u	u	m	u	u	u
low	u	u	u	u	u	u	u	m	u	u	u	u	m
lab	m	u	m	u	u	u	u	u	u	u	u	u	u
son	u	m	m	u	u	u	u	u	u	u	u	u	u

Hawaiian

	t	k	k^w	r	h	a	i	u
cons	u	u	u	u	m	u	u	u
ant	u	m	m	u	u	u	u	u
back	u	u	u	u	u	u	u	u
low	u	u	u	u	u	u	u	m
lab	u	u	m	u	u	u	u	u
son	u	u	u	m	u	u	u	u

Wichita

Figure 6.3: Some segmental systems in terms of markedness

establishes that marked back must be −back in this case, and unmarked back, +back. In effect, two "vowels" have been established, corresponding to two possible pathways through the hierarchy diagram.

In an actual segmental system, there must be some segment that actually prompts this split. That is, there must be some segment that is marked for anterior, some segment (perhaps the same segment) marked for back, etc. This constraint implies that every natural segmental system must have at least one segment that is marked for every feature in the hierarchy diagram. However, this constraint is too strong; as Kean observes, natural segmental systems do not seem to utilize all possible feature contrasts. A restricted version of the constraint does seem to hold, Kean notes. The features in the graph from sonorant and coronal upwards are attested in all natural segmental systems.

How does this process fit into a program size measure of acquisition complexity? Fixing a marked back/unmarked back distinction requires one bit of information. The total amount of external information required to fix a segment corresponds to the number of marks (m's) it receives. Thus, if no new classes were ever formed (hence, no segments ever marked), then no external evidence would be required to fix such a system (and it would have only the completely unmarked segments t and a). In contrast, if a segment such as ϕ is marked for three features, labial, continuant, and slack glottis, it demands three externally supplied bits of information to prompt three class splits.

In general the acquisition complexity of a particular segment depends upon its hierarchical relationship to other classes that have already been acquired. If the segment is immediately below an established class in the Kean hierarchy, then its specification is largely determined by the specification of the class above it. For example, a segment marked for back, low, and labial is just one mark different from the class established before it that is marked for back and labial; to specify this new class one need only draw a single new distinction rather than restate the entire chain of partitions. This information-theoretic redundancy is captured by the hierarchical relationship between the features back, low, and labial. In short, in the case of segmental acquisition one can show that the information-theoretic measure of acquisition complexity and the linguistic model of complexity coincide. The *size* of the developmental program for a segmental system is precisely the number

	X1	X2	X3	X4
consonantal	m	u	u	u
anterior	m	u	u	u
back	m	u	u	u
low	u	m	u	u
labial	u	u	m	u
sonorant	u	u	m	u

Figure 6.4: An impossible segmental system

of decision points that are required to fix the system—the maximum number of m's used.

The important feature of the partitioning process is that splitting occurs at the leading edge of the directed hierarchy graph, by successive refinement of existing classes of segments.

Because extension of classes occurs solely via the refinement of existing partitions, the set of segmental classes at step i will be a homomorphic image of the other class diagrams before it in the developmental sequence. Also note that the hierarchy tree is developed by marking just one distinctive feature at a time—not a necessary constraint, since it is not clear why one could not develop a new class by marking two or more features in one step. The result of this constraint is to guarantee that at any step i in the development of a segmental system the classes of segments will be at most one mark (m) different. For instance, this constraint excludes the array of marks in figure 6.4.

From one point of view the one-mark constraint is a puzzling one. It is not at all obvious why segmental systems should be designed so that the alteration of a single distinctive feature could convert an a into an i. This would seem to be an unwise design choice from the standpoint of error detection or error correction; as is well known, in order to be able to correct errors of k bits, then segments would have to be separated by a "ball" of radius $2k + 1$ (since one must guarantee that changes of up to k bits in any two segments still leave one able to determine the original segment). However, as will be discussed in more detail immediately below, the one-mark constraint is a natural one given a model of acquisition from positive-only evidence. Importantly, natural segmental systems seem to obey the one-mark constraint, as Kean observes. If this observation is correct, then the one-mark constraint fits naturally into a model of incremental, acquisition from positive-only evidence (rather than a model of error detection or correction).

Finally, because marking is always carried out at the immediate fringes of the existing class tree, the set of possible segmental systems is significantly constrained, and the information load of acquisition correspondingly reduced. Intuitively, this is so because the total information content of a segmental system is now encoded via *paths* through the developmental hierarchy rather than in a matrix of marked and unmarked features. By ordering the marking of segments one can focus attention on just one distinction at a time. Put another way, instead of setting all n features of each segment in a system plus or minus independently, a total of approximately 2^n decisions, one can fix the markings of a complete segmental system in a sequence of n decisions in a row.

For example, consider the difference between fixing a segment such as m in isolation vs. fixing it as part of a larger segmental system. Segment m is marked for the features labial and sonorant. But by the one-mark constraint, there must be some other segment in the system that is just like m, except that it is unmarked for labial; call this segment x. Segment x (or, rather, the bundle of marked and unmarked features that, so far, identify it as an equivalence class of segments) was identified earlier than m. To fix m we need only make one additional decision: is there a member of the old class that is marked labial or not? If it is, we obtain an m in the segmental system; if not, we obtain an n or something close to an n (segment x) but no m.

Put another way, the class of possible natural segmental systems seems to be more restricted than one might expect given a model where segments are obtained by selecting arrays of marked and unmarked distinctive features at random. Segmental systems are constrained in just the ways one might expect if they were acquired on the basis of an incremental fixing of segments according to the Kean feature hierarchy.[2]

---

[2] Readers familiar with techniques for compact storage of matrices will note that the markedness matrices are for the most part sparsely populated with m's, and those m's that do exist are systematically related to one another. But this is simply to say that there is a more compact representation of the matrix than an explicit list of u's and m's—namely, as a series of partition decisions

Let us consider this last point in somewhat more detail. Kean also notes that many segmental systems are not attested, and posits as a descriptive account of this fact what was called above the "one mark" condition.

(i) For each [m-obligatory] feature there exists at least one segment which is marked for that feature. (These features are numbered $i = 3$ to 8 and comprise consonantal, anterior, back, low, labial, and sonorant.)

(ii) For each pair of features F_i and F_j, $3 \leq i < j \leq 8$, if there is any segment which is marked for both F_i and F_j, then there are two segments S and S', such that S is marked for one but not both of F_i and F_j, and S and S' agree for all other features F_k, $3 \leq k \leq 8$, $k \neq i, j$. (1974:61)

This descriptive constraint has two effects. First, it ensures that every natural segmental system has a certain richness; there cannot be a system that has only one or two marks, hence only one or two segments. Second, no segment is two m's different from any other segment, at least for a certain class of primary distinctive features; every segment can be at most one m distinct from every other segment.

Kean observes that many unusual segmental systems, such as the Hawaiian system presented above, satisfy this constraint. In contrast, a system where m is two marks different from any other segment would be impossible.

Apparently the distinguishability condition is descriptively adequate. But there is no obvious reason *why* this condition should hold. Why couldn't there be a segmental system with segments that were two or more marks different from other segments in the system?

The one-m condition follows from the markedness hierarchy interpreted as an incremental developmental model. As we have described the way in which the hierarchy can be interpreted as an acquisition model, only one feature can be used to form a new partition of segments—only one *mark* is ever added at any given step. As a result, at any stage in the acquisition of a segmental system the partitions correspond to segments that are at most one m apart, automatically satisfying the distinguishability constraint. So Kean's observation might well be explained as a side-effect of the acquisition of segmental systems. Even so, it seems as though we have merely replaced a stipulation about the well-formedness of segmental systems with a stipula-

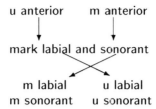

Figure 6.5: Incremental acquisition via markedness

tion about the acquisition of segmental systems. Why should acquisition be incremental?

There are several reasons why one-m acquisition steps should be the rule. A weak argument is that it would be natural for the smallest unit of a representational system to be able to function in a model of how changes to that representation can be made; if rules can make reference to the single unit **anterior**, then it is natural to expect that there could be rules to set just the value of the single unit **anterior**.

A stronger argument can be made on grounds of acquisition, as mentioned earlier. Suppose that acquisition is not incremental, so that two or more marks can be added at a single step. It would then be possible to form a new class partition based on marking both the features **labial** and **sonorant** without having first used the feature **sonorant** to form any segment classes. Figure 6.5 illustrates.

Now there is no class that will correctly accommodate a segment that is [u labial, m sonorant]. One way to remedy this problem would be to allow the procedure to go back and rebuild classes that have already been formed, but this would violate the developmental ordering that has been assumed. The fringe of the hierarchy tree would no longer summarize the possible next states that could be hypothesized, since there could be segments such as **n** that would demand the interpolation of new classes between older partitions and the current partition. In other words, the one-m constraint amounts to the demand that new classes be the minimally specific refinements of existing classes. This way of ordering hypotheses follows the Subset Principle. It is just what we would expect if segments are acquired by positive evidence.

Beyond the one-mark constraint, there are apparently other restrictions on segmental systems that may have an explanation in the domain of acquisition, though the connection is not so straightforward. Consider figure 6.6. This array of marked and unmarked [−syllabic, −consonantal] segments as exhibited by Kean (1974:47), where blank positions indicate an unmarked segment, m=marked.

While the details of this markedness matrix are not crucial, what is significant is that the matrix exhibits a high degree of redundancy. Apparently, even though there are 2^{24} possible patterns of distinctive feature values—over 16 million possibilities, as Kean notes—most of these are not exhibited in natural segmental systems. This sparseness is apparent in the regions of the matrix above that are uniformly unmarked. It seems as though the features stiff vocal cords, delayed release, and so on are not utilized in distinguishing among vowels. As Kean observes, some of these impossible co-occurring feature values can be accounted for since they would otherwise imply the existence of contradictory articulatory features. For example, a segment cannot be both low and high; hence, the value −low implies that high must be +high; a segment cannot be both flapped and trilled, hence +flap → −trill. But the great bulk of the redundancy remains unexplained, as Kean remarks:

> Any theory of phonology which assumes the current feature framework must have some mechanism for excluding these nonoccurring segments. The cases [of implicational constraints—rcb] are meant to be illustrative of the types of segments which must be disallowed in phonological systems. Further research in this area is called for. (1974:72 n. 6)

The constraint here could well be developmental. Recall that according to the rule for forming new classes the features nasal, stiff vocal cords, and back are all candidates for a partition of the basic vowel class into two new classes, and that the feature back is apparently selected. For whatever reason, the features nasal and stiff vocal cords are not used. Without accounting for this last fact, observe that by the definition of the developmental process, we cannot mark a feature (hence use it to create a new partition) unless the features above it in the markedness hierarchy have previously been used to create a new partition. But then, if nasal and stiff vocal cords are never marked, then none of the features below them in the hierarchy ever become available for forming partitions of the class of vowels.

	i	e	æ	u	o	œ	ī	ē	ā	ū	ō	c
cons												
ant												
back	m	m	m	m	m	m						
low			m			m	m	m		m	m	
cor												
son												
lab				m	m	m	m	m				
spr												
high		m			m			m			m	
nas												
cont												
StVc												
SlVc												
SG												
CG												
lat												
DR												
stri												
flap												
trill												

Figure 6.6: **A markedness matrix.**

Given the developmental model, the features slack vocal cords, constricted glottis, spread glottis, strident, continuant, lateral, and delayed release will all remain unmarked, as a body. This is precisely what is observed. Schematically, a whole section of the hierarchical tree becomes inaccessible because of the "blocking" effect of the u's positioned at the features stiff vocal cords and nasal.

It is claimed then that the systematic nonappearance of certain clusters of distinctive features is a by-product of the incremental acquisition model itself, and in that sense is explained by a developmental model. By restricting the way in which new partitions can be formed out of old ones, the model implies that once certain pathways are not selected for forming segmental classes, they will never be selected. This adds considerable constraint to the acquisition process itself. For instance, once a segment is known as [−syllabic −consonantal], only the following additional distinctions need be made: back, low, labial, coronal, nasal, stiff vocal cords, spread, high, for a total of 8. In contrast, if one cannot eliminate such pathways, then 19 features must be set.[3] The developmental program allows us to "compress" the table of u's and m's exhibited above into a ordered series of 8 step-by-step decisions. Each new class partitioning depends on the partition decisions that have gone before— as reflected in the Kean hierarchy. The current state of the class partitions reflects previous decisions; at each step, only a single new markedness decision (determining which distinctive feature should be marked "m") is made. By arranging the decisions sequentially over time yet in correspondence with the hierarchy graph, we reduce the problem of fixing a [−syllabic −consonantal] segmental system from one of choosing a single system out of 2^{16} possible systems to one of making just eight decisions.

The developmental model proposed here effects a considerable economy over an instantaneous model that would simply "project" an entire segmental system in a single step given a representative body of data for that system.[4]

---

[3]There are some complications to this picture that have not been directly addressed here. Some of the impossible alternatives are the result of impossible articulatory co-occurrences, as Kean observes. These result in a series of implicational demands, such as, −CONSONANTAL → +ANTERIOR. This complicates the account of which features are accessible or not. If a feature is set by implication, then features below it in the hierarchy can become accessible, just as if that feature had been used for marking.

[4]One could, of course, *simulate* a developmental model in an instantaneous framework, since one is free to specify any function whatsoever to project the initial data into a final segmental system. But this approach would seem to miss the point. We should also emphasize that this ordering effect is only a *logical* one; it need not be so ordered in

This is one case where a noninstantaneous model actually does better than an instantaneous one. By relaxing the idealization that acquisition decisions are made "in parallel" one can arrive at a better account of the observed segmental systems in natural languages.

The compression in the table of u's and m's for [−syllabic −consonantal] segments is made possible at the price of ordering the decisions about how distinctive features are to be marked. As a result, the model predicts that there should be observable *stages* in the development of segmental systems corresponding to the implicational structure of the markedness hierarchy. Chapter 5 claimed that developmental stages are in fact simply the visible surface residue of such implicational structure. If this model of category ontogenesis is correct, it suggests a variety of predictions about the externally observable course of acquisition of phonological rules. For instance, the model subsumes an early and well-known proposal of Jakobson's (1968) regarding the expected order acquisition of phonological categories within a distinctive feature theory. Those categories that appear earliest in the implicational structure of the developmental "program" as defined by Kean's markedness hierarchy are those that must be acquired first. According to Kean's distinctive feature hierarchy, the features segmental and syllabic would be set first, then the feature consonantal. This ordering predicts that t, p, and k would be among the first consonants acquired, and a, i, the first vowels. Note that this sequencing appears to be *roughly* verified by empirical work, though there has been controversy regarding Jakobson's more restricted, and probably overly-strong proposal. Of course, what developmental sequence is actually observed "on the surface" could depend on the interaction of other factors besides this hierarchy that is presumably a part of universal grammar. In particular, one would expect performance factors to intervene and complicate the actual developmental course. In the case of phonological categories, for example, the delayed appearance of t relative to p could possibly be due to the intrinsic difficulty of producing a dental consonant—a matter partially dependent on motor control, hence possibly subject to interference via maturational effects not a part of the specification of Universal Grammar per se. Jakobson's proposal also differs in some details from the model described here:

> Ordinarily child language begins, and the aphasic dissolution
> of language preceding its complete loss ends, with what psy-

---

time, though its interpretation as such leads to interesting developmental predictions, as discussed in the main text.

chopathologists have termed the "labial stage." In this phase, speakers are capable of only one type of utterance, which is usually transcribed as /pa/ .... The development of the oral resonance features in child language presents a whole chain of successive acquisitions interlinked by laws of implication.

the development of the spirants presupposes that of the stops in children's speech, and in the world's languages the former cannot exists without the latter .... The development of the back consonants presupposes in the speech development of the child the development of the front consonants, i.e. the labials and dentals trans. Olmsted (1971:106)

In Jakobson's theory, as in the model presented above, the development of phonological contrasts proceeds by homomorphic refinement of existing contrasts. It is cruder than Kean's theory because it does not incorporate the articulatory implications of Kean's hierarchy (such as −cons → +anterior) or the bifurcations of Kean's hierarchy. Scollon (1976:48–52), in the context of a study of a single child's productions, notes that Jakobson's stage predictions do not hold exactly:"it looks as if the stage 3, labial-dental split, seems to be not a contrast in position so much as a split between [+continuant] and [−continuant]." The Kean hierarchy has a richer implicational structure that may explain this kind of variation: the continuant feature could lie on a different line of triggering from a dental/labial contrast. It remains to explore in detail the predictions for segmental acquisition made by the Kean markedness hierarchy.

Natural classes and the developmental hierarchy

Kean noted that the hierarchy of distinctive features not only provides a blueprint for a developmental model of segmental systems, it also defines natural classes of distinctive features. For instance, Kean observed that there are no phonological rules of the following form:

−sonorant   →   [delayed release (DR) Constricted Glottis (CG)]
+consonantal →   [continuant labial]

The question is, Why not? There are other attested phonological rules that mention the features **delayed release** or **labial**, and other rules that change more than two distinctive features. The answer Kean proposed was that it seems as if there are no phonological rules that mention features that are not hierarchically related, according to the developmental program. **DR** and **constricted glottis** do not form a "natural class" of features, because they lie on different branches of the hierarchy tree; in contrast, the feature **labial** lies directly above **high**, and so there can be a rule that combines these two features.

This constraint makes sense from an information theoretic viewpoint, and actually ties together three major themes of this chapter: the definition of a natural class, disjunction, and acquisition from positive-only evidence.

Consider first how much information it takes to define some class of features. Suppose that the features are not hierarchically related according to the Kean diagram, as in the pair [CG DR]. To specify the value of **DR** we must give values for all the features above it in the hierarchy: **consonantal, anterior, back, low, labial, coronal, spread, sonorant, high, nasal, continuant, lateral**; for **CG** we must give values for **consonantal, anterior, sonorant, stiff vocal cords, nasal,** and **continuant**. Thus the specification of the pair, [CG DR] requires one to provide enough information to write down the entire hierarchy tree, save for the righthand section that pertains to the features flap, trill, etc.—a total of 13 distinct features. This is larger than the number of features it takes to specify either **CG** or **DR** separately, and thus violates the definition of a natural class, repeated below:

> N is a natural class if it takes the same or less information to specify N as any individual member of N.

In contrast, suppose that two features are hierarchically related, as in [anterior back]. Then the specification of back will almost entirely overlap that of anterior; once we have specified the value of **anterior**, it takes but one more decision to fix the value for **back**. Thus the specification of the class [anterior back] will take at most the same amount of information as that needed to specify [back], and forms a natural class. In general, it is easy to see that any pair of hierarchically related features will possess this compression property, and that any pair of nonhierarchically related features will not. It is, of course, the fact that the specifications for **anterior** and **back** are redundant, or overlap, that allows us to collapse the description of the pair [anterior back].

6.2 The *M* Constraint

We now turn to an important constraint on semantic representations proposed by Sommers (1971) and Keil (1979), the *M constraint*. We shall show that it fits into our model of incremental acquisition. As described earlier, Sommers proposes that if one arranges terms such as *dog*, *cat*, *love*, and so forth into a graph structure whose terminal leaves are terms and where each node is an item that can sensibly be predicated of the all terms below it in the graph, then one never, or rarely, finds human intuitions of sensibility resulting in *M* shaped graphs. Rather, the graph structures take the form of hierarchical trees. Figure 6.7 illustrates.

Cases of *M* shaped patterns are evidently rare, and are characteristically found with lexical ambiguity, as in the word *bat*, which can be either made of wood or a flying mammal (Keil 1979:13).

Keil points out that the *M* constraint may be motivated on the information theoretic grounds of compact representation: as observed by Katz (1966), the effect of using a hierarchical network to organize the properties of things such as cars, trees, and ideas is to save space by eliminating the need to list, redundantly, the predicates sensibly applying to both trees and cars. Keil also suggests that the constraint could reflect the demands of acquisition, without being explicit about just how the constraint would help. However, it is plain that the constraint aids acquisition because *M* shaped patterns correspond to disjunctive, unnatural classes. By avoiding such patterns, an acquisition procedure can ensure that its knowledge can be stated in a disjunction-free fashion—an important property if acquisition is to be based on positive-only evidence.

As noted by Iba (1979) and others, if disjunctive statements are permitted then one cannot always guarantee that acquisition will succeed without appeal to negative examples. In addition, the *M* constraint suggests a specific set of restrictions on the ontogenesis of categorization abilities, as discussed by Keil (1979). In particular, Keil found through empirical studies of children that the hierarchical tree structures demanded by the *M* constraint developed by nonerasing homomorphic mappings—that is, children formed new categories by splitting old ones, rather than creating entirely different tree structures.

Intriguingly, the restrictions on segmental and phrase structure systems also seem to obey the *M*-constraint. Both systems exhibit the characteris-

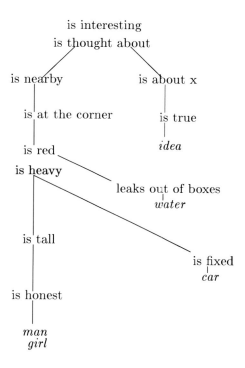

Figure 6.7: An M-constrained predicate hierarchy tree

tic M-constrained pattern of nondisjunctive categorization, suggesting that these systems, too, are constrained so as to be acquirable on the basis of positive-only information. Moreover, the developmental pattern in both systems is the same, with new categories developing out of old ones. There is no apparent radical restructuring of categorization trees. This confluence of constraint in two quite different rule systems can be taken as strong support for the category-splitting approach to phrase structure acquisition used by the acquisition procedure discussed in chapters 2 and 3.[5]

One can see that the M constraint embodies the same information-theoretic definition of what counts as a natural class as that advanced by the phonological model. For example, suppose that *zorch* was a word denoting either a blue pyramid or a red cube. According to the M constraint, *zorch* could not stand for a natural concept, at least not in the vocabulary of blocks used earlier. This is because *zorch* would fall under two separate hierarchy trees, violating the M constraint. *Zorch* is not a natural kind term because its specification according to the predicate hierarchy requires one to describe the entire predicate tree—each branch must be listed. But given that this much information could used to pick out the term *zorch*, then we could use the same capability to specify almost any pair of terminal items in the predicate tree, even if they were not covered by a single label. It is this property that distinguishes a natural from a nonnatural concept: if the information required to specify a term is such that a *random* class of items could be specified, then that term is nonnatural. Nonnaturalness corresponds to the lack of explanatory power, because so much information is required to pick out a nonnatural class that one could just as easily pick out a random collection of items that are connected in no apparent causal fashion.

Returning to the discussion of the M constraint, it is easy to see that there is a close connection between the developmental hierarchy for phonological segments and the trees discussed by Keil. Observe first that the connections among predicates established by sensibility judgments form a subsumption relationship, where a predicate P_1 subsumes entities X, Y just in case one can meaningfully predicate P_1 of X and Y. Thus if $P_1 = alive$,

---

[5]In the case of Kean's theory, there are several apparent exceptions to the M constraint that occur in the case of marked distinctive features (such as constricted glottis). Acquisition of items positively marked with distinctive features such as these would then require negative evidence or explicit correction to acquire—a legitimate possibility, considering the rarity of the feature. However, the core structure of Kean's system obeys the M constraint. Alternatively, the presence of M-shaped patterns in Kean's system might be taken as a potential defect that ought to be remedied.

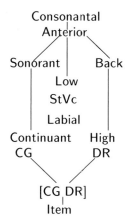

Figure 6.8: Segmental development follows the M constraint

$X=$ *tree*, $Y=$ *fish*, $Z=$ *rock*, then P_1 subsumes X and Y, but not Z. The subsumption relationship is the relationship of "domination" in the tree of possible predications. If there is some predicate P_2 such that P_2 applies to X but not Y, then P_2 dominates X, but not Y. But then, the domain of objects to which P_2 can be sensibly applied is a subset of those to which P_1 can be sensibly applied. We may take this subset relationship as establishing a partial ordering of predicates, just as in the phonological acquisition model.

Given this partial ordering of predicates, one can now see that M constraint violations correspond to nonhierarchically related, hence unnatural classes. For instance, consider the class [DR CG]. Represented in the distinctive feature partial ordering, we obtain an M shaped pattern. See figure 6.8.

More generally, one has the following result: a class X creates an M constraint violation with respect to a predicate hierarchy T iff X is unnatural in T, where *unnatural in* T can be defined information-theoretically, as above, or descriptively, as a term that is defined by nonhierarchically related predicates. Compare Keil (1979:161):

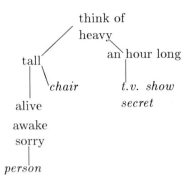

Figure 6.9: An example predicability tree at age 5–6

> For a concept to be natural it must be composed of predicates that denote the same category or categories that are supersets or subsets of one another.

Beyond this connection between the M constraint and natural classes defined information-theoretically, there are other correspondences between Keil's results and the general developmental model presented earlier. Let us review these briefly.

First, Keil found that predicate hierarchies developed via the refinement of existing classes of predicates, rather than by the radical reconstruction of predicate applicability relationships. This finding was supported by studies of the growth of predicate trees of young children. In other words, Keil found that the trees developed via the branching of the fringes of existing predicates—the same process of homomorphic refinement as was posited in the phonological model presented above. For instance, at the earliest ages studied (5–6 yrs.), some children's predicate trees looked like that in figure 6.9.

When second graders were tested, their trees were foliated versions of initial trees, as shown in figure 6.10. This developmental assumption is just like that of the phonological model. A new phonological partition is formed when it is realized that a segment is *not* like the segments of its classmates,

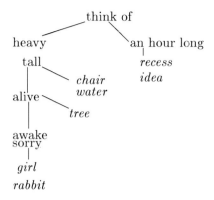

Figure 6.10: Foliated tree at later age

and hence must be marked. (The hierarchy tree dictates *how* it must be marked.)

Second, with rare exceptions, children were found to obey the M constraint. This constraint is also honored by phonological rules.

Third, the lattice of predications had an upper bound, an all-embracing predicate that could be applied to *any* object: e.g., *think about*. The corresponding predicate in the phonological domain is *syllabic* or, perhaps, *segmental*.

One of the key effects of the M constraint is to eliminate the possibility of disjunction in formulating descriptions of concepts, again as in the phonological case. For suppose that an item is described by predicates that are not hierarchically related, say by the chains P_1, ..., P_m and Q_1, ..., Q_n. Then that item falls under $(P_1, \ldots, P_m) \vee (Q_1, \ldots, Q_n)$, a disjunction that has no compact reformulation (assuming now a fixed stock of predicates). (The item could be trivially described by the general subsumer predicate *is thought about* just as the null set serves to bound from above all feature descriptions held in common, but this description would also admit many nonmembers of the class.) Thus M constraint violations must be expressed as disjunctions in the description language. Conversely, suppose that one has a description expressed disjunctively that is known to have no compact reformulation without the use of disjunctions. Then the description is of the form $P \vee Q$, where P

and Q are themselves hierarchical predicate chains. That is, the description violates the M constraint. Further, M constrained trees prohibit disjunction.

The relationship between lack of disjunction and compact representations raises the question as to whether it is possible to reformulate one's primitive vocabulary and arrive at a new system of predicates in which the formerly disjunctive description is eliminated. In a trivial sense this is possible: a disjunction $(A \vee B)$ can always be labeled by its own "name," e.g., C. This certainly leads to shorter descriptions. An approach of this kind has been adopted by some Artificial Intelligence researchers, notably, Langley (1977) as a heuristic for discovering new primitives: if one finds a recurring disjunction, then label it with a unique name. Note that if the M constraint is to be honored then the place at which the new "predicate" C is to be placed in the tree is clear; C must be spliced in at the point where A and B split. Note that this method, if allowed, would amount to a violation of the incremental, monotonic, approach to acquisition advanced earlier. The backtracking of the new category heuristic is much like that required to violate the one-m condition for segmental systems.

6.3   The Subset Principle

Chapter 5 outlined the formal details of the Subset Principle, as a general learning principle for acquisition using positive-only examples. It was claimed that this single principle underwrites most, if not all, specific learning principles about hypothesis ordering advanced in the linguistics literature. This section backs up that claim.

For our first case study, we will examine a problem that has been called Dative overgeneralization. The facts are these. (See Baker 1979; 1981; Pinker 1982.) With certain verbs one can interchange direct and indirect objects, but with others the switch is not permitted:

> *I told a story to Bill*
> *I told Bill a story*

The following examples show that the pattern of interchange is quite complex, varying from verb to verb in a subtle way even for verbs that are semantically quite similar.

X	V	NP	*to*	NP
1	2	3	4	5
1	2	5+3	∅	∅

Figure 6.11: A "classic" dative rule

I said a funny thing to Bill
*I said Bill a funny thing
I reported the crime to the police
*I reported the police the crime
I gave a book to Bill
I gave Bill a book
I loaned a book to the library
I loaned the library a book
I donated a book to the library
*I donated the library a book
I showed the book to Bill
I showed Bill the book
I demonstrated the typewriter to Bill
*I demonstrated Bill the typewriter

It is assumed that the acquisition procedure does not have access to the negative (starred) examples, which are never produced. The problem, of course, is how the acquisition procedure can avoid the overgeneralization that Dative alternation is always permissible. Suppose an example such as, *I gave Bill a book* triggers a rule hypothesis that such a shift is possible. On an *Aspects*-type account, as Baker (1979) shows, this would mean a rule something like that in figure 6.11.

This rule admits all of the starred examples listed above. Call the language generated by the rule system incorporating this rule L_i. If only positive evidence is available, there will be nothing to inform the acquisition procedure that it has overgeneralized; equivalently, there is language L_j that is also compatible with the example, *I gave Bill a book* and yet is a proper subset of

L_i. The Subset Principle is violated if the larger hypothesis is made first. If positive-only acquisition is to be maintained, then there must be some other triggering sequence of examples that avoids this pitfall.

Baker's solution to this problem is the obvious one: ensure that an interposed L_j *cannot* be generated. This he does by triggering the rule of Dative shift on a verb-by-verb basis. That is, if we associate with a verb's lexical entry its possible subcategorization frames, then the frame NP–NP (Dative shift) is associated with a particular verb if and only if a positive example exhibiting that frame has appeared with that verb. Thus, *give* would allow Dative shift as soon as *I gave John a book* was encountered; but since such verbs as *donate, demonstrate,* and *say* never appear with the Dative shift frame, the acquisition procedure would never generalize to include them. It should be clear that this "rule restricting" method eliminates the possibility of overgeneralization by positing the most conservative acquisition possible, thus ensuring that the Subset Principle obtains.

There is something unsatisfying about this approach, however. While it guarantees by fiat that acquisition by positive-only evidence will work, it leaves unexplained the apparent productivity of sentence variants like Dative alternation.[6] It also smacks of rote acquisition: if one admits the possibility of rule by rule acquisition with no generalization, then it should also be possible to acquire language on a sentence-by-sentence basis, save perhaps for a rudiment of recursion made possible by simple phrase structure rules.

More importantly, it does not seem to be even descriptively adequate, at least in the simple form that Baker provides. For, as pointed out in Stowell (1981), even a single verb such as *throw* sometimes permits Dativization and sometimes does not:

I threw the ball to Bill	*I threw Bill a ball*
I threw the ball to the ground	**I threw the ground the ball*

The subcategorization frame of *throw* would have to be annotated in some way to accommodate facts such as these.

Finally, conservative acquisition does not appear to be faithful to the facts about child acquisition, as noted by Pinker (1982):

---

[6]Baker claims that no productivity has been observed with Dativization in child language. Productivity is observed with other constructions, however, as discussed below.

It is held that children learn conservatively, entering predicate-construction pairs into their lexicon only upon hearing a particular predicate used in a particular construction.

Unfortunately, this solution will not work. It predicts that children will never generalize a known predicate to a new construction, and this predication is false. Bowerman (1974) documents her young daughter's productive mis-use of verbs in causative constructions, along the lines of "I jumped the doll," .... It seems then that children are neither purely conservative (item-by-item) nor purely liberal (lexical redundancy rule) learners. (1982:710–711)

To account for the apparent pattern of under- and over- generalization in child acquisition, Pinker (1982) proposes that productivity can be accommodated by the progressive loosening of "only if" conditions on the application of so-called "lexical rules" that have the effect of Dative alternation, making the Direct Object the Indirect Object, and vice-versa:

One possible explanation for these data is that children's lexical rules first apply only to narrowly defined semantic or thematic categories such as agent-of-action and patient-of-action. The difficulty with this account is in developing a plausible learning mechanism that will take the child from rules that operate on semantic or thematic symbols to the correct adult rules, which operate on grammatical functions [e.g., thematic roles are such terms as AGENT, PATIENT; grammatical functions are roughly the traditional notions of Subject, Object—rcb]. It could be that this change simply results from maturation, but I think one would want to implicate nonstationary mechanisms only as a last resort.

There is a better solution. One can invoke a certain property of lexical rules that is independently motivated by studies of adult grammar. In some languages, lexical rules may apply only if certain thematic conditions are first met. For example, a Passive lexical rule changing an object to a subject might apply only if the original subject and object were the agent and patient arguments of the predicate (Bresnan, personal communication). It could be that when children coin a lexical rule, the rule operates on grammatical functions, as it does in the adult grammar, but a set of "only if" provisos referring to the thematic relations of the arguments to the predicate are included with the rule . . . . If subsequently a sentence is encountered which inspires the learner to form a rule with the same function replacements, but which simultaneously violates one of the "only if" conditions (e.g. *Leon was considered by Cindy to be a fine yodeler*), that "only if" condition is deleted. Thus, the form of the rule remains constant, though its conditions for application might change depending on the particular target language. (1982:711–82)

Note that what Pinker is proposing amounts to a claim that the Subset Principle holds. The rule prompting Dative alternation is to be annotated with feature predicates that hold of semantically defined classes of verbs. A positive example exhibiting Dative shift acts as a trigger by showing that a certain semantically coherent class of verbs can undergo Dative shift— presumably, not the class that includes verbs such as *say*, *demonstrate*, or *report*. The problem now lies in uncovering the requisite distinctions. Pinker admits that this is a difficult hurdle:

Still, one problem remains. There seem to be pairs of semantically similar predicates in English such that only one member of the pair can be operated on by a lexical rule; for example, Dativization applied to *give* versus *donate*, *tell* versus *say*, *show* versus *demonstrate*, and so on. Assuming that there is no subtle semantic/thematic difference between all predicates that can undergo Dativization and all those that cannot, the only solution to this acquisition problem is to hypothesize some kind of information indirectly available to the learner that will inform him that a predicate cannot appear as a given lexical form. (1982:712)

As we shall see below, however, there seems to be no need to draw a *semantic* class distinction to account for these patterns of Dativization. Stowell (1981) observes that the distinction between *show* and *demonstrate* is apparently correlated with a Germanic/Latinate distinction in word formation, with word formation being in turn the key to the formation of Dative construction. Though some complications arise in this story—it is perhaps linked to deeper properties of residual Case assignment of Latinate forms—it at least indicates that semantic class distinctions among predicates are *not* crucial here.

Let us reanalyze this same acquisition problem from the standpoint of recent transformational theory, Government-Binding (GB) theory (Chomsky 1981). Contrary to some assertions that have appeared in the literature, GB theory actually provides a solution to the problem of Dative alternation acquisition, and in a way that surmounts the difficulties of the lexical approach.

First, one must point out that it is simply an error to assert that a transformational grammar cannot make reference to the properties of lexical items. All modern generative grammars, transformational grammars among them, consist of several modular components. A transformational grammar is not just a set of transformational rules; in addition, there is a lexicon. In particular, the properties of lexical items play a central role in Government-Binding theory, in virtue of the Projection Principle. The Projection Principle ensures that the properties of lexical items, including the subcategorization frames of lexical items, are available at every level of linguistic representation. Therefore, these properties may be assumed to be accessible at the point where annotated surface structure is built.

Suppose then a sentence such as, *I gave Bill a book* is encountered. What must be known in order for the sentence to be analyzed successfully? Plainly, there is a crucial prerequisite: the subcategorization frame of *give* must be known, at least in part. As Chomsky observes, to know what *give* means is to know at least that *give* takes an NP (Direct) Object, and an NP (Indirect) Object. Thematic roles must also be assigned correctly. Developmentally, an acquisition procedure could infer at least the presence of the NP direct object from the existence of sentences such as, *John gave a book to Mary*. Note that this means that there is then at least some ordering in the way examples are used for inference. Sentences where Dative shift has *not* applied are assumed to be used in acquisition before those where Dative Shift has applied. How can this ordering be imposed? Recall that we have ruled out the possibility of the external environment supplying this kind of constraint. However, ordering need not necessarily be supplied by the external environment itself, but might, rather, be imposed by the capabilities of the acquisition procedure—an intrinsic, rather than an extrinsic ordering. Chapter 3 discussed examples of this kind.

There are several ways this intrinsic ordering could arise. What happens when the procedure attempts to analyze a Dative shift *give* sentence? Assuming that some type of adjacency constraint on NP arguments has already been acquired (see below as to why this would be so), the NP directly after *give* will be taken as the main argument to *give*, i.e., it assumed to function the way *Mary* does in *John kissed Mary*. But this analysis gives the wrong annotated surface structure for *John gave Bill a book*, since it implies that *Bill* is what is given. Somehow, the acquisition procedure must be able to recognize that this is so. Here we assume that that the procedure consults an independently derived representation of thematic roles; *Bill* is not the thing given, so some change must be made. This assumption is also made in Pinker's model (1982) for the acquisition of lexical-functional grammars:

> I assume that the input to the child is a semantic text consisting of strings paired with "uncommitted" f-structures ["functional structures", the lexical-functional theory's analog of deep structures—rcb]. These f-structures differ from the ones that the adult would assign to sentences in that, clearly, they cannot contain information that is determined by rules that have not yet been learned. However, I assume that they contain information about the propositional structure of the sentence's meaning (such as the correct links between predicates and arguments), the topic-comment distinction defined by the pragmatics of the utterance, and whatever default grammatical information may be associated with the predicates and arguments (e.g., the assignment of SUBJ[ECT] to agent arguments) . . . . In this example ["John convinced the milkman to swat the dog"—rcb] the child is assumed to know that *John* is the topic of the utterance . . . that the principal predicate, *convince*, takes three arguments, corresponding here to *John, the milkman*, and *the milkman swats the dog*, that the predicate *swat* takes two arguments corresponding to *the milkman* and *the dog* that the same milkman is simultaneously the convinced and the swatter, and that the SUBJ[ECT] OBJ[ECT] and SCOMP[LEMENT], respectively, correspond to the agent, patient, and proposition arguments of the predicates. (1982:687–689)

Now we invoke the incrementality assumption adopted by the acquisition procedure, a principle of "inference from clear cases." Basically, the idea here is that no more than one decision is made in a single step. In the case of *John gave Bill a book*, two decisions must be made: one to add to the subcategorization frame for *give*, and one to permit a change to the default correlation between adjacency and thematic role. Since the sentence violates the canonical thematic-syntactic alignment, the acquisition procedure can conclude nothing about the subcategorization frame for *give*. In effect, the sentence is interpreted nonsyntactically, and prompts no change in the acquisition procedure's syntactic knowledge (in this case, the subcategorization frame for *give*). In contrast, suppose that the sentence *Bill gave a book to John* was encountered. Putting aside the problem of analyzing the indirect object, note that by the adjacency constraint and the default association between the NP adjacent to the verb as the thematic role of PATIENT, the procedure deduces that *a book* is the thing given—and this is confirmed by an independent reconstruction of thematic roles, or even a partial reconstruction in this case. It is this confirmation that allows the procedure to add an entry to *give*'s subcategorization frame. In the case of *John gave a book to Bill*, only the subcategorization frame of *give* must be altered, and so this is permitted. The result: the Dative sentence will be ignored as a source of information for syntactic acquisition *until* the unshifted form has been analyzed. Note that this assumption of incremental decision-making resembles the phonological one-mark constraint, and is in fact intended to order the space of acquisition decisions so that the Subset Principle is automatically satisfied.[7]

It has been assumed here that the adjacency requirement on Direct Objects is the default, unmarked case. This default assumption follows the Subset Principle; for discussion, see below. But in other languages this condition is weakened, even absent. Triggering data for this change could consist of interpolated adverbs: V–ADV–NP, where again the NP is confirmed as having the thematic role that an adjacent NP should have. For example, this is apparently the situation in French. Again there is only a single difference between this example and ADV–V–NP, a minimal pair that focuses attention on the decision to weaken the adjacency requirement. A Dative Shift sentence also seems to violate the adjacency constraint. Here too we may assume that positive examples give the child examples that adjacency is violated.[8]

---

[7] It is important to understand what incrementality means. Incrementality in underlying acquisition decisions does not necessarily imply incrementality in surface behavior, or rule-by-rule acquisition. This is because a single decision could set a parameter that could have far-reaching effects throughout a grammar, leading to noncontinuous changes in surface behavior.

[8] As will be discussed in more detail below, Stowell (1981) argues that this is the result of a word formation rule that "absorbs" the NP Indirect Object into the verb. If this view is correct, it might be that so-called "free word order" languages are simply languages that are freer in their word formation rules, permitting adjacency even across multiple Noun Phrases.

Alternatively, one could assume that the subcategorization frame for *give* is partially built when either a Dative or non-Dative sentence is encountered, in either case yielding the following:

> *give*: [NP, NP]

The *to* preposition ignored, as is apparently often the case in child language. The entry is unrefined, in that none of the distinctions required in the adult grammar are made—besides the lack of the *to* case marker, the restrictions blocking ungrammatical adult examples are not present.

This second alternative resembles Braine's (1971) proposal, in that a very general form is posited first, only to be replaced by refinements:

> *give*: [NP...]

The NP argument is assumed to be obligatory. This is the right choice if the Subset Principle is to apply. For if the NP was assumed to be optional, then two surface forms could be generated, one with the NP argument and one without. Call the language that includes these strings language L_i. However, the correct target language could be one including just obligatory NP arguments for this verb, L_j. Thus there is an L_j that is a proper subset of L_i for this class of triggering data, a violation of the Subset Principle.[9] Since the Subset Principle is a necessary condition for positive evidence acquisition, the acquisition procedure must be designed so that arguments are assumed obligatory unless specific triggering evidence is encountered that indicates that they may be optional, or absent from a verb's subcategorization frame.

The second portion of *give*'s subcategorization frame critical for the analysis of Dative constructions is the *to*-NP phrase. Once again, there would seem to be plausible available positive evidence for this kind of phrase:

> *I went to the store*
> *I took Mary to school*
> *I walked to school*

---

[9]This argument has also been presented informally by Roeper (1981:139–140).

We may assume that the acquisition procedure already has the rules to combine *to* and an NP into a Prepositional Phrase-type complement to a verb. If it does not, then Dative constructions with *to* will simply be unavailable as a source of information for syntactic acquisition, though of course the sentences may still be perfectly well *interpreted*.[10]

The order of the NP arguments is not fixed by subcategorization frames. In English at least, this order is set by an adjacency requirement on Case assignment: an NP receiving Objective Case must be adjacent to the verb that assigns Case:

*I gave quickly a book to Bill

How is the adjacency requirement acquired? Once again, the Subset Principle may be invoked. The most restrictive assumption possible is that adjacency holds, since this generates the *narrowest* class of output possibilities as a possible target language. Note that we hold all other parameters constant. A language satisfying the adjacency condition could be a proper subset of one that was not, and yet cover the same triggering data. The acquisition procedure thus assumes an adjacency requirement as the default, unmarked case, loosening it only if positive examples are encountered that indicate violations of adjacency. In English, since examples violating adjacency (*I hit hardly Bill*) will never be encountered, this strict requirement will never be dropped.[11] In other languages, positive examples exhibiting adjacency violations would prompt a relaxation of these conditions, perhaps along a continuum of possibilities. Thus one might expect to find languages where strict adjacency was relaxed according to a hierarchy of phrasal types. For example, since adverbs and particles are not assigned case, it would seem plausible that the smallest kind of adjacency relaxation would be to allow adverbs and particles to be interposed between a verb and its Object. In other languages, such as classical Arabic, a Subject NP can be interposed between verb and Object in surface forms. The most extreme violations of adjacency would occur in languages that have so-called "free word order,"

---

[10]There is some evidence that at an early age children in fact ignore *to* PPs; see Maratsos (1978).

[11]Perhaps the requirement is never dropped in any language. Then apparent adjacency violations are just the result of freer use of word incorporation rules. In this case, the Subset Principle would still hold—English would simply have a more tightly constrained set of incorporation rules.

such as Warlpiri. Here, the adjacency requirement is weakened to such an extent that a whole series of NP's can be interposed between the verb and the NP receiving Objective case.

It is interesting to observe that if an adjacency restriction is an unmarked, default assumption, then such a constraint could aid the learner even in so-called nonconfigurational languages where adjacency does not seem to play a central role in the adult grammar. For suppose that the learner assumes that adjacency holds. Then sentences in which the adjacency requirement happens to be met will be interpreted correctly, or at least more easily, than those where it does not. Establishing this case might permit the learner to determine other connections between the verb and its Object—namely, case agreement marking. Then, when a nonadjacent example is encountered, the adjacency requirement could be dropped in favor of the agreement marker. Note that this is essentially what has been assumed above about the acquisition of *to*-NP complements. The earliest examples are presumed to be sentences such as *John went to school*, where the constraint of adjacency and the prepositional marker *to* coincide. In English, the adjacency requirement is dropped in favor of case assignment via the Preposition—hence English Prepositional exhibit relatively free order, modulo the adjacency restrictions of other phrases. In effect, the primitive of string adjacency has been exploited as device to acquire another source of knowledge, that of case agreement.

In fact English has a weakened adjacency requirement on Prepositional Phrases of just this kind. On this account, there are no "configurational" or "nonconfigurational" languages, but simply languages that exhibit a range of adjacency requirements for one or another type of phrase. The adjacency requirement for NP Objects in English makes it characteristically configurational, because the assignment of thematic roles via the connection of grammatical relations remains structurally based.

Returning now to the main discussion, the acquisition procedure has so far built the basic subcategorization frame for *give*, and has established the (default) adjacency requirement on the NP Direct Object. To proceed further, one must make some assumptions about Dative in the adult grammar of English, within the Government-Binding theory. Here the approach of Stowell (1981) will be adopted. Stowell's theory of Dative Shift is a good model of the change in point of view from *Aspects* to the GB theory, from a theory based largely on a system of *rules* to one based on a system of *principles*. Instead of positing a rule of Dative Shift that is encoded as a transformation, Stowell advances several constraints on Case assignment and how thematic roles are determined so as to obtain the observed array of Dativization judgments.

Stowell assumes that Dativization is possible when two requirements are met, and that the *to*-NP form is possible under a third condition:

1. The verb-NP pair can be reconstituted as a complex verb. That is, one can restructure [$_{VP}$ [$_V$ *gave*][$_{NP}$ *Bill*][$_{NP}$ *a book*]] into [$_{VP}$ [$_V$ *gave* [$_{NP}$ *Bill*]] [$_{NP}$ *a book*]], thus preserving the adjacency condition on case assignment for the Object NP *a book*.

2. The NP can be incorporated only if it can "possess" the direct object of the verb, in some sense. Thus, one has *John gave Bill a book* (because Bill can possess the object, a book), but not *John sent Canada a telegram* (unless Canada is construed as an entity in some way that can possess a telegram, e.g., as an institution.) Note that an animate/inanimate distinction is not the right distinguishing feature here, since *I gave the dock a hard shove* is perfectly fine. Here, the dock can "possess" the quality of being given a hard shove.

3. Finally, a *to*-NP form can appear if the verb takes an object that is assigned the thematic role of GOAL, or a thematic role with some kind of inherent directionality. Thus, *I sent a telegram to Canada* is grammatical, because *Canada* is an appropriate NP to serve as a GOAL.

These restrictions (plus one final twist, described below) do seem to do the trick. For example, as Stowell notes, *That storm almost cost them their lives* does not have a corresponding *to* form, since a DIRECTIONAL or GOAL theme is apparently lacking. Conversely, the *Canada* example or **I threw the ground the ball—I threw the ball to the ground* seems to show that possession is nine-tenths of the Dative Shift law.

The question now is, How can these restrictions be acquired from positive evidence alone? Let us take up each condition in turn, starting with restriction (3).

There seems to be abundant evidence for an acquisition procedure to associate a thematic role of GOAL with a *to*-NP form. Many sentences appear with *to* indicating directionality. If we assume, as before, that the learner can independently recover the thematic role of such NPs, then the right association can be forged:

> *I walked to the store*
> store=GOAL (or DIRECTION)

Just how this directionality is recognized remains to be explicated. Perhaps it is recognized as a transfer of location, in some fashion. For example, *I walked to the candy* is bizarre unless *the candy* is construed as denoting a particular point in space. Similarly, *I gave a book to Bill* involves a change in the location of the book, in an extended sense. One might speculate that as with the case of phonological acquisition, it could well that the first step is to recognize that *to the store* does *not* serve in the same thematic role as *a candy* in *I ate a candy*. Only later would this new category be given a "name" of its own, e.g., "Goal." Just how this might happen will be left open here.

In any case, the assignment of a GOAL or DIRECTIONALITY theme to the object of a *to* Prepositional Phrase already rules out some problematic cases of Dative alternation. The *to*-NP subcategorization is assigned on a verb-by-verb basis, and occurs in adult speech only if inherent Directionality is thematically assigned. Therefore, *to*-NP forms are never found in conjunction with verbs in which directionality makes no sense, e.g., *begrudge, cost,* or *envy*.

What about the thematic distinction regarding possession? There is reason to believe that this distinction is one of the earliest made by children, as shown by Keil (1979). Children can draw distinctions between possession and nonpossession.

With the "possession" distinction available, one can now attack the problem of how the acquisition procedure can learn when to incorporate an NP, and when incorporation is impossible (given a particular verb). First of all, incorporation demands adjacency:

> *I gave the books away to John*
> *I gave away the books to John*
> **I gave away John the books*
> *I gave up the fugitive to the police*
> *I gave up to the police the fugitive*
> **I gave up the police the fugitive*

What does it mean to incorporate an NP into a verb? In part, incorporation has something to do with partial, but compositional, semantic interpretation; the verb and its (Indirect) Object NP are formed into a kind of semantic unit, as noted by Hornstein and Weinberg (1981) in the related case of preposition stranding. They point out that the existence of preposition stranding depends in part on the ability of a verb to "absorb" a preposition or prepositional phrase and form a single complex verb:

> *I decided on a boat*
> *What did you* [[$_V$ decide–on] *trace*]

This view has a natural interpretation in a model of online sentence processing. It amounts to the claim that semantic interpretation (whatever that comes to) is incremental, in the sense that completely constructed arguments to a verb are interpreted immediately as they are finished, rather than waiting until an entire argument structure, the complement of the verb, has been built. This new predicate (not a natural predicate, in most cases) is then applied to the next argument that is completely built, and so on.[12]

If this interpretation of incorporation is correct, then it is also natural to assume that the compositional formation of a complex predicate— incorporation—demands that thematic role assignment be correctly carried out as well. That is, in the adsorption of *a book* into *give*, *book* must be understood as receiving Objective case, so that the thematic role of PATIENT may be properly assigned; the predicate *give a book* with *book* as RECIPIENT is ill-formed. As we have seen, the proper assignment of thematic role in a verb that has a [NP *to*–NP] subcategorization frame exploits *to* as a Case marker, and an indicator of directionality. Therefore, it appears as though the correct assignment of case and thematic role requires *to* as a marker of some sort. But this marking is absent in the Dativized sentences. If incorporation is to be possible then, there must be some way to recover this deleted case marker. In other words, *I gave Bill a book* means *give–to Bill—a book*, and this meaning must be somehow recoverable. Thus this condition amounts

---

[12]This process is akin to that of Skolemization in logic, though the analogy should not be taken too literally; see Williams (1981a). The basic idea—adopting for a moment a model theoretic view, though this is not crucial here—is that the complex predicate *give a book* picks out just those possible worlds where *give a book* is true. There is then some function f corresponding to this selection. f in turn is applied to the remaining argument, *Bill*. Skolemization will also apply to non-Dative shift examples, but in this case a different function would be constructed.

to a recoverability of deletion restriction on incorporation. This is perhaps the reason for the *inalienable possession* restriction on incorporation. The thematic role of POSSESSOR is sufficient to recover the thematic assignment of DIRECTIONALITY, and so incorporation can proceed.[13]

How is knowledge of incorporation acquired? The impossibility of incorporation with verbs such as *report, say, demonstrate* is in fact revealed by positive examples:

*I reported Bill the crime	*I reported to Bill that John was sick*
*I suggested Bill the crime	*I suggested to Bill that John was sick*
*I said Bill something	*I said to Bill that John was sick*

For some reason, the marker *to* cannot be deleted in such cases. According to Stowell, this distinction between e.g. *show–demonstrate* is reflected in the phonological properties of Native vs. Latinate words. Native (Germanic) words are monosyllabic, or, if disyllabic, have primary stress on the first syllable (*give, threw, xerox*); Latinate words are the complement of this class (persuade, suggest, report). Native words can undergo Dativization; Latinate words cannot. Exceptions seem to involve Latinate words that now receive first syllable stress:

I promised Bill a bicycle
(cf. *I promised to Bill that I would not leave*).

Neologisms seem to follow this rule, as Stowell observes: *I xeroxed him a letter*; **I photocopied him a letter*.[14]

There are some apparent exceptions to the phonological classification of Native and Latinate words: **I said Bill a story* (one syllable, Germanic)— but perhaps this is because *say* involves direct "quotation." *I designed a new*

---

[13]Note that DIRECTIONALITY need not be recovered unless the verb is known to have a subcategorization frame [NP *to*–NP], however. One could speculate as to how is the POSSESSOR theme might be assigned. It could be derivative of the "typical" Direct Object assignment: *I kicked the dock*—*I gave the dock a kick*. Then any argument string adjacent to the Verb would be assigned this thematic role. Again, there is abundant positive evidence for this choice.

[14]The retention of *to* seems natural here. Perhaps it is a property of Latinate words that they retain a residue of obligatory case marking. Latinate verbs seem to demand a case marker, and take $\bar{S}$ and NP complements.

bathroom for my mother/I designed my mother a new bathroom (Latinate, bisyllabic, primary stress on second syllable.)[15]

What about *donate*? There are several reasons to believe that this word is exceptional. First of all, *donate* has a peculiarly American usage. Second, and more importantly, it appeared historically with the preposition *with*: *The settlers were donated with warrants for land* (OED). Indeed, its Latin root means, "to present X with Y". Just like "give away," then, perhaps donate is really "donate with," in which case the case marker "with" blocks verb incorporation, hence Dative Shift. But how could this subtle distinction be learned? Actually, as might be expected, *Bill donated the library the books* is accepted by some speakers (stress has shifted to first syllable).

Finally, for cases such as, *I threw the ground the ball*, observe that it has been assumed that the acquisition procedure can answer "possession" predicates such as, "Can the ground have a ball?" If this is assumed, then note that attempted "Skolemization" of the predicate form *give–Canada–a ball* fails, since the complex predicate *give Canada* is meaningless. (Cf. interpretations in which a denotation can be assigned, e.g., "I gave the United States a hard time.") Thus these examples may be ruled out.

In summary, the following sequence of examples and deductions are required to fix what is called Dative alternation:

Step 0. Establish Direct Objects for the relevant verbs. Evidence: *I gave a book* ...

Step 1. Establish the Adjacency requirement for Direct Objects (English). Evidence: Default unless proven otherwise.

Step 2. Establish *to*-NP as part of subcategorization frame of the verb. Evidence: *I gave a book to Bill.* (Rules out *cost*, *envy*, and the like.)

Step 3. Establish directionality of *to*-NP. Evidence: *I went to the store.*

Step 4. Establish the possibility of NP incorporation into the verb. Evidence: Given the adjacency constraint, and assuming independent reconstruc-

---

[15]Here are some others:

I assigned him the second row
(trisyllabic, stress on second syllable.)
I awarded Bill second place (Latinate OF)
I will radio Bill the answer
(trisyllabic, Latinate, but stress on first syllable)

tion of the thematic role of the Direct Object, then *I gave John a book* must collapse *gave—John* into a verb. Evidence for incorporation itself: *I picked up the book.*

Step 5. Establish "inalienable possession" for incorporated NPs, or deducibility of the theme of the indirect object. Establish possession distinction (possible predicates). Evidence: *Bill has a book.*

Now consider the apparent developmental dependencies implicit in this acquisition sequence. The adjacency constraint must come before incorporation is attempted—but it does, since it is the unmarked, default case. Second, the subcategorization frame of a verb must be acquired before incorporation is attempted, but this too is a constraint that will automatically be met, since without the subcategorization frame one is prohibited from syntactic inferences. The only other dependencies are to acquire the directionality of *to* and the constraints on incorporation. These come after the subcategorization frame is established. If directionality (or thematic role assignment to the Indirect Object) is not understood, then incorporation fails, so this fact must be established before Indirect Object incorporation. If incorporation itself is assumed to be a central part of semantic interpretation, then it must be acquired quite early and may be assumed to be the unmarked case, for Direct Objects. Finally, the notion of inalienable possession seems to be understood at any early age, though it is not clear where it fits into the above sequence.

The Subset Principle is invoked in several places: (1) to make the adjacency restriction the default; (2) to make NP arguments by default obligatory; (3) to demand incremental decision-making (and hence order examples intrinsically).

In the remainder of this section, we analyze several other uses of the Subset Principle in ordering acquisition hypotheses.

The PRO-drop parameter

Languages such as Italian exhibit a cluster of properties that languages such as English or French do not: among other things, they permit sentences with missing Subjects, and can invert Subjects freely:

>*Found the book
>*ho trovato il libro* ("I found the book")
>*ha mangiato Giovanni* ("Giovanni ate")
>(Chomsky 1981:240)

It has been suggested (see Chomsky 1981) that these differences may be the result of a "parameter" that is set to one value for Italian, and to another for English and French. Since the empty subject is presumably a pronominal element, this parameter has been called the "PRO drop parameter." Regardless of whether this is the correct analysis of this difference between, e.g., English and Italian, the question arises as to how the setting of the PRO drop parameter may be acquired, so that English and French can be distinguished from Italian. For purposes of exposition, let us say that the PRO drop parameter has just two values: 1 (if Subjects can be dropped, and PRO inserted, yielding an Italian type language); and 0 (if Subjects cannot be dropped, and PRO inserted, yielding English or French type languages). One proposal is that a principle of *indirect* negative evidence operates in this case: if no example sentence of a certain complexity or less is found to exhibit evidence of PRO drop, then assume that PRO drop is not permitted at all (Rizzi 1980). For example, one could adopt the Wexler and Culicover restriction and assert that the entire transformational system is acquired on the basis of sentences of degree of embedding two or less. Then, if no sentence of this depth or less exhibited PRO drop, the child could assume that PRO drop was not permitted. This method plainly works, assuming some kind of complete presentation sequence of all positive sentences less than some fixed complexity.

But there is a simpler approach that also works, and that does not require the assumption of negative evidence at all. Note that a language that permits PRO drop is *broader* than one that does not, since it can generate two surface forms where a non-PRO drop language can generate only one. This fact leads one directly to consider an alternative solution: why not force the Subset Principle directly, and insist that the unmarked (default) assumption for the PRO drop parameter be the one that generates the *narrowest* class of languages? Then the default setting would be 0—a non-PRO drop language. If the acquisition procedure ever encounters a positive example sentence where the Subject is absent, e.g., *Found the book* (meaning, "I found the book"), then the parameter can be set to 1 so as to generate the larger language. If the acquisition procedure never hears a sentence with PRO dropped, then the parameter remains set where it was to begin with. No negative evidence need be used.

S̄-deletion

Chapter 4 showed how S̄-deletion works to license an empty element in sentences like *John was believed to be wrong*. In the unmarked case, PRO is obligatory for infinitivals, since a full clause, S̄, acts as a barrier to government. Since lexically realized elements must be governed, we conclude that the position after *believe*, embedded in the S, is ungoverned. Thus the empty category is PRO, not trace. A marked property of certain verbs is to permit the sequence S̄–S to be collapsed to just S. Deletion of the S̄ now permits government of the embedded Subject, hence a trace or lexical NP, as observed.

Again the question of acquisition may be raised, as observed by Lasnik (1980). Since S̄-deletion permits a *broader* range of surface strings than no S̄-deletion—either an empty string or a lexical NP—it represents a superset hypothesis. Therefore, if the Subset Principle is to be maintained, S̄-deletion should be a marked option; the default assumption should be that S̄-deletion is not possible. If a verb is encountered where government can be observed, e.g., *John expected Bill to win*, then the acquisition procedure can assume that S̄-deletion is possible for that verb.[16] In chapter 4 we saw that this is just what the acquisition procedure does. It puts in one equivalence class all verbs (like *expect*) that allow an overt NP as the subject of an embedded sentence.

Note that an indirect negative evidence solution is possible in the case of S̄-deletion, just as with the PRO drop parameter. The acquisition procedure could assume that all verbs could undergo S̄-deletion; if it then examined all sentences less than two S's deep and observed that no forms such as *John tried Bill to win* appeared, it could conclude that S̄-deletion was impossible for this verb. Exactly as before, however, one can see that indirect negative evidence is not required to set this parameter. This result is expected, given the general result that any parameter identifiable from indirect negative evidence can also be set using direct positive evidence.

---

[16]The subset ordering makes a developmental prediction. The acquisition procedure assumes that a verb does not govern across an S boundary unless evidence is obtained to the contrary. If this is correct, and making the usual (difficult) assumptions that acquired rules should also appear in productive use, then (incorrect) forms such as, *I wanted* PRO *to win* should appear before forms that delete S̄, such as *I wanted Bill to win*.

Bounding nodes for Subjacency

In most current theories of generative grammar, one assumes that movement rules obey certain locality principles. Movement rules cannot cross more than a single clause boundary—the Subjacency constraint. (This is the case even if explicit "movement" rules are not permitted, but rather interpretive principles that co-index empty categories with their antecedents.)

> *John is certain e_i to like ice cream*
> * *John seems it is certain e_i to like ice cream*
> * *The man who I don't know who knows e_i*

Interestingly, this last sentence is grammatical in Italian, as discussed by Rizzi (1978):

> *L'uomo wh*-phrase *che non so chi trace conosca e_i*

According to Rizzi, this is because it is $\bar{S}$, not S, that is a bounding node for Subjacency in Italian. Therefore, the empty category *trace* can be co-indexed with the *wh* phrase because it crosses only a single full clause boundary; the second boundary is an S, not an $\bar{S}$. Apparently, the choice of a bounding node is yet another parameter that must be set in order to "fix" a grammar.

Suppose Rizzi's analysis is correct. How could the choice of bounding node be determined on the basis of evidence received by an acquisition procedure? Once again, let us apply the Subset Principle. If the bounding node for Subjacency is S, then a narrower class of languages is generated than if the bounding node for Subjacency is $\bar{S}$. If both of these languages are potential correct targets, then the first is a proper subset of the second (all other things being equal). By the Subset Principle the acquisition procedure's first hypothesis should be to set the bounding node for Subjacency to S. In other words, the default assumption is that all languages are like English in this regard. If this assumption is wrong, then a positive example will appear that violates S-bounding—as in the Italian example above. Then the acquisition procedure can reset the Subjacency parameter to the next "largest" value, namely, $\bar{S}$.

If Subjacency can be weakened from S to $\bar{S}$, then why couldn't there be a language that weakens the Subjacency condition one step further, allowing movement (or interpretation) to cross *two* or more clause boundaries? It may be that this follows from the evident *noncounting* property of natural languages. Apparently, the rule systems of natural grammars do not make use of predicates that count; there is no rule that moves an item so that it is three words from the end of a string, or, for that matter, checks to see if it has moved an element over three clause boundaries. It is well known, however, that *string adjacency* is a common predicate in grammars; witness the adjacency condition on Case assignment. Thus natural rule systems can state whether a phrase is adjacent to another phrase or not (and hence, in a derivative sense, can determine if a phrase is "one" clause away), but they cannot do more than this. If *adjacent clause* is a natural predicate and, say, *fifth clause* is not, then one could not even *state* an extra-subjacent condition, let alone acquire it.[17]

If specifying S as a bounding node for Subjacency is a tighter constraint than specifying $\bar{\text{S}}$, then it follows that making *all* categories bounding nodes would be an even tighter constraint; if the Subset Principle is strictly applied, then this should be the true default setting of the Subjacency parameter. What this would mean is that, in the default case, no movement would be possible out of A, V, P, or N phrases. This constraint could be weakened as positive evidence is received that violations can occur. See Koster (1978) and Baltin (1982) for evidence that a generalized locality principle like Subjacency is operative in domains other than S.

An even tighter constraint than this would be to assume that all (lexical) categories are bounding nodes. In effect, this would mean that no movement would be possible at all; that is, word order would be fixed as determined by any adjacency constraints.

In sum, the Subset Principle may be invoked to establish an ordering of hypotheses concerning the surface output of possible movement rules. The default hypothesis is that there is no movement, since this produces the smallest class of output sentences; each new hypothesis admits an incremental increase in the range of output sentences. At the other extreme, movement is completely free, subject to locality constraints such as Subjacency. By design, the acquisition model outlined in chapter 2 respects this ordering, and the locality constraints. As noted, the locality constraints themselves are restricted to use only certain predicates like "adjacent to." Together, these constraints tell us that new actions should be attempted in the following order.

---

[17]See Berwick and Weinberg (1984).

ATTACH   (without any permutation or movement.)
SWITCH
INSERT LEX ITEM
INSERT TRACE

This ordering reflects a hierarchy of decreasing restrictiveness on movement. The first assumption made is that *no* movement will be required, and that the constituent in the first position in the buffer can be attached to the current active node without further modification. If this action cannot succeed because of a subcategorization violation, then a purely local string permutation, SWITCH, is attempted.[18] Next the system tries the insertion of a lexical item. It is hard to see if this is more or less general than a SWITCH, so we might order it before SWITCH, but since it introduces new tokens it definitely allows a wider range of surface possibilities than ATTACH. Finally, if the attempted SWITCH rule fails, then a less restricted rule, INSERT TRACE. Note that in the case of both SWITCH and INSERT TRACE that only strictly *adjacent* predicates are invoked: adjacent buffer cells in the case of SWITCH, and adjacent S-domains in the case of INSERT TRACE.

$\overline{\mathrm{X}}$ acquisition of specifiers and complements

Williams (1981c) describes a special case of the Subset Principle as a potential model for the acquisition of $\overline{\mathrm{X}}$ specifiers and complements. It is very like the one described in chapter 2. (The two were apparently developed independently.) The idea is simple. The Subset Principle dictates a particular order in which hypotheses should be entertained. The first assumption is to assume that a phrase has no specifiers or complements, since this generates a subset class of languages. As usual, this initial assumption would be dropped in the face of positive evidence to the contrary—in this case, the existence of a complement or a specifier.

As Williams observes, there is no particular order in which specifiers or complements are fixed, relative to each other. Further, since either or both can be missing, the end state may be a phrase structure rule lacking in either specifiers or complements. More often, however, complements are obligatory

---

[18]Recall however that the second item in the buffer must be a complete constituent, so that it is not strictly accurate to say that SWITCH is a string operation.

arguments; hence the general order of acquisition will be to fix complement structure before fixing optional specifiers.[19]

Optional and obligatory arguments and rules

In the discussion of the acquisition of "Dativization" it was pointed out that the Subset Principle implies that the arguments to a verb (more generally, any Specifier or Complement) should be considered obligatory until positive evidence is received that indicates otherwise. This proposal has also been advanced by Roeper (1981). More generally, it has been widely pointed out (Baker 1979) that it is difficult, if not impossible, to determine whether a rule is obligatory or optional on the basis of just positive evidence. For instance, Baker observes that Subject-Auxiliary inversion is obligatory in main clauses. If an acquisition procedure guessed a subset language and assumed that inversion was optional, it could generate two forms, the second ungrammatical: *Who will John kiss?/ Who John will kiss?*

In part this difficulty can be side-stepped because the acquisition procedure *analyzes* rather than *generates* sentences. Since it will only encounter inverted main-clause questions (for whatever reason), its knowledge of the language (as embodied by rules of analysis) in effect presumes that the inversion rule is obligatory, as desired. Suppose counterfactually that the inversion rule was optional in main clauses. This causes no problem; the acquisition procedure will simply acquire a new rule of analysis to handle that situation as well. In short, one can see that by formulating the acquisition procedure as one of fixing new rules of analysis, one automatically orders hypotheses so that the default assumption is that a rule is obligatory until proven otherwise. This ordering satisfies the Subset Principle.

From a different point of view, Baker's criticism seems unfounded. Suppose that indirect negative evidence is permitted. In the example above, if a noninverted main clause question is not heard, then an acquisition procedure can assume that noninverted questions are ungrammatical. (The dual approach, using just positive evidence and the Subset Principle, was the one described in the previous paragraph.) In fact, all of the "projection puzzles"

---

[19]It is interesting to point out that children seem to frequently drop Subjects, behaving as if the language was a PRO drop language. Recently, Hyams (1983) has confirmed this proposal. It has also been suggested that this is an output (production) constraint of some sort (see Newport, Gleitman, and Gleitman 1977). Apparently, obligatory arguments—complements—are not dropped as frequently.

listed at the end of Baker (1979) are solvable in exactly this way, either by the use of positive evidence and the ordering imposed by the Subset Principle, or by the use of indirect negative evidence.[20]

The uniqueness principle

Chapter 3 briefly discussed the following acquisition principle proposed by Wexler (see Roeper 1981):

> Unless proven otherwise, assume that there is just one surface structure for every deep structure.

Note that this constraint has the effect of enforcing the Subset Principle, since whenever possible just one surface string is permitted instead of two. Since this is a proper subset of the case where both surface strings are possible, the narrowest language should be guessed first. As discussed in chapter 3, the Uniqueness Principle can be used to force the acquisition of surface filters, such as the *for-to* majority dialect filter of English.

This completes our survey of ordering hypotheses as used in the linguistic literature. In each case, the Subset Principle can be invoked to explain just why that ordering strategy is the right one.

6.4 Inductive Inference of the Auxiliary System

To conclude this chapter, we apply the theory of automaton inference to the auxiliary system of English. We shall see just how many positive examples

---

[20] A list of these puzzles:

(1) Negative exceptions to transformational rules (E.g., *I reported John the accident*). This is solved via the trigger, *I reported to Bill that-S*.

(2) Positive absolute exceptions to transformation rules (E.g., *John tried for Bill to win*). This is solved via the failure of $\overline{S}$ deletion in this case, as ordered by the Subset Principle.

(3) Obligatory status for some transformational rules, optional status for others. (E.g., making Subject-auxiliary inversion obligatory in main clauses). This puzzle is analyzed above.

(4) Extrinsic rule ordering.

(5) Language specific filters.

are needed to learn the right minimal target automaton for this system, uncovering constraints on the automaton that allow this learning to be done efficiently. We shall also compare this process to the computer model described in previous chapters.

First let us set the stage by outlining the major linguistic analyses of the English auxiliary system, given by Akmajian, Steele, and Wasow (1979:1):

> The analysis of the auxiliary in English grammar has been, and continues to be, a controversial area of research in recent theoretical linguistics. Since the original transformational analysis of the English auxiliary given in Chomsky's *Syntactic Structures*, a number of modifications and challenges of that analysis have been presented.
>
> It seems fairly reasonable to view previous research on the auxiliary as dividing into two general proposals—the phrase structure analysis (PS analysis) and the Main Verb analysis (MV analysis) ....The PS analysis was originally proposed in *Syntactic Structures* with essentially the following phrase structure rule:
>
> (1) AUX →Tense (Modal)(have + en)(be + ing)
>
> The facts to be accounted for can be stated quite simply: an English sentence can contain any combination of modal, perfective *have*, progressive *be*, and passive *be*, but when more than one of these is present, they must appear in the order given, and each of the elements of the sequence can appear at most once. 1979:17

Formally, it is easy to see that Chomsky's phrase structure rule amounts to the specification of a very restricted finite-state automaton (one that generates only a finite language); this is so because a grammar for this language can be written without involving any self-embedding rules of the form $A \rightarrow \alpha A \beta$, with α, β nonnull, simply by replacing the schema above with appropriately labeled nonterminals to form a right-linear grammar. If we add a rule for *do* insertion, and attempt to incorporate passive/nonpassive verb forms along with an object NP, then 92 sentences (46 active sentences and 46 passive sentences) can be generated. See table 6.1 for a partial list.

There are several more passive sentences just like the active forms that give us a total of 92 possibilities.

1. John gives a book.	2. John has given a book.
3. John is giving a book.	4. John has been giving a book.
5. John gave a book.	6. John had given a book.
7. John was giving a book.	8. John had been giving a book.
9. John can give a book.	10. John can have given a book.
11. John can be giving a book.	12. John can have been giving a book.
13. John could give a book.	14. John could have given a book.
15. John could be giving a book.	16. John could have been giving a book.
17. John may give a book.	18. John may have given a book.
19. John may be given a book.	20. John may have been giving a book.
21. John shall give a book.	22. John shall have given a book.
23. John shall be giving a book.	24. John shall have been giving a book.
25. John should give a book.	26. John should have given a book.

Table 6.1: Some auxiliary verb sequences in English.

A minimal finite-state system to generate this set of surface strings is depicted in figure 6.12. It has 10 states, including a reject state, if we lump recognition of *a book* together into a single state. Note that this automaton is deterministic.[21]

Since there are 10 states, it should suffice to provide an induction procedure with the value $n = 10$ along with all positive example sequences of length less than 21—all 84 example sentences. What is more interesting, as we shall see, is that all sequences need not be seen in order to induce the right target automaton. The very long and rare auxiliary sequences need not be used.

Clearly, a necessary condition for successful induction is that every possible distinction made by the minimal automaton be exemplified by at least one example. In other words, the graph depicting the finite-state automaton must be completely covered by examples: all transitions must be included in at least one example. If not, there is some token, e.g., *might*, that is not given in any example sentence. Then the correct target automaton cannot be inferred, because there is no way to know about this particular transition. The rule system would remain incomplete, but this is not a surprising result.

---

[21]The automaton description and results on reversible inference have been obtained in collaboration with Sam Pilato.

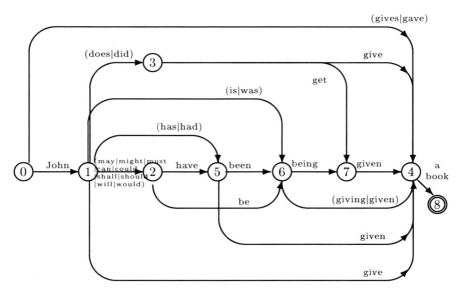

Figure 6.12: A minimal automaton for the English AUX system

If we calculate the covering sample required by this particular 10 state automaton, we see that it includes 27 examples. However, this sample is not sufficient. Consider a state that two or more identical tokens enter, e.g., *given* is entered via *was given a book, could be given a book, will have given a book*. These are different states, and we must now ask what prevents the induction procedure from concluding, incorrectly, that they should be collapsed.

Abstractly, consider a machine where two distinct states 1 and 2 have identical transitions via *b* to a third state. In addition, state 1 has transitions *f* and *g* into it, and transition *a* out; while state 2 has transition *h* into it. In this case a covering sample can consist of just three sentences: *ga*, *fb*, and *hb*, for example. But plainly just this evidence collapses *fb* and *hb*, resulting in the incorrect target where *f* and *h* lead into a single state, distinct from the state that *g* leads into. We need at least *fa* to force *f* and *g* into the same state. But then we also need *gb*, for otherwise we still have *f* and *h* incorrectly lumped together. In short, in this case we must include at least the crossproduct of input and output arcs from state 1 (4 examples instead of 2), where identically labeled exit arcs from distinct states (here, states 1 and 2) enter a common state. Otherwise, we run the risk of collapsing nonidentical states. In the case of the AUX system, if we do not take this into account, we would collapse *been* and *being* into a single state, for example. Note that because we assume a deterministic automaton, the same problem cannot arise in the *forward* direction: the same state cannot have two identically labeled exit arcs leading to distinct states.

One can continue this line of reasoning backwards from states 1 and 2, if necessary. For suppose that the only arcs entering states 1 and 2 were labeled *f*. Then, by the same argument, we would have to consider all possible combinations of arcs entering and exiting states leading to states 1 and 2, in order to guarantee that the correct target is established. Looking at the AUX system, we note that this kind of "lookbehind" is not necessary. At most *one* token distinguishes all such cases. For example, *given* is disambiguated by just one extra token of lookbehind, *being*, *been*, and *have*. *Give* is distinguished by *did give* and *would give*. No two-token lookbehind sequences are required.

Summarizing this argument, we note that we must expand the covering sample as follows:

i: For each unique token leading into a state;

ii: For each exit arc from that state (including the state if it is accepting);

iii: Form the sentence consisting of the minimal prefix to the unique token, traversing the token, taking the exit arc, and then a minimal suffix to the accepting state.

We have shown only that this kind of sample is necessary, not sufficient. Angluin (1982) demonstrates it to be sufficient as well.[22]

How many example sentences are required now? It turns out that only 48 positive examples are needed. Importantly, by using shortest-length prefixes and suffixes, we need not look at the length 5 auxiliary sequences such as *would have been being given*. These are covered by other examples. Basically, one needs at least one sentence for every modal (*could, should,* and so on); one to establish the relative order of *have* and *be*; one to fix the relative order of modals and *have*, and one example for the two *be* forms. [23]

The key constraint guaranteeing that a limited data sample will work, then, is that the target system be backwards deterministic within a limited radius. In the AUX system this is one token. If the inference procedure can distinguish active from passive sentences, then matters are better still. It is easy to see that the set of just active AUX sentences is backwards deterministic without using any lookbehind. Only 38 examples are then required. Such a system is learnable in nearly linear time, according to Angluin's (1982) general results. This situation underscores the advantages of descriptive modularity. If passive sentences need not be distinctly learned, but rather acquired as a fixed set of variations of active counterparts, then the amount of "brute force" induction is reduced to nearly the optimal case. If idiosyncratic sentence patterns describable by n states must be learned by brute force procedures, then looking at roughly n examples would be about the best one could do.

There are other examples of highly idiosyncratic or nonparametric subgrammars in linguistic descriptions. These include the NP specifier system and morphological rules. If these subsystems are all backwards deterministic with limited lookbehind, then they too will be easy to learn (in polynomial time) from examples. It remains to see whether this constraint holds, but if it does, then it would appear that where linguistic subsystems are not learn-

---

[22]One must add all sentences of length less than the lookbehind; in this case, length less than 1.

[23]The induction procedure works by first constructing a prefix tree for every example sentence and then collapsing equivalent states. Angluin (1982) describes the method in detail and shows that it works correctly; it runs in polynomial time proportional to the sum of lengths of input sentences.

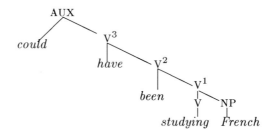

Figure 6.13: A branching verb analysis for AUX

able by simple parameter-setting methods, they are constrained to be easily learned by brute-force inference procedures.

Other analyses of the Aux system

As mentioned earlier, other analyses of the English Auxiliary system have been proposed. Do these make a difference for acquisition? We shall present some evidence indicating that these alternatives are on a par, at least with respect to automaton acquisition. For example, Akmajian, Steele, and Wasow have suggested that the AUX system is produced via simple phrase structure rules like the following, where the exponents of V refer to bar levels in an $\overline{X}$ system.

$$\text{Aux} \rightarrow \quad \{\text{Tense, } do, \text{ modal}\}$$
$$V^n \rightarrow \quad [+V +\text{AUX}] \; V^{n-1}$$

This yields right-branching structures like that in figure 6.13.

This grammar overgenerates, of course, since the order of *have* and *be* has not yet been encoded. Akmajian, Steele, and Wasow propose to capture the ordering restrictions via subcategorization frames. Perfective *have* will demand a V^2 complement, progressive *be* a V^1 complement, and passive *be* must be immediately followed by a main verb. Thus the 3-2-1 order of bar level nonterminals encodes the relative order of *have* and *be*, just as the *Aspects* phrase structure rule did.

From the point of view of inference, there is little difference between this proposal and the earlier one. The verb analysis forms a right-branching structure, generating only a finite-state language. The number of nonterminals, hence the number of states, is the same in both the traditional *Syntactic Structures* analysis and in the Akmajian–Steele–Wasow theory. That this should be so is not surprising. Somehow any grammar for the AUX system must encode the descriptive fact that the elements modal, *have*, and *be*, are ordered with respect to each other. This information must be acquired if it cannot be deduced from other (perhaps universal) constraints. In other words, any theory for AUX must generate the right *language*. If the language is regular (and finite), then it is not surprising that there are a variety of proposals that can represent a minimal finite-state automaton for that language.[24]

Any proposal that does not reduce the grammar of the AUX system to other, more general constraints is on roughly the same acquisition ground as any other proposal: it demands the induction of·a finite-state machine of about the same size as that demanded by any other descriptively adequate system that has been suggested in the literature.[25]

As a final example of an AUX analysis, Baker (1981) has recently advanced a variant of the Akmajian, Steele, and Wasow approach that attempts to do away with a three-level analysis of Verb Phrases. Instead, it generates all verbs at a V^1 level and introduces V^1 as a possible subconstituent of modals:

$$S \rightarrow \{M^1 \text{ or } V^1\}$$
$$M^1 \rightarrow \text{Modal } V^1$$
$$V^1 \rightarrow V V^1 \text{ or } V \text{ NP}$$

---

[24]Baker (1981) remarks that Emonds (1969) contains a proposal to deduce the ordering of elements of AUX from general constraints on verbs. This approach seems more plausible given the current Government-Binding theory, and we will return to it below.

[25]As Akmajian, Steele, and Wasow observe, there are other advantages to their analysis that go beyond an account of the order of elements in the auxiliary. For example, the rules are designed to provide a natural explanation of what the natural units should be for movement rules like verb fronting. Under their proposal, the phrases *study French, been studying French, have been studying French*, and *could have been studying French* are complete phrases, hence can be moved as complete units. This explanation is not immediately available to a system that generates a "flat" auxiliary. However, it may be possible to reproduce this effect by combining the government-under-adjacency constraint with the Hornstein-Weinberg notion of reconstruction.

To avoid overgeneration, Baker again resorts to subcategorization restrictions; he suggests that lexical entry for *have* contain the insertion frame context ___ V^1 *en*, that for *be* the context restriction ___ V^1 *ing*, that for *do*, ___ V-stem.

Plainly, Baker's rule system is also right-branching. There are some differences between it and the two previous theories, however. Evidently there are fewer nonterminals in this account than in either the previous two, since there is only one phrase of type V. This would seem to be an advantage. All of Baker's rules are of the form Head-Complement, where Head is modal or verbal. This form suggests that constraints on ordering may indeed be naturally captured via restrictions on allowable complements, and these perhaps may be derivable from other, more general constraints. On the other hand, the information content that is captured in other systems by using nonterminal labels still needs to be acquired in this system. Now this information is now associated with lexical items. This is to be expected in a system that attempts to eliminate phrase structure categories: to remain descriptively adequate, the information formerly encoded via nonterminal labels must be encoded somewhere. Each of the lexical restriction frames must be learned.

How much extra information is encoded in the lexical entries? As shown by Peters and Ritchie (1973), context-sensitive insertion frames of this kind can be simulated by a finite-state frontier-to-root tree automaton that checks whether the context conditions are met. The induction of this automaton replaces the induction of the finite-state machine of other analyses.

To compare the Baker system to the other proposals, we must see how large a tree automaton is required in order to simulate the lexical entries. If the trees defined by the base grammar are just right or left branching, then the resulting automaton is just an ordinary finite-state automaton, as noted earlier. But then, the number of states in this automaton must be at least as great as the number in the minimal (reduced) automaton for the AUX language, i.e., the same number or larger than that for the first two proposals above; otherwise, there would be a finite automaton smaller than the minimal automaton for this language, a contradiction. One cannot get something for nothing.

Thus the total number of finite automaton states that must be induced in Baker's approach must be the same (or greater) than the number involved in the *Syntactic Structures* or Akmajian, Steele, and Wasow approaches, despite appearances to the contrary. In fact, this conjecture is borne out. If one augments Baker's system so as to include *do* insertion, passive *be*, and NP,

start, and reject states, the the number of states required is the same as in
the generative approach:

Start, Accepting,
Nonaccepting states= 3

NP: *John*
NP: *a book*

do: [___ Vmainstem]

Vmainstem: [___ NP]

be: [___ Ving]
have: [___ Ven]
modal: [___ V-tense]

passive *be*

being: [___ Ven-passive]

This takes exactly 10 states, as before. However, it is important to stress
again that there is an advantage to the elimination of nonterminals if one can
derive these general context-sensitive insertion frames from general principles.
It is the overall acquisition complexity of a grammar that counts, not just
the complexity of one portion of it. This being so, then the overall grammar
is simplified if general principles can be used to explain the acquisition of
several of its components, instead of having specific principles of each separate
component.

Finite-state induction and the acquisition procedure

The acquisition procedure's approach to the AUX system is closest in spirit
to the acquisition of context-sensitive insertion frames, as in Baker's model.
This is true for two reasons: (1) the tree shape induced is the same, roughly,
an X^0–$\overline{X}$ complement structure; and (2) the pattern-action grammar rules
are local context-sensitive insertion rules. Rule predicate patterns are just

context-sensitive feature tests as used by Baker. The predicates are also strictly local, in the sense of Joshi and Levy (1977), the same sense that Baker intends. Specifically, a predicate is *local* just in case it is a Boolean combination of *proper analysis predicates*, where a proper analysis predicate is defined as in Joshi and Levy. First we define the set of proper analyses of a tree t, $P(t)$, inductively.

(i) If $t = 0$ (null tree), then $P(t) = \emptyset$;

(ii) If $t = $ root A, dominating subtrees $t_0 \ldots t_n$, then $P(t) = \{A\} \cup P(t_0) \cdot P(t_1) \cdot \cdots \cdot P(t_n)$, where $\cdot$ denotes set concatenation.

Now define contextual conditions via context-sensitive rules of the form $A \rightarrow \omega/\Phi$ ___ Ψ, if there is a proper analysis of the form $\rho_1 \Phi A \Psi \rho_2$, where ρ_1, ρ_2 are possibly null. This is a proper analysis predicate. Intuitively, a proper analysis predicate specifies a horizontal context "slice" through a tree that passes through the node being rewritten (node A), touching one representative node from each subtree in the horizontal slice. It should be apparent that any grammar rule predicate that contains only lexical tokens in its input buffer or perhaps a complete subtree in the first or second buffer cells meets this definition of local. Thus the pattern-action rules of the parser can be rewritten as context-sensitive proper analysis predicates. The acquisition procedure also follows Baker's approach in that there is just one kind of phrase structure schema used to develop the AUX system. Obviously, the order X–Complement-X must be acquired first.

Finally, the acquired rule system is right-branching, just as in Baker's model, and there are no levels of the form V^3, V^2, V^1, as in Akmajian, Steele, and Wasow. Level numbers denote simply different nonterminal names, hence are used simply to distinguish machine equivalence classes. But these classes can just as well be defined via context-sensitive insertion frames. What the parser learns, then, is closest to Baker's proposal for the AUX system.

6.5 Summary

In chapter 5 we presented several formal ways of looking at acquisition, while chapter 6 turned to concrete applications. To summarize both chapters:

• We advanced a theory of acquisition complexity based on the notion of program size as applied to linguistic systems.

- We compared noninstantaneous and instantaneous models of acquisition. It was found that in some cases, even in the acquisition of finite rule systems (e.g., segmental systems), noninstantaneous models are advantageous for acquisition. By positing acquisition as taking place over time one can provide a better account of the existence and nonexistence of segmental systems. Certain segmental systems are "inaccessible" because they are not reachable via natural developmental pathways.

- The noninstantaneous model can be envisioned as an ordered sequence of decision points moving through a lattice of possible systems. In this respect, it resembles concept acquisition models proposed in Artificial Intelligence research under the heading of "version spaces."

- The noninstantaneous model of acquisition predicts the rough surface appearance of the development of segmental systems. This suggests that observed developmental stages may simply be the reflection of the underlying "choice points" of the noninstantaneous model.

- We proposed a general learning principle, the Subset Principle. The Subset Principle accounts for a wide range of more specific learning principles that have appeared in the linguistics literature as constraints on evaluation procedures, e.g., that arguments are assumed by default to be obligatory, or the default assumption that there is at most one surface structure for every deep structure.

- We analyzed the AUX system as a problem in the induction of finite-state automata. Importantly, the AUX system is restricted so that its "brute force" induction is not hard. Several linguistic analyses of AUX were compared from the standpoint of this formal model. All of the approaches—phrase structure, lexical insertion contexts, and complex V analysis—were judged to be on a par, at least with respect to acquisition complexity. The acquisition model simulates the learning of a right-branching verb based analysis of the auxiliary system.

Chapter 7

Locality Principles and Acquisition

A central theme of this book is that constraints make learning possible. The computer model's restrictions aid learning by reducing the search space for new rule hypotheses. But natural languages are not just learnable, they are also parsable. The computer model respects this second functional constraint of natural languages as well: the system is always able to parse the language it has so far learned. This is a reasonable psychological demand, but there is in fact no *a priori* reason to believe that the demands of learnability and parsability are necessarily compatible. After all, learnability has to do with the scattering of possible grammars with respect to evidence input to a learning procedure. This is a property of a *family* of grammars. Efficient parsability, on the other hand, is a property of a *single* grammar. A family of grammars could be easily learnable but not easily parsable, or vice-versa. It is easy to provide examples of both. For example, there are finite collections of grammars generating nonrecursive languages that are easily learnable (just use a disjoint vocabulary as triggering evidence to distinguish among them). Yet by definition these languages cannot be easily parsable. On the other hand, as is well known even the class of all finite languages plus the universal infinite language covering them all is not learnable from just positive evidence (Gold 1967). Yet each of these languages is finite-state and hence efficiently analyzable.

Given this lack of necessity, what is surprising is the close connection between constraints that guarantee efficient parsability and constraints that guarantee learnability from simple data. One and the same set of constraints seem to work for both. This chapter explores this connection. We shall see that the connection between learnability and parsability constraints is not accidental. The same locality conditions that ensure deterministic parsability using k lookahead cells also ensures learnability from simple positive examples.

More precisely, we shall see how the constraints demanded in the Wexler and Culicover model for learning transformational grammars are replicated in the parsing-based acquisition model. We then turn to a formalization of the the locality constraints of the Wexler and Culicover model, the so-called Bounded Degree of Error (BDE) constraint. We formalize the locality constraint on parsing as a condition of Bounded Context Parsability (BCP). The key result is that BCP implies BDE. Here, "easily learnable" means "learnable from simple, positive (grammatical) sentences of bounded degree of embedding." In this case then, the constraints required to guarantee easy parsability, as enforced by the bounded context constraint, are at least as strong as those required for easy learnability. This means that if we have a language and associated grammar that is known to be parsable by a Marcus-type machine, then we already know that it meets the constraints of bounded degree learning, as defined by Wexler and Culicover.

Sections 1 and 2 of this chapter formalize the Marcus parsing model. First, we show how packet names and node annotations can be replaced by complex state-stack symbol combinations. Second, we show that the derivation sequence traced out by a Marcus parser is rightmost (using the results of Hammer (1974)). Third, we show how Marcus's "attention shift" mechanism is really just a version of Szymanski and Williams's (1976) noncanonical bottom-up parsing model. If only a finite number of attention-shifts are allowed, then Szymanski and Williams show that only the deterministic context-free languages can be handled.

In Section 2 we present a restricted two-stack parsing model, designed to extend LR(k) techniques to noncontext-free languages. Using the finite automaton representation for parsers suggested by DeRemer (1969), we present a necessary condition for a context-sensitive grammar to form the basis of an extended LR(k) parsing procedure: the set of *characteristic strings* of the grammar, roughly, the set of possible left-contexts that arise during parsing, must be a regular set.[1] Viewed as an extension of the Marcus parser, the

---

[1] When applied to a context-sensitive grammar, this condition forbids rule systems where canonical derivations involve nonterminal center-embedded rewrite sequences, i.e., successive sentential forms such that $\gamma AB\beta \rightarrow \gamma DAC\beta$, where A, B, C, D are nonterminals. This is so because then the set of characteristic strings cannot be regular, by a well-known theorem of Chomsky (1959). Note here that we consider a set of characteristic strings, and not the language generated by a grammar. This condition is plainly not

restricted two-stack model can handle some noncontext-free languages, e.g., $a^n b^n c^n$. To do this requires an arbitrarily long input buffer, however.

Section 3 of this chapter probes the relationship between the locality principles prescribed by the acquisition model and those advanced in linguistic theory. In particular, it examines the Wexler and Culicover constraints and the Lasnik and Kupin (1977) formalization of a transformational grammar. The majority of the constraints advanced in both the Wexler and Culicover and Lasnik and Kupin models are shared by the current acquisition procedure.

The last part of section 3 turns to the formalization of the Bounded Context Parsability and Bounded Degree of Error conditions, and sketches a demonstration that BCP implies BDE. (The converse result, that BDE implies BCP, seems unlikely, because it is easy to give examples of easily learnable languages that are not easily parsable.)

7.1 Formalizing the Marcus Parser

Our first task is to show that the Marcus parser is a restricted variant of a conventional LR(k) parser, namely, the LR(k, t) parser design first proposed by Knuth (1965).[2] There are two basic parts to this demonstration: (i) converting the Marcus transducer into a more typical parser; and (ii) showing that the Marcus parser observes a rightmost recognition order (neglecting the complication of attention shifts).

Using a parse tree as control

To begin we note that there is difference in the data structures used by the Marcus parser and parsers as they are usually presented in the literature. The basic difference is that the Marcus parser stores a partial representation

---

sufficient to ensure deterministic parsing, however, since not all context-free grammars are LR(k). In addition to the representability condition, DeRemer points out three other constraints required in order for a grammar to be LR(k): (i) its representation as a parsing automaton cannot have any so-called inadequate states, i.e., the transition diagram must be deterministic; (ii) the finite-state automaton must halt on all inputs, i.e., it must not loop forever on some inputs; and (iii) it must detect errors in input sentences as early as possible.

[2]Specifically, it is a LR(2,2) parser: it uses at most two symbols of lookahead and can reduce either one of two leftmost complete subtrees at any step. Below we will discuss exactly what this terminology means.

of the parse tree on its stack, and makes reference to that representation to guide its parse; however, most formalized parsers do not store an explicit representation of the parse tree. For instance, an LR(k) parser stores complex information on its pushdown stack: a table that acts like a miniature finite automaton dictating to what new state it should go and what action it should perform given some input symbol, lookahead symbols, and current state. The table stores all the possibilities of *where* the parser could be in a rightmost derivation. This is the work that the partial tree representation is doing in the Marcus parser. It should come as no surprise then that one could replace the explicit tree representation with an implicit state-symbol representation. Instead of building a tree, we simply number all righthand sides of productions, corresponding to the Marcus grammar rules that were labeled *Attach as X*. Each attachment made to a constituent in the active node stack corresponds to complete analysis of a phrase of type X; the modified parser announces this fact by emitting the number associated with the production. Similarly, suppose all other distinct rules are numbered. Then the output of a parse will simply be an (ordered) sequence of numbers, $p_1, p_2, \ldots, p_n$. This is one conventional way of describing a parser's recognition sequence, as described in Aho and Ullman (1972:264). Suppose we define a context free grammar in the usual way, i.e., as a four-tuple of nonterminals N, finite alphabet Σ, productions P, and start symbol S. Then Aho and Ullman define a *left* (right) *parse* as follows:

> Let $G = (N, \Sigma, P, S)$ be a context-free grammar, and suppose that the productions P are numbered $1, 2, \ldots, p$. Let α be in $N \cup \Sigma^*$. Then:
>
> A *left parse* (right parse) of a is a sequence of productions used in a leftmost (rightmost) derivation of α from S.

As Aho and Ullman show, we can think of a parser for a grammar G formally as a simple transducer that maps strings in the language of G to all their right or left parses. To actually build a device that does this work, one must implement this transducer, generally as a pushdown machine of some kind. Successive operations of the transducer (and hence right- or leftmost derivations) correspond to successive configurations of this processor, in the familiar way.

Formally, let us define a pushdown automaton (PDA) as a 7-tuple, $(Q, \Sigma, \Gamma, \delta, q_0, Z_0, F)$. Q is a finite set of states, Σ a finite input alphabet,

Γ a finite set of symbols that can appear on the pushdown stack, δ a finite set of transitions or productions, q_0 an initial state, Z_0 the initial symbol on the pushdown stack, F the set of final states. A *configuration* of the automaton is defined as $(q, w, \alpha) \in Q \times \Sigma^* \times \Gamma^*$. A move of the automaton, denoted $\models$, is a relation between two configurations; $(q, aw, Z\alpha) \models (q^*, w, \gamma\alpha)$ iff $\delta(q, \alpha, Z) = (q^*, \gamma)$. To convert the PDA into a transducer (PDT), we need only add an output of the transitions to write out the appropriate production numbers; *delta* will then map from $Q \times (\Sigma \cup \{\lambda\}) \times \Gamma$ to $Q \times \Gamma^* \times \Delta^*$, where Δ is the vocabulary of output symbols and λ is the empty string.

How exactly can the partial subtrees used by the Marcus parser's grammar rules be encoded into the configurations of a PDT? Let us show informally how this is done. If the subtree consists of just a single symbol, then the answer is clear: the corresponding stack symbol of the PDA will just be the same. So G must include all the possible active node stack items—NP, VP, S, PP, etc. Further, since an active node labeled, say, +*passive* is different from a node not labeled *passive*, we must distinguish between the two; we do this by forming complex symbols, e.g, [VP +passive], [VP]. There are only a finite number of such complex symbols, since there are only a finite number of such feature annotations. What if an active node is a partial subtree that has several daughters? Only the immediate daughters of an active node are assumed to be accessible to grammar rules. This means that if, say, an NP and a PP have been attached to a VP node that is being built, then these nodes are part of the VP subtree. However, none of the syntactic material below the NP or PP—the Noun or its complements, for example— can affect the parse. As discussed in chapter 4 and in Berwick and Weinberg (1984), this constraint has the effect of enforcing the linguistic constraint of *constituent command* (c-command).

Whatever the source of this constraint, what c-command means is that the *internal* syntactic detail of an NP or PP node attached to some active node cannot change the parser's moves. But this means, in turn, that one can encode the subtree attached to an active node as a single complex symbol: if the active node consists of a mother node X and daughters $Y_1, \ldots, Y_n$, simply form the bracketed expression $[XY_1 \ldots Y_n]$. If the number of possible daughters of a node is finite, the number of such complex symbols is finite, and the encoding is possible. Does this last condition hold? At first glance, because of adjunction, it does not seem to hold. For example, a VP can have an indefinite number of (adjunct) PPs attached to it: *I saw Bill behind the table beside the bed near my house* .... To eliminate this possibility, we must be able to claim that such adjunct expressions can be finitely encoded as a single complex symbol, at least for the purposes of affecting the future course of a parse. Fortunately, in English this seems to be the case. A potentially infinite sequence of PPs, Adjective phrases, or other adjunct sequences occur in the form X^*. Suppose we represent adjunct sequences of this kind as such. That is, form the complex symbol $[X]^+$ whenever two or more such adjuncts appear. For example, the sequence PP PP PP PP attached to VP may be collapsed to $[VP\ PP^+]$, indicating that some nonzero number of adjunct PPs has been attached to a VP. Let us call this an adjunct cluster.

The requirement that the elements are adjuncts here means that true NP arguments to a Verb will not be so collapsed. This implies that the number of true arguments must be finite; e.g., that a verb can have at most a finite number of arguments that are assigned thematic roles. In contrast, the adjunct cluster is assigned just a single thematic role. Given these assumptions, then the annotations on an active node are finite.[3] Therefore, we can encode any subtree relevant to parsing transitions as a single complex symbol.

What about the packet names? Again one can just factor them into the complex "state" that is saved on the pushdown stack. So for example, the packet **Parse-Head-infl** will become simply the state q_i, and the packet **Parse-Complement-infl** the state q_j. The actual stack symbol stored will be simply the pair $[X, q]$, where X = the complex symbol described earlier and q = the state as just defined.

At the beginning of a parse, the stack will contain the special start symbol *Start*. Acceptance is defined by an empty stack plus the symbol *Start* plus an end of sentence marker in the first two cells of the input buffer. The machine then enters an accept state and halts. An error condition is signalled if, at any point in the parse, no actions can be taken but the machine is not in the accepting state.

Finally, since grammar rules can make reference to not only the top element of the stack, but also to the so-called *current cyclic node*, we must have some way to encode this information as well. When a new active node

---

[3]Observe that nothing rules out sequences of the form, adjunct cluster —true argument— adjunct cluster—true argument, and so on. But then, since the number of true arguments is finite, eventually one will obtain a finite sequence of alternations followed by some indefinitely long adjunct cluster—still finitely representable as an annotation.

This method assumes some way to distinguish between true arguments and adjuncts. Some such method is required in any case, in order to determine whether, e.g., a verb's subcategorization frame has been fulfilled.

is formed, its current cyclic node is simply the cyclic node of the node that was just active, unless a new cyclic (NP or S) node has been formed in the meantime. In either case, we can simply code an active node as the pair (active node, cyclic node). Since the annotations on any cyclic node are finite, this representation is finite as well.

Complex symbol formation is closely related to the standard development of LR(*k*) parsing. Let us review this material here, since it will be important in the sequel. First we consider the following intuitive definition of an LR(*k*) grammar: "We say that [a grammar] *G* is LR(*k*) if when examining a parse tree for *G*, we know which production is used at any interior node after seeing the frontier to the left of that node, what is derived from that node, and the next *k* terminal symbols" (Aho and Ullman 1972:379). Formally, we may say that a context-free grammar is LR(*k*) if:

(1) $S \xrightarrow{*}_R \alpha A w \to_R \alpha \beta w$;

(2) $S \xrightarrow{*}_R \alpha B x \to_R \alpha \beta y$; and

(3) the first *k* symbols derivable from *w* = the first *k* symbols derivable from *y*

imply that
$\alpha = \gamma, A = B$, and $x = y$, i.e., that only one reduction is possible.

A key hurdle to cross is that the lefthand context α that we need to make our parsing decisions could be arbitrarily long. However, it can be shown that if a grammar is LR(*k*) then a finite table associated with any topmost stack element is sufficient to uniquely determine what to do next. This result makes use of the fact, cited above, that the sentential forms of a rightmost derivation of any context-free grammar (and some noncontext-free grammars) form a finite-state language. Following DeRemer (1969), this property allows one to represent the finite control table information required by an LR(*k*) parser as a finite automaton. Consider an example of this provided by Harrison (1978:526):

Grammar:

$$S \to aAd \quad S \to bAB$$
$$A \to cA \quad A \to c$$
$$B \to d$$

As may be verified, the set of right-sentential forms with respect to this grammar is: $\{aAd, acc^*A, bAd, bAB, bcc^*\}$. This set is regular. Therefore, we can represent it via a finite transition network (Harrison 1978:528), where the T_i are states to be defined later and transitions between the states are tokens like a, b, or A. Each path in the transition diagram terminates in the completion of a particular constituent. These terminal states are called reduction states, because they signal the completion of constituents according to the rules of the grammar. For example, T_6 announces the completion of an S, since it corresponds to the sentential form aAd; likewise, T_8 corresponds to the completion of an A, T_7 to an S (via bAB), and T_9 to a B (via d).

As DeRemer (1969) observes, this control information is not enough to carry out a parse because a reverse derivation consists of a sequence of right-sentential forms. In general we must make several "passes" through the network, and use a stack to keep track of recursive calls to the control network. First we define the transitions of the control network, adding the actions to either (i) shift input items and state names onto the pushdown stack; (ii) pop some series of input items and state names (indicating a reduction); or (iii) indicate an error condition.

Let $G = (N, \Sigma, P, S)$ be a (reduced) context-free grammar and let $k > 0$. Let T be a set of states. Σ_λ^k denotes the set of strings from the alphabet of length k, including the empty string. Define two functions f and g as follows.

f, the parsing action function, is a mapping from $T \times \Sigma_\lambda^k$ into {shift, error} $\cup$ {reduce, $\pi | \pi \in P$}.

g, the , is map from $T \times N$ into $T \cup$ {error}.
(Harrison 1978:527)

The function f looks at the state as indicated by the current stack symbol T_i and the current input symbol(s), and decides whether to push the symbol (along with the associated T_i) onto the stack, pop the stack (reduce), or declare an error. It corresponds to the grammar rule actions of the Marcus parser. A *shift* is just like a *create node* action; a *reduce* corresponds to *dropping* a node from the active node stack into the buffer. The function g is the transition function of the finite-state network representation of the parser. It indicates to which state the parser should go, given some current stack symbol T_i and input symbol(s), and declares an error if no move can be made. In the Marcus parser, this information is carried by the grammar rules and the packet system. Each packet network for a particular phrase is just a finite transition net.

What information is contained in these tables? Each holds a (finite) representation of where in the analysis of a right sentential form the parser could be, given that k tokens of lookahead information are available. For example, given our example grammar, after seeing a b the parser must be in one of the following states: (1) it could have just finished the b portion of the rule $S \rightarrow bAB$, with A and B completely built or A built and d to check; (2) it could have seen b and already have built the last A in a string of As, with B or just d to check; or (3) it could have seen b and not yet built an A (or possibly many As). These possibilities are called the *set of valid* LR(k) *items*, for this grammar, production, and lookahead. An LR(k) item is defined with respect to a grammar G, as the pair $(A \rightarrow \beta_1 \cdot \beta_2, w)$, where $A \rightarrow \beta_1 \beta_2$ is a production, and w is a lookahead of at most k terminal items (words) that can be derived from A. (Intuitively, as observed by Harrison (1978), we have already checked that the derivation up to the dot is possible, and the lookahead is w.) An item $(A \rightarrow \beta_1 \cdot \beta_2, u)$ is *valid* if there exists a derivation in G such that $S \xrightarrow{*}_R \alpha A w \rightarrow_R \alpha\beta_1\beta_2$, with u a valid lookahead. The computation of the set of valid items, and the proof that they define the states of parser in the right way so that the resulting machine works correctly is the key to the LR(k) parsing method. For proofs, see Aho and Ullman (1972).

Note that there are no conflicts in the resulting machine as to which transition to make. Specifically, there is never a conflict between a reduce or shift move, nor is there ever a choice of which reduction to make. If this is the case, we say that the resulting set of LR(k) items is *adequate*, otherwise, *inadequate*. An inadequate state has a conflict between whether to enter a final state, thereby reducing a set of items to some nonterminal, or to keep going with the analysis of the phrase.[4]

It is the sets of LR(k) items that form the control network T_i. The ten sets that form the states of the finite control required by the grammar above are drawn in figure 7.1 (From Harrison (1978:535); λ denotes the empty string).

---

[4]More formally, as defined by DeRemer (1969:47): Any state having two or more transitions, at least one of which is a transition to a final state, is called an inadequate state.

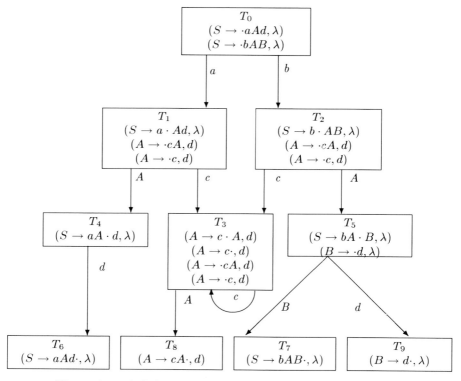

Figure 7.1: A finite transition network for an LR(k) parser

The dot is used to mark the current location of traversal through the righthand side of a phrase. This corresponds to the use of packets in the Marcus parser. For example, consider the expansion, NP→ Determiner Adjective N Complement. If the packet **Noun** is active, then this means that we have already traversed the Determiner and Adjective portions of the rule. But this means that the dot should be located as follows: NP→ Det Adj · N. Packet deactivation and subsequent packet activation corresponds to moving the dot, since this means that we have completed the construction of a constituent or determined that some constituent is optional. Moving the dot leads to a new state of the finite control network, as indicated above, with a new group of LR(k) items active. The set of LR(k) items is just the set of possible rule expansions that are possible at a given point in the parse. We see then that a packet of grammar rules, in Marcus's sense, corresponds simply to a set of LR(k) items. The stack of active nodes and packets plus buffer contents of the Marcus parser correspond precisely to the stack of appropriate dotted rules plus lookahead items (valid LR(k) items). Neglecting for the moment the apparent use of topdown predictions in the Marcus parser and its use of nonterminal lookahead, we can summarize the discussion so far by saying that the Marcus parser is a restricted LR(k) parser. It is restricted because we can use only a literally finite expression in nonterminal and packet names as the left context representation, rather than general regular expressions. In other words, the lefthand context can be a finite language, but not a general regular (and possibly infinite) language.

Encoding top-down predictions

Let us now consider these last two issues in turn. First of all, it seems as if the Marcus parser could not be LR(k)-based because, as Marcus himself claims, sometimes it makes top-down predictions rather than working in a strictly bottom-up fashion. For example, if the item *the* is seen in the input buffer, then a Noun Phrase is predicted and placed on the active node stack, without ever waiting for the remainder of the right-hand side elements that confirm the existence of an NP. Of course, the parser then proceeds to check that in fact an NP can be found; since the system is assumed to be deterministic, though, this check is presumably guaranteed unless the sentence is ill-formed. (For example, a nonsentence could be, *the gave the book.*)

As pointed out by Hammer (1974), however, one can design a bottom-up parser that integrates top-down prediction in the same fashion as the Marcus parser:

> Prediction is a concept usually associated with top-down parsing, rather than bottom-up. The entire process of top-down parsing consists of nothing more than making a sequence of predictions and then seeing them come true. Given a nonterminal and a lookahead string, we predict which rule of the grammar must be applied to the nonterminal in order to effect the eventual generation of the lookahead string.
>
> On the surface, this concept seems completely alien to the approach embodied in bottom-up parsing. There, nothing whatsoever is predicted, no anticipation of the future ever plays a role in the progress of a parse. It is only when we have reached the end of the handle that we recognize it as such and discover to which nonterminal it is to be reduced .... But in one important sense, there is an air of prediction to the entire proceedings. Before the bottom-up parse of a sentence begins, we are effectively predicting that we shall reduce it to S, the sentence symbol .... We will generalize this approach and utilize prediction not only at the beginning of a bottom-up parse, but at selected points throughout. That is, at various times we shall predict that the bottom-up parser, proceeding in a normal fashion, will eventually reduce some prefix of the remaining input to a specified nonterminal. (1974:27–28)

Hammer goes on to show that we can regard this interweaving of top-down prediction with bottom-up reductions as in effect a set of possible subroutine calls. At certain points in the parse, the "main" parsing machine can hand over the job of finding a particular, predicted nonterminal to a subroutine. Again to quote Hammer:

> It is easier to think of [the new machine] ... as representing a generalized kind of parsing machine, in which it is possible for one state to transfer control to another part of the machine and get it back when that part has completed its predefined task. Each time a call transition is made, a new stack is created for the

benefit of the called submachine. This submachine will use this new stack as its parsing stack, and will destroy it when control is returned to the calling state. Since (as we shall see) it is possible for submachine calls to be nested (i.e., for one submachine to call another, or itself recursively), it is more convenient to think of the machine at large as really having a stack of stacks.

It should be observed that the order of recognition by such a machine is still strictly left-to-right, bottom-up. All the extra work of making predictions and fulfilling them, of creating and suspending stack levels, as of yet makes no appreciable difference .... Note that there are two more steps in the predictive parse, to account for the prediction and fulfillment steps, but otherwise the parses and stack configurations are essentially the same. In particular, the final states are entered in precisely the same order, thus preserving the order of recognition in the parse. (1974:37–39)

Sets of LR(k) items correspond to packets. The exit from a set of LR(k) items (= a state in the diagram) corresponds to the deactivation of a packet, and entry into a set of items corresponds to the activation of a packet. Completion of a phrase (= entry into a final or reduce state of the control automaton) corresponds to dropping a phrase into the input buffer in the Marcus machine.

Given this correspondence, the use of top-down prediction in the parser is subsumed by the Hammer formalization. Attachment of a node to an active node occurs in precisely the order specified by Hammer, that is, in a bottom-up, left-to-right order, even though we may predict the existence of a node and place it in the active node stack before it is completely recognized.[5]

Marcus only allowed this "stack of stacks" approach in the analysis of Noun Phrases. To take a simple example, consider how NPs are parsed by

---

[5]This statement is not quite accurate, in that there are a few places where the Marcus machine predicts a node and attaches it to its proper place in the parse tree. In particular, VP nodes are created and attached to the S's that dominate them without first completing the construction of the VP. This cuts against the grain of the rest of the parser, however, since the VP node still remains in the active node stack. If uniformity and a strict bottom-up recognition order is to be maintained, then we must change this so that nodes in the active node stack cannot be attached to any mother nodes. The only way for attachment to a superior to occur is to (1) complete the construction of the node then (2) drop the node into the buffer and finally (3) attach the completed node. Direct attachment would complicate the acquisition procedure.

the Marcus machine. A "leading edge" of an NP, like a determiner, sparks entry into the packet system for NPs. Marcus recognized this as a kind of subroutine call, what he dubbed an "attention shift." If an attention shift occurs, then the current parse is suspended, and the parser entered recursively to handle the NP. The packet for NPs corresponds precisely to Hammer's notion of a submachine—the parser is called recursively. When an NP has been successfully parsed, it is returned to the input buffer, and the parse picks up where it left off. If the attention shift occurs with a triggering item in the first buffer cell, then this is exactly Hammer's approach. For now we ignore the fact that the NP could be recognized noncanonically. As we will see, this occurs if an "attention shift" is allowed to occur on an item in the second or third buffer cells.

Besides NP attention shifts, there are other places in the parser where top-down prediction occurs. These cases correspond to what was earlier called the "automatic" creation of nodes, for example, the creation of a PP node given that a preposition has been detected in the input buffer. These node creations plainly fall under Hammer's design as well. Since NP attention shifts and node creation via grammar rules (now handled by detection of lexical Heads) are the only places where top-down predictions are used in the parser, we can conclude that Hammer's formalization subsumes Marcus's use of top-down prediction, and that in fact the recognition order of phrases is strictly bottom-up.

Nonterminal lookahead

Finally, let us consider the possibility of noncanonical recognition sequences. Chapter 1 discussed a case where one had to delay the recognition of an item in the input until a complete constituent to the right of that item was completely recognized. The example was a situation where *Have* could be either an auxiliary verb or a main verb: *Have the students take/taken the exam.* The parser can decide between these only after parsing *the students* as a complete NP; then it could look at the lookahead item *take/taken*). In this case then we have delayed deciding about the rules Auxverb→*have* or Main verb→ *have* until the Subject NP has been recognized. This recognition sequence is noncanonical; a reverse rightmost (or leftmost) recognition sequence is not followed. Nevertheless, the parse is still bottom-up.

Szymanski and Williams (1976) have studied parsing models of this kind. The approach is based on a suggestion of Knuth's (1965) called $LR(k,t)$ parsing. In a standard $LR(k)$ parser, one must always attempt to reduce the leftmost complete subtree. For example, in the case of *Have the students, have)* is the leftmost complete subtree, and therefore one is limited to deciding what to do with *have* before one proceeds to analyze *the students*. However, in $LR(k,t)$ parsing, one is allowed to reduce any of the t leftmost subtrees. For example, an $LR(2,2)$ parser can handle the *Have the students* case, because it is permitted to reduce the NP starting with *the students*, the second leftmost complete subtree, and then use a lookahead of two items, NP and *takes/taken*, to decide what to do next:

> Parsers for $LR(k,t)$ grammars can be constructed using a technique similar to that used for building $LR(k)$ parsers .... The only major difference is that the lookahead string associated with an individual $LR(k)$ item is allowed to contain nonterminals as well as terminals. Whenever an inadequate item set (i.e., one in which the correct parsing action is undefined due to the presence of conflicting items) is reached, the parser postpones any implied reduction(s) and shifts to a new set of items. This new item set includes in its closure any items produced by expanding the leading nonterminal in the lookahead string of any postponed items ....
>
> Since the process of postponing an individual item can be repeated at most t times, no lookahead string need have a length that exceeds kt. Hence the above construction is finite and we have the next theorem.
>
> Theorem 4.2 It is decidable whether an arbitrary CFG is $LR(k,t)$ for fixed values of k and t. Furthermore, an $LR(k,t)$ grammar can be parsed in linear time. (1976:241)

Szymanski and Williams observe that $LR(k,t)$ grammars can be parsed by deterministic pushdown automata, since one need back up at most a finite number of times in succession, over a finite distance. Therefore, $LR(k,t)$ languages are deterministic languages. (For every $LR(k,t)$ language, there must be some weakly equivalent $LR(k)$ language, by the equivalence of $LR(k)$ and deterministic languages.)

How does this result fit in with Marcus's notion of attention-shifts? Note that the LR(k, t) restriction says that only a *finite* number of attention shifts should be allowed. This is in fact what Marcus proposed. His machine was limited to three attention shifts. What happens if we allow an unlimited number of attention shifts? Szymanski and Williams show that then some (unambiguous) nondeterministic languages become parsable, for example, the non-LR language, $L = \{a^n b^n c^m d^{m-l} | n, m, l \geq 1\} \cup \{a^n b^{2n} c^m d^m | n, m \geq 1\}$.

As Szymanski and Williams note, this language cannot have an associated LR(k) grammar for any lookahead k because "any grammar for [L] will require the handle of some sufficiently long sentence to be at the *a-b* interface, and the context required to distinguish between two alternative parses, namely, whether there are more d's than c's in the remaining portion of the string, cannot be determined by a partition into regular sets" (1976:232). But there is a noncanonical deterministic parser for this language: one need merely postpone the decisions about the a's and b's until we find out about the d's and c's. This is precisely what happens in the *Have the students* case. Note that the analysis of L may in general demand an unbounded number of postponements, or attention shifts. and Williams go on to show that if one limits the parser to an unbounded number of postponements, restricted to the case of left and right contexts that are representable as regular sets, then the resulting parser still operates in linear time on a two-stack deterministic pushdown automaton.[6]

If the Marcus parser fits into Szymanski and Williams's model as described, then it is actually an LR(2,2) parser: at most one non-nested attention shift is allowed, and two lookahead symbols are used. A single non-nested attention shift translates into the ability to reduce one of two leftmost complete subtrees, at any step. Why do only two symbols count for lookahead, when the parser's buffer can hold three elements? The first item in the input buffer serves as a locus for reductions; it is actually an input token that prompts control transitions, rather than a lookahead symbol per se. For example, even an LR(0) parser, one that uses no lookahead, must read input symbols from time to time; these would fill the first buffer position. Therefore, it is more accurate to say that the Marcus parser uses two lookahead tokens, and one input token.

---

[6]If general left and right contexts are allowed, or if noncontext-free grammars are used, then n^2 time may be required. An example is given in the next section.

Let us summarize the analysis so far. The parser that forms the basis of the learning procedure is essentially an LR(2,2) parser. Its use of top-down predictions can be folded into its bottom-up operation along the lines suggested by Hammer (1974), adding at most a linear number of steps to a parse. Packets and associated grammar rules correspond to sets of LR(k) items, as conventionally described. The parser's attention shifting mechanism for NP's amounts to the use of a limited noncanonical parsing technique. A finite amount of attention shifting does not add to the class of languages that can be parsed, namely, the deterministic context-free languages; it could add to the transparency or naturalness of the grammars that could be written for those languages, just as it is often the case that a language is better expressed as an LR(3) rather than an LR(1) grammar, even though all deterministic context-free languages have LR(1) grammars.

7.2   Two-stack Deterministic Parsing

In this section we define a two-stack parsing model that mimics the stack and buffer system of the parser. The machine is defined to have the early error-detection capabilities of an LR(k) machine. We will see that if we extend the buffer stack so that it is arbitrarily long, then certain noncontext-free languages become parsable, in time n^2.

First, we observe that the parser has in effect two stacks: (1) its active node stack; and (2) its input buffer. The input buffer functions as a stack because items are pushed from the active node stack onto the input buffer when an item is dropped into the buffer, and popped from the buffer onto the active node stack when a completed constituent is attached to some active node. Crucially, the input buffer acts as a stack only if we assume that what Marcus called the "left-to-right" hypothesis holds, namely, that items are attached from the input buffer to the active node stack in a strict left-to-right order.

A formalization of this machine proceeds along standard lines. Instead of just a single set of stack symbols Γ, we include a separate set of symbols for the active node stack and for the input stack. Active node stack symbols are of the form (X, q), where X is a nonterminal that can appear in the input stack, and q is a state of the finite-state control. A configuration of the machine at step i (a snapshot of its state) can be written by concatenating the two stacks together along with the state at step i; this follows Walters's

(1970) notation for his extension of LR(k) parsing to a two-stack machine. The instructions of the machine can be either: (1) a reduction, in which case the active node stack is popped and the completed nonterminal pushed onto the first cell of the buffer, and the state is possibly changed; (2) a lookahead transition, in which case the state of the parser may change without altering any items in the input buffer or node stack; or (3) a read transition, possibly using lookahead, in which case an symbol from the input stack may be placed on the active node stack, and a state transition can occur. In addition, we must define an accepting configuration, in the usual way. Note that this parser can use nonterminal lookahead symbols, since nonterminals may be dropped into the input stack, only to be used as lookahead material.

To see how this device works in practice, consider how we might build a machine to handle the noncontext-free language $a^n b^n c^n$. As usual, the productions are numbered, 0, 1, etc.

Grammar 1

Start $\rightarrow$	S •,	0	Aa $\rightarrow$	aa,	4
S $\rightarrow$	ABSc,	1	Bb $\rightarrow$	bb,	5
S $\rightarrow$	Abc,	2	BA $\rightarrow$	AB,	6
Ab $\rightarrow$	ab,	3			

We still have the analog of a rightmost derivation for context sensitive grammars. Although the problem here is complex, the following notion will suffice here: following Walters (1970) define a derivation as rightmost if the successive lines of a context-sensitive derivation are formed without ever performing a rewrite that lies wholly to the left of an immediately preceding rewrite. For example, figure 7.2 shows a rightmost derivation in this sense, where the boxes indicate material being rewritten at the current step, and angle brackets indicate the output material from the previous step. Note that a box is never *completely* to the right of an angle bracket.

As usual, the parse of this sentence will be in the reverse order of its generation; aa will be reduced back to Aa, etc. We can now define a finite-state control to recognize the right sentential forms generated with respect to this grammar. There are 13 states in this machine. As with the LR(k) machines, transitions between states are sparked by recognition of either terminal words (like a, b) or nonterminals (A, B). Such a parsing machine takes 41 moves to

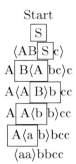

Figure 7.2: A canonical context-sensitive derivation

process $a^3b^3c^3$. Table 7.1 gives excerpts from these transitions, using a [node stack, state, input stack] triple representation.

This parser drops completed constituents back into its input buffer, in the same way that the Marcus parser does. It goes beyond the Marcus parser, though, because its input buffer must be arbitrarily long in order to perform the interchange of A's and B's. With its fixed input buffer, the Marcus parser cannot handle this kind of example. It is also easy to show that the analysis will take at most proportional to n^2 steps, where n is the length of the input sentence. Details are given in Szymanski and Williams (1976).

There is an important condition on sentential forms that permits this finite-state control model to work. This is that the set of right sentential forms (now in the extended sense) must be a finite-state language. This is plainly a necessary condition to be able to write down the required control network as a finite-state automaton. In contrast to all context-free grammars, some strictly context-sensitive grammars do not have right-derivations that form regular sets. Therefore, these grammars cannot be parsed using this method of encoding left context. (There might be some other method of parsing them, of course.) The previous context-sensitive grammar did have a finite-state left context. In contrast, consider an alternative grammar for $a^n b^n c^n$, from Turnbull 1975. We'll show that right derivations in this grammar do not form a finite-state language.

	Configuration	Action
1.	$\emptyset, state1, aaabbbccc$	Read a, go to state 4.
2.	$[a, 1], 4, aabbbccc$	Read a, go to state 9.
3.	$[a, 1][a, 4], 9, abbbccc$	Reduce via production 4.
4.	$\emptyset, 1, Aaabbbccc$	Read A and go to state 3.
5.	$[A, 1], 3, aabbbccc$	Read a, go to state 4.
6.	$[A, 1][a, 3], 4, abbbccc$	Read a, go to state 9.
7.	$[A, 1][a, 3][a, 4], 9, bbbccc$	Reduce via production 4
8.	$[A, 1], 3, Aabbbccc$	Read A, go to state 8.
9.	$[A, 1][A, 3], 8, abbbccc$	Read A, go to state 8.
10.	$[A, 1][A, 3][a, 8], 4, bbbccc$	Read b, go to state 10.
11.	$[A, 1][A, 3][a, 8][b, 4], 10, bbccc$	Reduce via production 3.
12.	$[A, 1][A, 3], 8, Abbbbccc$	
	.	.
	.	.
	.	.
31.	$[A, 1][B, 3][A, 6][B, 3][A, 6][b, 3], 7, ccc$	Read c, go to state 12.
32.	$[A, 1][B, 3][A, 6][B, 3][A, 6][b, 3][c, 7], 12, cc$	Reduce via production 2.
33.	$[A, 1][B, 3][A, 6][B, 3], 6, Scc$	Read S, go to state 11.
34.	$[A, 1][B, 3][A, 6][B, 3][S, 6], 11, cc$	Read c, go to state 16.
35.	$[A, 1][B, 3][A, 6][B, 3][S, 6][c, 11], 1, 6c$	Reduce via production 1.
36.	$[A, 1][B, 3], 6, Sc$	Read S, go to state 11.
37.	$[A, 1][B, 3][S, 6], 11, c$	Read c, go to state 16.
38.	$[A, 1][B, 3][c, 11], 16, \emptyset$	Reduce via production 1.
39.	$\emptyset, 1, S\emptyset$	Read S, go to state 2.
40.	$[S, 1], 2, \emptyset$	Reduce via production 0.
41.	$\emptyset, Start, \emptyset$	Done.

Table 7.1: Noncanonical parser action sequence

Grammar 2

S →	aSBc,	1	bC →	bc,	2
S →	aBC,	3	cC →	cc,	4
aB →	ab,	5	CB →	BC,	6
bB →	bb,	7			

The right sentential forms of this grammar are not regular, since they include strings of the form $a^n b^m bc$, with $n \geq m + 1$. If one compares the successive lines of a rightmost derivation in this case versus the preceding grammar, one can see just why this happens. The successive lines are self-embedding, that is, include nonterminal material completely to the left and right of material being rewritten. Again, boxes mark the rewriting intervals for a given step, and angle brackets represent the output of the rewriting rule from the previous step.

Grammar 2 (self-embedding)	Grammar 1 (nonself-embedding)
Start	Start
⟨a S Bc⟩	AB S c⟩
a⟨ aB C⟩Bc	A B⟨A bcc
a⟨ab⟩ CB c	A⟨A B⟩b cc
aa b⟨B C⟩c	A A⟨b b⟩cc
aa⟨bb⟩ Cc	A⟨a b⟩bcc
aabb⟨cc⟩	⟨aa⟩bbcc

Grammar 1 never derives nonterminal material to the right of successive lines marked by the rightmost edge of a box, whereas Grammar 2 does, in lines 3 and 5. By a well known theorem (Chomsky 1959), this means that the derivation lines of Grammar 2 cannot be represented by a finite-state machine, as required for our parser control. This restriction is plainly not a sufficient condition for deterministic parsing, since there are context-free grammars that are not $LR(k)$, for example, ambiguous grammars. We must add other conditions to ensure that there will be no parsing conflicts. When we do this for the two-stack parser presented above, we find that we may simply define that the machine will (1) detect errors as soon as possible, that is, on the smallest prefix x such that xy cannot be in $L(G)$, for all possible y's consistent with the lookahead seen so far; and (2) not loop indefinitely. This development is covered in Turnbull (1975) and will not be discussed here.

How could the Marcus parser handle this example? If we extend the input buffer, then there are two possibilities. One could simply use the switch operator directly, interchanging A's and B's in the input stack. This analysis would mimic the parser just described above. It requires an arbitrary number of "attention shifts." Alternatively, one could generate a base structure with a terminal string $(ab)^n c^n$ and then displace the a's to the front, via a kind of obligatory *wh*-fronting. This is roughly the analysis proposed by Wexler (1981) for such cases. Wexler also shows that this language is learnable, given the assumptions of the Wexler-Culicover Degree-2 theory (See the next section for additional discussion.) Therefore, the constraints imposed by the Degree-2 theory are weaker than those imposed by the Marcus parser: the Marcus parser, with fixed input buffer, cannot parse this language (using the grammars described above). At least in this case, then, the constraints that guarantee learnability do not guarantee bounded input buffer parsability. In the next section we shall sharpen this result by probing the parsability–learnability connection in detail.

To summarize the results of the preceding sections: The Marcus parser is basically a restricted variant of an $LR(k, t)$ machine as proposed by Knuth (1965). It is a restriction of that design because the parser itself cannot encode unbounded left-context as an arbitrary finite-state language (folded into the parser's finite-state control); rather, it uses bounded if-then rules that refer to the literal tokens of the grammar such as NP or S. It is more accurate, then, to call it a variety of Bounded Context Parser. Additionally, the parser introduces top-down prediction into a bottom-up parse as outlined in Hammer (1974). Given an unlimited input buffer, such a machine can handle some strictly context-sensitive languages in quadratic time. Evidently, the constructions of English that Marcus handled did not demand this capacity.

7.3 Parsability and Learnability

With this formal analysis behind us, we can now turn to the key question of the functional role of locality principles. Our analysis has two parts. First, we shall look at two independent, specific proposals about the constraint on natural grammars, the Lasnik and Kupin (1977) formalization of transformational grammar, and the Wexler and Culicover (1980) Degree-2 theory for the learning of transformational grammar. We shall see that the constraints advanced in both theories are quite similar to those of the current learning procedure. Second, we shall take a closer look at the constraints guaranteeing learnability and parsability, and why these two "functional demands" on language apparently yield closely related locality constraints. A key result will be to suggest that one and the same set of locality constraints that give Bounded Context Parsability also suffice for learnability from simple positive examples. Locality constraints like Subjacency, then, not only help parsing, they help learning.

Locality constraints in other models

Our first step is to look at the constraints on grammars advanced by other models. We look at just two of the most explicitly formulated formalizations of transformational grammar, the Wexler and Culicover Degree-2 theory and the Lasnik and Kupin theory.

Wexler and his colleagues have developed a specific mathematical model of the acquisition of transformational grammar. The aim of the theory is to define constraints such that a family of transformational grammars will be learnable from "simple" data; the learning procedure can get positive (grammatical) example sentences of depth of embedding of two or less (sentences up to two embedded sentences, but no more). The key property of the transformational family that establishes learnability is dubbed *Bounded Degree of Error* (BDE). Roughly and intuitively, BDE is a property related to the "separability" of languages and grammars given simple data: if there is a way for the learner to tell that a currently hypothesized language (and grammar) is incorrect, then there must be some simple sentence that reveals this—all languages in the family must be separable by simple positive example sentences.

The way that the learner can tell that a currently hypothesized grammar is wrong given some sample sentence is by trying to see whether the current grammar can map from a deep structure for the sentence to the observed sample sentence. That is, we imagine the learner being fed with series of base (deep structure)–surface sentence (**b**, **s**) pairs. If the learner's current transformational component, T_l, can map from b to s, then all is well. The acquisition computer model has a somewhat different job than this, since it must *parse* an input sentence and come up with an underlying representation, corresponding to the deep structure b in the Wexler and Culicover model. Still, both models are assumed to have access to an independently constructed representation of the thematic structure of simple sentences. Both models do nothing at all if this recovery of thematic structure can be carried out by current syntactic knowledge—a forward generation of the sentence, for Wexler and Culicover, and an inverse parse of the sentence, in the computer model.

What if the learner's transformational component is not yet correct? Then $T_l(b) = s' \neq s$. A *detectable error* has been revealed. The Wexler-Culicover learning procedure knows that something is wrong; it adds or deletes a transformational rule at random (with uniform probability over the class of rules) from its current transformational component, and proceeds. Eventually, as Wexler and Culicover show, if certain conditions on transformational rules are met, this learning procedure converges to the right transformational component with probability one. The key property that is sufficient to guarantee convergence is BDE:

> A family of transformationally-generated languages L possesses the BDE property iff for any base grammar B (for languages in L) there exists a finite integer U, such that for any possible adult transformational component A and learner component C, if A and C disagree on any phrase-marker b generated by B, then they disagree on some phrase-marker b' generated by B, with b' of degree at most U. (Wexler and Culicover 1980:108)

If we substitute 2 for U in the theorem, we get the Degree 2 constraint, the one actually established by Wexler and Culicover. Once BDE is established for some family of languages, then convergence of a learning procedure is easy to proved. Wexler and Culicover (1980) have the details, but the key insight is that the number of possible errors is now bounded from above.

The question then becomes how BDE may be ensured. Wexler and Culicover found that in order to guarantee learnability one had to impose a number of principles on transformational rule functioning. These are summarized in table 7.2. Wexler and Culicover proposed two kinds of constraints: (1) constraints on the application of a single rule; and (2) constraints on the interaction of rules from one S domain to the next.

The constraint on single rules is easy to understand: no single rule can refer to unbounded context. Specifically, no single rule can refer to more than two s domains, the current s and the next higher s. This Wexler and Culicover call the Binary Principle. It is clear just why this constraint is necessary. If it were not imposed, then a single rule could refer to an arbitrarily large context. Not only would this be a difficult situation for parsing, but since an arbitrarily context would have only a small chance of appearing, the rule context would not be encountered with high enough probability and the rule would not be acquired. The Binary Principle is essentially the Subjacency constraint, though Wexler and Culicover discovered this principle independently.

The effect of Subjacency is to limit rule context to just the current s that is being analyzed, plus the next higher s. This constraint has a natural and direct interpretation in the acquisition parser. Grammar rules can refer only to their current active node (possibly an s) and the current cyclic node above that (also possibly an s).[7] The result is that grammar rules cannot refer to unbounded context. In fact, rules must trigger on precisely the same domain as the operations spelled out by Subjacency.

The constraints on multiple rule interactions are more complex and make up the bulk of Wexler and Culicover's work. Basically, one must guarantee that an error made on one s domain cannot be propagated indefinitely far as a "hidden" error, only to be revealed on some large, hence rare, sentence structure.

There are two possible classes of such interactions: (1) an interaction of *material*—a transformation can move an entire lower context into a higher context; and (2) an interaction of *context*—a transformation can be triggered or inhibited by the context of another cycle. How could a series of rules interact? A multiple rule chain could be arbitrarily long and hence provide unbounded context to trigger or inhibit a rule arbitrarily far away. This clearly would have the same undesirable effect as a single unbounded context. Thus one aims to limit the amount of material that can be passed from one s domain to the next; several constraints are required here.

First, since a transformation can move an entire tree, an arbitrary context could be moved in a series of jumps, only to be torn apart later on. To rule out the movement of arbitrary context, the Degree-2 theory advances constraints that in effect render a phrase inaccessible to further syntactic

---

[7]Recall that here we have modified the original Marcus definition so that Subjacency is in effect enforced directly by the parser.

action after it has been moved across an S boundary. Again, there are two senses of "accessible" here: the tree itself might be torn apart or syntactically manipulated; or it might be used as the context for some other rule. These two possibilities are ruled out by separate constraints posited by the Degree-2 theory. The *Raising Principle* plays a key role in eliminating such manipulation. Roughly speaking, it states that after a tree has been moved across an S boundary, its internal syntactic constituents cannot be moved by any later rules.

Now observe that this is precisely what goes on in the Marcus parser after a node is lowered into another S. This is because, by assumption, a node can be lowered into another clause only by first dropping that node into the input buffer, then creating the new clause node (an S), and finally attaching the node to be lowered to the new clause node. But this means that the node that was lowered had to have been completed, as is always the case, so that it could be dropped into the input buffer. This means that all the *internal* details of the node so lowered cannot be altered; that material has already been attached to the NP. Thus the Marcus parser enforces the Raising Principle.[8] Williams (1981d) shows that the Raising Principle can be strengthened to do nearly all the work of a second principle advanced by Wexler and Culicover to eliminate unbounded syntactic manipulation, the Freezing Principle.

The second constraint, limiting interacting contexts, is dubbed *No Bottom Context*. It says, roughly, that if a transformation acts across an S domain, moving an element from a lower S to a higher S, then it cannot refer to context in the lower S in order to act. Only the target S can have a context restriction. (Transformations operating *within* an S are obviously unaffected.) This requirement is imposed so that material raised from yet another previous (lower) S cannot be used as a triggering context, thereby creating a situation where context material can be successively "cascaded" from one domain to the next.

Because parsing is the inverse of generation, just as before we must be careful in seeing how this constraint might be reflected in parsing. The analog of "raising" in the original Marcus parser is the following "lowering"

---

[8] One could propose that completed nodes are "opaque" to further syntactic manipulation because they are shipped off to another module of sentence processing for semantic interpretation. This constraint enforces the c-command restriction, and leads to an interesting functional account of indexing of pronouns, as outlined in Berwick and Weinberg (1984).

Wexler and Culicover Constraints	Acquisition Procedure Constraints
Incremental rule acquisition	Incremental rule acquisition
No negative evidence	No negative evidence
No memory for past sentences	No memory for past sentences
(only current sentence used	(only current sentence used
as data)	as data)
Small number of	Small number of
new rule hypotheses	new rule hypotheses
Simple sentences used	Simple sentences used
Deterministic generation	Deterministic parsing
Binary principle	⎫ Determinism plus locality
Freezing principle	⎬ restrictions imposed by buffer
Raising principle	⎭ and pushdown stack context
No bottom context	

Table 7.2: Wexler and Culicover constraints compared to computer model

action sequence: (1) create an NP trace; (2) insert the trace into the buffer; (3) create an S; (4) attach the trace somewhere in the lower S. Note that all operations are clausebound (see Marcus 1980 for additional discussion); that is, no single grammar rule acts across an S, using context in the higher domain. All rules that do lowering act within a single S. Of course, this is not enough to force something like No Bottom Context. It might still be possible to write a grammar rule that violates this principle, however unnatural that rule might be. Such a demonstration remains to be carried out.

These three restrictions—the Binary Principle, the Raising Principle, and No Bottom Context—are the central Wexler-Culicover constraints that enforce BDE. They also appear to be met by the computer model. There are other restrictions advanced by the Degree-2 theory that play a role in establishing the learnability of a transformational system. Most of these have to do with the data input to the learning procedure rather than constraints on the form or function of grammar rules themselves. Most are reflected in the computer model as well. The first six entries of table 7.2 summarize this relationship. Both models rely on simple data and positive-only evidence. Both analyze one sentence at a time. Both operate deterministically.

Lasnik and Kupin constraints	Acquisition constraints
Rules not marked as optional or obligatory (no extrinsic ordering)	Rules not marked as optional or obligatory (no extrinsic ordering)
Rule patterns use only one string condition; no arbitrary Boolean conditions	Rule patterns use only one string condition; no arbitrary Boolean conditions
Subjacency	Subjacency
More specific rules trigger before more general rules	More specific rules trigger before more general rules
Small number of rule actions	Small number of rule actions

Table 7.3: Comparison of Lasnik & Kupin to acquisition procedure constraints

The remainder of this section turns to a second formalization of transformational grammar, that of Lasnik and Kupin (1977). Table 7.3 lays out the comparison between this account and the constraints of the acquisition procedure. Again, the close connection between the two systems should be apparent. The two models both severely restrict the form and functioning of grammar rules. Both models obey Subjacency. Both add constraints that aid learning directly: they do not mark rules as being obligatory or optional, since this would be hard to learn from positive evidence. Both models order rules so that specific rules get a chance to execute before general rules. This too is a requirement based on positive example acquisition. The only constraint that needs some explanation is the restriction to no arbitrary Boolean conditions. The acquisition procedure matches rules based on positive features—whether an NP is present, or whether a VP is of a certain type. It is not allowed to carry out a negative existential search, triggering a rule if there is just one such element present, or if such an element is present anywhere in the left-hand context of the parse. Thus it too cannot resort to complex existential conditions.

7.4 Learnability, Parsability, and Locality

At least two independently designed grammatical models—models built with learnability in mind—have close ties to the computer model outlined in this book. A deeper question remains: just why should the computer model, grounded on the goal of efficient parsability, reflect these learnability constraints so directly? How are the constraints of parsability and learnability linked?

For this comparison to make sense at all, one must precisely define efficient parsability and learnability. We already have good candidates for each of these. As a working definition of what is efficiently parsable, we shall take the class of Bounded Context Parsable (BCP) grammars, which we define as the LR(k) or LR(k, t) grammars restricted to use literally bounded left and right contexts for parsing decisions. Intuitively, a grammar is BCP if it is backwards deterministic given a radius of k tokens around every parsing decision. That is, it is possible to find deterministically the production that applied at a given step in a derivation by examining just a bounded number of tokens (fixed in advance) to the left and right at that point in the derivation. This is a restriction of the general LR(k) constraint, since in the LR(k) case, we need not examine actual tokens to the left and right of the current position, but may actually base parsing decisions on some finite-state encoding of previously encountered context. In contrast, a bounded context parser must refer to the actual tokens of the grammar for its decisions.

Following Aho and Ullman we have this definition for bounded right-context grammars, which we immediately extend to cover the Marcus parser:

> G is bounded right-context if the following four conditions imply that $A = B$, $\alpha' = \gamma$, and $\epsilon = \iota$:
>
> (1) $S \xrightarrow{*} \alpha A \omega \rightarrow \alpha \beta \omega$ and
> (2) $S \xrightarrow{*} \gamma B \iota \rightarrow \gamma \delta \iota = \alpha' \beta \epsilon$ are rightmost derivations in the grammar;
> (3) the length of ι is less than or equal to the length of ϵ; and
> (4) the last m symbols of α and α' coincide, and the first n symbols of ω and ϵ coincide.

We will use the term "bounded context" instead of "bounded right context." To extend the definition to the Marcus parser, we drop the requirement that the derivation is rightmost and use instead noncanonical derivation sequences as defined in the previous section. The effect is to have a lookahead that can include nonterminal names like NP or VP.

As our definition of what is easily learnable, we shall simply take the families of grammars that meet the BDE condition, as defined earlier.

We can now at least formalize our problem of comparing learnability and parsability. The question now becomes: What is the relationship between the BDE property and the BCP property? Intuitively, a grammar is BCP if we can always tell which of two rules applied in a given bounded context. Also intuitively, a family of grammars is BDE if, given any two grammars in the family G and G' with different rules R and R' say, we can tell which rule is the correct one by looking at two derivations of bounded degree, with R applying in one and yielding surface string s, and R' applying in the other yielding surface string s', with s not equal to s'. This property must hold with respect to all possible adult and learner grammars. So a space of possible target grammars must be considered. The way we do this is by considering some "fixed" grammar G and possible variants of G formed by substituting the production rules in G with hypothesized alternatives.

At least informally, then, the close connection between parsability and learnability might follow from an overlap in locality constraints, at least as formulated here. The theorem we want to prove is this.

> If the grammars formed by augmenting G with possible hypoth-
> esized grammar rules are BCP, then that family is also BDE.

The theorem is established by using the BCP property to directly construct a small-degree phrase marker that meets the BDE condition. Select two grammars G, G' from the family of grammars. Both are BCP, by definition. By assumption, there is a detectable error that distinguishes G with rule R from G' with rule R'. Let us say that rule R is of the form $A \rightarrow \alpha$; R' is $B \rightarrow \alpha'$.[9]

Since R' determines a detectable error, there must be a derivation with a common sentential form Φ such that R applies to Φ and eventually derives sentence s, while R' applies to Φ and eventually derives s', different from s. The number of steps in the derivation of the the two sentences may be

---

[9]More generally, we should right this rule using the Marcus parser form, with a bounded left and right context.

arbitrary, however. What we must show is that there are two derivations bounded in advance by some constant that yield two different sentences.

The BCP conditions state that identical (m, n) (left and right) contexts imply that A and B are equal. Taking the contrapositive, if A and B are unequal, then the (m, n) context must be nonidentical. This establishes that the BCP condition implies (m, n) context error detectability.[10]

We are not yet done though. An (m, n) context detectable error could consist of terminal and nonterminal elements, not just terminals (words) as required by the detectable error condition. We must show that we can extend such a detectable error to a surface sentence detectable error with an underlying structure of bounded degree. An easy lemma establishes this:

> If R' is an (m, n) context detectable error, then R' is bounded degree of error detectable.

The proof (by induction) is omitted; only a sketch will be given here. Intuitively, the reason is that we can extend any nonterminals in the error detectable (m, n) context to some valid surface sentence and bound this derivation by some constant fixed in advance and depending only on the grammar. This is because unbounded derivations are possible only by the repetition of nonterminals via recursion; since there are only a finite number of distinct nonterminals, it is only via recursion that we can obtain a derivation chain that is arbitrarily deep. But, as is well known (compare the proof of the pumping theorem for context-free grammars), any such arbitrarily deep derivation producing a valid surface sentence also has an associated truncated derivation, bounded by a constant dependent on the grammar, that yields a valid sentence of the language. Thus we can convert any (m, n) context detectable error to a bounded degree of error sentence. This establishes the lemma and the basic result.

What are the implications of this result? First of all, it confirms the intuition that locality constraints important for parsing could also aid learning. Once a family of grammars as defined above meets the BCP condition, it already meets the BDE condition. Thus we might use the BCP condition as a touchstone for the BDE property, without resort to Wexler and Culicover's combinatorial demonstration. Second, the result demonstrates that

---

[10]One of the other three BCP conditions could also be violated, but these are true by assumption. We assume the existence of derivations meeting conditions (1) and (2) in the extended sense, as well as condition (3).

the acquisition model described in this book is, in fact, closely related to the Wexler-Culicover BDE model.

From a computational point of view, the language acquisition faculty and the language processing faculty appear particularly well-designed. Natural languages must be both learnable and parsable, and the same constraints aid both goals. In this book we have seen how to build an explicit computational model that can learn language as it learns to parse. The procedure works because of strong constraints on the descriptions of rules that it can build. These same constraints also ensure that what it learns will fit naturally into an efficient parser. Echoing the approach set out in the first chapter, we have gone at least part of the way to a true *computational* theory of language use and acquisition. That computational theory has illuminated the reasons for locality constraints in natural language, both for learning and parsing; provided a general theory of development and certain predictions about the course of child language acquisition; and led to important engineering constraints on a flexible parser. Most of all, it has forged a vital bond between our understanding of *what* knowledge of language is and *how* it is put to use—two central goals of the theory of grammar and natural intelligence.

References

Aho, A. and J. Ullman, 1972. *The Theory of Parsing, Translation, and Compiling.* Vol. 1. Englewood Cliffs, NJ: Prentice-Hall.

Akmajian, A., S. Steele, T. and Wasow, 1979. The category Aux in universal grammar. *Linguistic Inquiry* 10:1–64.

Anderson, J., 1977. Induction of augmented transition networks. *Cognitive Science* 1:125–157.

Angluin, D., 1978. Inductive inference of formal languages from positive data. *Information and Control* 45:117–135.

Angluin, D., 1982. Inference of reversible languages. *Journal of the Association for Computing Machinery* 29:741–765.

Aoun, Y., 1979. On government, case marking and clitic placement. MIT Department of Linguistics, unpublished ms.

Baker, C.L., 1979. Syntactic theory and the projection problem. *Linguistic Inquiry* 10:533–581.

Baker, C.L., 1981. Learnability and the English auxiliary system. In *The Logical Problem of Language Acquisition*, C. Baker and J. McCarthy, eds. Cambridge, MA: MIT Press, pp. 296–323.

Baltin, M., 1982. A landing site theory of movement rules. *Linguistic Inquiry* 13:1–38.

Berwick, R., 1979. Learning structural descriptions of grammar rules from examples. *Proc. 6th International Joint Conference on Artificial Intelligence*, Cambridge, MA.

Berwick, R., 1982. Locality principles and the acquisition of syntactic knowledge. PhD dissertation, MIT Department of Electrical Engineering and Computer Science.

Berwick, R., 1983. A deterministic parser with broad coverage. *Proc. 8th International Joint Conference on Artificial Intelligence*, Karlsrühle, Germany.

Berwick, R. and A. Weinberg, 1982. Parsing efficiency, computational complexity, and the evaluation of grammatical theories. *Linguistic Inquiry* 13:165–191.

Berwick, R. and A. Weinberg, 1984. *The Grammatical Basis of Linguistic Performance*. Cambridge, MA: MIT Press.

Biermann, A., 1972. On the inference of Turing machines from sample computations. *Artificial Intelligence* 3:181–198.

Biermann, A. and J. Feldman, 1972. On the synthesis of finite state machines from samples of their behavior. *IEEE Transactions on Computation* C-21, June, 592–597.

Blum, M., 1967. A machine-independent theory of the complexity of recursive functions. *Journal of the Association for Computing Machinery* 14:322–336.

Blum, M. and L. Blum, 1975. Towards a mathematical theory of inductive inference. *Information and Control* 28:125–155.

Book, R., 1970. Time-bounded grammars and their languages. *Journal of Computer and System Science* 5:397–429.

Bowerman, M., 1974. Learning the structure of causative verbs: a study in the relation of cognitive, semantic, and syntactic development. *Papers and Reports on Child Language Development No. 8*. Palo Alto: Stanford University.

Braine, M., 1971. On two types of models of the internalization of grammars. In *The Ontogenesis of Grammar: A Theoretical Symposium*, D. Slobin, ed. New York: Academic Press.

Bresnan, J., 1972. The theory of complementation in English syntax. PhD dissertation, MIT Department of Linguistics.

Bresnan, J., 1982. *The Mental Representation of Grammatical Relations*. Cambridge, MA: MIT Press.

Brown, R., 1973. *A First Language*. Cambridge, MA: Harvard University Press.

Brown, R. and C. Hanlon, 1970. Derivational complexity and the order of acquisition in child speech. In *Cognition and the Development of Language*, J. R. Hayes, ed. New York: John Wiley, pp. 155–207.

Chomsky, C., 1969. *The Acquisition of Syntax in Children from 5 to 10*. Cambridge, MA: MIT Press.

Chomsky, N., 1951. Morphophonemics of Modern Hebrew. MS dissertation, University of Pennsylvania.

Chomsky, N., 1959. On certain formal properties of grammars. *Information and Control* 2:137–167.

Chomsky, N., 1965. *Aspects of the Theory of Syntax*. Cambridge: MIT Press.

Chomsky, N., 1970. Remarks on nominalization. In *Readings in English Transformational Grammar*, R. Jacobs and P. Rosenbaum, eds. Waltham, MA: Ginn and Co., pp. 184–221.

Chomsky, N., 1975. *Reflections on Language*. New York: Pantheon.

Chomsky, N., 1981. *Lectures on Government and Binding*. Dordrecht, Holland: Foris Publications.

Chomsky, N. and M. Halle, 1968. *The Sound Pattern of English*. New York: Harper and Row.

Crespi-Reghizzi, S., 1971. An effective model for grammar inference. *Proceedings of the IFIP Congress 71*, Amsterdam: North-Holland.

Crespi-Reghizzi, S. Guida, and G. Mandrioli, 1978. Non-counting context-free languages. *Journal of the Association for Computing Machinery* 25:571–580.

DeRemer, F., 1969. Practical translators for LR(k) languages. PhD Dissertation, MIT Department of Electrical Engineering and Computer Science, Laboratory for Computer Science Report MAC-TR-65.

Emonds, J., 1969. A structure-preserving constraint on NP movement transformations. In *Papers from the Fifth Regional Meeting of the Chicago Linguistic Society*, R. Binnick, A. Davison, G. Green, and J. Morgan, eds. Chicago: University of Chicago.

Farmer, A., 1980. On the interaction of morphology and syntax. PhD Dissertation, MIT Department of Linguistics.

Feldman, J., 1972. Some decidability results on grammatical inference and complexity. *Information and Control* 20:244–262.

Fiengo, R., 1974. Semantic conditions on surface structure. PhD dissertation, MIT Department of Linguistics.

Fiengo, R., 1977. On trace theory. *Linguistic Inquiry* 8:35–61.

Fillmore, C., 1968. The case for case. In *Universals in Linguistic Theory*, E. Bach and R. Harms eds. New York: Holt, Rinehart, and Winston.

Floyd, R., 1964. Bounded context syntactic analysis. *Communications of the Association for Computing Machinery* 7:62–66.

Fodor, J., T. Bever, and M. Garrett, 1974. *The Psychology of Language: an Introduction to Psycholinguistics and Generative Grammar*. New York: McGraw Hill.

Fodor, J. D., 1979. Superstrategy. In *Sentence Processing: Psycholinguisitc Studies Presented to honor Merrill Garrett*, W. Cooper and E. Walker, eds. Hillsdale, NJ: Lawrence Erlbaum.

Frazier, L., 1979. On comprehending sentences: syntactic parsing strategies. PhD dissertation, University of Massachusetts Department of Linguistics, Amherst.

Fu, K. and T. Booth, 1975. Grammatical inference: introduction and survey. *IEEE Transactions on Systems, Man, and Cybernetics* 4:95–111.

George, L., 1980. Analogical generalizations of natural language syntax. PhD dissertation, Department of Linguistics, MIT.

Gleitman, H. and L. Gleitman, 1979. Language use and language judgment. In *Individual Differences in Language Ability and Language Behavior*, C. Fillmore, D. Kempler, and W. Wang, eds. New York: Academic Press.

Gleitman, L. and E. Wanner, 1982. Language acquisition: the state of the state of the art. In *Language Acquisition: the State of the Art*, E. Wanner and L. Gleitman, eds. Oxford: Cambridge University Press.

Gold, E., 1967. Language identification in the limit. *Information and Control*, 10:447–474.

Goodall, G., 1984. Parallel structures in syntax. PhD dissertation, Department of Linguistics, University of California at San Diego.

Grimshaw, J., 1981. Form, function, and the language acquisition device. In *The Logical Problem of Language Acquisition*, C. Baker and J. McCarthy, eds. Cambridge, MA: MIT Press, pp. 165–182.

Halle, M., 1961. On the role of simplicity in linguistic descriptions. *Proceedings of Symposia in Applied Mathematics*, 12.

Halle, M., J. Bresnan, and G. Miller, 1978. *Linguistic Theory and Psychological Reality*. Cambridge, MA: MIT Press.

Hamburger, H. and K. Wexler, 1975. A mathematical theory of learning transformational grammar. *Journal of Mathematical Psychology*, 12:137–177.

Hammer, M., 1974. A new grammatical transformation into deterministic top-down form. Cambridge, MA: MIT Project MAC TR-119.

Harrison, M., 1978. *Introduction to Formal Language Theory*. Reading, MA: Addison-Wesley.

Horning, J., 1969. A study of grammatical inference. Stanford AI Report CS–139.

Horning, J., 1971. A procedure for grammatical inference. *Proceedings of the IFIP Congress 71*, Amsterdam: North-Holland, pp. 519–523.

Hornstein, N. and A. Weinberg, 1981. Case theory and preposition stranding. *Linguistic Inquiry* 12:55–92.

Hyams, N., 1983. The acquisition of parameterized grammars. Department of Linguistics, CUNY.

Iba, G., 1979. Learning disjunctive concepts from examples. MIT Artificial Intelligence Laboratory Memo 548.

Jackendoff, R., 1972. *Semantic Interpretation in Generative Grammar*. Cambridge, MA: MIT Press.

Jackendoff, R., 1977. $\overline{\text{X}}$ *Syntax: A Study of Phrase Structure*. Cambridge, MA: MIT Press.

Jakobson, R., 1961. *Selected Writings, I*. The Hague: Mouton.

Jakobson, R., 1968. *Child Language, Aphasia, and Phonological Universals*. The Hague: Mouton.

Joshi, A. and L. Levy, 1977. Constraints on local transformations. *SIAM Journal of Computing* 6:272–284.

Joshi, A. and L. Levy, 1978. Skeletal structural descriptions. *Information and Control* 39:192–211.

Katz, J., 1966. *The Philosophy of Language*. New York: Harper and Row.

Kean, M., 1974. The theory of markedness in generative grammar. PhD dissertation, MIT Department of Linguistics.

Keil, F., 1979. *Semantic and Conceptual Development: An Ontological Perspective*. Cambridge, MA: Harvard University Press.

Kimball, J., 1973. Seven principles of surface structure parsing in natural language. *Cognition* 2: 15–47.

Kiparsky, P., 1973. Elsewhere in phonology. In *A Festschrift for Morris Halle*, S. Anderson and P. Kiparsky, eds. New York: Holt, Rinehart, and Winston.

Knuth, D., 1965. On the translation of languages from left to right. *Information and Control* 8:607–639.

Kolmogorov, A., 1965. Three approaches to the quantitative definition of information. *Problems of Information Transmission*, 1:1–7.

Koster, J., 1978. *Locality Principles in Syntax*. Dordrecht, Holland: Foris Publications.

Labov, W., 1970. The study of language in its social context. *Studium Generale* 23:30–87.

Labov, W. and T. Labov, 1976. Learning the syntax of questions. *Proceedings of the Conference on the Psychology of Language, Scotland*, July 1976.

Langley, P., 1977. BACON: A production system that discovers empirical laws. Pittsburgh, PA: Carnegie-Mellon University, CIP WP 360.

Lasnik, H., 1980. Restricting the theory of transformations: a case study. In *Explanation in Linguistics*, N. Hornstein and D. Lightfoot, eds. London: Longmans, pp. 152–173.

Lasnik, H. and J. Kupin, 1977. A restrictive theory of transformational grammar. *Theoretical Linguistics* 4:173–196.

Levine, B., 1981. Derivatives of tree sets with applications to grammatical inference. *IEEE Transactions on Pattern Analysis and Machine Intelligence* 3:285–293.

Liberman, A. and A. Prince, 1977. On stress and linguistic rhythm. *Linguistic Inquiry* 11:511–562.

Lieber,R., 1980. On the organization of the lexicon. PhD dissertation, MIT Department of Linguistics and Philosophy.

Lightfoot, D., 1981. The history of Noun Phrase movement. In *The Logical Problem of Language Acquisition*, C. Baker and J. McCarthy, eds. Cambridge, MA: MIT Press.

Lightfoot, D., 1982. *The Language Lottery*. Cambridge, MA: MIT Press.

Limber, J., 1973. The genesis of complex sentences. In *Cognitive Development and the Acquisition of Language*, T. Moore, ed. New York: Academic Press.

Maratsos, M.P., 1978. New models in linguistics and language acquisition. In *Linguistic theory and Psychological Reality*, M. Halle, J. Bresnan, and G. Miller, eds. Cambridge, MA: MIT Press, pp. 247–263.

Marcus, M., 1980. *A Theory of Syntactic Recognition for Natural Language*. Cambridge, MA: MIT Press.

Marr, D. and K. Nishihara, 1978. Visual information processing and the sensorium of sight. *Technology Review*, October.

Marr, D. and T. Poggio, 1977. From understanding computation to understanding neural circuitry. *Neuroscience Research Program Bulletin* 15:470–488.

Marshall, J., 1979. Language acquisition in a biological frame of reference. In *Language Acquisition*, P. Fletcher and M. Garman, eds. New York: Cambridge University Press, pp. 437–453.

Mayer, J., A. Erreich, and V. Valian, 1978. Transformations, base operations, and language acquisition. *Cognition* 6:1–13.

McDermott, J. and C. Forgy, 1978. OPS: a domain independent production system language. In *Pattern-Directed Inference Systems*, D. Waterman and F. Hayes-Roth, eds. New York: Academic Press.

McNeill, D., 1966. Developmental psycholinguistics. In *The Genesis of Language*, F. Smith and G. Miller, eds. Cambridge, MA: MIT Press.

Milne, R., 1983. Lexical ambiguity in a deterministic parser. PhD dissertation, University of Edinburgh Department of Computer Science.

Mitchell, T., 1978. Version spaces: an approach to concept learning. PhD dissertation, Stanford University Department of Computer Science.

Moore, G., 1956. Gedanken experiments with sequential machines. *Automata Studies*, Princeton: Princeton University Press, pp. 129–153.

Morgan, J. and E. Newport, 1981. The role of constituent structure in the induction of an artificial language. *Journal of Verbal Learning and Verbal Behavior* 20:67–85.

Newport, E., H. Gleitman, and L. Gleitman, 1977. Mother, please, I'd rather do it myself: some effects and non-effects of maternal speech style. In *Talking to*

Children: Language Input and Acquisition, C. Snow and C. Ferguson, eds. New York: Cambridge University Press, pp. 109–150.

Olmsted, D., 1971. *Out of the Mouth of Babes: Earliest Stages in Language Learning*. The Hague: Mouton.

Peters, S. and R. Ritchie, 1973. Context-sensitive immediate constituent analysis—context-free languages revisited. *Mathematical Systems Theory* 6:324–333.

Pinker, S., 1979. Formal models of language learning. *Cognition* 7:217–283.

Pinker, S., 1982. A theory of the acquisition of lexical-interpretive grammars. In *The Mental Representation of Grammatical Relations*, J. Bresnan, ed. Cambridge, MA: MIT Press, pp. 655–726.

Plotkin, G., 1970. A note on inductive generalization. In *Machine Intelligence*, B. Meltzer and D. Michie, eds. 5. Edinburgh: Edinburgh University Press.

Reinhart, T., 1976. The syntactic domain of anaphora. PhD dissertation, MIT Department of Linguistics.

Rizzi, L., 1978. A restructuring rule in Italian syntax. In *Recent Transformational Studies in European Linguistics*, S. Keyser, ed. Cambridge, MA: MIT Press.

Rizzi, L., 1980. Comments on Chomsky. In *Proceedings of the June 1980 Conference on the Cognitive Sciences*, J. Mehler, ed. Paris: CNRS.

Roeper, T., 1981. On the deductive model and the acquisition of productive morphology. In *The Logical Problem of Language Acquisition*, C. Baker and J. McCarthy, eds. Cambridge, MA: MIT Press, pp. 129–150.

Ross, J., 1967. Constraints on variables in syntax. PhD dissertation, MIT Department of Linguistics.

Scollon, R., 1976. *Conversations With a One Year Old*. Honolulu: University of Hawaii Press.

Shipman, D., 1979. Phrase structure rules for Parsifal. MIT Artificial Intelligence Laboratory Working Paper No. 182.

Slobin, D., 1966. Grammatical transformations and sentence comprehension in childhood and adulthood, *Journal of Verbal Learning and Verbal Behavior* 5:219–227.

Solomonoff, R., 1964. A formal theory of inductive inference. *Information and Control* 7:1–22.

Sommers, F., 1971. Structural ontology. *Philosphia* 1:21–42.

Starke, P., 1972. *Abstract Automata*. New York: American Elsevier.

Stowell, T., 1981. Origins of phrase structure. PhD dissertation, MIT Department of Linguistics and Philosophy.

Szymanski, T. and J. Williams, 1976. Noncanonical extensions of bottom-up parsing techniques. *SIAM Journal of Computing* 5:231–260.

Tavakolian, S., 1981. The conjoined clause analysis of relative clauses. In *Language Acquisition and Linguistic Theory*, S. Tavakolian, ed. Cambridge, MA: MIT Press.

Thiersch, C., 1978. Topics in German syntax. PhD Dissertation, MIT Department of Linguistics and Philosophy.

Turnbull, C., 1975. Deterministic Left to Right Parsing. Toronto: University of Toronto Computer Systems Research Group Report CSRG-46.

Vergnaud, J. and M. Halle, 1980. Three dimensional phonology. *Journal of Linguistic Research* 1:1–10.

Walters, D., 1970. Deterministic context-sensitive languages. *Information and Control* 17:14–61.

Wexler, K., 1981. Some issues in the theory of learnability. In *The Logical Problem of Language Acquisition*, C. Baker and J. McCarthy, eds. Cambridge, MA: MIT Press, pp. 30–52.

Wexler, K. and P. Culicover, 1980. *Formal Principles of Language Acquisition*. Cambridge, MA: MIT Press.

Wexler, K., and R. Manzini, 1984. Independence of parameters in language acquisition. Unpublished ms, University of California, Irvine.

Williams, E., 1981a. Predication. *Linguistic Inquiry* 11:203–260.

Williams, E., 1981b. On the notions "lexically related" and "head of a word." *Linguistic Inquiry* 12:245–274.

Williams, E., 1981c. Language acquisition, markedness, and phrase structure. In *Language Acquisition and Linguistic Theory*, S. Tavakolian, ed. Cambridge, MA: MIT Press, pp. 8–34.

Williams, E., 1981d. A readjustment in the learnability assumptions. In *The Logical Problem of Language Acquisition*, C. Baker and J. McCarthy, eds. Cambridge, MA: MIT Press, pp. 64–78.

Winston, P., 1975. Learning structural descriptions from examples. In *The Psychology of Computer Vision*, P. Winston, ed. Reading, MA: Addison-Wesley.

Yngve, V., 1960. A model and an hypothesis for language structure. *Proceedings of the American Philosophical Society* 104:444-466.

Index